n0565912

For information about special discounts for
bulk purchases please contact SKW Publishing
at 847-816-0831 or info@animalwarrior.com

The Animal Warrior
A product of SKW Publishing
A division of SKW Enterprises

Copyright © 2008 by Sandy Kamen Wisniewski

All rights reserved, including the right to reproduce this book or portions thereof in any form whatsoever.
For information address The Animal Warrior c/o AEAR, P.O. Box 7343, Libertyville, IL 60048.
www.aear.org

Book edited by Mary Spidle - www.AAEditing.com
Book design and photography by Stephanie Chizek - www.FetchDesigns.com

Library of Congress Cataloging-in-Publishing Information:
Wisniewski, Sandy Kamen   The Animal Warrior   ISBN 978-0-615-25795-2

Dog on front cover is Braille. Dog on back cover is Nacho.
Both dogs' stories are featured in this book and have since been adopted to new and loving homes.

THE ANIMAL WARRIOR

One Woman's Quest To Protect The Lives of Animals

By Sandy Kamen Wisniewski

Edited by Mary Spidle

Book design and photography by Stephanie Chizek

This book was written in memory of my rescued dogs

Mota, Heidi and Rascal.

The Early Years

Pet Sitters of America

Animal Education and Rescue

Acknowledgements

Without the help and support of so many people, Animal Education and Rescue would be just the fantasy of a self-professed, slightly different, big dreamer and major animal lover. First, I must thank my husband Chuck. He has always been perfectly content working in the background, but little do many people realize, he is a huge part of the success of Animal Education and Rescue. He has taken on so much of the work that still provides us an income so that I can live my passion (but as of this writing make no money doing it). He is a top-notch, dedicated father to our two children and our many pets.

Next, I'd like to thank my extended family that has continued to support me in all my endeavors. Thanks especially to my mom and dad who, while not big animal lovers themselves, saw the importance of animals in children's lives. Without my childhood dogs, gerbils and birds I know my path would have been very different and I may not have ever realized my passion.

Special thanks goes to Stephanie Chizek, who designed the inside and outside of the book. With her exceptional creative and technical talent she was able to capture the essence of the book. Thanks equally goes to my editor, Mary Spidle, who did an outstanding job editing my book. She is a gem.

Lastly, I would like to thank the dozens of people who have given their time, spent their money and shared the vision I have to bring animals and people together through education, rescue and therapy. You all have my deepest gratitude. There is no way I could have saved all those lives and brought joy to so many without you. While I am the trunk, you are the branches and leaves that cause our growing tree to blossom.

To protect people's privacy all the names, towns, streets and locations in this book have been changed. I did use the real names of most of the animals. The stories shared here are a summary of actual events that happened, to the best of my memory. This book is not meant to act as a medical guide. Please consult your veterinarian about any medical issues.

Introduction

Animal abuse and neglect is a fact. It happens. It's an upsetting fact that, when I think about it, makes me that much more driven to do what I am doing. Animals have no voice or way of telling their human families to stop hitting them, stop neglecting them and stop abusing them. They cannot call 911 or file charges against the people who are supposed to love them.

That's where I step in. I am one of the voices for the animals. I am their protector. I am fiercely determined to right the wrongs done to animals.

Sometimes it's just about educating the human family. Maybe they don't understand that they can't tie a dog outside all day without water, food and shelter. Maybe they don't understand that what they are feeding their dog is not enough. Maybe they need assistance in getting the medical care their animal needs. I am a teacher. I am willing and able to teach human families, if they are willing to listen and implement change.

But to those people who are selfish, ill at heart or evil and take their anger and frustration out on the helpless and weak: Meet me, Sandy Kamen Wisniewski, Animal Warrior. I will do whatever I can to stop you.

The Early Years

The Early Years

The swirl and whirl of my hectic life has me wondering how this all happened. Yet my life, when I look back on it, was destined to meet me here where I am today. I am one of the many people driven to change the lives of as many heartbroken, lonely, wrecked, beaten, starved, rejected, homeless and might-as-well-be-homeless animals as possible. I am but one of a group of people who are driven by a passion to make changes in the way we as humans treat the animals that share this world with us.

How did I end up doing what I am doing? I guess I can say that I believe you can fumble through life unsure of where you are going but content (or maybe not) with the idea of just living day by day. I was never that kind of person. From early on I yearned to make a difference in a huge way. I built up some small businesses that are modestly successful. I volunteered my time consistently throughout the years, joining committees and boards of directors, leading support groups and even creating a support group. I became president of a local chamber of commerce, was honored with numerous awards in business and rubbed elbows with local popular business-types. I shuffled my children to their share of after-school activities, and I planned elaborate birthday and holiday parties. I had a full, hectic and progressive life.

But even with all that I was doing I was never satisfied. I felt unfulfilled and knew there had to be more for my life. Inside my very being I always had a deep, passionate need to make a huge difference. I knew I hadn't found my calling, but I didn't know what it was exactly or how I'd get there. But now all that has changed and continues to evolve as I am finding my calling and my vision through a series of happenings that brought me to where I am today.

This book is sprinkled with hope, pain, love, strength, laughter and so much more. The first part may seem sad, but it is important to have written because it is through pain that we can choose to find our path, our strength and our calling.

• • • • •

Donning my armor, carrying my sword, I hold my arms out and open for those animals calling for help. I have found this journey personally profoundly difficult and questioned many, many times why I do it. But I keep coming back to the reason. It's during those moments of doubt that all I have to see is the sad eyes of an animal in need to keep me going. It is not an option for me to sit back and let things be; it is only an option for me to set in motion positive change. That is my duty as a good human being on this earth.

I often ask myself, why do I choose this difficult path?

There are certain memories from my childhood that have always stuck with me, strong and vivid with raw, pressing emotions attached to them. Many of these memories revolve around animals. In hindsight I believe that what I had to experience as a child, in part, in all its heartache and pain, was essential to making me who I am. I believe that we can choose to learn from our mistakes, taking a negative and turning it into a positive. That is my philosophy that I try to live by every day.

Sisters and Pepsi-Cola

An early fall day, the leaves dry and brittle under my feet, I crunched down the makeshift rock path at the back of our house, following my big brother Gerry. I was skipping along, looking down at my white leather shoes with their silver buckles and three tear-dropped shaped holes on top. The refreshing feeling of the cool wind was exhilarating on my bare legs; my dress moved about daintily. In my seven-year-old mind I was thinking about everything and nothing at the same time, my brain chattering away. Mostly I was busy just trying to keep up with nine-year-old Gerry. He marched ahead of me, wielding a stick he was using as a sword.

"La la la," I sang out as I skipped and hopped along.

Suddenly Gerry turned and looked past me at something. His blue eyes grew round and his mouth opened wide and twisted in a grimace of fear. My heart jumped in my chest as I abruptly stopped and turned to look. I saw it...well, him. A black, curly fluff ball on four legs–tail wagging furiously and a wet red tongue–was charging at us like a commuter train. Gerry let out a scream, so I joined in chorus, and we both ran from the charging ball of fur, hysterical and terrified.

After that initial meeting we must have gotten used to Pepsi because he quickly became an important family member. Pepsi, a Standard

Poodle, was a high-energy, fun-loving pup. In the first months he spent his days in the kitchen as my mom taught him bathroom habits and how not to chew everything he could get his mouth on. As he became trustworthy he gained more freedom. He also chose his favorite human, my 12-year-old sister Margie, who became his very best friend.

The two were inseparable. Everywhere Margie went Pepsi was her shadow. He looked up at her with I-love-you-more-than-heaven-and-earth eyes. At night he curled up with her in bed. It was an awesome relationship to watch. I was intrigued by the love they shared and hoped some day that I, too, would have such a relationship.

· · · · ·

Our home, a gorgeous Frank Lloyd Wright cottage-style home, was built in 1905. It was a wonderful home to grow up in. There were seven bedrooms, five baths, lots of room for hide-and-seek. Harold, our milkman, would climb the long back stairs once a week, put milk and eggs in a silver milk box beside the door, open the screen door and poke his head inside. Then he'd call out, "Milk Man!" slapping closed the door behind him as he hurried to his next stop.

Our home was situated on top of a rolling acre of land. The neighboring homes were large like ours and also on expansive lawns. Huge trees formed canopies throughout the neighborhood, providing shade from the sun and a lovely backdrop. My younger brother Billy and I loved to explore the nearby ravines and kick up sand by Lake Michigan, only a steep, curving road away.

Spring arrived and Pepsi was growing into a big, goofy, clown-like dog. He quickly learned how to push the back screen door open with his nose and head outside. Our yard was not fenced so he explored it and our neighbors' properties as well. As he became more confident he came and went from home as he pleased, romping through the neighborhood, and being un-neutered, likely meeting many lady dogs.

Pepsi played a game that kept him entirely amused. He decided he would chase cars. He would wait in the bushes at the front of our house, and when a car drove by he would burst through the bushes and run full blast behind the innocent driver. I can only imagine what our neighbors thought when they saw Pepsi running behind them in the rearview mirror.

Pepsi would be gone for longer and longer periods of time, running around the neighborhood and exploring. I knew no different; I thought this was normal. When dinnertime rolled around my mom or sister would yell out the back door, "Pepsi! Pepsi! Come, Pepsi!" Within minutes Pepsi would appear at the door breathless and ready for his supper.

Meanwhile I filled my days with long bike rides, pumping my legs faster and faster, ignoring the burn of my thigh muscles as I tried to keep up with my younger and more energetic brother Billy. Billy and I explored the ravines, grabbing onto trees and roots as we climbed up and down the steep slopes. Occasionally we discovered treasures, like an old bottle or a rubber ball, dumped carelessly into a ravine. Squirrels and chipmunks skittered about, busily climbing trees and digging for bits of food in the ground. Birds sang loud and clear, like a natural symphony just for me every day. It was a glorious time.

Autumn rolled around and the huge, old trees in our neighborhood blessed us with leaves painted in shades of red, orange and green. I spent many days kicking up the leaves and sifting through them, finding those I thought were extra special. With my mom's help we pressed the leaves into books as a keepsake. My siblings and I raked leaves into piles and then jumped into them. The pungent, rusty, burnt-iron smell of the leaves was strong in our nostrils. The world outside was as though God spilled magnificent colors, textures and sounds lovingly for us all to enjoy. The entire season Pepsi enthusiastically bounded through leaves and life, enjoying every minute of every day exploring the world around our home.

As the Midwestern climate always promises, wind, rain and cold came. The last few shriveled brown leaves still clinging on the trees one-by-one blew away like a sad and lonesome song. The sun slept earlier and outside my home I saw my world as spooky and full of scary things. Shadows grew long as night approached. Days were eerily quiet and squirrels frantically scurried about, looking for the last remaining food buried in the ground. Powerful winds made the trees creak and groan, their branches rubbing and scraping together like dead, dry bones grinding together.

One day that late fall Pepsi didn't come home for dinner. Margie and my mom called for him on and off that evening. "I don't know why Pepsi's not coming home," Margie said to Mom as she worriedly looked out the kitchen window.

Scrubbing a dinner dish in warm soapy water, Mom replied, "I'm sure he'll come home soon."

The next three evening dinners consisted of discussions about Pepsi. Each discussion began with Margie voicing concern for Pepsi and ended with Mom's reassurances. I could feel a sinking dread in my chest. The house itself felt empty and heavy with worry.

The third night, after dinner, we drove around the neighborhood with the windows rolled down. Sticking our heads out the windows we yelled, "Pepsi! Pepsi!" After two hours of driving around and not seeing Pepsi we pulled into our driveway dejected. I could tell my mom was worried too. Picking up the phone my mom began calling all the neighbors. One by one our hopes were squashed; no one had seen Pepsi.

The fourth night Pepsi was missing I went into my brother Billy's room and plopped myself down on his lower bunk, watching as he tinkered with some toy. After a few minutes I got up and looked out his bedroom window. It was a black, windy night, the howl of the wind and the rustle of the trees was the perfect backdrop for a scary story. After some time I thought I heard a forlorn cry above the noise of the wind. It sounded awful. "Listen," I said to Billy. "Do you hear that?" He stopped what he was doing and listened.

"No." And he went back to his work.

I listened some more. Moments passed and I heard it again. It sounded like a cry and a moan. It was a horrible sound, the sound of something in great pain, something crying out for help, alone and terribly frightened. "Do you hear that?" I asked him again.

Hunkered down still engaged in his toy he said, "No."

"Could it be Pepsi?" I asked cupping my hands on the window's glass, trying to see through the darkness. He didn't answer. He was done listening to me. "Should we go out and see if it's him?" I said still peering outside at the creepy blackness. He didn't answer. A short while later I headed for bed, and lying there I had a fitful night's sleep.

The next morning was sunny and pleasantly crisp, a reprieve from the cold winter to come. I was in the kitchen when I heard some commotion outside the back door. I opened the screen door and headed down the long flight of stairs towards the noise, the screen door slapping shut behind me. Two steps from the bottom of the stairs I looked to my left–the very spot where Gerry and I ran away from Pepsi when he was a pup a year and a half earlier. Crouched down among the dead leaves I saw Dave, our live-in Mother's Helper, looking at something. Then, as if in slow motion, I turned back to my right and saw Margie walking towards Dave.

As Margie got closer her face contorted in pain and a cry left her belly as she lunged forward on wobbly legs. Dave ran to her and grabbed her arms and held her up as she sobbed and sobbed. I walked down the last steps and slowly moved closer to them and looked over to see what was beyond Dave and Margie. There lying on the path was Pepsi, lifeless. His fluffy ears were splayed out, his mouth open with his tongue hanging out. The reason for his death was obvious; his stomach was torn open and his guts were lying outside his body. I had never seen anything so horrific before. I stood frozen in place and it felt as if I was standing above my body looking down.

Margie screamed and screamed, like a mother bear whose cub suddenly died, her voice echoing through the lawns, trees and ravines. She crumpled to the ground, her head hanging low and tears streaming down her face. And I stood there, the guilt I felt beyond measure, still hearing the moans and cries of our dog from the night before. I knew he had suffered terribly and I blamed myself for his death and my sweet sister's pain.

God, help me, I thought, *I was weak. I was a coward. Why didn't I tell my mom? I didn't help my dog when he needed me.* The guilt washed over me like a suffocating blanket.

For weeks afterwards every night Margie clutched Pepsi's collar in her hand as she lay in bed crying herself to sleep. The mood in the house was tense; every slap of that kitchen door was a reminder of our beloved dog. None of us knew how to cope with that kind of loss. I was so intensely sad and ridden with guilt. Eventually Pepsi's collar was hooked on Margie's wall as a memorial, an indication she was moving through her grief. I felt Pepsi's spirit stay with us, lingering for a while until he ran off, probably to play. To this day, some 30 years later, Margie still has Pepsi's collar, a reminder of her best friend.

Baby Sparrow

When I was ten I found myself responsible for the life of a baby sparrow. I don't know how I ended up with that responsibility, but there sat a bird on the bottom of a small birdcage, in Billy's bedroom. I marveled that nature could make something so tiny, adorable and so vulnerable. She was the size of a chicken egg with black bead-like eyes, brown feathers with pinfeathers and downy feathers poking out everywhere, indicating that she was still a baby.

It was Friday afternoon and with no school for the next two days I was sure I could mother this bird. I was thrilled to have her but equally– or more so–desperately concerned about how to take care of her. She sat on the floor of the cage, her chest heaving in and out. She made this baby chirping/crying noise that made me think she was hungry, but I had no clue what to feed her.

She kept looking towards me and opening and closing her muted yellow-colored beak as if to say, "Please, someone feed me." I found nuts and seeds in the house and scattered them on the bottom of the cage. I cut a paper cup in half and put water in the bottom. I placed it in the cage beside her, and I watched her in frustration as she ignored the food and water. She just kept on making that mournful noise and opening and closing her mouth. "Come on, baby," I begged, "eat. Come on, eat."

Billy dug up some worms for me and I placed them on the bottom of the cage. She didn't look twice at the worms and just kept on crying. I knew she was hungry and it was breaking my heart that she wouldn't eat. I had no idea who to ask for help. I took the little bird out of the cage and tried to hand feed her to no avail. I thought, *well maybe she'll eat if she gets hungry enough.*

That evening we were supposed to go to my aunt's house for dinner. I begged my mom to let me stay home. I explained that the baby bird needed me, but Mom insisted that I go. Throughout the evening, which included a dinner that dragged on and on, I thought of the baby bird and watched the clock as the seconds crept by. Finally we left and 30 minutes later arrived in front of our house.

Running across the long porch I flung open the front door and bounded two steps at a time up to Billy's room. His light was on and the bird cage was straight ahead. I quickly walked over and peered inside. Lying at the bottom of the cage was the baby bird–dead. She looked so sad, so alone, so abandoned and having had no one to love her, she died alone. Her cage seemed so big, the bars creating a prison in which she died. I was crushed. I felt terribly guilty that I was responsible for the little bird's death.

That night as I lay in bed I couldn't get the image of the bird alone and dead in the cage out of my head. My heart was heavy with grief and my checks wet with tears. After tossing and turning I finally fell into a fitful sleep.

Louie the French Poodle of Ravine Drive and Beaches

Shortly after Pepsi died my mom found a breeder and bought another Standard Poodle. When the pup moved in it was bittersweet. The little black bundle was adorable and sweet but it felt wrong to love him, like we were betraying Pepsi. But in a short time we fell in love with our new dog, appreciating him for his unique personality. After some brainstorming on names for the new dog, my mom came up with the best of all our suggestions: Louie. My mom felt that Louie was a nice French name for a French poodle.

Louie's puppy-hood was spent largely in the kitchen with newspapers on the linoleum as a method of housebreaking. I remember times when Louie was caught chewing on something he shouldn't my mom smacked a rolled up newspaper on the kitchen table with a *WACK,* scaring the daylights out of not only the dog but everyone else within ear shot.

That puppy was trying my mom's patience at times, but the worst was when he was left in the kitchen with my brother's birthday cake sitting on the kitchen table. When it was time to go get it my mom went into the kitchen and found big chunks of the cake missing. My mom put her hands on her hips and looked at Louie. Louie stood there with this innocent look on his face, his tongue hanging out and his tail happily wagging like a rudder. But Louie couldn't hide the white frosting all over his muzzle and big, floppy ears. My mom tried to hide a smile and called out, "Kids, come here!" We came running. "See what that dog did?" She pointed at the cake.

Looking from Louie to my mom and back again we saw the smile my mom was trying to suppress and we all said in unison, "Louie!" and started giggling. "Look what you did!"

Trying to look stern Mom said in an angry tone, her lips pursed, "Louie, what did you do?" He just wagged his tail harder at his name and our giggles. It was impossible to be mad at that dog!

By the time Louie turned a year old he was housebroken and could be trusted to have the run of the house when we were gone. Louie found a spot to watch us come and go. It was a large window on the landing between our first and second floors. Anytime we returned to the house and looked up from outside, Louie was at that window wagging his tail, jumping up and down and barking. What a wonderful welcome! As soon as we stepped out of the car he bounded down the stairs and met us at the door. When we came inside he leaped up at us, practically knocking us down.

When I was 11 Louie and I started walking the long winding road through the ravines to the beach below. At the foot of the long road an old, gray cement water pumping station loomed silently and hauntingly near the parking lot. The beaches spanned on either side of the pumping station, with Lake Michigan water as far as the eyes could see. Silver fish washed up on the shore in large numbers, hundreds of rocks covered the beach and sea glass sparkled in the sunshine. To my benefit beach goers long ago found other more suitable beaches, allowing me to take my dog to enjoy the sun, sand, water and solitude.

Louie and I especially loved going to the beach when it was windy because the waves roared to the shore. Louie found it greatly amusing to leap after the waves as they hit the shore and bite them. "Go get it!" I'd encourage him, laughing. I walked along the shoreline, my hair and clothing blowing in the strong wind, with Louie running, sniffing and chasing about me. There was a mystic and eerie feeling on those days, and the water seemed vast and menacingly strong. But I always felt safe and secure as long as Louie was with me.

Billy and I dressed Louie up in T-shirts, bandanas and shorts. Whenever he was wearing one of our get ups he had a look of resignation on his face. Because the T-shirt often times was too big he would walk off tripping on it as he went. We also discovered Louie liked to fetch the beam of a flashlight. We spent many would-have-been-boring hours amusing our dog and ourselves as he chased the light in the dark.

Ever since the tragedy of Pepsi's death my mom made sure the hook was latched on the back screen door. But one of the other causes of Pepsi's more than enthusiastic personality was the fact that he was not neutered. It was the 1970's and at that time the education wasn't there about the benefits of spaying and neutering. So, because we didn't know any better, we never neutered Louie either. That would prove to be a very bad decision.

One of the more mild side effects of an un-neutered male dog was that Louie humped many guests who visited our home. My mom would warn us before a friend arrived, "Don't let your friend stand too long in one place," or "Have them sit down."

But if the opportunity allowed him Louie would go at the victim's leg with a vengeance. The person whose leg he was flirting with would shuffle their free leg away while kicking out the humped-on leg like they were trying to shake out a kink. But Louie was not easily deterred and with steel determination would clamp on tighter. Finally one of us kids (after getting a big laugh at the victim's expense) would come to the rescue of the person who was the object of Louie's attention and grab Louie by the collar and pull him off.

By the time Louie was seven he had slowed down considerably.

He no longer mounted people, and taking a walk in the neighborhood was much more to his liking than romps at the beach. His curly hair was turning gray and his eyes were slightly cloudy. He was perfectly content to just follow my mom from room to room and plop down when she quit moving.

That year we sold our big house and bought a smaller one on the other side of town. At the new house Louie didn't have the big window to sit in front of and watch for people coming over. His new post was at the top of the back steps where he could see out the back door, the most frequently used entrance of the house, and greet anyone who came through it. He handled the change without fuss because the people he loved, especially my mother, were still with him. Even though my mom didn't gush love all over Louie (she wasn't a dog lover; Louie was bought for us), I often times heard her talking to him when she didn't think anyone could hear her. She really loved that dog.

A few years later I got married and moved out of the house. There was still plenty of activity at my mom's house because my younger brother and sister still lived at home. We also had most of the family get-togethers there. Louie greeted me with a warm welcome. Even though I never got used to the fact that we no longer lived in my childhood home I was comforted that my childhood dog was still there.

One morning I received a call from my mom. "Louie has been throwing up. He doesn't seem right." Louie was ten years old at the time.

"What else is he doing?" I asked.

"Well, he's sleeping a lot more and seems listless." She sounded very concerned.

"Okay, we should take him to the vet and see what's wrong." She agreed and said she would call me after she made the appointment. My gut told me something wasn't right.

The following day I met my mom and Louie at the animal hospital. The veterinarian was concerned about his symptoms so he ran some tests. Some time later the vet came into the exam room. He had a solemn look on his face. "I'm sorry but Louie has testicular cancer. It has advanced and there is no treatment." He paused, searching our worried faces. "Um, I'm so sorry, but he has maybe six months at best."

"What does that mean exactly?" I asked, realizing right away that I had just asked a stupid question.

"You can keep him quiet and his condition would be manageable for a time." He pushed his glasses up the bridge of his nose and scratched nervously at his temple. Looking at us with kind eyes he added, "Or we can put him to sleep any time before."

"Let me talk to my kids," my mom said. I was trying hard not to cry. We walked into the small waiting area to talk. My mom expressed her concern about leaving Louie home alone all day while she was at work. She said, "I just can't handle working full time and taking care of him if he's sick. It's just too much."

"I can bring Louie home to my house," I said. Even as I said it I knew it wasn't a logical option. I already had two dogs of my own and they were young and rambunctious. Chuck and I lived in a very small, three-bedroom, ranch-style house, and I was eight months pregnant. I seriously considered making up the spare bedroom for Louie, but I knew he wouldn't be happy. The only home he had ever known was with my mom, and I couldn't see him adjusting to my home.

My mom called my siblings to get their input. We all felt like we had no choice. My mom spoke to the vet and told him we decided to put our precious Louie to sleep. I couldn't imagine how hard that was for my mom–until years later when I had to do the same thing with my own dogs.

The vet's assistant brought my mom and me into a private room void of everything but a few chairs. She brought Louie in the room and we were greeted with the usual tail wagging and little tap-dancer dance.

I wanted to bring him home so badly. My mom stood by as I knelt down and put my arms around Louie's shoulders. I put my face by his curly head and nuzzled up to him. Breathing in his oily, dandruff-y old man smell I said, "Louie, I love you so much. Thank you for going to the beach with me, for greeting me every day after school and being our best friend." I was fighting back tears.

My mom said, "I can't take this," in a cracked voice and walked out. We all handle grief differently.

After she left I felt more free to cry and tears spilled down my cheeks as I held on tight a bit longer. I imagined our hearts meeting, felt the warmth of our souls touching. "I will carry you with me always." Saying goodbye was horrible and I miss him to this day some 17 years later.

Billy met us at the animal hospital and agreed to be with Louie when he was put to sleep. I was so grateful. I didn't want him to be alone but felt that I would literally lose it if I stayed, and in my condition that wasn't a good idea. Billy told me later that he held Louie the whole time and he died peacefully.

For months afterwards when I visited my mom I occasionally thought I heard Louie's tags from his collar jingle. One afternoon my mom and I were sitting at the kitchen table enjoying some coffee and a snack. I asked her, "Mom, do you ever hear Louie's tags making noise?"

"Yeah. It's kind of creepy, but yes, I hear him."

For months when visiting my mom I felt comforted by hearing the tags jingle. Whether a figment of our imaginations or Louie's spirit not ready to move on, I don't know, but after a time I stopped hearing his tags. When I asked my mom if she still heard them she just shook her head no.

Today when I do speeches about the importance of spaying and neutering I tell my audience about Louie and how his life was cut short because he was not neutered. I can only hope by doing that it will give pet owners one more reason to understand the importance of spaying or neutering their pets.

Fly, Fly Away

When I was 16 I moved in with my dad, his wife Clare and their baby Mikey. The home was situated on five hilly acres, with mature trees and an apple orchard. As young children my brothers, sisters and I visited our dad when he lived there, before Clare was in the picture. We enjoyed long days of adventures–which included playing tag, fishing at the neighbor's pond and climbing trees. The house was miles from the nearest gas station and 15 minutes by car to the nearest shopping mall. But this time living there would not create happy memories…well, except for one.

Clare was not at all happy that my dad invited me to live with them. Frankly, Clare would have preferred if all five of us kids from his first marriage simply disappeared. She was stoically icy to all of us. She made it clear since we met her that we were the Cinderellas and she was the stepmother. Knowing how she felt about us, I didn't like her one bit.

The two of us living under the same roof in the middle of nowhere created a huge amount of tension in the house. My dad was gone a lot so more often than not it was just Clare, Mikey and I. She didn't speak to me, so in turn I didn't speak to her. When my dad was home often times I could hear them fighting about me living there. More than a few times my dad would come into my room and blame me for his wife's unhappiness. There was no doubt in my mind that Clare was just working on a way to get me out of their house for good.

It was the beginning of the school year. After school and on weekends I stayed in my bedroom reading or writing. Surrounding me was this feeling of incredible loneliness, as if I was wearing it as a heavy coat. Nothing now, or back then, is worse than feeling unloved and forgotten. And there at that house, amid apple trees and land that should have been joyous to be living in, I felt like I was in a dank cave, by myself, the white noise of loneliness raw like a wound.

One day I went by myself to the mall and wandered into the pet store. I loved to look at the animals there and watch with fascination as they communicated with everyone and everything around them. That particular pet store had puppies, birds and fish, as well as supplies of all kinds.

Making my way to the bird section I stopped at a large cage filled with cockatiels in many colors. There were gray, pied (speckled and freckled in white, gray and yellow), yellow, and yellow and white ones. All of them had a perfectly round, orange circle on each cheek. The male cockatiels had brighter orange cheeks than the females.

The cockatiels had their own social network that was fascinating to watch. They communicated with different chirps, hisses and screeches. They fluffed their feathers in excitement or in flirtation. They took turns eating and drinking. They preened each other and themselves. Sometimes spats broke out among them where they would screech angrily at each other, beaks open and pecking at the offender. One would fly off, ruffle his feathers as if saying, *Well, how dare!* and then go about his business.

I kept eyeing one cockatiel with a stark white body and yellow head. He was so beautiful and seemed gentle and sweet. After watching the birds for a while I decided I wanted the little bird. I would have to find a way to convince my dad.

My dad was not a big animal lover and his house was spotless, so convincing him would be tough. The following day he agreed to go to the pet store with me to meet the bird. To my surprise he not only let me have the bird, but he also bought the bird along with a birdcage and accessories. I felt so special in that moment. It was truly a miracle.

A store worker expertly caught the bird in a net–the bird protesting with angry screeches–and gently placed him in a cardboard box with holes punched in it for air. I carefully held the bird in the box against my chest as my dad carried everything else we got to the car and drove home.

Alone in my room I placed the box on the carpeting in my bedroom. I quietly opened the top of the box and peered inside. The little bird looked up at me his beak open, hissing. I reached into the box and put my hand gently around the bird. He promptly latched onto my finger like a crocodile and would not let go. I pulled my hand and bird out of the box and cried out in pain. That bird would not let go! I had to shake my hand to get him to let go, and he dropped to the floor and scurried away.

I was shocked at his viciousness. A lump grew heavy in my throat and I started to cry. Then I felt stupid for crying, which made me cry even more. At that time in my life I was so lonely the rejection I got from my new bird was just too much.

But with nothing else to do, and hours of boredom ahead of me, I was determined to get the bird to like me. I thought naming him something that would symbolize an optimistic outlook to our relationship would be a good idea, so I named him Buddy.

Any time I moved my hand towards Buddy his eyes would narrow, he would hiss and his beak would open as he braced to bite. As I got closer he would back up and then make a run for it. He scurried away and stopped only when he felt he was at a safe distance, his tiny chest heaving. (He couldn't fly because the pet store clipped off the last layer of feathers in order to limit flying ability. This was done as a means of taming a bird, the theory being that if they can't fly they are forced to learn to like people.) It had been three long days since I brought him home. I was discouraged and felt terrible for the scared little guy.

We were both still afraid of each other (I recalled with great vividness the bite that drew blood), so I found a thick glove and placed it on my hand. I got down on my hands and knees and slowly reached my gloved hand toward him. He ran off and to a corner where he was trapped. I crawled slowly towards him and gingerly reached out a finger to him, placing my finger under his chest. "Up, up, Buddy," I encouraged. Buddy raised a claw up in protest and then hesitantly put it on my finger. Gaining his bearing he shifted his weight to the foot on my finger and then moved his other foot up onto my finger. "Good boy, Buddy!" I exclaimed in a whisper, smiling widely. Victory!

Within a few days I had him stepping up. He still hissed at me with cross-eyes, but we were making progress. I bought a book about cockatiels and learned that Buddy was fearful and aggressive because he wasn't "hand raised." A hand-raised bird is taken away from his mom before it even has feathers and is fed by a human, thus imprinting a human as the bird's mommy. Buddy was raised by his bird-mom so I couldn't blame him for not liking me. The book I read about birds said it could take hours and hours of working with him to make him tame and to move slowly so the bird would learn to trust me. I was determined to make a friend.

After a week I no longer needed gloves and he no longer made angry noises at me. When I approached he chirped a happy hello. We settled into a daily routine. Each morning I reached into his cage and he climbed up on my finger. As I walked across the room he scampered up my arm and onto my shoulder, where he perched. He sat busying himself preening and picking out dead skin and tiny pinfeathers.

Within a month I could gently run my fingers down his feathers and kiss his beak. He loved to hang out on my bed with me as I read or wrote, scurrying about and picking at the pages of the book I was reading or nibbling on the pen I used for writing. We were best friends, my loneliness a thing of the past. He lifted me up and filled me in. My room was no longer sterile and empty but filled with life and love.

A few months later Buddy and I moved back to my mom's house. He took residence with me in my old bedroom. I was back at my former school and spending time with my old friends, but Buddy remained center stage in my life. He rescued me from a dark loneliness and helplessness and brought me a light. In turn I rescued him from fear and confusion.

I let the feathers on his wings grow out so he could fly and he would fly around my room as much as he pleased. I decided Buddy needed a friend, so I went to a pet store and bought a gray female cockatiel that was not nearly as pretty as Buddy. I picked her out because I knew that since she wasn't as pretty as the others in the cage she would have a harder time finding a home. I named her Ashley. Within weeks I bought another bird, a little green conure that I named Lancelot. I was thrilled with my bird family.

Unlike the cockatiels, who did everything with dainty dignity, Lancelot was a shameless clown. He hung upside down like a monkey and hopped clumsily from place to place. He climbed up curtains, grabbing the cloth with his claws and beak, and when he reached the top he would scream out in exuberant domination and bob his head up and down like a bobble head in a bumpy car.

His screaming was so loud it was heard throughout the house. Luckily for me (and him) my mom's room was all the way on the other end of the house. I didn't care about his ear-piercing scream; he was my baby–loud baby, I had to admit–but mine. The birds hardly ever were in their cages and my room was their playground.

Routinely, I took Lancelot outside on my shoulder so he could enjoy the warm, fresh air and bright sunshine. Part of me felt bad that these birds were living so differently from what was natural for them, and I wanted them to have the best possible life. Buddy and Ashley never went outside in their cage because even with their wings clipped they could still fly and I didn't want them to fly away. But I did clip Lancelot's wings. I paid close attention to Lancelot in my bedroom and when he began to fly a little I would clip his wings again so that I knew when we went outdoors he couldn't fly away.

One morning as the sun shone brightly on a perfect late spring day, I picked Lancelot up, placed him on my shoulder and headed outside. We went through the screened-in porch. I opened the back door and as it slammed behind me Lancelot shot off my shoulder and flew up into the air like his wings had never been clipped at all.

Up, up and away Lancelot flew, his wings pumping up and down swiftly. The whole time I could hear his screechy cry of happiness. I stood there dumbfounded, sick to my stomach. I cupped my hands over my mouth and yelled, "Lancelot, come back!" He landed on a giant oak tree, screeched back and then flew to another tree farther away. He was green, the tree's leaves were green, and I could barely distinguish the two. I ran down the deck stairs, "Lancelot, please come on. Come on, baby. Lancelot, please!" I begged. I raced from tree to tree, following his call as it continued to move farther away. By now tears were streaming down my face. I felt so betrayed by him. How could he not want to come back to me? "Lancelot, you come now," I ordered, sobbing as tears fell down my face.

My mother must have heard me because she ran outside. "What happened?" she asked me.

"Lancelot flew away," I moaned, searching her face for help.

"I'll call the neighbors. That way if someone spots him they'll call. Which direction did he go?" I pointed towards the ravines.

While she headed for the house I hurried down the winding road that led to the ravines, which were filled with giant old trees. Looking up tree after tree, I called out to my little boy. The air was eerily quiet.

I stayed out until after dusk. His cries were long gone, as was he. I knew I would never see him again. I was angry with him for leaving me and wondered what our love for each other meant after all. But I also knew in my heart that birds weren't meant to be pets and this one needed to be free. I worried that he wouldn't survive by himself and prayed that someone would find him and take him in.

Over time the pain of losing him was less raw and I lavished additional love on my cockatiels. One morning I took Buddy outside in his cage. Cleaning their cages was a mess so I figured one morning that I would clean Buddy's cage outside. Doing so, I reasoned, would serve two purposes. It would make the process less messy because it was outside, and Buddy would get some fresh air and sunshine.

The wind was strong but balmy. I set the cage on the white iron patio table and pulled the tray on the bottom out half way. I didn't realize that the whole bottom would be open until it was too late. It happened so fast that if I had blinked I would have thought he had magically disappeared. Instead I saw Buddy swoop out the bottom, and with one chirp goodbye, he was gone.

I called up into the trees, "Buddy!" Remembering too clearly what happened with Lancelot I groaned out in pain and frustration and anger at my stupidity. I also felt betrayed once again that my beloved best friend had left me. I opened the back door, sobbing and nearly bumped into my mom.

"What happened?" she asked.

"Buddy flew away," I said between clenched teeth choking back tears.

"Oh, no, Sandy, I'm so sorry. Maybe he'll come back."

"No he won't," I said firmly. *He just wanted to be free,* I thought. I left the bird-cage outside, empty and soulless, as I climbed the stairs to my room, crawled under the covers and fell asleep.

Less than a month later I was in my room when Ashley began thrashing around in her cage. I picked her up and attempted to calm her. I held her as she died in my hands. My bird family was gone. What I learned is that birds don't want to be caged and when given the choice will choose to be free no matter how much you love them or you think they love you. They have wings to fly and their spirits need to soar, just as we need to use our legs to walk, to run and so much more. I am eternally grateful for my birds, especially Buddy, who lifted me up when I lived in darkness and showed me love when I needed it most.

Gerbil Overload

When I was eight we got our first gerbils, Blintz and Sour Cream. They lived in a glass aquarium in our spare bedroom/sewing room/guest room/Aunt Gertie's room (all of which the room was called at one time or another). The room was located on the eastern side of the house, one of the rooms above the garage and behind the kitchen.

Blintz and Sour Cream were Margie's gerbils. Quickly they reproduced, providing me with my much-loved Peanut Butter and Jelly. Well, in a short time both food choices then made more babies and so on and so on and so on. Each time a momma had a litter it was so exciting. I'd come into the room (which was beginning to have a distinct odor) and look in the cages (now there were two cages) and upon close examination would see teeny, blind, deaf, squirmy, pink gerbils spilling out from under a gerbil mom. Running out of the room I announced with great excitement and pride, "We have babies!" I can just picture my mom standing in the kitchen elbow deep in dirty, soapy water, stopping what she was doing for just a second when she heard me. I am positive she was NOT thinking happy thoughts about our ever-increasing gerbil family.

In short order both cages were overrun with gerbils, way too many for the cages, and the smell was now seeping down the hall and into the kitchen. My mom was threatening to let the gerbils loose in the ravines if we didn't clean their cages. I didn't have the foggiest idea how to clean those cages. Where do you put the gerbils when you have to dump the filthy, poo- and pee-soaked shavings at the bottom of their cage? You couldn't possibly hold them all. But about every other week I would go into the room to spend time with the gerbils and the cages would be magically clean. My guess is my mom probably got sick of the stink and cleaned them herself.

The gerbil's room was a fun place to go and hang out and watch the gerbils scurrying about. The babies grew brown hair and their eyes opened–pint-sized versions of the adults. I held them every day so they would get used to being held, marveling at their tiny size.

There was one particular gerbil baby that I became extremely attached to. I named him Cuddles because he always cuddled up in the palm of my hand. I was able to pet his belly with my finger and even carry him around in my shirt pocket. Most of the gerbils were too squirmy for that. But when he was about two weeks old I noticed that he seemed quieter than usual and my gut told me something wasn't right. I watched him with worry as he sat quietly in the palm of my hand.

The following day I went to visit the gerbils and looked for Cuddles straight away. Searching the cages I made mental notes on who was who and couldn't seem to find Cuddles. Then, in the corner of the cage underneath two of his siblings, I spotted Cuddles. I peered closer. He was curled up in a ball, eyes closed and motionless. I knew he was dead. I cried and ran from the room.

The gerbils were multiplying at such a rate that there had to have been over two dozen in four cages that lined the room. They couldn't have been happy in their overcrowded homes and we were starting to lose interest, which didn't help matters. I have no idea why they weren't separated so they didn't continue to reproduce. (I can only guess that none of us knew how to tell which were boys and which were girls. I know I sure didn't.) Well, one day they must have decided that enough was enough and the whole lot of them made a jail break and were loose in the house.

All five of us kids scattered and combed the house from top to bottom looking for those gerbils. It was the ultimate game of hide-and-go-seek. Our home had seven bedrooms and five and a half baths, plus a full basement, so there were endless places to search. We did find a few of the gerbils, but most of them remained free. Looking back I know we should have separated the gerbils and not allowed them to reproduce so many times. I have never made that kind of mistake again with any critters I had in the future. But whenever I see gerbils in pet stores they bring a smile to my face. As I stand there looking into the cage watching their busyness I am reminded of Blintz, Sour Cream, Peanut Butter and Jelly and a sweet heartbreaker named Cuddles.

Calico Blessings

Tagging along with Gerry one summer day we ended up at the front door of a neighbor. "Mr. and Mrs. Donkers are really nice," Gerry informed me. "Sometimes they give me candy or chocolate. They like me to visit. They'd like you to visit, too." Stepping onto the cement stoop of the white, cottage-style home, Gerry knocked on the door. Looking around as we waited, I noticed all the different flowers that were blooming in their front yard.

The front door opened and a tall, skinny, balding man answered. He smiled down at us. "Well, well," he said. "Hello, Gerry. Who did you bring with you?" he asked, peering around Gerry at me standing just behind him.

"This is my sister, Sandy."

"Hello, Sandy."

"Hi," I answered shyly, looking down at the ground.

"How old are you?"

"Nine."

"Would you both like to come in? My wife is making a delicious dinner. You're welcome to join us."

"No, thanks," Gerry answered. "We have to go now. I just wanted you to meet my sister."

"Alright. Will you come back, Sandy?" I nodded my head but wouldn't look at him. "Gerry, come by again soon."

"Bye," Gerry said and turned to leave.

"Bye, bye," Mr. Donkers waved, as we headed home. Gerry waved over his shoulder. I turned towards Mr. Donkers and as I walked a few steps backwards I waved a bashful goodbye.

The next summer my mom suggested I visit Mr. Donkers. I had not been back since the summer before. "His wife just passed away. He might like some company." Having nothing else to do I skipped down the hill and two doors down to his home.

When Mr. Donkers's wife died it was a huge blow to him. He missed her terribly. I entered his life at a time when he needed someone. I, too, needed someone, and strange as it might seem we filled a void in each other's lives. In just a short time our relationship turned into a unique and special friendship.

Being a reclusive type, uncomfortable to near panic in social situations, Mr. Donkers rarely left his home. He went to church once a year for the blood drive and visited the local grocery store on a weekly basis. Other than that he stayed home and either listened to his portable radio or made a bite to eat.

I was his only visitor for weeks, if not months, at a time. Two of his three adult children lived within driving distance, but with their busy careers they couldn't visit often. From time to time I'd bring a friend with me, whom he would welcome with open arms. But mostly I went there by myself.

Mr. Donkers loved to buy me sinful foods to snack on. Throughout the years I had a variety of delicious snacks. He bought one-pound Hershey's chocolate bars, the black cover and shiny silver inner wrapper a delight to open. I'd get the whole thing for myself. He never wanted any of the food. I'd snap off one square at a time and let the chocolate melt in my mouth, then I'd wash it down with 4-ounce Coca Colas. Then there was the phase where he bought me Jay's potato chips, which I gorged on. The whole time I ate he would say, "I hope your mom won't be mad at me that I let you have all this." I assured him she wouldn't mind. After the Jay's period were the bags of miniature Snickers bars. During any of these snack fests we sat and chatted, and if weather permitted, we sat on the old wicker chairs on the back porch, rocking away as I ate.

We spent many afternoons examining and talking about his vast stamp and coin collections. He pulled old photo albums out of drawers with black and whites of his family and pointed to each photo and told me the story of the image we were viewing. He had 78 years of life so his photo albums were filled with fascinating history. When he got to a photo of his wife he would pause, gently tap the side of the photo and say, "She was the most beautiful woman I ever knew. I don't know what she saw in an ugly duck like me. This old man was one lucky guy."

A few years passed and I was becoming increasingly busy with school, friends and a part-time job. I was outgrowing Mr. Donkers and felt terribly guilty. I visited him far less often than in the past. There were times when I would walk past his house on the way to a friend's house and he would see me through the window and run into his kitchen to get one of our regular treats. Then he'd fling open his front door and wave the food at me and say, "Hi, Sandy! Do you want to come in and have some candy?"

"Can't now, Mr. Donkers. I have to go somewhere. Maybe to-morrow."

His face would sink, his arm holding the candy would fall to his side heavily and he would say, "Okay, maybe next time," and close his door. I felt just awful.

The summer of my 14th year my neighbor Matt came running up to my house. Out of breath he gasped, "I found a litter of kittens outside my neighbor's back porch. Wanna help me find homes for them?"

"Sure!" I answered excitedly.

We rode our bikes to the house where the kittens were and dumped the bikes over in a hurry. I followed Matt behind the house and we peered under the small back deck. Sure enough, four sets of eyes shined back at us.

Somehow we were able to lure the kittens out, and unable to find the mother, we put the four kittens in a box and went door-to-door trying to find people to take them. I didn't even bother asking my mom if we could keep a kitten because I knew the answer would be no. One by one we found homes for three of the four kittens. Stuck with one kitten I thought of Mr. Donkers.

I put the tiny kitten inside my jacket and rang his bell. He opened the door and exclaimed, "Well there's my special girl. Come on in." Not noticing my bulging jacket he went to his usual spot on the olive green sofa as I took my seat opposite him in the old wingback, the dust clouding up as I sat down. I smiled like a Cheshire cat.

"I have a surprise for you." I wanted so badly for him to love the kitty that my heart was beating quickly as I took the kitten out of my jacket.

"Oh my!" he exclaimed. "A kitten. You brought a kitten to visit me!"

I got up and walked over to him, the tiny calico kitten in my hand. I handed her to him. He tentatively reached for her and then withdrew his hand. "It's okay, she won't bite," I said, placing the kitten in his lap. "Oooh!" he exclaimed in delight as the kitten darted up the back of the couch and then to his shoulder. I giggled.

"See, she loves you already." She rubbed up against his pale face, knocking his dark-rimmed glasses crooked. He smiled and straightened them and lifted a long thin finger up towards the kitten.

"Soft," he commented.

"Yes, she is." I paused, bracing myself for the next important question. I began, "Mr. Donkers, this kitten has nowhere to live. She needs someone and I have checked with all the neighbors. No one wants her and she has no home to go to. (Little did I know that the plea for the kitten would be the first of hundreds of times in the future I would plead for a homeless animal.) I was hoping, well, hoping that you would keep her."

"Oh no, no, no. Can't do," he said frightened, shaking his head from side to side. "I can't take care of a cat."

"Why?" I asked feeling defeated.

"Because I just can't, that's all."

"But why?" I pressed.

"I don't know the first thing about taking care of a kitten."

"I can teach you. I'll go with you to the store and get supplies. Please," I begged.

I wanted him so badly to have this kitten for both selfish and unselfish reasons. The kitten needed a home. He needed someone to take care of and be responsible for. I just knew that would brighten up his life, give him purpose. And selfishly it would lighten the burden I felt always having to go visit with him and be responsible for taking away all his sadness and loneliness. I had every intention of continuing to see him, but I had school and friends and I wasn't visiting as often. I felt guilty about it and this could be an answer to my dilemma.

"You'll go with me to get supplies?"

"Yes."

"You'll show me what to do?"

"Of course."

"When should we go?"

"No time like the present!"

"Well...."

"Come on, Mr. Donkers," I encouraged. "We can do this. Remember, she needs you."

That was my very first experience, and thankfully the last, going to the grocery store with Mr. Donkers. He drove an old, dark blue car that looked like a wind-up toy. It was stick shift. The roads around our neighborhood twisted and turned, dipped and were dotted with stop signs. The entire ride we jerked and swerved and sped on, barely missing other vehicles, road signs, pedestrians and curbs. By the time we got back I was a bundle of nerves, thankful to be alive and still determined to help the homeless kitten and the lonely old man.

Mr. Donkers and the cat he named Mittens lived in blissful harmony. When I came to visit he would motion towards Mittens and say, "Who gave me this kitten?"

I would smile and say, "I did,"

"Yes, I believe you did. She is the best kitten. She is so smart."

We discussed how quickly she was growing and he made sure I heard the continual purring as she walked back and forth on the back of the couch rubbing up against his head. Other times she sat quietly perched on the back of the couch, green eyes at half mast, as he listened to his daily news reports with the portable radio on his lap. She followed him up to bed at night and slept in bed with him. They were two peas in a pod.

Mittens couldn't have come at a better time. I was now relieved of my guilt because Mr. Donkers had a new best friend. He no longer looked for me as I passed his house because he was too busy with his kitten. We were still buddies, but my role was no longer daunting. Mr. Donkers and his calico cat Mittens showed me first hand the power of pet therapy. Pets joined with people can create friendships like no other.

Sammy the Bassett Hound

Sammy was an adorable, big clod of a Bassett Hound that lived around the block from us. A few years earlier I had babysat for Sammy's human sister quite regularly, a little girl whose entire vocabulary at three and a half was "NO!" Sammy may have learned that stubbornness from his human sister because "NO" was all he seemed to be saying as well.

Driving up the street with my family it was not unusual to see Sammy sitting and sunbathing square in the center of the road. The first few times we saw him my mom would tap on the horn expecting Sammy to get up and move to the side of the road. No such luck. If we were to even enter his conscious mind he would look at our car passively, and with obvious distain he would go back to looking around while sunbathing. Eventually, and only when he felt like it, he would meander to the side of the road and let us creep past.

It became an exciting game betting my siblings as to whether or not Sammy would be in the road. In short order Sammy no longer eventually moved to the side after a gentle tap, tap of the horn. Now my mom had to blare on the horn to even get him to look at us. Then again, when he felt like it he would slowly walk, head held high, big, black nose sniffing the air, to the side of the road. If I was outside playing I would occasionally hear a car's horn honk and smile, knowing it had to be Sammy in the road again.

One day Sammy decided that the blaring horn was NOT going to make him move, and so we sat in the car waiting as my mom blared on the horn. Sammy lay there, eyes at half-mast, soaking up the rays. After a few minutes of this my mom put the car into park and told us kids to yell out the window for Sammy to move. "Sammy! Go on! Move Sammy!" It didn't work.

So my mom asked Billy to go get Sammy and put him on the side of the road. Billy jumped out of the car, grabbed Sammy by the collar and gently guided him to the sidewalk. Boy would we laugh and laugh watching Billy lead Sammy to the side of the road, nose out of joint and tail held high.

Billy was Sammy's personal escort for a while until we no longer saw Sammy in the road. I'm not sure what happened to him, whether Sammy's family finally wised up that Sammy was causing a problem in the neighborhood, or if he had succumbed to a car's wheels. I was tempted to ask my mom but opted against it. I wanted to believe Sammy was safe inside his home with his little human sister–both causing grief for their parents as they continually said, "NO!"

Hiding from Horses

When I was three-and-a half my dad owned some racehorses. One day he brought my sister, my brother and me to the track to meet his horses. He picked me up and held me close as we went face to face with a horse. "Look at the pretty horse, Sandy," my dad said. But he didn't get the reaction he expected. The big animal scared me and I began to cry. He tried reassuring me but I cried harder until he moved me away from the animal.

Five years later my dad, who loved to expose his kids to all different kinds of things, decided to start taking us on Sunday excursions to a horseback riding place. During the car ride to the stables my siblings chatted excitedly with each other. "Margie, who are you going to ride?" Gerry asked.

Margie thought for a minute, tilting her head slightly, eyes furrowed in thought. "Oh, I don't know, maybe Jinx. He's a neat horse."

I listened to these exchanges completely puzzled by their fearless attitude. I had it in my mind from the very beginning that horses were dangerous. Likely the fear was instilled those many years before when visiting the horseracing track.

The car hit the gravel and a billow of dust blew up around the car as we arrived in the drive where the horse stables were. The smells of hay and manure were strong. I was sure I would soon throw up from the fear that was rising in me. Everyone scrambled out of the car except me. I decided I was NOT getting out of the car. I sat where I was, clutching the seat belt strap in case my dad tried to physically force me out of the car. Both back doors were open making me feel completely exposed. I was sure that some horse would come racing over ramming his head into me or stomping on me with his giant legs.

My dad turned around in his seat to face me. "Come on Sandy, let's go. You don't want to sit here the whole time we're riding."

"Yes, I do," I answered stubbornly, crossing my arms over my chest, my right fist white knuckled around the seat belt strap. The first bead of sweat raced down my temple.

"It's too hot in the car. At least stand outside or go over to the picnic table." He pointed to the picnic table fully exposed outside.

"I WANT TO GO HOME!" I burst into tears, panic making my skin tingle with tiny electric shocks.

"Sandy," my dad said lowering his voice to show he was serious, "this is ridiculous. Go sit on the bench. The other kids are waiting."

I shook my head and pinched my lips together. I wouldn't look at him.

"Suit yourself then," he said while getting out of the car. "We'll be back in an hour."

The first thing I did was slam the still open doors and roll down the windows just enough so the horses couldn't get into the window with their big faces and bite me. The car was already very warm, and beads of sweat sat on my forehead and between my shoulder blades.

Keeping my eyes fixed on the outside world I tried breathing slowly and calming myself. The heat in the car was increasing and it was becoming more difficult to breathe. I rolled the window down just a bit more and daringly stuck my face by the opening. The air outside was slightly less dense, at least from my point in the car, but was hardly bearable. I was terribly sad and scared and frustrated by the whole thing. Minutes inched by until my family came skipping and giggling back to the car.

After a season of horseback riding–in which I never participated and stayed sweltering in the car–to my relief my dad chose different things to do with his kids. Horses were a thing of the past for me, or so I thought.

Several years later Margie, Gerry and two of our friends, Julie and Debbie, spent a summer at a horseback riding camp. The camp, named Hoofs & Barn, was about four and a half hours away in Wisconsin. For months afterwards they talked about what a wonderful time they had. I decided that the following summer, when I was 13, I wanted to go there too. Enough years had passed that I had forgotten that I was *TERRIFIED* of horses.

We arrived on a hot Saturday. The bus pulled onto the long drive and parked beside two large cabins. The girls shared one cabin and the boys another. We unpacked and had the day to explore the gorgeous property. Running down the hill my friend Debbie and I explored the vacant outdoor horse corral. Then we went back up the hill and to the west of the cabin and checked out the cafeteria. "Isn't this place great?" Debbie commented, smiling broadly.

"Yeah, this is cool. It's so pretty here," I said looking out on the vast piece of land, pine trees flanking it. The rich shades of green grass, shrubs and trees dotted the slight rises and falls of the acres around us. It was magnificent! We ran into other campers and quickly made new friends. That night we had a bonfire and roasted marshmallows over an open fire pit, pulling the burnt, sweet mess off sticks and popping them in our mouths. The smell of grass and dirt was sweet, gritty and heavenly.

The next morning we got up bright and early and were instructed to go to the barn. The barn, located out of view of our cabins, was on the top of a hill. A large corral was at the bottom of the hill. A group of seven of us filed into the barn and up narrow stairs to the barn's dusty loft area.

While we sat on rickety, box-shaped benches a camp counselor patiently taught us about the horse's anatomy, passing around horse bones, photos of horse breeds and x-rays of horse injuries. She showed us a Western and English saddle and explained the differences of riding Western and English. I found it fascinating and looked forward to reading my homework sheets and memorizing all of the horse's body parts. I went back to my cabin that evening excited by what I had learned and anxious for the next day.

The next morning we all headed back to the barn. I was looking forward to another day of learning. When we entered the barn, instead of heading up the stairs, we followed our leader to horse stalls inside the barn. We were told we could pick out a horse that would be assigned to us for the length of our stay. *How much fun is this?* I thought.

We filed down the long row of stalls slowly looking at each horse, the kids giddy with anticipation. I stood seven paces back and admired the beautiful animals. After a time each child picked a horse to try out—everyone except me. We were told if we decided to switch we could, but only once. I stood shifting from foot to foot. The counselor turned her attention to me and said, "Sandy, there are these two horses left. Which one do you want to try?" That's when my heart began to race.

I explained, "I came to horseback riding camp because my sister and brother said they loved it last year. My best friend Debbie was going so I wanted to go, too. But, I really don't want to ride horses. I can just watch everyone else ride and just do everything else," I said matter-of-factly. She motioned for me to follow her outside.

"Sandy," she said, "you are at a *horseback riding* camp. You must work with the horses. You have to ride a horse."

"I can't," I stated, stunned at her response.

"Well, you'll have to."

"I, I, I'm…well," I stumbled, my voice beginning to rise, "I am really afraid of horses. Really, really afraid."

"Oh, come on, they won't hurt you."

"You don't understand. I can't, really, I can't." I felt a lump grow in my throat. Tears began to fill my eyes and my heart began to pound. "I can't!" I shouted. My blood was rushing to my head.

The counselor looked at her watch. "The other kids are being shown how to put on a bridle and a saddle. Then they are going down to the corral. I have to help everyone else now. Hang on. Just stay here. I'll get back to you." I stood there numb, for the first time realizing what I had gotten myself into. I was a long way from home out in the middle of nowhere. *Hitchhiking. I could hitchhike.*

A good half-hour later I was still just standing outside. All the other campers were gone, having left the barn on their designated horses. Relief swept over me when I thought they must have forgotten me. *What should I do now?* I tiptoed back into the barn. I paced the sawdust-covered ground, kicking it up with my cowboy boots. *I kind of like the smell of the barn.*

Through the door of the barn I saw the silhouette of a person, the bright light of the sun creating but a shadow of whoever it was. Like a John Wayne Western I heard the dreaded music that always plays just before a shoot out. The silhouette approached me slowly, slowly until she was close enough that I could make out the face of my counselor. She hadn't forgotten me.

"I spoke to the camp director," she began. "We'll start you out by having you just walk a horse down the hill to the corral."

"But…"

"Come on, let's go," she stated sternly. She began walking towards the stalls. I reluctantly followed, feeling like any moment I would throw up. My knees were shaking.

Stopping at a stall holding a medium-brown horse with a gorgeous chestnut mane, the counselor said, "This is Star. He is a very nice horse and will not give you any trouble." I stood mutely listening. "I'll get the bridle on him and show you how to lead him."

She proceeded to open the stall door and entered, swallowed up in the darkness. After a few minutes, during which I decided I needed to pee really, really badly, she opened the door and led the horse out. Clippity clop, clippity clop. I heard his big feet stomp the floor with each step. I stepped backwards, keeping a fair distance between us. I was sure I was going to be trampled. I followed behind, my knees still terribly weak, as she led the horse near the barn's door.

"Come on, Sandy, I have things to do. Hurry up," she stated crossly.

I made a big loop around them and was now six feet away alongside of them.

"Come here," she commanded.

"I can't."

"Yes, you can."

I knew it was irrational but I couldn't help it. I couldn't believe what I had gotten myself into! I thought of the long bus ride and how hard it would be to get home. I took a deep breath, swallowed the spit in my mouth and stood beside her.

"All you have to do is take the reins like I have them," she held them out to show me, "and just walk. The horse will follow. You can talk to him, too, in a nice way." She stuck the reins in my hand. Abruptly she walked away leaving me with the huge beast.

"Wait!" I called after her. She kept walking away and out of the barn. "Oh, God," I said out loud. I wouldn't look at the horse for fear of serious panic. I stepped forward one step and heard the horse move. CLIPPITY "Oh, no!" I moaned. I took another step–CLOP–and so did the horse. I realized the sooner I got down the hill the sooner I would be done with this so I began walking, looking at the ground directly in front of me.

Tears began streaming down my face as I walked. I just kept thinking, *I am leaving this horrible place right after this. I can't do this. I am going to get trampled. I am going to die.* The horse lightly stepped on my cowboy boot. I cried out (though it didn't hurt at all) and started bawling harder. I was about halfway down the hill and I knew the other campers were down there. I was so ashamed about my blubbering that I wiped the tears from my cheeks with the back of my hand, dirt streaking my face, and reassured myself that I was almost there. When I finally got to the corral I looked up and all the campers and a few counselors were looking at me. They were a blur of smiling faces and then they cheered me on, saying, "You can do it!" "Good job!" and "Yeah, Sandy!" as I took my final steps. The counselor took the reins from me. I looked at my friends sheepishly, touched by their support. I thought, *I can do this one more day.*

On day three the staff decided they would break me in by having me ride a pony. Seeing the horse was no bigger than a very large dog, I was thrilled with the idea. I was almost 5 feet 8 inches tall. The counselor showed me how to put my left foot in the stirrup and swing myself up over the pony's back. I did so with ease and sat proudly atop him, my feet still touching the ground. I giggled. "Now go down to the corral and meet the other kids there."

For the first time ever I pressed my heels lightly into the pony's side and she began to walk. Up and down, up and down, I was bouncing like a basketball being dribbled two inches from the ground. My brains felt like they were slowly being scrambled. I tensed up, trying to deal with the painful up and down earthquake motion of my body. That only made it worse. So as the horse walked on I tried to relax and she carried me down the hill. I looked down at my fellow campers, filled with pride and grinning from ear to ear. My head was like a ping-pong ball. I zoned in on my friend Debbie, who was expertly sitting atop her horse.

She looked at me and started laughing so hard I thought she'd fall off the horse. I laughed back. I realized I must be a hilarious sight.

In the next few days I became comfortable around regular-sized horses. Before long I was sitting atop my horse Star. I decided to ride Western and learned how to move on top of him, our bodies working together. I clicked with my tongue to get him to move and grew confident directing him with my reins. I loved the smell of the barn, the hay, the dirt and the musty, sweet-sweaty smell of the horses. I loved the feel of my horse as I stroked his silky, muscular neck. I groomed my horse and he became my friend.

We were preparing for a competition. We would be competing in different games. We could sign up for one or two games and practice the games with our horse, in the hopes of winning a ribbon. I chose barrel racing, where you guide your horse around two barrels, set about 20 feet apart, and are scored for the best time and the best form. I practiced every day and felt ready when the day came to compete.

Planted in a bleacher bench in the indoor arena I watched each game with great interest and enthusiasm. There was a fresh layer of dirt on the floor, which was kicked up by the horses as they and their riders performed. My name was finally called so I climbed down the bleachers and made my way to my horse. "Hey, Star, how ya doing, buddy?" I gave him a pat on his neck and mounted up. I rubbed and patted his neck and side. Even though I was nervous Star and I were now friends and I knew I could trust him to take good care of me.

I steered Star up to the starting line and waited. When I heard the signal to "go" I pressed my heels into Star's side while making a click, click with my tongue. He took off towards the first barrel. Nearing the barrel I pulled the reins to the right and guided him around it. Clearing the first barrel I gave Star another nudge with my heel and we galloped towards the next. I was conscious of my form. Molding my body to his, we rounded each barrel, going around and around. We were one, performing a choreographed dance number. It was one of the most amazing things I have ever experienced. Nobody else was there, just my horse and me.

I heard the ending signal "stop" and I slowed Star down and to a stop. He danced around excitedly as I slapped his side and praised him. I couldn't believe I had actually done it. The rest of the games were a blur, as I sat with my friends waiting for the end. After the last rider finished their game we all waited for the results. Anticipation and excitement were in the air.

Sitting in the stands in the indoor arena, one of the judges stood up and thanked everyone for their participation and commended everyone for a job well done. Then she started awarding the ribbons. I watched with interest as each person who won walked up to the judge to receive his or her ribbon. Each winner received a complimentary brief applause by the audience.

"Now I'll announce the winners of the barrel racing." I looked up. "Third place goes to Susan Jones." Susan jumped up and went over to take her ribbon. "Second place goes to Marcus Salzmen." Marcus sauntered up to the judge with a grin on his face. "Now, for first place. Sandy Kamen, come get your ribbon." I looked up stunned, as a lump formed in my throat. As I walked up to receive my first place ribbon applause erupted around me, people whistled and some stood up.

All of my fellow campers, as well as the counselors, knew how far I had come. It was flattering and touching to have their support. As I walked up to receive my ribbon I couldn't believe that I had done it. I had conquered my fear.

Hard Lessons Come in Furry Packages

Julie, a new friend freshman year, invited me to a party she was having at her house. There were half-a-dozen girls there when I arrived and I was welcomed enthusiastically. The party kicked off with rock music, finger foods and chatter. Then one of girls asked if she could see Julie's sister's pet rabbit.

"Sure," Julie said. "I'll go get her." She came back a minute later with a big, light brown rabbit kicking and squirming in her arms. "Settle down, Sammy!" she commanded, struggling to keep her in her arms. We all crowded around the rabbit. I was immediately drawn to Sammy because of her spunky attitude.

"Where'd your sister get her from?" I asked.

"A pet store. Now she doesn't want her anymore."

"I'll take her," I said quickly. I was fully aware I would have to hide Sammy from my mother. She would NEVER allow me to have a rabbit.

So the next day, a sunny and warm summer day, I snuck Sammy into my room and set her up in the bathroom. I had no idea how to take care of a rabbit so I just gave her the whole bathroom to hop around in. I bought her rabbit food and put down fresh water. But within a short time the floor began to smell of urine and the little pellet poops were all over.

I swept and scrubbed but within minutes there would be more poop and pee on the floor. I also noticed that Sammy was eating the wallpaper.

A few days later I decided Sammy needed a friend because she was lonely. I went to a pet store in the mall and picked out a beautiful, cottony-white, purebred Angora rabbit. They put her in a ventilated box and I snuck her home. I put her in the bathroom with Sammy and named her Princess. Knowing what I know now about rabbits it's a miracle they didn't fight when I put them together. Rabbits can take weeks of slowly introducing them to each other before they can live together.

By week's end the rabbits successfully ate the wallpaper halfway up the wall, ruined the Italian tile floor, and the whole bathroom stunk like an unventilated barn that had seen better days. If I had known to cage them when I couldn't watch them and to provide litter boxes for them to go potty in, the damage never would have occurred. But I didn't know any better and didn't know of anyone to ask.

Princess was by far calmer and gentler than Sammy. Many days, while my mom was gone, I took Princess outside and put her in our front yard and sat with her and petted her silk-like fur. I talked baby talk to her, cuddled her in my arms and within moments any worries I had would melt away. I was madly in love with that bunny. To this day I can still remember how she felt and the smell of her musty hair as it tickled my nose.

It took only three weeks for the strong odor of the rabbits to seep into the hallway and alert our cleaning woman, Nessie. I asked her not to clean my room or bathroom knowing she would tell my mom my secret. While I was gone one day Nessie entered my room and followed the smell to the surprise in my bathroom. I was busted.

"You will get rid of those rabbits immediately!" my mother screamed. "They ruined everything in the bathroom. Now it'll all have to be replaced and it will cost a lot of money," she went on. "I want them out now!"

"But I don't have anywhere for them to go," I said meekly.

"Well, you better find somewhere, and fast."

"Can't I keep them?" I knew the answer already.

"Absolutely not!" She stormed off.

Because Sammy was "wild" I thought she could just make it on her own. I remember vividly walking with her in my arms down the steps of our deck and setting her down on the grass. "Go on now," I told her. She looked at me like, "What?" and then hopped off. I had no idea that domesticated rabbits should never be turned loose and would surely die from a predator, starvation or thirst. They had no idea how to fend for themselves. They cannot make dens and do not know how to hide from enemies.

Months later I learned from Billy that he and my mom came upon Sammy that afternoon, hopping around the grass below the deck. Billy picked her up and they brought her to the forest preserve where they let her go. I am just sickened to think of what happened to her. It is most unlikely that she survived, and it still haunts me to think about how ignorant we were and what I did to this animal that relied on me.

Princess, I knew, was far too fragile to "make it on her own." Following my mom's instructions to get them "out of the house immediately" I put her on the deck to give me some time to try and figure out where she could go live. That afternoon, depressed, I chose to take a nap to escape my sadness. Far into a dreamless sleep Margie came into my room and woke me up.

"There's a horrible noise outside, like a child screaming."

"Leave me alone, I'm sleeping," I replied grouchily, turning away from her and putting the covers over my head. I heard the door close.

Two hours later I woke up and went to check on Princess. I went out to the deck calling, "Princess! Princess!"

Looking behind some wooden boards lying up against the house was my rabbit Princess torn to pieces, her guts spilled out and most of her head gone. An animal must have come onto the deck and killed her.

If I could have disappeared at that moment I would have. The pain was so great it was as if I had been kicked by a 300-pound man clear in the chest. The wind was knocked out of me. The world around me spun and spun and I stumbled backwards.

It is my fault she died. Why hadn't I woken up when she was screaming? God, that's what Margie heard. My poor baby, so helpless, so alone. She suffered. I was supposed to protect her. I killed her. She counted on me. I let her down completely and totally. I am the worst person in the entire world. I kill rabbits. My baby. My Princess.

I stumbled into the house, my breathing labored, my chest ridden with sharp pain. Why I thought to call my mom and tell her I don't know. Part of me blamed her and part of me needed my mom to reassure me.

"Mom," I cried into the phone. "Princess got killed! Oh my God, Mom! I killed her. She died because of me!" I sobbed into the phone, my body shaking uncontrollably. I leaned against the wall for support.

"I'm so sorry, honey," my mom said, sincerely sad for me.

"You have no idea how much she meant to me," I continued.

After a few more minutes my mom suggested I calm down and asked to speak to Margie. Later I learned she had instructed Margie and our summer helper Dave to dispose of Princess's body.

The rabbits were never discussed again. But I never forgot them and harbored guilt and regret at their demise. Today every rabbit I save and foster makes me think of Sammy and Princess. Each time I teach children how to care for rabbits properly I believe I am paying Sammy and Princess back for the mistakes I made.

Leo the Lion

In the spring of 1984 problems at home led me to make the decision to move in with a friend in Chicago. Since I was still attending high school I commuted to my hometown school 30 minutes away. It was a scary time. I suffered from depression and I felt lonely and totally disconnected from everyone and everything I knew.

One Sunday morning my friend and I decided to visit a pet store that sold puppies. In short order I left the store with a three-month-old, chocolate brown Cairn Terrier/poodle mix puppy with big, brown eyes and a chocolate-colored nose. I named my new pup Leo. The minute Leo was placed in my arms my depression and loneliness lifted.

When we went into the pet store and ultimately picked out Leo the pet store sold us the dog no questions asked. I was being financially supported by a friend and couldn't afford my own place. Even if I could have supported myself I would have had a heck of a time finding an apartment to rent that would allow a puppy. I surely had no idea what I was getting myself into. It's very disturbing to think that without any screening at all from the pet shop employees, anyone could take a puppy home that had the money to pay for one.

Shortly after purchasing Leo my mom and I patched things up and I moved back home. But my mom made it clear that Leo was not welcome at her house. I wasn't about to give him up so I came up with a temporary plan. It was springtime so I kept him in my car when he couldn't be with me. It wasn't ideal but he seemed happy and I still had my Leo. At night I didn't feel comfortable leaving him in the car, so I snuck him into my bedroom.

It didn't take long for my mom to realize that Leo was in my bedroom overnight, and since she didn't say anything about it I reasoned that was approval for Leo to move in. But unfortunately it wasn't so easy.

From the start whenever I left Leo in the bedroom he whined and barked loudly and frantically scratched the door. Returning some time later, to my dismay I saw that Leo's nails created deep gouges in the door. Every time I left the room I came back to more damage to the door. *Maybe she won't notice,* I thought as I stared at the long, deep slash marks in the door. My mom discovered the marks on the door and stated sternly, "Either you get rid of the dog or you both have to leave."

Without a place to go and desperately wanting to keep Leo, I worked on finding a solution to his behavior. I reasoned that if I fixed the problem my mom would give in and let Leo to stay. To stop the destruction to the door I went to the pet store and purchased a crate. The next morning I put Leo in the crate and closed the crate door. I instructed him, "Be a good boy," and added, "I'll be back later." I walked out and gently shut the bedroom door behind me. Leo started barking. *He'll settle down,* I thought.

I returned home a few hours later. My mom was in the kitchen getting dinner ready. Not looking up from the green pepper she was chopping she said flatly, "The dog is still barking." *Ugh!* I hurried upstairs to check on him. When I opened the door Leo was panting and whining in his crate. I bent down and opened the crate door. He scrambled out and jumped up and down and spun around in circles, excited to see me. Petting him I noticed his front legs, chest and face were soaking wet. *Why is he so wet?* I wondered.

The following day I decided to find out if Leo would settle down in his crate after a while. I placed him in his crate and closed the door. I instructed him sternly, "Now, Leo, be a good boy," and I left the room. I stood outside the door and listened. I could hear him moving around in his cage, whining. Within seconds the whining escalated to a high-pitched yelp. Within a minute his anxiety grew and he began barking and yelping and what sounded like scratching and digging in his cage. He sounded like a wild animal stuck in a trap. I stood there for 15 minutes listening to the noise, hating hearing his misery. Enough was enough. I opened the bedroom door and let Leo out of his cage. He was soaking wet. That poor dog was so freaked he had drooled all over himself. *What was wrong with him?*

After doing some research I learned that what Leo had was separation anxiety–a condition that is very difficult to remedy. My solution: I began sneaking him downstairs when my mom left for work and putting him in the kitchen with our Standard Poodle Louie. That solved the anxiety problem, but a new problem occurred; he started chewing my mom's kitchen cabinets. It didn't take my mom long to notice the cabinets. "That dog has to go," she yelled, finally and totally fed up with the dog and me.

Leo's anxiety may or may not have been due to poor genetics. Regardless, he was from a pet store and most pet stores buy puppies from breeders that mass produce their puppies. People who mass produce puppies are also commonly known as puppy mill breeders. They breed their females over and over again, caring little, if at all, about the quality of the parent's genetic line, the dog's temperament and what that would mean to the puppies or the people who bought one. Nor do they care how physically hard it is on the female to have litter after litter.

To top that off the breeder dogs are housed in small quarters, this, of course, causing stress to the all the dogs. Many publicized cases of puppy mills show dogs in crowded and filthy conditions. There are laws in some states about puppy mill breeding but each state is different and often puppy mill breeders go undetected. When the breeder dog no longer produces puppies she is discarded. She could be given away to anyone who will take her, given to a shelter or euthanized.

I bought Leo–which wasn't a smart idea considering I didn't have a home stable and suitable for a dog. I also unknowingly took the risk that I would have a dog with behavior or physical problems. To make matters worse I contributed to keeping puppy mill breeders in business by buying their "product." In the end I learned a very tough lesson.

The threats of becoming homeless became more frequent by the day. Unable to afford my own place I began to panic. Giving up Leo was like saying goodbye to my child, my best friend and my family all in one. The thought made me feel so desperately lonely it reminded me of how I felt when I lived at my dad's house before my dad bought me my cockatiel Buddy. On more than one occasion my mom found a family to take Leo, but I refused to give him up. I didn't know how to solve his behavior problems and I felt like I had no one to turn to for help.

Every night before going to sleep I gathered Leo up in my arms, hopped in bed and put him on my chest. We had a nightly ritual that helped us both fall asleep. I stroked his baby-soft, curly hair, taking in his unique Leo-pup odor. He looked at me with his milk chocolate-colored eyes like I was his everything. After a time his eyes would grow heavy and he would fall asleep on my chest, our breathing in rhythm with each other. Shortly thereafter I would drift off into a peaceful sleep. He was my drug, my therapy and my little boy. I was sick about the thought of losing him but in the back of my mind, I thought, *Does Leo deserve better?*

Our cleaning woman, Nessie, loved dogs. She always had dogs of her own and was the only person who gave Leo any attention besides me. She talked to him while she was cleaning my bedroom and always took a minute to pet him. One day I broached the subject about her taking

Leo. She said she'd love to adopt him.

It was a Saturday afternoon when Nessie and I arranged for her to come and get Leo. The day she was scheduled to get him I was exhausted after a night of crying on and off and was jumpy and edgy all day. I held Leo in my arms most of the day. I kept glancing at the clock watching the minutes tick by until Nessie arrived that late afternoon.

Nessie came inside with her usual "Hallo!" in greeting. I stood in the kitchen with Leo still in my arms. Without hesitation I handed Leo over to Nessie. Taking him in her arms she said, "Don't you worry, Sandy, Leo will be just fine, just fine." Unwilling to cry I just stood there, my heart feeling as if it was shattered into a million pieces.

Every week that Nessie came to clean the house she gave me updates on Leo. She said Leo was able to go wherever he chose in the house and sleep wherever he pleased. Someone was almost always home and he was showered with love. Nessie said she loved his self confidence. "That dog," she'd say, shaking her head and smiling. "He thinks he's all that. He walks around like he's king, his big butt in the air."

Nessie told me a funny story that clearly showed Leo's confident attitude. She had a mail slot in her front door where the mail carrier shoved the mail through every day. The first week Leo lived with Nessie he discovered that an offender was shooting papers through his front door. He watched the mail drop through the slot and fall to the ground. He wagged his tail in an agitated way, sniffing the mail. But as the week went by Leo got more and more irritated at the offending mail slot and mail.

He decided he was going to find out what was going on by his front door. He waited on the back of the couch looking out the living room window. He sat there tensed and at-the-ready. At noon sharp a man in what Leo saw as a suspicious uniform, carrying a big bag and wearing a hat, rounded the corner and headed for his front door. *That intruder does not belong here!* Leo thought, his tail wagging fiercely. Like a missile he dove off the couch and ran towards the front door, barking ferociously and lunging *bam, bam, bam* into the door and the mail slot. The mail came through the door like spaghetti out of a pasta maker. Leo leaped up and grabbed the mail, and growling like a wolf that's made a kill, shook and tore the mail into shreds.

Leo had found a daily job he was very proud of–killing the mail. Each day he took his task very, very seriously. Routinely late in the morning he sat on his perch on the back of the couch by the window. When the mailman arrived he was already positioned underneath the mail slot, ears perked up and tail twitching like a propeller. After each mail killing he walked away with his nose in the air and his rear end swaying from side to side.

But, Nessie told me, it became a real issue because every day they had to try and tape their mail back together again. They yelled at him when he attacked the mail, but that didn't stop him from destroying it. Unable to come up with a way to correct the behavior Nessie and her family made sure someone was by the mail slot when the mailman arrived so they could get the mail before Leo did.

The last memory of that day at my house when Nessie took Leo was Leo slung over Nessie's shoulder, his paws draped onto either side of her neck. He looked back at me curious but unconcerned. *He should have cried, barked or looked distraught,* I thought, feeling betrayed. I knew Leo loved Nessie and would be just fine–which was the only way I would have given him up. It was me who felt torn to bits by that loss. That night I hugged my pillow to my chest and only drifted off to sleep after being spent from crying. It took a very long time to heal from that loss and I learned a very valuable lesson about responsible pet ownership.

Pet Sitters
of America

A Turning Point

It was the mid-eighties when hair was teased stiff with hair spray and gel–scared straight up. Many boys and men had mullets–short hair in the front and sides and long hair in the back. There were big shoulder pads, leg warmers and parachute pants. Pop stars like Michael Jackson and Madonna were hot and *Footloose* and *Flashdance* were huge hits in the movies. There was MTV and acid-washed pants.

I was 19 and still excited about my freedom after graduating high school the previous June. I was nervous and anxious about this new stage in my life and unclear where my future would lead. But if I was asked I would have said, "I see myself making a huge difference in this world, somehow, some way."

I worked nine hours a night as a cocktail waitress, dodging an occasional bar fight and a flying beer bottle, ignoring the constant goggling and pretending I didn't notice the drug use in the bathroom. Living wild I was really walking the ultimate tightrope between light and darkness. One wrong move and I could have fallen off and been sucked into the pits of the drunken, dysfunctional world of bars, where lonely and destructive people went to forget their sorry lives. A couple times I indeed did step into a pothole or two. I was young and thought I was indestructible. But underneath the chaos of that time a fire was burning inside me. I knew where I was then was not where I was going to be in the future.

One late winter morning, when it seemed people were coming out of their skin, so sick of the long, drab, cold Midwestern winter, I was in the kitchen, toasting a bagel, preparing to start the day. No bells rang and no horn sounded. Probably if there had been one, I wouldn't have noticed. (I may not have noticed a fly landing on my nose.) A moment of clarity filtered through my self-absorbed brain, like a tap, tap, tap on my shoulder, when my attention swerved to my mom on the telephone at the opposite end of the kitchen. She was talking to Laura, our next-door neighbor. "Sure," she said. "I can ask Billy if he'll take care of the cats when you go on vacation."

Overhearing the conversation it was as if a voice in my head said, "Sweetie, this is it...follow the yellow brick road. It'll lead you to where you are meant to be." Sensing this I took action. To catch my mother's attention I began waving my arms wildly in her direction. She looked over at me. I pointed a finger to my chest mouthing, "Me, me." Such is history. That is the moment that led me to create The Pet Sitters of America and Compassionate Dog Training. And only because of that could I have found my way to one of my true passions, Animal Education and Rescue, where I am a crusader for animals and am making a big difference in a positive way.

Professional Pet Sitting

The Midwest sun shined brightly through my bedroom window, warm and welcoming, one morning in the spring of 1987. I sat at home by the telephone on pins and needles, waiting. I had placed my first ad in a local weekly paper, back in the classified section, the week before.

It read:

Going out of town?
I'll take care of your pet while you vacation.
Call 555-2638.

The telephone rang abruptly, sharp and insistent. I snapped up the phone. "Hello?" I said quickly.

"Yes, hello. I was calling about the ad I saw in newspaper," the voice on the other end said.

"Yes, hi, how can I help you?" I asked sounding way too eager and trying to sound much older than my 19 years.

"I have a vonderful Golden Retriever. He is our baby. Ve love him very much. My vife and I need someone to valk him Monday to Friday in da middle of da day while ve vork." Concept–I hadn't thought of walking a dog in the middle of the day while the owner was working. I thought it could have its possibilities. In all honesty I would have taken his dog for tea every day dressed in a tutu had he asked. I arranged a meeting with him for that afternoon.

"I see you then and you meet our vonderful dog. Okay?"

Must be one awesome dog, I thought. "Okay, thank you. I'll see you then."

After replacing the receiver on the phone base I got up from the floor where I had been sitting while speaking to the dog owner and jumped up and down and giggled, thrilled at the prospect of having my first client. Little did I know what dog was really awaiting me.

His house was in Glen Oaks, an upper class suburb, north of the city of Chicago. The town was garnished with lavish and robust trees and sidewalks snipped clean of any weeds or any trace of debris. Many homeowners had maids, lawn service and weekly laundry pick up. Parks had magnificent green-carpeted lawns with mature maples and oaks peppered expertly throughout the park and perfectly manicured shrubbery. Sparkling new playgrounds rounded out the pristine landscape, with children swinging from swings, running around and squealing down slides into the waiting arms of either the mother or a nanny.

My windows were down and the fresh air smelled heavenly. It flowed freely through the car, whipping my blond hair around my face. I continued down the road in my light green 1983 Honda Accord–rusted around the wheel wells–giving away that I couldn't possibly live in Glen Oaks but was in fact one of the many servants that worked there. I pushed my hair aside and cranked up the radio, singing along with *Higher Love* by Steve Winwood. A grin tipped up the corners of my lips as I savored the inspirational music combined with the beautiful passing world. *Today*, I decided, *will be a good day.*

Finding the house easily, I slid out of the seat of my car, paper and pen in hand, and headed for the door. My mind jumped forward to the moment a beautiful Golden Retriever would bound happily to the door, diving on me with big, wet kisses. I rang the bell. A middle-aged, short man with a rumpled, button-down shirt and silver-rimmed glasses answered the door. "Hi, I'm Sandy," I said smiling.

"Hello. Come in. I am Mr. Peterson," he said without smiling back. I stepped inside the dark house. No leaping, bounding Golden Retriever. Puzzled, I followed Mr. Peterson past the entranceway and to the left to what appeared to be a living room area. The house was very dark, especially after being outside in the sunshine. I blinked over and over again trying to adjust to the dimness. The curtains, heavy and drawn shut, closing out all but slivers of light that burst inside in blinding slits, only making it harder to see. The air was musty and smelled like dust, mold and mothballs. I followed him through the house near blind. *Where is the dog?* I thought.

I followed Mr. Peterson to a small room barren of any furniture except for a bench placed against a wall. He sat down and motioned for me to sit beside him. *Strange house. Where is the furniture? Why is it so dark in here? And where the heck is the dog?* It was a strange and awkward place to settle in but I accepted it gratefully. Still waiting for the dog to appear I settled my paper and pen on my lap–trying to appear professional and at-the-ready. I shifted awkwardly and waited, the silence making my ears ring.

Suddenly the quiet was pierced with Mr. Peterson saying, "There's Teddy!" Squinting at the door I saw a furry, shadowy figure meandering towards us. Coming closer the dog came into full view and the Golden Retriever I had imagined was really a mixed breed–a 35-pound mutt that was probably a Golden Retriever, Cocker Spaniel, who-knows-what mix. He ambled slowly towards us, big, black eyes fixated mutely on me. He had long, wavy, thick, yellow- and sand-colored fur sticking out all over that made me think that he hadn't been brushed or groomed in a while.

"Oh, he's so cute!" I exclaimed, a tad too enthusiastically. I bent forward and as Teddy drew nearer I reached out to give his head a two-finger scratch. As I placed my fingers on his head it was as if a button was pushed on the top of his head causing his lips to rise up, exposing yellow teeth. He narrowed his eyes, stood tensely and transmitted a low growl. I quickly withdrew my hand, "Does he always do that?"

"Not always. Only sometimes," he responded calmly. *This is the strangest man, house and dog probably in all of Glen Oaks.* Not very reassured, I thought, *Okay, this is my very first job and I will make it work.* I put my hand out and touched the top of his head again. I must have hit that button because once again the lips curled in a snarl and I retracted my hand.

I wanted the job so badly I reasoned that he would likely behave better for me once he got to know me. I left shortly thereafter, agreeing to come back the next day to start my daily walks, but not without deep reservations.

Riding home weary and deflated with a sense of dread I thought about the prospect of going back the next day. My first client's pet went from being the friendly, happy-go-lucky dog I thought he was, to the reality of it–an old, scruffy, little monster. Refusing to stay in that negative frame of mind, I convinced myself tomorrow would be a better day.

The next morning, I got in my car and retraced my drive of the day before. Arriving at the home, I parked and stepped out of my car. An image suddenly popped in my mind–a wild, blond-haired beast flailing his body towards me, yellow teeth exposed like the killer shark in the movie *Jaws*. I shook my head and walked up the steps and used the key Mr. Peterson provided me to enter the home. I heard the lock click and I slowly (and I mean very slowly) eased open the door. I imagined the dog slamming his body against the inside of the door, causing the door to fling me backwards off the front stoop and send me falling to the ground.

The image of the attacking beast still vivid in my mind, I opened the door wide and cautiously entered the front hall. I squinted my eyes, trying to adjust to the dim light. "Tedeeeeee?" I called out in a sugary sweet singsong voice. No dog. "Tedeeeee" I called out again. No dog.

I thought, *Okay, he's stalking me. He is now going to barrel around the corner, teeth gnashing together, lips drawn in a menacing grin. Now stop running off with your crazy imagination*, I said to myself. I forced myself to try and relax and walked from room to room with no sign of Teddy. I made my way to the kitchen.

The small kitchen had a table pushed against the far wall with a bouquet of plastic, dusty, greasy-looking blue flowers in a grimy vase in the center. There was no sign of the dog. I walked over to the table and slowly lifted up the tablecloth to look underneath. No Teddy. I turned around and took a step forward and practically ran into Teddy. I gasped. At the same time I forced a grin from ear to ear.

In my I-am-a-sweet-and-friendly-person voice I said, "Well, heeeellooo, Teddy! Wanna go for a walk?" He just stood there staring at me, no response. *Okay*, I thought, *maybe he's going to be fine*. Picking up his leash off the countertop I slowly reached down for his collar–leash clasp ready. I touched his neck preparing to snap on the leash. Up went the lips, teeth exposed, and his eyes jumped to life. I pulled back. "That's it," I told Teddy. "I'm not messing with you. So much for a career in pet sitting." I was that scared of him. Dejected I put the leash back on the kitchen table and walked out of the kitchen, down the hall and out of the house without looking back at killer-dog. Before closing the door I called out, "Good luck finding a pet sitter, Teddy."

Arriving home I called Mr. Peterson at his office. "I'm sorry, Mr. Peterson, but Teddy is growling and baring his teeth at me. I am afraid he will bite me. I can't walk him."

He didn't seem remotely surprised. "I vould like it if you try again," he said, appearing to be accustomed to begging for Teddy's sake.

"No," I said adamantly, "I can't."

"Please reconsider," he said.

"Let me call you back." We hung up and I stood back and pressed my back heavily against the wall. *Just my luck*, I thought to myself. *This whole pet-sitting thing is a no-go.* But the guy seemed really desperate. *I'll call my boyfriend Chuck.*

After explaining to Chuck my dilemma he agreed to go to Mr. Peterson's with me the next day to see if he could walk Teddy. Chuck was far braver than I. He had a practical and logical nature. Besides, he was physically strong, and if my vivid imagination was correct he stood a better chance of not getting hurt if Teddy attacked. I called Mr. Peterson back and told him Chuck and I would give it one more try. He recommended that we walk Teddy off leash. "Pick up the leash and carry it and Teddy vill fallow you."

Nowadays that would be impossible because most towns have leash laws, not to mention the liability risk of walking a dog off leash, but it was a different time. When Chuck and I arrived at the house we went into the kitchen and within minutes Teddy appeared in the doorway. I stood behind Chuck. "Come on, Teddy," Chuck commanded. Teddy snarled. I grabbed onto Chuck's arm. "Knock it off, Teddy," Chuck said firmly and picked up the leash off the table.

"Be careful," I said squeezing his arm.

"It's fine, Sandy, relax. Let's go, Teddy." Chuck walked past Teddy with me attached to his back. I moved to his side, Teddy now standing behind us looking up with a glare on his face. Chuck kept walking. I was still clutching his arm and looked back at Teddy. "Let's go Teddy!" Chuck said. Teddy meandered behind us.

"He's coming!" I said excitedly.

"Good. Come on, Teddy."

That was how my career–much credit given to Chuck–began. For over three years, up until Teddy's death of old age, Chuck and I walked Teddy. I can still remember like it was yesterday, the leash clutched in one of our hands as we walked in slow deliberate steps around the block, Teddy following just slightly behind us with a glower and an I-am-too-good-for-you attitude on his face.

We never won Teddy's heart. We were his mere servants and he made sure on a daily basis that if we dared try and touch him he would let us know it. But it did teach me a lot, my experience with Teddy. I learned that if I couldn't do something or if it seemed out of my realm of expertise (in this case fear of a biting dog) to delegate to someone who has the ability to do what you can't do. Secondly, it taught me tolerance and not to give up so easily, because often times you can find a way to do something.

Lastly, I learned that any dream of small business ownership being perfect or easy was far from reality. Being a business owner is full of challenges that would test my resilience to go on over and over and over again.

· · · · ·

The first year of business I fumbled through each day, trying to build a business on nothing but a dream–literally. Just out of high school, I had no training in business and relied solely on my common sense, intuition and the advice from my father, who was a very smart businessman. He in turn got his attorney Larry involved.

On a fairly regular basis, at my dad's urging, I asked Larry for legal as well as general business advice. Each time he talked to me in an irritated and condescending way. I couldn't figure out why he spoke to me that way. Each time we spoke I tried adjusting my tone and my way of speaking to him, hoping that it would change his attitude. That didn't work.

Looking back in retrospect I suppose Larry just had that kind of personality. I truly don't know how he kept clients. But I was young, naive and felt like I needed him and had no one else besides him and my dad to get advice from. It was pure torture talking to Larry. At the time I reasoned that I could learn something from Larry if I could wade through his verbal crap. It was at the great expense of my dignity, but I did learn a few things from Larry that stuck with me all these years.

One of the things he told me was, "Be patient. Success doesn't happen overnight." So between all the verbal slams I did get that nugget of quality advice, which I chose to keep. He was right about that. Patience would serve me well over and over again. But I did learn something else from Larry. He taught me that I should never let another professional, whose services I was paying for, treat me like dirt again.

Dooie the Old English Sheepdog

My business grew steadily the first year. It was an exciting time of hopes and dreams for a prosperous career. One of my early charges was Dooie, a big, shaggy Old English Sheepdog. I walked him for quite a few years in the middle of the day while his owner was at work. When I came each day Dooie loped to the door to greet me, his tail-less, big butt wiggling excitedly. During our many walks he pulled, not enough to strain my shoulder, but just enough to tug me along annoyingly.

At the park Dooie and I played fetch. Well, I take that back. Fetch usually consists of a human throwing a ball/Frisbee/toy/whatever and a dog going to get it and bringing it back to the human. In all reality I was throwing the ball and most of the time getting it too. It took a while for me to catch on until the one day as I went after the ball one more time I noticed Dooie standing still, pink tongue lolling sideways, intently watching me through his long, shaggy bangs. He found my fetching skills quite entertaining.

Morning and evening seven days a week Dooie's entire diet consisted of canned beef stew. The sickening sour stench of the spoiled beef stew on his muzzle caused me to gag reflexively when he nailed me with a big, sloppy kiss. Even the furniture smelled of the stuff because Dooie would rub his face back and forth along each piece of furniture, trying to rub his face clean. As I watched him rub up against a couch one day I noticed the dark, dirty beef stew all along the furniture. I wondered if Mr. Handleman, Dooie's dad, knew what he was doing. A dog's best sense is his nose so weeks and weeks worth of beef stew on his muzzle must have driven him batty. It would be like smearing a line of gravy under our noses and keeping it there for a week.

The story would end there if it weren't for the fact that Dooie lived with two male humans who gave me a run for my money. Mr. Handleman was a bachelor and father of one teenage son. The first year I cared for Dooie Mr. Handleman's 16-year-old son lived elsewhere. About a year into the gig the son, Jon, moved in with Dad, and I was asked to stay with both Jon and Dooie while Dad traveled. Being an enthusiastic young entrepreneur I was always willing to go the extra mile and try new things. Even though kid sitting was not one of my normal job duties I agreed to house-sit with the two. I was 20 and had no experience being in charge of a teenager. Let's face it, the previous year I *was* a teenager. But I went into it with gusto and immediately tried to make friends with Jon.

Jon, I would learn later, thought he hit the jackpot. I was young— probably appeared to him like a naive Suzie Mary Sunshine (the big smile, head tilting and singsong voice will give you the correct image) and he took advantage of my authority.

Arriving at their house the second evening I opened the door and was greeted, as usual, by Dooie and his wiggly butt. I could hear hard rock music filtering down from upstairs but thought nothing of it; Jon was a teenager after all, no big deal. I proceeded to walk Dooie and came back about twenty minutes later. I put the leash on the counter by the door and headed upstairs to check on Jon. I knocked on the bedroom door, the boom-boom-boom of the music so loud my feet were vibrating. Unheard, I slowly opened the door and peeked in.

Waves of thin, sweet-smelling smoke wafted out at me as I opened his door. The smoke entered my lungs, making me instantly light headed, and I hesitantly opened the door all the way, letting a cloud of smoke into the hallway. Dooie, who had followed me upstairs and was by my legs, brushed past me and trotted into the room (so confidently, I observed, that Dooie may have been as accustomed to the weed as Jon was). In that split second I had to make a decision about what to do. I marched into the hazy room, blinked and squinted my eyes and saw four teenagers sprawled out in various poses around the small room. I yelled over the music at Jon, "Shut the music off!"

In a state of dulled fear, Jon, eyes droopy, hobbled to the stereo. His friends slowly sat up as straight as they could, and he shut it off, bringing instant silence to the room. He stood in the deafening silence, head bent forward so his shaggy hair covered half his face, clearly sub-missive, swaying from side to side like a slow-moving flag in the wind. Hands on my hips, I lectured Jon about marijuana use and told his friends that they were to leave immediately. Meanwhile during the mayhem I forgot that Dooie, minutes earlier, had scooted past me into the room.

The teens stumbled for the door, down the stairs and out of the house in a matter of seconds, while I glared at Jon, telling him his father would be notified. It was only then that I glanced over and by the foot of the bed was Dooie, half on his back, half on his side, his muzzle open in what, I swear, was a smile. He was panting mildly, taking in the second hand smoke and loving the effects it was giving him. Yes, it was a stoned Old English Sheepdog! I grabbed his collar and had to pull the 85-pound dog out of the room. He weaved down the stairs without a care in the world.

Months later Mr. Handleman stopped paying his bill so I had to take him to court to get paid. He was very upset with me because I took him to court and told me "he no longer required my services." It was a disappointing way to end a friendship with a very special and unique canine friend. But all in all I choose to remember that dopey, comical dog with a fat butt that wiggled at me in greeting, who ate beef stew and taught me the fine art of fetching.

Not-So-White Socks

Early on in my career I experienced some of the pitfalls of running a service business. Sometimes it's the challenges of the animals you service, like Teddy the nasty, old mixed breed, other times it's the attitude and demands of the pet owners that create the obstacles. I'll never forget clients of mine, husband and wife Thomas and Christine Nobbs, a couple with two Yorkshire terriers, who asked me to stay overnight in their home while they vacationed to Hawaii. I was just 20 years old and still green around the gills and willing to do most anything to please a client.

Before the Nobbs left for vacation we set up a date for me to stop by and meet their dogs and see what I needed to do while staying at their home. On the date of our initial visit I arrived at their home promptly as scheduled and rang the bell. After a few minutes Mrs. Nobbs opened the door and invited me inside. Stepping into the entranceway I was greeted by her adorable and perfectly groomed Yorkshire Terriers. Noting the shiny, wood floors I took off my gym shoes at the door. I looked down at my not-so-white socks with embarrassment. *Add bleach next time,* I noted to myself.

The dogs and I trailed behind as Mrs. Nobbs went about giving me a tour of her home. The home, tastefully decorated and classically elegant, looked like it could have been featured in *Better Homes and Gar-*

dens magazine. The rooms smelled of baby powder, roses and lemon oil, the floors so smooth I resisted skating along in my socks.

Following her upstairs we stepped into a bedroom I was told I was to sleep in. She said that the dogs would be sleeping with me at night. "Certainly," Mrs. Nobbs said, "you do not have to share your blanket with them, but it is essential they are on the bed with you all night long." She tucked her chestnut hair expertly behind her diamond-studded ear and went on. "They have their own comforter. They'd much prefer it to yours." As if on cue the dogs jumped onto a leather-covered stepstool, then an antique trunk and onto the bed and daintily lay down.

"Equally," she added, wagging her manicured nail in my direction, "if not more important you must, and I stress must, set your alarm for 1:00 a.m.," she pointed over to the alarm clock on the mahogany side table, "and take them outside to go do their wee-wee and too-too."

"You mean let them out at one in *the morning*?"

"Yes, promptly."

"Oh, okay," I said trying to hide my dread.

She brushed her hands down her wrinkle-free trousers before turning and leaving the dogs and me to follow her out of the room. I looked down at my own pants–paw-muddied blue jeans–and discreetly tried to brush them clean as I hurried behind her.

During my stay at their home I trudged downstairs dutifully at 1:00 a.m. sharp, one tiny dog tucked under each arm and waited outside in my bare feet while they went potty. By day three the equivalent of jet lag plagued my mind and body. I couldn't understand why she would have such a schedule for her dogs and wondered how she did it herself on a regular basis.

I was told I was only allowed to leave the house "for an hour a day." I obeyed and the long days left me feeling imprisoned and intensely bored. I tried playing fetch with the dogs but they just stared passively at the toy as I threw it past them. I brushed them daily until they walked away and petted them often. I watched them sleep, lick themselves and play quietly with their toys. I couldn't even get a reprieve from the long days by taking the dogs for a walk because I was specifically instructed that I was "never to walk them but just let them outside in the backyard to do their wee-wee and too-too." I watched television so often the screen became blurry and all I heard was blah, blah and blah. I read until my eyes burned with weariness and I fell asleep. I felt terribly uncomfortable in their home and very much like a menial servant.

At 2:00 p.m. every day I was told to bring the dogs into the living room. I was told NOT to answer the telephone because they would be calling to talk to their dogs through the answering machine. The calls went something like this: "Hi, sweet babies, it's mommeee. Are you having a good day? We are having so much fun on our trip, but we miss you terribly." Then came kissing sounds and a sigh. "Here's Daddy." Silence.

In disbelief I rolled my eyes and shook my head. I looked across the room at the dogs to see if they were listening. One dog was licking his crotch and the other was sleeping. "Hi, pups, it's your dad. I hope you're having fun with your babysitter and we miss you. Bye, kids."

The seven days I lived at the Nobbs home felt like an eternity. I was relieved when they returned and I could leave. The first night at home I slept like a rock and woke up in the morning so very grateful for a full nights sleep and even my not-so-perfect house. I did learn some very important lessons from that experience. I learned that I would treat everyone that works for me with dignity and be realistic with my expectations. I also learned that I prefer being not so perfect. It feels more real, more alive and far more interesting.

Jelly Bean

On March 12, 1989, Chuck and I got married and moved to a town 25 minutes away. I expanded my business and in short order had our two children, Shari and David. In 1993 Chuck quit his full-time job to stay home with the kids and help me run Pet Sitters.

It was a busy morning in the office when the phone rang for the fifth time in a half an hour. "Good morning, Pet Sitters, how can I help you?"

"Yes, hello. My name is Esther Walterstein. I have a pot-bellied pig I need taken care of while I vacation." I recognized the woman's name right away. Her family owned one of the most successful retail chains in the country. I knew it was the right person because I also knew their family lived in the area. *This could be a very good client.*

"Okay, well, I'd be happy to help you. Now what kind of pet did you say you have?"

"A pot-bellied pig."

"You have a what?" I asked.

"A pot-bellied pig. Her name is Jelly Bean."

"Jelly Bean?"

"Yes."

I stifled a laugh. *This has got to be a joke.* "Okay," I cleared my throat. "Where do you live?"

"Lake Forest. And I need someone who will stay overnight and Jelly Bean has to be able to sleep with whoever stays at night."

"Sleep with her?"

"She sleeps with us every night."

"Um, okay, well, where does Jelly Bean go to the bathroom?"

"In a litter box."

"In a litter box?"

"In a litter box. The litter box is in our room."

"Your *room*?"

"Yes. Excuse me, is this connection okay? You seem to be having a hard time hearing me."

"No. No, I'm not. Sorry. I hear you, but I have to say we've never taken care of a pot-bellied pig."

"Well, we must have the best."

"They're all great sitters but none of us has taken care of, um, a pig."

"I'll show them what do to. You have to understand Jelly Bean is our baby. She needs very specific care."

"Okay."

"I want to meet the person first."

"Of course."

We contacted Karyn, a pet sitter of ours who lived in Lake Forest. Karyn, always willing to take on any kind of job, scheduled a visit with Jelly Bean. She called us after she had met Jelly Bean and Esther and sure enough everything was as the client had said. "How big is Jelly Bean?" I asked Karyn.

"Oh, she's only around 15 pounds but she's supposed to get big. You have to be really strict with a pig, have a set routine. They're really smart."

"Really?"

"Who would have known I would learn so much about a pig? But you know with how difficult they can become it's a lucky thing they are having me start taking care of her while she's so little, because once she's big, well, that could be a real problem."

"Is Jelly Bean vegetarian?" I asked her, knowing that Karyn was vegetarian.

"Yep, no meat."

"Really? And do you have to have her sleep with you, really?"

"Yep."

"Does she smell?"

"Not at all."

"Wow, is this weird. What's the house like?"

"It's huge."

"Huge?" I was doing it again.

"Yep."

"Like a mansion?"

"Yep."

Shaking my head I said, "A pig in a mansion sleeping in a bed going potty in a litter box."

"Yep."

So, for a year we heard stories of Jelly Bean. Karyn became a pro at taking care of her. She did lots of research about pot-bellied pigs and seemed to be more of an expert than the owners themselves. By that time, Jelly Bean tipped the scale at over 150 pounds and was testing everyone's patience. "If they're not careful," Karyn told me one day, "Jelly Bean is going to bite someone. She is getting really bratty."

The next day I received a call from Karyn. "Jelly Bean bit me."

"What?"

"She bit me."

"Are you okay?" I asked, concern in my voice.

"I think so. I just cleaned it really well. It's just a nip."

"What happened?"

"Her parents play this game with her where they wave their arm out kind of to the side where the fat under their arm is exposed."

"What?"

"You know where that fat is that swings under arms of women?"

"Yeah," I answered, not believing what I was hearing.

"I was holding my arm out and she bit me under my arm."

"Why the heck would they play some game with their underarms? I don't get it."

"They thought it was funny to see her open her mouth and pretend to bite," she said, sounding disgusted.

"That's about the stupidest thing I have ever heard," I sighed and shook my head. "Do you need to see a doctor?"

"No, I think I'm okay. I'll just keep an eye on it."

"Karyn," I said, "you have to cover your arms from now on." *That sounds so strange.* "Also, call the client and let them know what happened."

"I already did."

"Okay, talk to you later. Call me if you need me." I hung up.

The following morning I was walking into my office when my office worker, Donna, stopped me. "Sandy, I just got a call from one of Karyn's friends. Karyn is in the hospital. I guess the pig bite got really badly infected and her arm blew up, really huge I guess."

"You're kidding?" I said dumbfounded, worry quickly taking over the shock. "Is she okay?"

"She's on IV fluid. Her arm's huge."

"Oh no!"

"She gave me Karyn's phone number at the hospital. But she can't talk now."

"And the client isn't answering their phone where they're at?"

"No. Someone needs to cover taking care of Jelly Bean. They're still out of town."

"Do we have an extra key to their house?"

"Yes," she said dangling a key on a ring with a big, fat, pink pig on it, swinging it back and forth for me to see. "This is it."

I called Chuck at home and told him what happened. "I need you to go with me to take care of Jelly Bean."

"When do we have to go?"

"Four, this afternoon. I have no idea what we have to do to take care of the pig, and I heard she can be mean with strangers."

"Great," he said sarcastically.

"Yeah, and she's over a hundred pounds now, about 150."

He paused and then said, "What kind of teeth do pigs have?"

"Hopefully not too big. But," I reminded him, "Karyn's in the hospital."

"Great."

We arrived at the home and pulled into the circular drive. Looking around I was in awe at the size of the house, not to mention the elaborate stone and marble facing. It looked like a home that could have easily been used for a 1950's Hollywood movie. "Wow, look at this place!" I said in awe. "What would it be like to live like this?"

"I don't know," Chuck answered, getting the key out of his pocket as we walked towards the side door.

"If I had this house I'd sell it and buy a farm. Come to think of it *she* should buy a farm." Chuck turned the key in the lock. "Wait!" I put my hand on his arm. "We have to have a game plan." I was starting to get nervous.

"What do you mean?"

"What if the pig charges us?"

"She won't charge us," Chuck said in his Sandy-don't-be-stupid voice.

"Okay, well, then you go first."

He turned the key and slowly opened the door and peered in. I had my hand on his shoulder. "Where is she?" I whispered, squinting, trying to adjust my eyes to the dim light.

"I don't see her." We were both inside a large mudroom where we were told we would find Jelly Bean. Just then Chuck said, "There she is."

"Where?" I whispered.

"There." He pointed to the far side of the room. "Hi, Jelly Bean!" Chuck said with his best I'm-your-best-friend voice. He began walking farther inside.

My eyes finally focused in on Jelly Bean. "OH, holy big pigs!" I hissed. "She's HUGE! It's a real pig in a mansion. I can't believe it!"

Chuck kept moving slowly towards the pig, saying in a soft sing-song kind of voice, "Good piggy, good piggy." The pig looked at him passively with small beady eyes.

"She's not moving at all," I informed him, as if he didn't know.

"Good Jelly Bean," Chuck kept crooning.

Just then Jelly Bean slowly and deliberately turned her head towards me. "She's looking at me," I whispered, feeling the panic in me rise. I noticed I was standing alone no longer safe behind Chuck. "Chuck," I said agitated, "she is looking at me!"

"So what?" he said, annoyed. "Hey, Jelly Bean!" He said in a syrupy voice, "How you doing?"

I said, not moving my mouth and between clenched teeth, "Chuck, I am starting to freak out!"

"Calm down," he said.

"I cannot calm down." I felt my knees starting to knock together. "She's staring at me. She's going to come after me."

"Sandy," he commanded, "calm down. Just walk past me and– see that gate–go over it." Just then Jelly Bean began walking towards me.

"Oh no!" I began sidestepping towards the gate while Chuck put out his arms to try and keep her from moving.

"Stay, Jelly Bean," Chuck said sternly.

Quickly I made a dash for the gate and leaped over it. Unfortunately there was a step down. I fell and the gate fell on top of me. "Help!" I screamed.

"Stay, Jelly Bean, stay, stay," Chuck commanded behind me. Jelly Bean confidently waddled past Chuck and began heading towards me, still on the ground. "No, no, bad pig. GET UP, Sandy, GET UP! RUN!"

"Oh, Oh, Oh, Ah!" I chanted, scrambling to my feet and running–to where, I didn't know. Straight ahead was the kitchen. There, right in the middle, was an island oasis, away from the rampaging Jelly Bean. I ran for it, leapt on top and breathing heavily turned and saw Jelly Bean trotting towards me. She slowed to a stop and looked up at me with placid beady black eyes as if to say, *Oh, I guess I can't EAT HER*!

Relieved beyond measure I slowed my breathing and smiled. "Ha!" I said to her, "Can't get me up here can you?" Jelly Bean and I turned and looked at Chuck, who was sauntering up behind her. Jelly Bean turned her enormous body around and moved towards Chuck. "LOOOOOOKKKKK OOOOOUUUUTTTT!" I yelled, seeing this all happen in slow motion. "Rruuuuuuunnn!!!" Chuck began running with the pig trotting in pursuit.

They both ran out of sight and moments later Chuck came running back towards me with Jelly Bean following behind him. This time her mouth was open and two huge teeth–and I mean huge–were flashing. *Those could do some serious damage.* "Get up here," I told Chuck. But no, he wasn't going to hide from the pig. Instead he trotted in circles around the island with the pig, obviously amused, trotting behind. Chuck thought this was hilarious. He was getting into this whole chase-me game. He tucked his arms in tight to his sides, pumping up and down, and brought his knees up and down like he was run-marching, or maybe a horse on a pole on a merry-go-round, every now and again glancing back at Jelly Bean.

"Call Mrs. Walterstein," Chuck told me. "Ask her if the pig will bite."

"Chuck. Hello, the pig already bit. It bit Karyn. I don't know how the heck we are going to take care of her."

"Call her."

So I leaned over to the counter where I saw a note and a phone. I scanned the note. "Feed Jelly Bean three times a day. The food is in the refrigerator," I read. "The lock on the refrigerator is because Jelly Bean can get into it and help herself to food." I paused, scanning the letter for a phone number. "Here it is." I picked up the receiver and dialed.

"Hello, Mrs. Walterstein, this is Sandy with Pet Sitters."

"Hello, Sandy."

"Hi. We're at your house. Jelly Bean doesn't seem too happy to have us here. Chuck wants to know if Jelly Bean bites."

"Bites?"

"Bites."

"Is your husband wearing blue jeans?"

"Yes."

"Jelly Bean hates blue jeans," she said matter-of-factly.

"Oh?"

"Yes, he really shouldn't have worn blue jeans."

Okay, well then we should have known THAT. I'll just have him whip them off. Whatta 'bout his underwear? Does she hate those too? But instead I said, "Is that why she is chasing him with her mouth open?"

She giggled, "Yes, isn't she funny?"

"Funny." I paused and cleared my throat. "Will she bite?"

"She may nip."

"Chuck," I turned to Chuck still jogging around the island, "she said that Jelly Bean might nip."

He was getting out of breath but was obviously now too macho to get on the island. "Ask her if nip means nip with blood."

I asked her, "Nip with blood?"

"Just tell him to roll up his pants."

"Roll up your pants, Chuck."

He didn't answer. His face said, *I'll figure this one out. Some people are real idiots.*

I hung up with the pig's owner. "I have an idea," Chuck panted. He took off down the hall and out of sight. I waited on the island. A few minutes later Chuck returned, sauntering into the room.

"Where's Jelly Bean?" I asked looking behind him.

"Well, I figured out where the bedroom is and running through it I found out there are two entrances to it. So I ran in one and ran to the other and quickly closed the door behind me with Jelly Bean still inside. Then I ran to the other door and slammed it shut, so she's inside the room."

"Brilliant!" I told him.

"Yeah, I figure I'll get all the food ready and have her chase me downstairs. The food should distract her for a few minutes while I run upstairs and clean the litter boxes, and then I'll have her chase me upstairs and do the same thing I just did."

"Brilliant!" I said again.

So that is how Chuck took care of Jelly Bean the pot-bellied pig. That was also the last time we serviced that client. I hear Jelly Bean is still living with Mrs. Walterstein. It's been over ten years. But now I understand Jelly Bean got too aggressive even for her so she built a special shed outside. She also adopted a few more rescue pigs to keep Jelly Bean company. Ever since that experience I've never looked at a jelly bean the same way again.

Queen Anna

The wind kicked up suddenly, blowing her wavy, white hair around her head that autumn day in 1991 as she was wheeled inside her new residence. The sign on the door read: SPRING OAKS NURSING HOME. An event seemingly so small carried with it a woman who lived over 90 years. My grandma Anna was entering a building, as well as a stage in her life that my family and I knew was the beginning of the end of the life of a very special lady.

Time was moving way too quickly. It seemed like it was just yesterday my grandmother was a strong and vital woman who made delicious chicken soup and one-of-a-kind chocolate cake. She was blessed with a daughter, and four years later, a son, but her adult life was marred with hardship. Her husband was ill most of their marriage, leaving it up to her to work full time as well as raise their two children. Tragically, her husband succumbed to his long illness when my dad, Anna's younger child, was a teenager. But she persevered in life and was thought of highly for her hard work at her job and was adored by her children.

Both my dad and his sister grew up and married and had children of their own. Anna continued to be the queen bee, head honcho and CEO of her expanding family unit. Anyone describing the 4-foot 10-inch woman would say, "Don't let her small size fool you into thinking she's not big. She had the gumption and guts of a person twice her size." There was no doubt she was the boss. She routinely told anyone in earshot what to do, delegating tasks and voicing her opinion. She had a way of doing it though that was neither irritating nor mean tempered.

Her children and grandchildren were always her top priority, and we all felt her deep love. When I was a child my siblings, cousins and I spent many weekends sleeping over at Grandma's apartment in Chicago.

Shortly after Grandma moved into the nursing home I stopped by her old apartment to help relatives pack up her things. Turning the knob I entered her apartment and pulled the door closed behind me. The hushed voices and the rustling, quiet movements set the tone as I stood there watching them pack her belongings. It seemed surreal, like watching a movie in slow motion. I sat down next to my cousin Molly and picked up a bowl and began wrapping it in newspaper.

Grandma's dishes were being packed in cardboard boxes, knick-knacks gently wrapped in tissue, her bedding folded in a pile. Many of the items had memories attached to them, all being tucked away in boxes and bags. Each person packing them–my cousins Molly and Trudy, my sisters Alyse and Margie–was sitting in their own sad quiet.

Weekly my children, Shari, three, and David, two, visited Grandma in the nursing home. The kids thought it was a fun adventure taking the 45-minute drive to visit Great Grandma Anna. They loved running down the long hall to room 101 where Grandma was either in bed or in her wheelchair. She greeted us with glee, sometimes knowing who we were, other times not. I'd prompt the kids to talk to her. More often than not she was unable to hear them so I would parrot what they said to her in a loud voice.

Every time we went to visit her as part of the routine the four of us journeyed down the long hall, the kids on either side of the wheelchair, holding tight to her hand while I pushed from behind. The walk was a quiet way for all of us to connect emotionally without saying anything at all.

One morning while flipping through a magazine I came upon a picture that caught my eye. In it a senior citizen was smiling and hugging a fluffy Golden Retriever. The caption read: "Sadie Gives Love To Local Senior Home." Intrigued, I read the article. It appeared that a small group of animal lovers in Santa Barbara, California, was bringing their dogs to a nursing home to visit with the residents. The article talked about the positive psychological and physical benefits of what they called "Pet Therapy." The story said, "Pet therapy has been shown to lower blood pressure and relieve depression. There can be a significant positive affect on a person spending time with an animal."

Always trying to find a way to give back, I approached the activity director at Grandma's nursing home and pitched the idea of starting a pet therapy program. At that time the concept of pet therapy was brand new and my vision was received with some skepticism. "Couldn't the animals transmit diseases to people?" she asked me.

"I'll make sure the dogs are vaccinated and don't have fleas. The dogs will come from families where they are well taken care of."

"But can't a dog bite?"

"I'll make sure to screen each dog myself and will oversee the event each time we come. If any of the dogs are having a hard time or acting inappropriately I'll ask the owner to take their dog home."

"What about the people that are allergic?"

"Can you let us know in advance who those people are? That way we'll avoid them."

"I can."

"Okay, anything else?" I asked.

"Well…"

"Let me show you this article I saw in a magazine. They are doing pet therapy in California and it's been very successful." I handed her the article.

She opened up the folded clipping and scanned the article. "Hum, well, I think we can try it. Then we'll see. If it is a good experience then we can talk about doing it again. Okay?"

"Sounds great!" I said enthusiastically.

"Thanks for putting this together, Sandy."

"No problem. It's a way for me to be involved, get to know the staff too. That way they'll take extra good care of my grandma. Not that you don't now," I added quickly.

"I understand." She handed me back my magazine clipping. "Good luck. And thanks again."

"Glad to do it."

My next task was to find volunteers. Looking through my list of people who used our pet sitting service as well as sifting through my personal address book, I began making calls. Some 40 calls later I had seven volunteers with their dogs. They were all dogs I already knew and I felt confident they would do well with the residents of the nursing home.

The night of the first pet therapy my Chow mix Mota and I met the volunteers and their dogs in the cramped front lobby of the nursing home. I thanked the volunteers for coming and gave them a rundown of what we would be doing. Everyone was excited to be there. We headed up the elevator and to a large all-purpose room. Within a few minutes the room was filled with gray-haired, some bald, some wheelchair-bound folks.

We began the hour by having each volunteer and their dog stand in front of the group and talk about their pet. They told the audience what breed their dog was, what their dog ate and what their dog's favorite toy was. Some of the dogs did simple tricks like sit, shake and beg, which brought about enthusiastic applause.

It was my turn to address the audience and introduce Mota. I took my place in front, Mota by my side, and just as I was about to begin

Grandma yelled out from the back of the room, "That's my granddaughter! That's my granddaughter!" She was raising her arm and waving it in big, broad strokes, like a flag flying in the wind. Then she threw dozens of loud kisses in my direction. "Hi, Grandma!" I answered, waving and smiling, tickled by her enthusiasm and grateful for her moment of clarity.

The atmosphere that night was festive and joyous. The staff saw the positive results of our interactions and joined in the excitement. Every resident who chose to be part of our program left for their rooms with a smile on their face. The night ended better than I ever expected. It was a huge success. The activity director told us to come back as often as we liked.

So we began bringing animals every month. After a couple of months in addition to the group presentation we began visiting resident's rooms. The one-on-one contact with the people was intimate and moving. Hands that were riddled with arthritis appeared to become more flexible as they stroked a dog's head. People that couldn't even sit up in bed felt the warmth and softness of a dog lying in bed with them. Their pained and sad faces softened as they stroked the dog and reflected on the pets they had in the past.

Since the time the program started it has blossomed into a volunteer program that touches countless numbers of people. We have visited many different nursing homes with many different volunteers and their pets.

Ironically, my grandma was not an animal lover, and further yet, was afraid of them. When I was younger the only dog I knew that Grandma tolerated was my aunt's little mixed-breed dog, Coco. My Standard Poodle Louie was too much for her. But during our visits at the nursing home she did join us for the presentation every time we came with the dogs. But she sat all the way at the back of the room, far enough away from the animals that she felt safe. Although my grandmother died a year after the program began, whenever I think of pet therapy I think of her. She never knew that she was that spark that ignited a program that, to this day, still touches many, many people's lives.

I learned that a person could never tell where blessing will come from or what sad situation can and does bring about happiness at the center of the sorrow.

Movin' on Up

In 1993 we moved Pet Sitters to a beautiful, 1000-square-foot storefront. Prior to us renting the storefront it was a beauty salon. It had pink carpeting throughout the space and a big U-shaped reception desk at the front. It was classy and sophisticated, a unique facility for dogs.

We decided to expand our services and offer dog grooming. But after interviewing over a dozen dog groomers I realized a common theme among groomers was their lack of people skills. I was not willing to settle for a person that would offend our staff or our clients. So Chuck went to dog grooming school at the local college and after extensive training started grooming dogs. He was a natural at it and he quickly gained loyal clientele. I concentrated on increasing the dog training part of our business by working on marketing techniques and increased advertising. We made a small playroom for the kids and brought them to work with us every day.

By 1995 our business was really booming. We had 30 pet sitters, two full-time office workers and a fully functioning and busy grooming salon. I was doing a lot of dog training as well. By this time there were over 50 articles written about our company. I was grateful for our success, but the long hours, seven days a week (our business never closed), as well as the everyday care of our kids, our own pets and our home burnt me out.

After two years our lease was due for renewal. We decided the money we were spending on leasing that unit was not cost effective. So instead we prepared to move the business back home. Chuck built a separate entrance just for clients and added a wall on the main floor to separate our personal space from our business. One quarter of our living space was devoted to business services.

I had mixed feelings about moving the office back home. I was relieved that our expenses would decrease, but I knew what it was like to run a business from my home because I had done it for years. But this time I hoped that having completely separate living and working environments would allow me some private time away from the business. The move went smoothly but I still felt like something was missing.

During the next few years I tried different business ventures, groping around for what would satisfy me. I became a beauty care consultant. Cosmetics and skin care couldn't have been more boring to me, not to mention superficial. After six months I quit.

Shortly thereafter I was introduced to a couple that brought their dog in for grooming. I noticed the Cadillac they drove. They promised me if I worked hard I could be rich like them. They explained that if I bought products from specific catalogs and got other people to do the same, then I would get a portion of the profits of what I bought as well as what everyone else I got into the business bought. Like the beauty care company I had tried before this, too, was a multi-level marketing company. I saw this couple with the nice car and thought that maybe if I had more money I would be happy.

For months I spent hours and hours trying to build that business. I spent long evenings going to meeting after meeting, conference after conference and trying to sell the concept of the business to others so they too would get involved. After seven months I wasn't making any money. So I quit that business as well. The whole time I was trying those other businesses I managed Pet Sitters and Compassionate Dog Training.

In 1998, after years of volunteering at my local chamber of commerce, I became president. Through that venue I realized my love for public speaking, where I regularly spoke in front of hundreds of business professionals. My next business challenge was in 2000 when I started a small business consulting company, helping small business owners with marketing and promotions. While all along I had done freelance writing, I stepped that up and wrote more often. I was hooked up with the local high school adult education department and began teaching seminars on freelance writing, customer service, personality profiling and even vegetarian cooking. I loved the writing I was doing as well as the teaching and consulting. But still something was missing.

Passion
The dictionary defines passion as an intense emotion or desire.

Mota and Heidi

September 12, 2003, the clock in the car read 5:06 p.m. as Chuck, David and I drove away from the animal hospital after putting our 14-year-old dog Mota, a Chow/shepherd mix, to sleep. Just minutes before, I stood shaking and crying in the neighboring exam room as the procedure was done, Chuck holding Mota as he took his last breath. The dog we had adopted from Creatures of The Storm Animal Shelter 13 years before was now dead.

In the fall of 1989 Chuck and I had visited the shelter intent on adopting a dog. This dog would be my first from a shelter and I couldn't care less what kind of dog we came home with just as long as we adopted one. Walking along the rows of dog runs looking at each dog Chuck kept coming back to a big, shaggy black dog. The card on the cage read that he was a chow and shepherd mix. Each time we walked past that run the dog was lying down and looking at us and wagging his tail. "Look, Sandy," Chuck hollered over the deafening barking. "This one's really calm and he's really nice looking too. How about him?" Chuck said standing beside the cage.

"Sure, if that's the one you want. Fine by me."

During the ride home our new dog sneezed stringy, green snot all over the back of Chuck's neck, and after each sneeze shook his body, causing his filthy, long, black hair to go flying through the air like a heavy rain. It was a long and disgusting ride home.

We realized the dog was sick and after a round of antibiotics the calm and reserved dog we met at the animal shelter was no more. We were now faced with a hyperactive, strong-willed, goofy and brilliant dog–a combination of personality traits that would prove endearing yet challenging in the years to come.

After some thought and research Chuck named our new dog Mota, a Native American name meaning Little Bear. He indeed did look like a little bear. We learned almost right away not to expect Mota to be a good protector. One night, early in our marriage, Chuck chose to stay out late going to bars with his buddies. To teach him a lesson for his late night escapades I locked him out of the house and shut off all the lights. About 1:00 a.m. I was in bed and could hear some noise by the bathroom window. The window was slowly being opened. I knew it had to be Chuck trying to get in through the unlocked window. Our bed was opposite the bathroom. The window was above the bathtub and in full view of my bed. The window was a good six feet off the ground. I was enjoying Chuck's struggle getting through the window and was pleased to make him suffer.

Mota heard the noise of the window slowly opening and cautiously crept from the bedroom towards the window. The only light came from the full moon outside. Mota suddenly froze, crouched down and backed up slowly and crept back into our bedroom. He dove onto the bed and hid behind me shivering. "You big wimp," I whispered as I put an arm around him. As Mota hid behind me I watched Chuck fall with a thud into the bathtub, groan and stumble out of the bathroom. I closed my eyes pretending to sleep, a slight smile on my lips.

We had a wooden, privacy fence around our entire backyard and I never left the dogs outside for longer than it took to load the dishwasher, answer the phone or run the vacuum. Mota spent the first seven years of his life devising ways to escape the backyard. No matter how we secured the yard it took just a few moments for Mota to figure out how to squeeze through tiny spaces. It perplexed me over and over as I scanned the fence after having fetched him from outside the fence one more time.

It didn't take too long for me to figure out that Mota could contort his body in ways no other dog I knew ever could. I saw him do it from the kitchen window more than once. It seemed like I was constantly grabbing the kids, the three of us running out of the house to catch Mota. His nickname was Houdini, and Houdini was making me crazy with worry and frustration on a daily basis.

We took Mota to the forest preserve as often as possible so he could run around and expel some of his endless energy. He sailed through the preserve at full speed, stopping to stick his nose in nooks and crannies, bounding up and down small hills and leaping through bushes and groupings of trees. He found every mud puddle, splashing euphorically through them and jumping gracefully over fallen tree limbs. I loved watching him run and explore, the happiness clearly written on his face.

At home Mota sometimes urinated in the house. When the kids were babies it was on their diaper bags or on the wheel of a stroller. Sometimes while visiting a friend or relative I would get a whiff of urine in the air near where I sat. All I'd have to do is look to my side and see the offending diaper bag with Mota urine on it. When the kids were a little older occasionally I heard one of them holler, "Mom! Mota peed on my backpack!" Other times I would find a small puddle next to a cat litter box or on another object Mota decided was his. The urinating on things and in the house drove me batty.

One summer day Mota squeezed through a small gap in the fence where I hadn't noticed that the wind had blown a plank loose. I was standing on the deck when he made his escape. Yelling at Mota to stop only caused him to slither through the crack that much faster. "Darn!" I yelled in frustration. "That dog is going to be the death of me!" I ran out the side porch door and onto the driveway. Mota was trotting happily down the end of the driveway and rounded the corner onto the sidewalk that butted up to the very busy road in front of our house. I sprinted after him yelling, "Mota, come! Mota, come!" *Deaf, he was always deaf when he had his freedom.*

Jogging ten paces ahead of me I called his name again. Just then Mota swerved into the road and was hit by a car. To my horror he was flung through the air five feet, landed on his side and bounced. But like a cartoon where nobody ever gets hurt he hopped to his feet and trotted around the corner unscathed. The driver of the vehicle stopped and looked at me with tragic eyes. I shook my head and called out, "It's fine. He's fine," and motioned for them to keep driving. I am sure they had a good story to tell when they got home.

Another time after seeing Shari and David off to school one spring morning, where they met up with their friend Michelle and then went to school, I went about the business of the morning dishes when the phone rang. It was Michelle. "Sandy, Mota is in the principal's office and they told me you have to come pick him up."

Not processing I said, "What, Michelle? Wait, what did you say?"

"Mota followed us to school and now he's with me in the principal's office."

"He followed you to school?" I thought, *He's in the house.* I began searching my brain. *Where did I see him last?* It all began to sink in. I was mortified.

"Michelle, why didn't you guys bring him home? How could you let him follow you all the way to school?"

"We were going to be late. We kept telling him to go home but he just kept following us. So I brought him to the principal."

I groaned, "I'll be right there."

Leash in hand I jumped in the car and drove to the school. Entering the building I went to the principal's office preparing to be reprimanded. I opened the door and there was Mota, pleased as could be, sitting by the principal's desk. Seeing me he wagged his tail. "I'm really sorry," I said to the principal. "I…"

She cut me off, brushing off my concern, "That's okay, he brightened our morning. He's a very sweet dog."

"Yeah, I know," I said snapping his leash on him. "That's what saves him every time."

For 13 years Mota's good qualities saved him time and again when I wanted to throttle him. He was the first dog to join our pet therapy program and loved visiting the residents of the different nursing homes we frequented. He tagged along for educational programs I did in schools, loving the attention he got from the children. It was a joy sharing time with him at the forest preserve where we took long and refreshing walks. Mota was gentle and sweet with my children.

As Mota's body aged his spirit remained young. At times he looked puzzled as he struggled to get up. By early 2003 Mota began to deteriorate dramatically. His breathing was labored whenever he moved. He had lost a lot of his muscle mass and his once thick and glossy coat was now thin, dull and scruffy. We took Mota to the veterinarian for an exam. The doctor told us that his breathing problem was caused by heart failure. "He will slowly deteriorate," the doctor warned us. It was a tough thing to hear but we weren't surprised; we were beginning to accept his aging. But he still wagged his tail, his eyes were bright and alert, and he was eating and going potty outside. He still had quality of life so we were biding our time with him, but I also knew his days were numbered.

During the summer his breathing became much worse. I seriously began thinking about putting Mota to sleep–which would promptly make my heart jump. Chuck couldn't talk about it. I started asking other animal lovers how they knew when it was time. I received different answers, none of which helped me make the decision. Then one day while at the vet with a different dog I asked the doctor, "What does it feel like for a dog when he has heart failure?"

"It's like trying to breathe under water," he answered matter-of-factly. Mota was seriously suffering and I had to make that final call soon.

We adopted our German Shepherd mix Heidi shortly after Mota. She was also about 14 years old and I had to lift her up to her feet to go outside to relieve herself. More often than not she was lying down in her urine. She was lethargic and had little quality of life, spending the majority of her time just lying in the kitchen. I thought that maybe it was Heidi's time as well.

The day I called the vet's office to make the appointment to put Mota and Heidi to sleep I got out, "I have to make an appointment to…" then, "Hold on." I took the phone away from my ear and tried to gain my composure. My hands were shaking and my eyes were welling with tears. I took a few deep breaths. After a minute I got back on the phone. *I can do this.* "I have to make an appointment to put my dogs to sleep."

I wrote down in my date book:

Friday, 4:30 Mota and Heidi to vet, and felt sick with grief.

Friday, 3:43 p.m. Before leaving home for the vet's office I decided to take Mota and Heidi for a short walk. They loved walks and I wanted a few more minutes with them doing something we all loved to do. I put Heidi on leash and she slowly led the way through the grassy backyard out the back gate to the parking lot and to the bike trail behind our house. She walked stiffly but her tail was high and swaying, with a smile on her face that told me she was happy to be walking.

Mota trailed behind us, hobbling along and breathing heavily but determined to be with us. His raspy, throaty cough reminded me of his ongoing struggle. But in true Mota fashion, determined, he kept chugging along.

We stopped on the grass at the edge of the trail where I pulled out tufts of Mota's hair as I had for all the years he had lived with me and watched the gray-black hair fly and tumble around the grass. The act brought some normalcy to a completely un-ordinary day. He looked up at me, his breathing heavy and hard, with tired, black eyes. I petted his head and knelt down to look in his face. I gently leaned into him, placing his muzzle against my chest in a soft squeeze. "I love you, babes," I whispered choking back tears. *How bizarre, I have made the decision to end this sweet dog's life today. I can't believe in just an hour he will be gone. Should I have such power? But should I just let him suffer so?*

4:34 p.m. "We are late to our 4:30 appointment," I stated to Chuck, as he drove down the road in the stifling heat. I was in the back of our Dodge caravan with our son David, mentally cursing our van for its broken air conditioner. David and I took turns petting Mota and Heidi on their heads. A combination of sweat, the rancid odor of urine from Heidi's regular accidents on herself and the vehicle's gas fumes filled the interior. I grabbed David's hand and squeezed and then put my arm around his shoulder and squeezed that too.

Arriving at the animal hospital Chuck parked and gently picked Mota up and carried him into the hospital. He set him down slowly onto the linoleum. I helped Heidi out of the car and put a leash on her. She lopped inside the building with me following behind. The lobby area was empty so David and I sat on the plastic chairs provided. Chuck remained standing. Within moments a vet tech walked through the doors that led to the back and gave us a knowing, sympathetic smile. A second vet tech came through the same doors and also smiled. *They know why we're here.* I kept my sunglasses on. That intimate time in our lives felt uncomfortably exposed.

Before we made the final decision to euthanize Heidi we wanted the doctor to evaluate her just to be sure we were making the right decision. I was sure Mota was suffering but I wasn't so sure Heidi was. I glanced at my watch. *4:43 p.m.* I looked down at Mota, standing beside me on his stilted legs, his chest heaving in and out laboriously. Chuck, who had been pacing back and forth, walked up to Mota and began pulling clumps of shedding hair from his fur.

First, the doctor motioned us into a room and examined Heidi. After some thought the doctor said if she lost weight she would get around better. He felt that we could wait, that she still had time. I was so relieved. *Today I only lose one dog.* I made it my mission to get Heidi in the best shape of her life.

4:56 p.m. Moments ticked by, the blood at my temples pulsating to the rhythm of my heart. The dreaded time finally arrived when the vet tech motioned for Chuck and Mota to go into a room. I wouldn't be going. I just could not handle his death being my last memory. But before Mota left I bent down and looked into his spent, tired eyes. My mind went back to the Mota as a young, robust dog tearing through the woods in the forest preserve, flushing out birds, deer and other wildlife as he ran, harmlessly just wanting to play with them. I remembered the years of his escaping the backyard, his free spirit bursting forth into his world, and me walking the neighborhood calling him to come home.

I remembered the unconditional devotion he had to our children. I remembered Mota as my pet therapy partner, always enthusiastically visiting with the elderly, tail wagging softly, a smile on his happy-go-lucky face, doing his part to bring sunshine to people who needed it most.

I gave him one last hug and I whispered in his ear, "I love you so much," and "Now you be good," because I knew Mota would be causing the same chaos in his afterlife as he did in this life. Chuck and Mota were led to a room. The vet tech told David and I we could go into another room so we would have privacy. Standing in the stark room with David and Heidi, I tried to muffle my crying. It felt like time was moving so slowly and that I was having a bad dream I couldn't wake up from.

5:06 p.m.

A light dimmed that day. My family lost a very special soul. My baby boy-dog was no more.

Looking at the clock that evening it read 5:55 p.m. I wrote in my journal:

As I sit here, my dog of my young adult life, the first of the union of our marriage, is gone. Another segment of my life–our life–forever changed. A loss only people who have loved a pet can understand. But how could I deal with such loss? Was he just a dog, a big, black throw-away mutt? No, he was our dog-child, our canine charge, and our bundle of endless energy with the childlike wonder. How do I make sense of this? I miss him so much it feels like a searing hot knife is in my chest.

•   •   •   •   •

It was flickers of images that hit me one day as I sat in my office. I remembered being in the basement office writing out a business plan. It was on an old Mac Plus computer. I was typing out random thoughts and ideas. It was a plan for a non-profit humane society. The concept was to bring people and animals together through pet therapy, educational programs about animals and to rescue and re-home homeless pets.

I envisioned a place where homeless animals would live in home-like environments like cottages or small buildings. In my mind I also saw some of the volunteers who helped. They were older folks who were searching for a sense of purpose and troubled youth given supervised tasks. I knew the power of pet therapy because of all the years Mota and I visited various nursing homes. I saw efforts in helping animals could be a way of also helping people. People of all ages would volunteer. We could also focus on young kids, teaching them skills and responsibility in caring for animals–a built-in educational tool.

In 1994 when I first thought of the idea I knew starting a nonprofit like that was not possible. I was raising two small children, had a full-time business and financially was barely making ends meet. Bottom line was I had no time or money to give. But that day in September of 2003 my life had changed. While we were by no means wealthy, nor was I living my life at a slow pace, something had always been missing in my life–a passion to change the world, to *really* make a difference in a huge way. Maybe this idea from years before was the way.

Could I now? Looking at old files in my computer I tried to find the original plan from all those years ago but wasn't able to find it. I started writing down possible names for the humane society on scrap paper. As I kept rolling the idea around in my head I thought of Mota and the two thoughts collided. I could start the humane society and name it in memory of Mota. I had a concrete way to deal with my loss.

Meanwhile I turned my focus on Heidi. Heidi and Mota came from the same shelter. Mota was adopted first and Heidi came into our family six months later. I first met Heidi when Chuck and I visited Creatures of the Storm Animal Shelter on a Sunday afternoon to just look at the dogs. I liked visiting the local animal shelters, as strange as that might sound.

We browsed the cages one by one. Chuck was bending over petting a dog through the bars when a dog across from the one Chuck was petting attempted to sniff Chuck's butt. That butt-sniffer was Heidi. I looked down at the dog in that cage.

Heidi was a one-year-old, 80-pound German Shepherd mix. She had floppy ears and hair colored in muted shades of black and brown. She was bow-legged, had a wide butt and sad, black eyes. I thought all dogs were beautiful but she was the type of dog I knew would likely get passed over again and again. She looked plain to the eye and maybe even homely. Unlike the dozens of dogs that showed off for the visitors by jumping up on their cage door, barking and wagging their tail or others who looked sweetly up at visitors with their tail wagging, Heidi just stood in her cage expressionless, taking little notice of people. When I stuck a few fingers through the chain link wanting to pet her she just looked at my fingers passively.

On the way back home I mentioned to Chuck that I might want to adopt a shepherd mix I saw at the shelter. I said, "No one will adopt her 'cause she's homely."

"You don't want that dog," he told me.

"Yes, I do."

"Why?"

"Because, I *SAID*," I emphasized irritated, "no one will adopt her. Come on, you picked out Mota and you picked him 'cause he's pretty. Now I want to pick one out 'cause she's ugly, at least ugly to most people. Besides she sniffed your butt."

"You want to adopt a butt-sniffer?" he said amused.

"Yep."

"No, I don't think it's a good idea."

We rode the rest of the way home in silence with both of us in our own thoughts, but I couldn't get that dog out of my mind.

After stewing about the dog for a week, imagining her sitting quietly in her cage, not trying to gain anyone's attention, and unable to see the seriousness of her situation, I drove back to the shelter determined to rescue the dog. Walking with certainty I pulled open the front door of the shelter and headed back to the cage where I had seen the shepherd mix. I found her cage easily. She looked up at me with a dopey, placid stare. I said, "Well, sweetie, it's your big day. You are going home!" I walked back to the front where I told a woman behind the desk, "I want to adopt the dog in cage # 24."

"Would you like to walk her first to see what you think?"

"No, I'll take her."

"You sure?"

"Yes, I'm sure." I filled out the necessary paperwork, paid the adoption fee and followed the woman to my new dog's cage.

The dog dragged me out of the shelter nearly causing me to wipe out on the concrete. I didn't know the first thing about this dog. *Would she be okay with Mota? What about my daughter?* I began to wonder if I had made a good decision, but that only lasted a second. I reminded myself that I had made the only possible decision. I was a good judge of dogs and something was special about this one. She was supposed to be mine.

On the way home the dog stunk up the car, her long hair blowing around, the distinct, dirty, shelter-dog smell filling the car and saturating the upholstery. She sat solemnly in the front passenger seat and took in the scenery; her big, dark brown eyes looked hopeful. I was happy, elated really.

Arriving home I parked the car on our gravel drive. The dog pulled me out of the car where I lurched forward in a run-walk behind her onto the front lawn. *My God*, I thought, *she is strong*. I got that prickly feeling behind my neck when you feel like someone is watching you and knew it had to be Chuck looking out our big living room window. Years later Chuck told me that at the time I arrived home with Heidi he was on the phone and told his friend, "She actually did it. She went and got the dog." Chuck learned early on in our relationship that when he married me, he married any and all of the critters I brought home.

Chuck came up with the name Heidi. He said, "Heidi's a good German name." I liked the name right away. Heidi settled in nicely into our little home. She turned out to be a house-only dog, preferring to be inside the house most of the time. I was able to coax her outside to go potty, where she would eliminate quickly and head right back for the house.

Puzzled by her determination to spend as little time as possible outside I called the shelter to see if they had more information about Heidi's history. They provided me with the name and phone number of her previous owners. I called the previous owners and explained who I was. I asked, "Can you tell me a little about her, where she stayed and why you gave her up?"

"Oh, yeah, sure. We got her as a small pup. She got bigger and bigger quick-like and knocked the kid over. We put her outside. We couldn't have her knocking down our daughter. She stayed in the back-yard. Then she just got too big. We didn't know she'd get so big." He went on, "We just couldn't keep her anymore so we brought her to the shelter."

No wonder Heidi didn't want to stay outside. Dogs are pack animals and when a dog is isolated from his or her pack (which in this case was a human family) they can become emotionally withdrawn and even anti-social.

"Thank you for your time," I said and hung up. They never asked how Heidi was doing or thanked me for adopting her. It was obvious she was just a disposable object to them. Poor girl.

Heidi was loyal from the start. She followed me from room to room and wherever I stationed myself she lay by my feet. She was a great watchdog, alerting us when people came to the house with her ears perked up and a serious and protective bark. It was nice to have a dog you knew would protect you. Unlike Mota, Heidi made me feel safe at home.

Even with all of Heidi's positive qualities, she did not like being hugged. She tolerated it from me but not without her body tensing. If anyone else tried hugging her she would growl a warning. I didn't want to test the growl so I taught my kids from the beginning that they were not allowed to hug Heidi.

One afternoon the kids and I were relaxing at home. Four-year-old Shari was in the dining room having a snack. Three-year-old David and Heidi sat side by side on the living room floor watching *Barney* on television. I was sitting in the easy chair behind David and Heidi trying hard not to fall asleep. David looked over at Heidi sitting beside him and decided to put his arm around her. Heidi voiced a low growl. The next thing I knew David leaned over and bit Heidi in the ear. In the blink of an eye Heidi turned and bit David on his ear. David grabbed his ear and screamed in pain.

I jumped up from the chair and ran over to David and pulled his hand away from his ear. Sure enough the ear lobe was bleeding. "She bit me!" he screamed.

"I know she did. We have to go to the hospital." I swept him up and carried him towards the door. "David, why did you bite her?"

"She growled at me," he said in an angry, slobbery voice.

"Well, I guess you'll think twice about biting her again, won't you? Let's go fix you up." I grabbed my car keys. "Shari, sweetie, you have to help Momma. We're going to the hospital."

At the hospital David's little face was set in firm seriousness, perfectly behaved, as the doctor stitched him up. As he was working the doctor asked me what happened. "David bit our dog in the ear so the dog bit him back."

"How's the dog's bite?" the doctor asked slightly amused.

"Didn't bleed. David's teeth aren't as sharp."

The nurse, who was assisting the doctor, didn't find it amusing at all. In an angry tone she asked, "So are you going to get rid of the dog?"

"Of course not," I answered quickly, slightly irritated. "David bit her first. It wasn't her fault." I could tell the woman thought I was an awful mother. But I couldn't care less. I knew that any dog could bite if pushed. Heidi could have done far worse. *I will just have to be more careful.* Heidi was family and David had learned a valuable lesson. Less than six months later Heidi redeemed herself tenfold.

On a warm and sunny summer day, the sun poured through the windows in the house. It was one of those invigorating days where the whole world seemed energized and buzzing. I left Shari, five, and David, four, in the living room to play with their toys while I loaded the dishwasher. Standing at the sink, singing a show tune, I heard barking coming from outside. I stopped singing and listened. *Strange,* I thought, *it sounds like Heidi.* Puzzled I dried my hands and went onto the porch to look outside. I noticed that the porch door that led to the driveway was ajar. My heart jumped as I ran out the door. Something was wrong.

Leaping down the stairs I looked down the driveway and there was David toddling towards the street, Heidi barking and running around him in circles. David was heading towards the busy street at the front of our house. Heidi, sensing the potential danger, was trying to corral him back home.

Sprinting towards David I grabbed his hand and pulled him around. David looked up at me surprised. "What are you doing? Why did you leave the house?" I scolded crossly.

"I was going for a walk, Mommy," he answered in his serious, matter-of-fact, old man voice.

I bent down to his level and took his face in my hand. "David, you cannot EVER do that again. This is a very busy road and a car could hurt you."

"But Mommy, Heidi was with me."

"I know, but you still can never do that again." Heidi was my hero.

Heidi loved food. Unlike Mota's style of nibbling, Heidi inhaled her meals, sometimes gagging and coughing up kernels that shot across the room. I indulged Heidi in more food than she needed because I loved her. I also gave all my dogs rawhides occasionally as a special treat. By the time I took her to the vet for a consultation when I was contemplating euthanizing her, Heidi was close to 15 pounds overweight. The extra weight was literally killing her.

After the horrible ordeal euthanizing Mota, we drove home with sadness heavier in the car than the stifling heat. We arrived home and as I helped Heidi out of the car I made a silent vow to her that I would help her lose weight. I was not ready to let her go.

Every meal I measured out small portions of reduced calorie dog food and limited her treats to carrots. We began walking every day. The first week Heidi was only able to walk a block. By the second week we were walking a little further. By the third week we were walking a half-mile. She was losing weight and no longer had to be lifted up from a lying down position. I was thrilled and encouraged by her progress.

Meanwhile as she was getting healthier I was feeling closer to her than I ever had before. Each day we walked together it was a slow, ambling walk. I was forced to slow down and observe my dog and everything around us. We ambled along on our walks, that sun-filled, glorious spring. I noticed how Heidi's ears swiveled slightly when she heard a noise. I noticed how she occasionally twitched her nose smelling the fresh air.

I noticed the birds as they flew about, mostly shades of brown with an occasional cardinal, blue jay or woodpecker. The crows loud and insistent caw, caw, caws communicated with each other, overshadowing the daintier chirps of the other feathered friends. The brown squirrels were comical as they climbed and jumped from tree to tree like acrobats. They chattered to each other, their tails twitching excitedly. Heidi observed all this with quiet curiosity, teaching me to observe those subtle exchanges in the environment around us. Life, I learned, didn't always have to move so fast. I was profoundly grateful for my soulful sweetheart.

As a special treat one evening I decided to give all my dogs a rawhide. Heidi notoriously ate her rawhide slower than the other dogs (by now I had added two more rescue dogs to my home–two Pomeranians), so to give her privacy I walked her to the patio outside. I gave her the bone and went back inside. She walked away and settled down to eat it.

Back inside I made a quick phone call. Finishing my call less than ten minutes later I went back outside to check on Heidi. Looking down the deck stairs to the patio I saw Heidi lying motionless on her side. I knew in my gut, she had choked on the rawhide. I raced down the stairs and screamed, "Heidi! Heidi!" Looking at her face I saw that her eyes were open and staring at nothing. I put my hand on her chest. She didn't appear to be breathing.

It was dusk as I knelt down beside her. My nightgown fanned the ground, mud and rocks digging into my knees as I yelled out, "No way, Heidi, you are not leaving me like this." I began crying. "You are NOT LEAVING ME LIKE THIS!" I pried open Heidi's mouth with shaky hands and reached inside with my fingers. Searching her throat my fingers reached around a wet and slimy object. I pulled the object out and felt a suction of air follow. I flipped the slimy, piece of skin from my fingers. Heidi remained motionless. "Heidi!" I screamed at her. "Heidi!"

By then Chuck, who heard my screaming, came running. I was nearly hysterical by then. I told him what happened. He bent over Heidi trying to think of what to do. I had taken numerous classes on first aid for pets, so I knew how to do chest compressions. Stooped over my dog I placed the heels of my hands on her chest where I knew the heart was. I began chest compressions the whole time saying, "You are not going this way, you are not going this way," tears falling onto her still body.

After a few minutes I could tell she was coming around. Her eyes looked around. "Heidi, baby, are you okay?" I sat on the ground beside her. She looked at me and I smiled a weak smile. "Hi, sweetie, my poor baby," I crooned. After a while Heidi struggled to get up. I helped lift her to a standing position. She took some careful steps.

To be safe I decided to take Heidi to the emergency clinic just to make sure she was okay. We got in the van and I sat in the back with Heidi while Chuck drove. The whole ride there I stroked Heidi and told her everything would be okay. She looked around solemnly.

The doctor examined Heidi and then brought her in the back for a blood test. After what seemed like ages the doctor came back in and explained softly, "Heidi is in very bad shape. All her organs are failing."

"They are?" I asked in disbelief.

"Yes, they are."

"Do you think she is suffering?" I asked him.

"Dogs hide their pain far better than us humans do." He paused, thinking. "Yes, I believe she is suffering." He suggested we put her to sleep. That was the last thing I wanted to hear.

The time had come to say goodbye and I was not prepared. But who ever is? I asked Chuck and the doctor to leave while I said goodbye. I needed time alone with her. After they walked out I got down on the floor beside Heidi. I took her baby-soft, gray face in my hands and looked in her milky eyes and said, "You gave me the most amazing nine months. You taught me to slow down, to live in the moment and that growing old is okay. You did it with dignity and grace." I paused, tears falling. I wiped my nose on my sweatshirt. "Thank you for being in my life and being a big part of my family. Thank you for your loyalty and for protecting David. You are my dear, sweet friend. You will always be in my heart."

Moments later the doctor's assistant came in and asked me if I wanted to be with Heidi when she was put to sleep. I have never, even as of this writing, been able to handle being there when our pets are put to sleep. I ask the reader not to judge me for that. I cannot emotionally handle seeing my pets die. As one kindly veterinarian said to me once,

"What you decide to do is a very personal decision and one that no one should judge. All the years you had with each other far outweighs the few minutes at the end." He added, "They sleep, they just sleep."

So I asked the vet's assistant if she would hold Heidi while she was being put to sleep. She said, "Of course I will."

Driving home in silence, a familiar heaviness hung in the air. I couldn't speak I was so full of grief. I realized then that my grief was somewhat solitary because Heidi was mostly my dog; no one else had bonded with her like I had.

Chuck parked in the driveway and I got out and began walking, away from the house towards the trail where Heidi and I had walked so many times before. Chuck, not knowing what he could do for me, followed me for a while until I motioned for him to go away. I headed for the trail, that thick and muddy night. I walked and walked and walked. I experienced two major losses in less than a year–my two pals, my canine friends and loyal companions.

Animal Education and Rescue

New Adventures Test Resilience

September of 2003, the same month my dog Mota was euthanized, I began the necessary work to make my dream of starting a humane society from over a decade ago come true. Jotting down dozens of ideas for names I chose what seemed most logical, Animal Education and Rescue. I completed all the necessary legal paperwork and received non-profit status. Thinking back to my initial business plan I wrote a mission statement. In a nutshell the mission was to bring people and animals together through education, therapy and rescue. From the start I believed strongly that it wasn't just about helping animals; it was about strengthening the animal/human bond through our services.

The services we were going to provide were: 1. We would take animals that were homeless and place them in temporary homes until we could find them permanent homes. 2. We would provide educational programs to the public, concentrating heavily on venues involving children. 3. I decided to shift the pet therapy program from Pet Sitters of America to Animal Education and Rescue. Through our pet therapy program we would continue to visit nursing homes as well as expand our program to homebound folks that would benefit from pet therapy.

I designed our first brochures and business cards and sent out press releases announcing our opening as well as requesting volunteers.

I used my own money for start-up expenses, and Animal Education and Rescue's office was squeezed into the same space I used to run my other small businesses. By November I was ready to roll.

Through conversations with other people who rescue animals I learned the difference between shelters, rescue groups and humane societies. Shelters, I learned, are places where animals go that are homeless. Typically they are buildings with dog runs and cages and they have staff that work in the shelter. Every shelter looks different and houses a certain number and type of animals.

Rescue groups typically are run out of an office, out of someone's home. They can be any size from very small, operated by one person, to large groups operated by hundreds. There are breed specific rescue groups and all-breed rescue groups. Some rescue groups only rescue a certain species of animal while others rescue all types of animals.

There are rescue groups (and shelters) for dogs, cats, rabbits, ferrets, rats, guinea pigs, reptiles and birds, just to name a few. Because rescue groups don't have a shelter they rely on volunteers to agree to foster the homeless animals in their homes until they are adopted. Rescue groups may have a fall back if they get an animal and don't have an open foster home, such as a boarding facility, animal hospital, doggy day care or even a person who has a barn on their property.

Humane societies are organizations that focus on the education and prevention of animal neglect and cruelty. So essentially any shelter or rescue group can call themselves a humane society if they follow the principle understanding of what a humane society is. But just because an organization goes by the principle of a humane society doesn't mean that they are necessarily a no-kill humane society. The most widely accepted definition of a no-kill shelter is a place where all adoptable and treatable animals are kept alive and where the only animals that are euthanized are those that are unadoptable or not capable of rehabilitation.

Through Bev, a woman who was involved in German Shepherd

rescue for years, I learned about groups you could join on the Internet that share information about animals that need to be saved, as well as exchange helpful information about animals. Through one of the Internet groups I joined I learned about a shelter in a rural area in southern Illinois that needed help, called Pane County Humane Society. Their new director and shelter manager, Michelle, was determined to change things at the shelter.

The previous director did nothing to try and find homes for the dogs and cats that flooded the shelter. Worse than that often times he took the dogs in the back of the shelter and shot them dead. It was like a sick horror movie. The death rate at the shelter before Michelle took over was 95%.

I called Bev and asked her if she knew anything about why shelters asked other rescues and shelters for help. She said, "Yes, there are shelters in rural and financially depressed areas that desperately need shelters and rescues in more heavily populated and affluent areas to take animals from their shelters."

"Why would they need that?" I asked.

"Because they have very low adoptions in their area."

I thought about that for a minute and said, "But with shelters and rescues taking dogs and cats from the rural and depressed areas and relocating them and adopting them out in the more adoptable areas, the problem they face then becomes all our problems."

"Yes, it does," she said bitterly. She paused and then said, "Listen, Sandy, I wanna give you some advice about what you are going to do. I have been involved in rescue for five years. I didn't run a rescue but was very, very involved. I had to back off because it took over my life. It was like a sick addiction I ended up having. My family and my work suffered at one point. I became bitter and angry all the time. I had to quit. It was just too much."

"I'll keep that in mind, Bev. I really do appreciate the advice."

I also knew from working with Bev that she always saw the glass as half empty. Also, everything in Bev's life was always a drama. I hoped that my positive attitude and ability to communicate in an effective and professional way would outweigh what would be thrown at me. But Bev's words would come back at me time and again, testing my resilience and my positive attitude.

I spoke to Michelle from Pane County Humane Society and agreed to foster two dogs. My requirements were that the dogs had to be good with dogs, cats and people of all ages. I didn't care what size they were. Because big dogs take up the most amount of space at the shelter Michelle picked out two of the biggest dogs. But finding a way to get the dogs from the shelter to my house–which was an eight-hour drive– opened my eyes to what is called Animal Transporters.

There are people all over the country that network with each other–mostly through Internet circles–and agree to transport animals for a certain number of miles (or as we in the rescue world say, "leg(s) of a journey"), ultimately to safety. It's an awesome concept and vital that we honor this special group of angels who drive hours and hours for homeless animals.

Transporter's vehicles, if they do transport regularly, get ruined. I have seen the vehicles they drive. The wear and tear is way beyond what is normal due to the nicks and dings inside and outside from rocks, crates, dogs and more. By and large the dogs are completely stressed out when they get into the vehicle and some throw up or have diarrhea in their cages, the mess spilling out into the car itself. The animals may have fleas and ticks, which also can be in the vehicle. Plus, dog hair and filth from their prior living conditions leaves the car reeking and dirty. When the dogs are transferred from one vehicle to another they may snap out of fear or flatten themselves out, requiring the transporter to lift them up, which can be a back-breaking task.

These wonderful people put hundreds of miles on their cars and spend dozens of hours transporting animals for no money and just because they want to contribute in their own way. They are road warriors with a shared mission–to bring animals to safety. I have met some of the most kind-hearted people when I've done transports and felt an immediate kinship with them.

There was a lot to prepare before receiving the dogs. Michelle and I coordinated transporters who would drive the dogs up. It looked like it would be two people driving more than three hours each. I found a few pet stores that were willing to let me bring the dogs into their stores so people could meet them. I faxed press releases to the newspapers announcing our new meet-and-greet dog adoption events at the pet stores.

The day my new charges arrived I was filled with excited and nervous anticipation. I received a call from Joyce, the last transporter. She would be arriving at my house at around 5:00 p.m. Ten minutes to five she called and said she'd be on time. So at five sharp I waited in the driveway for Joyce and my very first foster dogs.

Joyce pulled up in a dirt-splattered, light blue, beat-up Dodge minivan. She parked and got out of her car. "Hi," Joyce said. "The dogs were really quiet for the ride. Pretty uneventful." Seeing inside the front of her car I noticed crumpled fast food wrappers strewn on the floor and seat of the passenger side. There were empty water bottles, balled-up papers and a film of animal hair covered everything. Squeezed in the pocket of the door was a half-used paper towel roll and what looked like a garbage bag.

"How long have you been on the road?"

"Nine this morning."

"You must be exhausted."

"I don't mind," she said, "but yeah, I'm tired. At least this time the run I had went smoothly. Unlike last week's. That was awful." She shook her head back and forth. "I had a litter of puppies that got sick all over themselves and each other and a hundred-pound shepherd mix that wouldn't stop barking."

"Oh, no."

"Anyway, your guys seem very nice. Big, and they stink, but you know." She sighed, adjusting her glasses. "You're my last stop."

"I can't thank you enough for bringing them."

"It's okay. Gotta get 'em out." She shook her head sadly. "That shelter's got issues. Just trying to help save a few." Joyce flipped up the back of the van. Lined from top to bottom were cages of all sizes and shapes. I never knew so many cages could fit in one car. In the two biggest cages were the shadowy silhouettes of dogs moving inside. I gave Joyce one of the two leashes in my hand, and we both opened a crate door and slipped a leash around a dog.

The dogs jumped to the ground. One of the dogs was a very pretty, female yellow lab mix. She had a blaze of white that went from the top of her brownish-red nose up to her forehead. It was quite striking. The other dog was a big, black male lab and Collie mix whose body was longer than it seemed it should have been, like he had been pulled and stretched. He had a long, Collie-like muzzle. "Hi, guys! You are so pretty. But you stink." I crinkled my nose. "I bet you have to go potty." Their tails wagged in response to my baby talk. To Joyce I said, "I'll take it from here," and reached for the female dog's leash. "Thanks again."

"Oh, here," she scarched her back pocket, "the medical records." She handed over two rumpled pieces of paper. I stuck them in my back pocket.

"Thanks," I smiled. "Get some rest."

"Will do." She got in her car and backed out of the driveway.

I walked the dogs to the backyard to go potty and stretch their legs. Going back inside I gave them baths, the water running black, and after another jaunt in the yard I crated them for the night. I named the black dog Stretch and the yellow dog Daisy. I went to bed excited that two new dogs were in my home and that I had saved them from death. Having the power and ability to save souls was an amazing feeling.

The first week the dogs were treated for diarrhea, received their vaccines and were neutered and spayed. I spent a lot of time getting to know their personalities. They liked other dogs and liked people of all ages, which made them very adoptable.

The next week I received a call from a woman who had met Daisy at an adoption event. She was a married, stay-at-home mom of a toddler and had a Jack Russell Terrier named Blue. She was looking for a friend for her dog Blue and fell in love with Daisy's sweet and gentle personality. I had her fill out an application online, and after reviewing the application and checking references, I scheduled a time to bring Daisy over to their home for what is called a "home visit." A home visit is where a volunteer goes to the prospective owner's home to make sure it looks suitable for the dog. If the home was suitable then they could adopt Daisy that night.

The sidewalks wound around the curvy and quiet, tree-lined streets. Big homes and well-kept properties passed by as I drove Daisy into the subdivision where she would hopefully be moving to. Thinking back to the shelter that Daisy came from I said to her, "Girl, you have moved up in the world. I hope this works out for you." I patted her head, a queasy feeling in my stomach. This would be my first home visit and my first dog that I would be placing. It was a monumental moment. The gravity of the responsibility was heavy. After finding the correct home I pulled into the driveway and we got out and went to the door.

Two men and two women, the shorter woman had a toddler on her hip, greeted us at the front door and let us inside. They were all talking at the same time and gushing over Daisy, overwhelming the poor dog. The Jack Russell, Blue, came bounding around the corner and Daisy and Blue began the butt-sniffing dance.

After some deciphering I figured out that the shorter couple were the people who wanted to adopt Daisy. The other two were their neighbors. Ted, the neighbor, was talking a mile a minute and loudly. "I read about your group. It's really great what you are doing. This is a nice dog, really nice. We want to support you, too. We have a dog now but maybe sometime we'll get another." He went on and on as I followed the group towards the kitchen. Daisy's tail was tucked between her legs. Her ears were back and the whites of her eyes shone like white gumballs. She kept looking up at me for reassurance.

"I'm sorry, but I think all this, um, noise is hard on Daisy. Is there anyway we could just meet with the family now and if everything works out you can see Daisy later? I would like to concentrate on Daisy and Blue," I pointed to their other dog, "and make sure Daisy will be okay with the baby."

"Oh, sure, sure," the neighbor said. "Yeah, makes sense, I get it. Sure. Just love what you're doing."

"Thanks a lot," I said smiling.

"Before I leave can I write you a little donation check? Do you take donations? Well, you must. Let me write one real quick."

"That's very kind of you."

"No, no, this is kind of you." He broke out his checkbook from his breast pocket and grabbed a pen off the kitchen counter. Meanwhile the dogs were out of sight. All of a sudden the strong smell of poop rushed into the room.

"Oh, I think Daisy pooped," Suzie, the potential owner, said looking towards the dining room. The dogs were doing laps around the house.

"Oh, no. Sorry, I'll get it," I said.

Maybe they won't want her now, I worried to myself.

"No, no," Bob, Suzie's husband, insisted, heading towards a roll of paper towels on the kitchen counter. "I'll do it."

Thank goodness. No big deal.

Ted tore the check out of his checkbook and handed it over. "It's not much but it'll buy you a bag of dog food."

I took the check and glanced down at it. I noticed it was for $50. "Thank you, that's very generous of you."

He waved me away and headed for the door with his wife. "We're out of your hair. Hope we didn't cause any problems."

"No, no. It was nice meeting you." I felt like a tornado was leaving. He shut the door behind him and I turned to Bob and Suzie. Bob was washing his hands after cleaning up Daisy's mess. The smell still stunk in the air.

"Let me show you around the house a bit," Suzie said.

I smiled, looking at Daisy as she ran around the corner after Blue. With the neighbors gone Daisy was totally relaxed. The dogs were having a blast.

"Sounds great," I said, "but would you mind putting the baby down to walk around, to make sure Daisy will be okay? I've tested her with kids before, but just to be sure."

"Of course, sure." She put her daughter down.

"What's your daughter's name?"

"Daphne."

"She's adorable."

"Thanks. Yeah, she is."

"How old is she?" I asked, watching Daphne walk with wobbly legs.

"She's 23 months." *Twelve is one year, 24 is two years. One month shy of two years old. Why do parents do the month thing?*

Meanwhile Daisy and Blue were still running circles around the house. Their daughter seemed oblivious to the chaos, which was a good sign. But I made a mental note to watch out for her if the dogs ran her way. I'd make sure she was snatched up before she got trampled.

"The dogs are getting along great," Bob said, watching them as they cruised through the kitchen. "Follow me, I'll show you around."

They gave me a tour of their downstairs. It was a big house with elegant furniture, Oriental rugs, and the knickknacks strategically placed here and there. They had a 30-foot ceiling in the living room with a loft visible on the second floor.

Daphne was toddling towards a box of toys on the floor when Daisy, in the midst of another lap around the house, noticed Daphne and stopped beside her. She sniffed the girl's diapered butt and wagged her tail. Daphne looked at Daisy, jumped up and down and squealed in delight. Daisy's tail wagged faster as she moved from the girl's butt to where the funny noise was coming from. Daisy proceeded to lick Daphne's partially opened mouth, which made Daphne go into a fit of belly laughs. We all laughed.

"I have to show you this," Suzie said, leading me to the dining room. She pointed to a leash, collar and two dog bowls that were on the floor beside the dining room table. "It's Burberry."

"It's burring?" I looked at the items. Each item had diagonal and vertical lines in muted browns and reds. I had no clue what she was talking about.

"Burberry. You know, Burberry," she exclaimed with glee.

"I'm sorry, I don't understand," I said feeling really stupid. "Is it a kind of dog brand or something?"

"Oh, no!" She said astonished. "It is a very well-constructed and well-known name brand."

"Oh, I see." I nodded my head, trying to sound enthusiastic.

"I spent a fortune on it. Two hundred dollars," she whispered, like she had committed a sin. "But when I saw it I just HAD to have it. Won't she look stunning in it?"

I looked over at Daisy and thought, *$200 could pay for four dogs to get neutered. What a waste.* "Yes, she'll look very nice," I said.

After we finished the tour I knew Daisy would be very well cared for. I had them sign the necessary paperwork and Bob handed me a check. The $150 donation barely covered Daisy's spay and shots. I thought of that Burberry stuff. *Oh well, she's in a good home.*

They walked me to the door. Daisy was following along, looking up at me and wagging her tail. At the front door I bent down to her level and put my arms around her. I kissed her cheek. Holding her head between my palms I looked in her face and said, "Now, Daisy, be a good girl. I love you and you have a wonderful life." My eyes filled with tears and I cleared my throat. I gave her one more kiss and stood up. "Thank you so much for adopting," I said, shaking the couple's hands.

"We'll take very good care of her. Thank you."

"I know you will. You are welcome." I walked out and to the car and drove away. *Daisy is now safe and happy. One dog saved.*

Within two weeks Stretch was adopted to a wonderful couple in a similar-looking subdivision to the one that Daisy lived in. With my first experience under my belt I was ready to do it again. Little did I know at that time, but the following 12 months would test my resilience and commitment to my mission. The following weekend we arranged to rescue one puppy and one adult dog from Pane.

I made arrangements to meet the last leg of the transport an hour away from our home. Chuck agreed to go with me. We were to meet Pat, a seasoned transporter, well known and respected in the rescue world. I had been instructed she would be in a black SUV on the south side of All Creatures Animal Hospital's parking lot.

At the designated time we parked alongside a black SUV that we assumed belonged to Pat. The SUV's door opened and a middle-aged woman with short, brown hair and wearing blue jeans jumped out of her car. With a clip hello, the woman I surmised was Pat helped the black lab mix out of the back of her car. We scrambled out of our car and opened the side door of our van. Pat guided the lab to our car and with one fell swoop expertly placed her in the crate in the back of my car. Pat explained that the puppy (that was supposedly a Rottweiler mix) cried nonstop in the crate so she held him on her lap the whole time. I took the little, eight-week-old bundle in my arms and got into the passenger seat of our car, placing the pup on my lap. We offered Pat some cash, which she refused. We thanked her for all her hard work and headed home.

We arrived home and settled the adult dog into the offices, which were being used to house our foster dogs, and carried the puppy into the other side of the house where my family and I lived. We had friends staying with us at the time so I passed the pup to a visitor who gladly accepted the babysitting duties. We named the puppy Scrappy. He was just adorable. He had short legs and a long body and emotional, expressive, big, brown eyes. Every night Scrappy slept curled up in bed with me, and during the day his feet rarely felt the ground as I carried him from place to place.

Meanwhile I was running both my businesses, Pet Sitters of America and SKW Enterprises (my small freelance writing/consulting business), in addition to volunteering close to 40 hours a week for AEAR. I was stubbornly focused on building the humane society, even though I knew I was beginning to get burned out.

After a few adoption days the black lab found a loving home, but no one wanted to adopt Scrappy, who we listed as a Rottweiler mix. Rottweilers were not desirable in our area. That was okay, though, because I decided, Rottweiler or not, Scrappy was with me to stay. He was my little buddy.

A week went by and I felt that emotional pull to help the helpless locked in shelters and wanted to rescue again. I looked at Pane County's web site and scrolled through all the dogs they had available for rescue. It was like a kid in a candy store–*who to save, who to save?* I had taken in three dogs that were given up by their owner so I didn't have room to take any more dogs. After a few weeks and begging many, many people

I found two people willing to foster.

The following weekend I agreed to take two puppies, siblings that looked like hound/husky and lab mixes, and a very large, adult German Shepherd mix named Patriot. I had foster homes for all three dogs. Carla, one of my employees through Pet Sitters of America, agreed to foster the two puppies, and a new volunteer, Kelly, agreed to take Patriot.

Mary, an AEAR volunteer, and I met the transport at a gas station two-and-a-half hours away. We arrived promptly, parked and opened the back of the SUV in preparation to put the dogs in crates in the back of the car. The woman who drove the other car handed me the female puppy. Holding the pup to my chest she urinated all over my front, the warm liquid trailing down my pant legs. Holding the pup out in front of me I looked down at my wet body and thought, *This will be a long ride back.*

Mary walked the little boy pup to a grassy area where he proceeded to have blasting, horrible-smelling diarrhea. I asked the transporter if the dogs were okay and she replied, "They're just stressed out from the ride." Something didn't feel right. Both pups looked very sick. Their ears were plastered behind their heads, their tails tucked under their back legs and they appeared lethargic. We loaded up the dogs and were about to leave when the transporter came to my window carrying a very sad-looking little Beagle.

"We thought this dog was going with someone else but they wouldn't take her. I was wondering if you wanted her. She was just separated from her puppies and is very sad. I'd hate to take her back to the shelter."

I looked at the little Beagle with the profoundly sad eyes, her muzzle pointed towards the ground, and said to Mary, "I don't want to leave her."

"Let's take her. We'll figure it out," she answered. So I got out of the car and took the dog from the transporter and got back in, placing the dog on my lap.

The smell in the car was near stifling. The mixture of the urine that was slowly drying on me and the smell of filthy dogs filled the car. The whole ride back as I breathed through my mouth and continually shifted, annoyed by my wet self, I worried about what I would do with the Beagle. I also had a nagging feeling of dread about the puppies. All my worries were magnified because of my life in general. I was running on overload and perpetually exhausted. I was trying to juggle everything– my businesses, my home, my kids and my pets. I wasn't exercising anymore, which had been a very important part of my self-care. *Why am I doing this?* I needled myself. But as always I saw some imaginary animal's eyes in my mind, looking to me to save him.

We arrived at my house–the drop-off and pick-up point for the foster animals–where Carla was already waiting. We let all the dogs walk around my backyard. The two puppies had more blasting diarrhea. The boy, whom we named Harry, kept trying to hide under everything in the yard–the bushes, plywood propped up against the fence and the dog agility equipment. It was strange behavior and very worrisome. I knew something was wrong with the puppies but I had no idea how bad things really were.

It was Sunday and the regular vet's office was closed so I asked Carla to get the puppies to the vet first thing in the morning. I tried re-assuring myself, remembering what the transporter had said about the puppies just "being stressed from the long car ride." The Beagle went home with Mary, and Kelly picked up Patriot, the big shepherd mix, at my house.

The next morning I received a call from the doctor at the animal hospital. "The puppies are very sick and may not make it," he said. "They have parvo, a highly contagious viral infection. The cost to treat them will be a lot." (At that time we were working with a vet who had outrageous prices and was barely supportive of the idea of us rescuing animals.) I am sure he thought I, and anyone associated with me, was nuts. He preferred working with the wealthy folks who bought dogs from breeders rather than what he saw as the dregs of the canine world. But we sometimes used their services because they weren't as busy as some of the other vet's offices (no surprise based on his attitude). Plus, they were just two blocks from my house.

"What kind of money are we talking about?"

"Hundreds. Hard to tell, maybe five, six hundred or more."

I was reeling from the news. I leaned over my desk, head propped up by my hand. *How could we afford this? I cannot go into personal debt over this. But how can we not try and save them? Those poor, sweet puppies.* I told the vet, "Do what you have to do to save them."

By the afternoon the doctor called me back and said Harry was doing very, very poorly and he felt he was suffering. He said the girl that Carla named Pippin was holding her own and had a chance. He suggested that we euthanize Harry. Giving him permission to euthanize a 12-week-old puppy was a horrible thing to have to do but I knew that I had to do what was best for Harry. "Okay, go ahead and euthanize him." I paused, swallowing down my tears. "But can you make sure someone is with him?" He assured me he would. Later that day I found out that while I was on the phone with the doctor Harry passed away on his own.

Harry has been forever etched in my memory, the little, sad pup that never knew happiness or good health. He never knew the love of a family and died a very painful death. Harry was the first animal that I memorialized as an AEAR forever dog. To be defined as an AEAR forever dog, it had to be an animal that was loved by us, was cared about deeply and died before getting adopted. Every single animal that becomes our responsibility will belong to someone, even if it's us.

Determined to learn as much as I could about parvo I combed the Internet, spoke to the doctor at length and talked to people who ran other rescue groups and shelters. I learned about its devastating effects. It was estimated that 50% of puppies die from parvo. It is highly contagious and in a shelter environment it can run rampant. Parvo is transmitted through the feces of an infected dog. One tiny particle of feces could kill an unprotected dog. The key to recovery is early intervention. The symptoms of parvo are blasting diarrhea, vomiting and lethargy. The diarrhea also has a distinct, strong odor, far different from regular diarrhea.

Pippin was still hanging on. By the third day the doctor said he thought she would make it but needed hospitalization for five more days. Our medical bill was more than $800. If we didn't stop racking up the bill we would be out of business. Graciously Carla agreed to take Pippin to her home and nurse her there. So the morning Carla brought Pippin home I met Carla and her husband Brian over at their house and showed them how to give Pippin sub-q fluids (water under the skin through an IV needle). I loaded them up with medical supplies and medicine and gave them a big hug before heading home.

The Beagle we took on that transport within days was adopted to a retired couple, while Patriot stayed with his foster mom Kelly. I met Kelly through a friend and she was rough around the edges to say the least. She had a permanent scowl on her face and sounded angry all the time. But in her actions through her volunteering her heart seemed to be in the right place, and I trusted my friend who knew her. I was desperate for foster homes and I knew Patriot would be okay until I could get him adopted. But my view of Kelly would change for the worse in short order.

A group of volunteers wanted to have a garage sale to raise some money. Kelly offered to have the garage sale at her house. Each day as I drove to her home to prepare, dropping off donated things and sorting and pricing, Kelly had Patriot on a tether outside. I would go over to him and pet him and talk to him. He relished the attention, leaning his big body into me.

But the entire four days I spent at Kelly's house all Kelly did was yell at the poor dog. It was "PATRIOT, GET DOWN!" "PATRIOT NO!" "PATRIOT, PATRIOT, PATRIOT!" Really, he was yelled at when he was doing nothing at all. I felt very sorry for him and decided he needed to be moved to someone else. My house was full of dogs so Lynda and Carl, volunteers that had never fostered before, agreed to try it out for a night. Kelly agreed to take him back if it didn't work out for them.

The following morning the couple that was fostering Patriot overnight said that he was too much dog. Lynda said in confidence, "Every time Carl pets Patriot, Patriot rolls over and pees a stream of pee like a water faucet. Carl just doesn't have patience for him." I wanted to tell her that they should probably never have kids, but I bit my lip instead and decided to be nice and said, "Okay, well, I'll call Kelly." I called Kelly for two days and left messages, but she never returned my calls. It looked like poor Patriot was homeless so I squeezed him into my house.

Three weeks into Pippin's recuperation I was upstairs changing clothes. As I dressed I watched my little shadow, Scrappy, walking around the room. Scrappy was growing up to look more like a Basset Hound/Beagle mix than a Rottweiler. I just thought he was the cutest mutt I'd ever seen. *Something seems wrong. Why are his ears back? Why does he look sick?* The sparkle in his eyes wasn't there. As I stood in my bedroom looking at him and thinking, he threw up clear bile on the floor. I knew my baby had parvo.

I carried Scrappy downstairs and presented him to Chuck. "I think Scrappy has parvo." I could feel panic rising in my throat. It was a Sunday night and the regular veterinarian's office wasn't open so I said, "I am not taking any chances. I am bringing Scrappy to the emergency clinic." *How much will this cost? The emergency clinic was so expensive.*

He looked at me with Scrappy protectively held in my arms and said, "You're overreacting."

"Too bad. I'm going with or without you." I grabbed my car

keys off the dining room hutch and with Scrappy secure in my arms headed down the stairs and to the car. Chuck followed behind us and to the car.

The whole way to the animal hospital I thought, *Scrappy cannot die. This is NOT an option.* We entered the hospital. I told the person behind the desk, "I think my puppy has parvo." Not taking any chances of spreading the virus, we were immediately escorted into an exam room.

As I waited in the exam room for the doctor I thought about what I learned about parvo. It was passed on to another dog when a healthy dog ingests the infected dog's feces. Puppies get a series of three shots their first year to protect them from parvo. If they have yet to receive all their vaccines then they are at most risk of getting it. I recalled that Pippin and Harry had diarrhea all over my backyard. So my yard essentially was a toxic, puppy-killing area. Scrappy was five months old and had received two boosters of the parvo vaccine but hadn't received his third yet. The shots were spaced one month apart and so he wasn't due for another shot for two weeks.

The doctor finally came into the room after what seemed like hours, and we explained our situation and Scrappy's behavior. The doctor took Scrappy in back to test him for parvo. A short time later the doctor returned and as I already knew the doctor said, "The test came up as a strong positive." You might as well have ripped my heart out. Scrappy had never spent a day without me and slept on my chest every night. Now I was leaving him in a strange place by himself, sick and fighting for his life.

Chuck drove home with neither of us speaking. The silence was thick and rancid. As soon as we got home I filled up a bucket with water and bleach. Bleach was the only cleaner proven to kill the stubborn virus. Tears were streaming down my face as I grabbed a garbage bag and threw out all the dogs' toys, blankets, beds, towels and bowls, anything that could have that horrible virus on it. I mopped each and every room from top to bottom with the bleach water, the whole time seeing my house as a virus-infected death trap for dogs.

The whole time I was cleaning I could barely see through the tears. I felt so many emotions hit me at once. I felt guilt for getting involved in rescuing animals, terrified at the prospect of losing Scrappy and resentful that Harry and Pippin had dumped toxic waste in my yard, spreading the stuff to my baby. More than anything I didn't feel the 100% support from my family and felt very, very alone.

I spoke to the doctor at 1:30 a.m. He said sadly, "Right now it's touch and go." My heart sank. But by the morning Scrappy was stable enough to be moved to our main veterinarian hospital. I dreaded calling our vet because I knew how that doctor felt about rescue animals. He had said to me more than once, "Maybe you shouldn't take dogs from shelters. You know you can't save them all."

Scrappy spent four days at the animal hospital. The bill was enormous and I was well aware I was in the same predicament as before, the possibility of running out of money. So, with the okay from the vet I brought Scrappy home and planned to nurse him there. But the problem was that I couldn't risk having parvo in my house again after I had bleached my whole house down. My dogs were likely protected because they were older and had their annual vaccines for numerous years but any new dog I brought in to foster could get infected.

My yard was off-limits until spring. Hopefully the freezing temperatures the coming winter would kill the virus in the yard. Gratefully we had separated the grassy area of my yard by a fence and there was a section of driveway that was fenced in and secure and could be bleached, where the dogs could go out and go potty.

Daily I received updates on Pippin's recovery and slowly but steadily Pippin was healing. Meanwhile I was determined not to infect my home with parvo again so I came up with a plan. Scrappy and I would go to a dog-friendly hotel. I didn't want to infect the grassy area around the hotel so I would bring a spray bottle filled with a bleach and water solution. The plan was that I would spray down any area where Scrappy pooped. Someone lent me a playpen. The playpen could be easily cleaned, eliminating the possibility of Scrappy having diarrhea on the hotel room's carpeting and infecting the room. If Scrappy wasn't in the playpen he would either be in my arms or outside going potty.

My children wanted to go with us and bring a few friends so we loaded up the car and drove across town to our local Best Western. Scrappy was still very, very sick. When we got to the hotel he was physically depressed and still had the typical parvo poop. I set up the playpen and placed Scrappy in it. I helped the kids unpack. While my kids ran up and down the halls with their friends, went swimming and clowned around, I watched television in the hotel room and took care of Scrappy.

By the third day of sub-q fluid and medication Scrappy's stools were firming up a bit and he was perking up. But he hadn't eaten in five days. The doctor suggested I buy some low-salt deli turkey at the store and see if he'd eat it. The kids and I went to the store and loaded up on snacks for all of us and turkey for Scrappy. When we returned from the store I offered Scrappy a sliver of sliced turkey. He took it in his mouth and then dropped it on the floor of the playpen. He looked at the piece of turkey and picked it up with his front teeth. The look on his face was like what he held between his teeth was a sour lemon slice. He stood up and began digging at the pad in the playpen. Pulling the corner up with his paw he dropped the tidbit of food underneath the pad and let the pad drop back down. He was hiding the food!

That afternoon he hid three other pieces of food and the sparkle was beginning to twinkle again in his eyes. The next morning I looked under the pad and all the pieces of food were gone. By the afternoon he was eating small meals and his stools were more solid. The same day I received a call from Carla. Carla and Brian decided to adopt Pippin so she was home to stay. It was a great day.

That afternoon we checked out of the hotel and headed home. A flood of relief hit me as I drove along and petted Scrappy, who was sitting in my lap. Looking down at my sweet bundle I thought, *Yes, this was tough but I got through it.* That time anyway I got the taste of victory and victory was oh so sweet.

Top Ten Stupid Things People Say About Dogs (and Cats and Other Small Critters)

1. My dog (or cat) had babies because it's important for the animal to experience motherhood. *Why put your pet through the pain and risk of a pregnancy? Pets don't need to experience pregnancy.*

2. My dog (or cat) had a litter so that my children can experience the animal having puppies (or kittens). *This is one thing your kids don't need to see. There are 3-5 million homeless dogs and cats that will die this year because there are not enough available homes. Teach your children about the bigger picture. Be part of the solution, not the problem.*

3. My dog (or cat) got pregnant by accident. A neighborhood dog (or cat) got into my yard. *An unaltered male will smell a female from blocks away and do anything they need to do to get to that animal. Get your pet spayed and you won't have that "accident" happen.*

4. I haven't had my dog (or cat) spayed because I heard they should "go through one heat cycle." *Why? Give me one really good, logical medical reason. This leaves the door wide open for an accidental pregnancy. (Refer back to #3.)*

5. I let my cat roam outside because that is the natural thing to do. It's cruel to have a cat confined to a house. *Do you let your toddler go*

outside alone? Cats don't know how to look both ways for cars. In the winter cats find warm car engines quite cozy. Also, they hold no chance against a dog, raccoon or a coyote.

6. My dog lives outside because he likes the isolation, solitude and fresh air. *Dogs are pack animals and thrive on spending as much time as possible with their pack. Isolating them will cause depression at the very least and often behavior problems as well.*

7. I chain my dog to a tree 24 hours a day because he keeps escaping the yard. I do visit my dog once a day or when I have time. *Read # 6. Now to add to that, how would YOU like to be tied to a tree? Either have the dog inside the house as a member of the family or give him to someone else who will.*

8. I couldn't take care of my cat/bird/rabbit/small critter anymore so I set him free in a forest preserve. He'll fend for himself just fine. *These animals are domesticated animals and will never be able to fend for themselves. They will likely die of starvation or will be killed by a predator or by a car.*

9. I spank/hit my dog when he is naughty. How else can I get him to listen? *Try dog-training classes. Dogs don't understand spanking.*

10. When my dog "goes to the bathroom" in the house I drag him to the place where he went and stick his nose in it and holler, "No going to the bathroom in the house!" *A dog's memory is short. All he understands is he is being dragged back to some poo or pee and his nose is being stuck in it and his owner is very mad. He makes no other connection.*

Sick Puppies and Kittens

Through my Internet contacts I learned about an animal rescuer named Colleen who rescued dogs in the Springfield, Missouri, area. She was a one-woman operation, driving hundreds of miles a week, going from pound to pound, shelter to shelter, rescuing dogs before their allotted time was up and bringing the dogs to safe places. Additionally the area she covered was overwrought with puppies and nowhere for them to go. One morning when I opened my e-mail I received a note from Colleen begging all rescuers within cyberspace of her e-mail to take a look at a large number of puppies that were going to be put to sleep.

Reading about all the puppies in dire living conditions I felt like I needed to do something to help, so after reading the e-mail I wrote back that I would take five puppies. As soon as I clicked SEND I had a sinking feeling. *What did I just do? Where will these five puppies go?* After thinking about my small number of volunteers, most of which did not foster dogs, I quickly realized there was nowhere else for them to go but my house.

So I prepared my offices with crates, bowls and food. The whole time I was getting ready I felt a sense of dread and worry wondering how I would manage five puppies. I had many of my own dogs, plus had to manage my businesses and everything for my family on a daily basis.

Ugh! But I kept reminding myself that I would make it work.

I was still trying desperately to find a home for Patriot. Meanwhile I decided the poor dog needed a name change. Every single time I said his name I heard it screamed in my ear by Kelly, his first foster mom. So I named the dog Charlie after the main character in *All Dogs Go To Heaven.* Our Charlie was the spitting image of that dog.

Charlie's submissive urinating was kept at a minimum as long as we approached him slowly and talked sweetly. We lavished him with attention and he seemed very happy at our home. At the time, though, I didn't want another dog. We had two Pomeranians, a German Shepherd mix named Sophie, a Rottweiler we had adopted after Mota and Heidi died and before starting AEAR, and Scrappy.

When the puppies I had agreed to take arrived, it was utter insanity. There were two adorable black lab mixes, one shepherd/hound-mix pup, a Chow/who-knows-what mix with copper-colored hair and an Airedale-type pup. The dogs were stressed out from the long transport and were barking, whining, squirming and jumpy. They were filthy, the smell of dirty dog filling the air. I was panicked trying to figure out how I was going to manage five puppies in a space that was less than 300 square feet. Chuck looked at me as if I was totally insane. His face alone told me not only was he NOT happy about what I had done but that I wouldn't get his help at all. I kept reminding myself over and over that it was temporary.

Three pups were settled in one extra-large cage and two puppies were set up in another slightly smaller crate. They had fresh water and food along with toys and blankets. Just as I was settling them down Victoria, a volunteer, came by to see the puppies. She decided she would foster one. *Yes! Thank goodness,* I thought to myself. She picked out the Chow mix and headed home. Less than 24 hours later they adopted her.

The following day I loaded the four remaining puppies in my van and brought them to our local mom-and-pop pet store for an adoption event. By now I had named the four remaining puppies. Bert and Max were the black lab mixes, the Airedale mix was Brandy and the shepherd/ hound mix was named after my beloved aunt that passed away, Naomi.

I set up a round, wire puppy pen and with the help of a few volunteers took them from the car and placed them inside the puppy pen. A family who lived in town stopped by and picked out Brandy. Arrangements were made for a home visit that would take place that afternoon. By the end of the four hours at the pet store all the pups were exhausted, as was I. Scooping each one up we loaded them back in the car and I brought them back home. But as I placed Max and Bert in their crate I thought that they didn't seem quite right.

Sitting on my fax at home was an application for Charlie. I was excited as I read that it was a family with two kids. The kids were very young but the husband had always had big dogs so he wasn't fazed by Charlie's big size. After checking references I brought Charlie out for a home visit. They lived in a small townhouse and I was slightly worried about the small space, two kids and a big dog, but after much discussion they were very confident that the space wouldn't be an issue. The house was no smaller than my first house and I had three dogs, two cats and four birds in that house, plus two small kids, so I knew it could be done. So I leaned down and gave Charlie a big bear hug goodbye and left.

A few days later was our monthly pet therapy night. I brought Naomi with me with the intention of showcasing her as one of our dogs that needed a loving home. I stood in the lobby area with Naomi sitting beside me as the volunteers and their dogs trickled in. Will and Susanna arrived, a couple I met when they adopted my foster dog, Bandit, a tenacious Yorkshire Terrier. I was thrilled the previous month when they joined us for pet therapy for the first time. I greeted everyone and we went around and introduced ourselves. There were seven regular volunteers and two new couples with their dogs. For the benefit of the new volunteers I briefed everyone on what to expect during our visit.

Just before we headed to the elevators to begin visiting residents I looked down at sweet little Naomi and had a thought. I zeroed in on Will and Susanna like a spotlight was shining right at them. I thought playing matchmaker with them and Naomi might result in a love connection. *What do I have to lose?* I picked Naomi up and walked over to Will and thrust Naomi at him. With a smile on my face I said, "Would you mind holding her for me?" Then without waiting for an answer I placed her in his arms and rushed away to the front of the group. I then called out, "Okay, everyone ready?" I snuck a peek at Will. Just then little Naomi looked up at Will with trusting, warm, brown eyes and he looked down on her and smiled. The very next day Naomi went to their home to stay. I have been blessed to see Naomi and Bandit on a regular basis. Will and Susanna decided to keep Naomi's name, which meant so very much to me because I loved my aunt Naomi so.

The following day I was sure that Max and Bert weren't feeling well, so not taking any chances that they might have parvo, I took them to the animal hospital to have them checked out. I carried one pup under each arm, followed a receptionist to a small exam room and waited for the doctor to come in. I sat on the floor stroking both pups that were sitting beside me quietly. As I waited I thought of all the work I was supposed to be doing at home. I had a dozen messages on my desk, I had to clean the house–it was a disaster–and I had promised David I'd take him to the video store.

The doctor came into the room. "Who have we got here?"

"This is Max," I pointed, "and Bert. They're not feeling well. Something's not right. I can't put my finger on it. They just don't act like normal puppies," I said looking up at the doctor.

One at a time the doctor examined both pups. "I don't see anything wrong with them." He scratched his head, thinking. "I don't know. Well, just keep an eye on them and if they get worse bring them back."

I felt good knowing at least I was doing all I could for them. But the next 24 hours they continued to seem listless and they weren't eating well. Their little ears hung back like they weren't feeling well and their brown eyes looked soulfully sad. I was convinced they were sick. The idea that they may have parvo kept running through my head. *I am not losing another puppy to parvo.*

The next day the pups still seemed sick so I brought Bert, the sicker of the two, back to the vet. I was worried about Max but there was nothing really to nail down as far as symptoms were concerned. Bert was worse, more listless and his stools were loose. The doctor was baffled and said, "I really don't know what's wrong with him but I agree he shouldn't be acting like this." Then he paused, thinking. "They may have the start of parvo." Not what I wanted to hear.

The doctor went on, "The puppies had their first parvo vaccine. If we tested them for parvo it could come out as a false positive because the vaccine is in their system. So there is really no way to know."

"Then shouldn't we treat them as if they have it? Give them antibiotics and fluids? I can do that myself."

"Yes, sure you can."

Here we go again, I thought. But I was determined I wasn't going to lose those two. When I got home I picked Bert up and brought him to the bathroom where the bag of fluid hung from a hanger on my shower curtain. I sat on my bathroom floor and held Bert on my lap and inserted the needle under his skin. I watched the life-saving fluid flow under his skin. His skin raised from the liquid underneath like a hump on his back. The whole time I stroked his head and his face and told him everything was going to be fine.

Just as Bert was beginning to perk up a few days later, Max looked sicker. He started having diarrhea and stopped eating. He stayed in the corner of his cage looking pathetic. I called the vet and was prescribed antibiotics. I had both pups on fluids for the next 24 hours. Once again my house was a sick hospital and everything felt contaminated. I was mentally and physically exhausted and received very little help from anyone. But a burning desire to help the helpless did not waver. A force drove me that I had no control over.

Bert started to act like a normal puppy, playing with toys and bounding around the yard. I was thrilled with his progress. He had a wonderful, even-tempered, sweet personality. It was amazing seeing him flourish, knowing that it was me that helped him bloom.

Sitting at my computer doing office work the phone rang. "Sandy, hi, this is Jeff. We adopted Charlie. Listen. I have to give him back. He is peeing and pooing all over my house." I sat there stunned, sickened.

"But he stopped doing that at my house."

"I'm telling you I swear he does it because he doesn't like it here. Maybe he wants to be at your house."

"But I can't keep him."

"Sorry, but my wife's gonna kill me. I have to bring him back."

"Okay." I counted all the animals I was in charge of in my head. "How about tomorrow afternoon?"

"See you then."

A young couple, Jennifer and Tarence, expressed interest in adopting Bert. They lived in Chicago in a condo. I reviewed their application and checked references. Everything approved, I loaded Bert into the car and we headed out to meet Jennifer and Tarence at their condo.

Nearing their home I noticed that the neighborhood they lived on was lined with square, brick buildings and three-story homes or homes converted to duplexes. The streets were clean and sidewalks kept tidy. There were coffee houses, cafes and small shops, all looking newly updated. I noticed many of the cafes and coffee houses that had outdoor areas had numerous dog bowls outside for dogs.

It was a magnificent, sunny fall day. The sun fell through my windows like a warm bath and everything outside looked fresh and sparkling. Bert and I entered a long, square, red brick building and began our walk up the two flights of stairs to the couple's condo. The hallways were tastefully painted and the woodwork on the banister rich, dark and shiny. There was a faint smell of lilac in the air. As we trudged up I kept encouraging Bert to climb, keeping a step ahead of him. Every so often Bert stopped mid-step and looked at me with those deep brown puppy eyes. My throat tightened just a bit that I might have to say goodbye soon.

My knuckles were prepared to knock on the door when it opened, with Tarence and Jennifer standing in front of me smiling nervously. Tarence introduced himself and immediately picked Bert up and said, "Hey, little buddy."

Jennifer, a red-headed, petite woman in her mid-twenties shook my hand and smiled warmly. "Did you find it okay?" she asked.

"It was easy."

"Great," Jennifer said sincerely. We stood silently awkward. I could feel the couple's nervousness because of the home visit and didn't blame them one bit. I would have been nervous, too. I would be making the decision whether or not they were allowed to adopt Bert. That was a lot of pressure for them. Trying to make them more comfortable I looked towards their living room and said, "Oh, you have a beautiful living room. I love the woodwork."

"We love it too. We love old buildings. It's what attracted us to the place."

Meanwhile Tarence continued gushing over Bert. Jennifer turned her attention to them and petted Bert on the head cooing, "You little sweet boy. You are just too cute." Then to me, "He is adorable!" Bert looked at her with his eyes soft and half closed, enjoying the gentle touch.

After a tour of their quaint condo we headed out the sliding glass doors in the kitchen and onto their small patio that overlooked a huge, U-shaped courtyard. Scanning the outdoor patios I noticed many people out on their patios taking advantage of the beautiful weather. Tarence called out to a neighbor who had a small, brown, scruffy terrier mix scampering around with him. "Hey, Fred," Tarence called up towards his neighbor. He picked Bert up by the armpits and held him out, Bert's back legs dangling. "This is Bert."

"Aw, he's cute. Let's see how Nikki and Bert get along." Their neighbor headed down the stairs to the courtyard, Nikki gleefully following. Tarence looked at me for approval.

"Sure," I said enthusiastically.

We walked down the steel stairs, Bert taking slow, deliberate steps to the bottom. As we stepped on the ground the buildings loomed around us. The courtyard was completely fenced in, a concrete hub for socializing. Nikki greeted Bert, her stubbed tail wagging fiercely. Bert responded casually waving his tail back and forth. Nikki bowed inviting play and Bert returned the bow. They were off, first Nikki chasing Bert, and then Bert chasing Nikki while Nikki yipped with excitement.

After a while we headed back up. Pulling the kitchen sliding glass door closed behind me I looked at Jennifer and Tarence and smiled. "So, would you like to make this official?"

They both smiled broadly and looked at each other and back at me. Tarence bent down to give Bert a hug and Jennifer nodded, "Yes! Of course, yes!"

I went over paperwork and we discussed housebreaking and solving other puppy behavior challenges, such as chewing and jumping. They signed the adoption contract while Bert sat contently in Tarence's lap. I put my arms out towards Bert. Tarence handed him over.

"Well, this is it, sweetheart," I told him as I held him close. My mind went back to the hours and hours I nursed this pup, the worries and the bond we shared. "You have a wonderful family that will take great care of you." Then, what would become my signature farewell, I said, "I love you. Now you be a good boy and have a wonderful life." I kissed him on both cheeks and handed him back.

I choked back the tears as both Tarence and Jennifer gave me hugs goodbye. I walked slowly down the stairs, my heart heavy with melancholy. I thought about the pup I saved from death. *This is why I do this,* I thought as I marched down the stairs with my head held high and my heart full.

When I got home Max was still curled up in the corner of his cage in the same spot he had been in when I left. When he saw me he looked up at me with sad puppy eyes. "Hey, little Maxy, how you feeling?" I opened the cage door and scooped him out. "Time for fluids, baby." We headed for the bathroom where I settled him on my lap. As the fluid seeped into his body providing the necessary life-saving liquid, I put my arms around him and closed my eyes and imagined my life's energy entering him and healing him.

After finishing with Max I walked around to the other side of the house and there was Charlie, as he had been before he was adopted out, roughhousing with our Rottweiler Shrek. Chuck was sitting on the couch watching TV. "So how was it when he dropped Charlie off?"

"Charlie went racing for the side door. Didn't look back, not once. I don't think he wants to leave."

"Really?"

"I think he was devising a plan to get back here, misbehaving on purpose."

"But I don't want another dog."

"I don't think Charlie cares what you want."

Max started getting bald patches around his eyes. I brought him to the vet. After a skin scraping he said, "Max has mange. It's a skin condition where mites multiply and cause bald patches. Fortunately it isn't the kind that is contagious to other dogs. But he will need oral medication for three months." That setback didn't faze me. Even though he had hair missing around his eyes he was beginning to act like a puppy should.

My next step was going to be to find Max a great home.

Meanwhile I heard through my Internet rescue circles that a mom cat and her one-week-old kittens needed a foster home–and quick. They were being housed in a shelter that was small, overcrowded and had contagious viruses running wild. The person pleading on behalf of the cat and her kittens wrote, "There was no way this momma and babies would survive there."

It was an exciting prospect, caring for the little family. My daughter Shari said she would take care of them in her room. So I wrote the shelter saying we would take the cats. Preparing for the cats' arrival I found a cardboard box and lined it with blankets and put it beside Shari's bed. I placed a litter box near Shari's closet and put bowls of food and water near the cardboard box.

Joyce, the same woman who had transported Daisy and Stretch, brought the cat family. After Joyce unloaded the carrier that the cats were in she suggested that we swap equal-size crates so that I didn't have to move the cats from one crate to the next. I handed her an empty crate and thanked her once again for her help.

I carried the heavy crate, Shari following behind, to Shari's bedroom. I placed the crate in the center of the small room and we both sat on the floor and peered into the crate. The mom, a shorthaired, black and white, mixed breed cat, looked at us with her sea glass-colored eyes. I slowly reached in and pulled her out.

It was like Christmas at the Wisniewski house as we pulled out one kitten after another. The first kitten I took out of the crate was all black. I looked him over while Shari exclaimed, "Oh, he's so cute!" Then I handed him to Shari, causing even more squeals of delight. The next one was a black one with stark white spots on her feet. I looked at the little kitten as she meowed and blinked her eyes. The third was a tortoiseshell kitten, her colors like a patchwork quilt. The fourth was a longhaired, gray and white kitten, significantly bigger than the others, with powder-blue eyes. "This one's Fred," Shari cooed, kissing the end of his pink nose. He pushed her face away with his front paws. The last kitten was a small calico. Only nature could make such perfect earth tone colors of rust, cream, brown and orange. The crate empty, we looked at the colorful family settled in the box with their mom.

"This one I am naming Ashley," Shari announced pointing at the calico nursing. "And let's see…" She waved her finger by the cats. "The littlest one," she pointed at the tortoiseshell kitten, "will be Gem because he looks like a pretty ring. The black one is Jet and the teeny tiny one will be Tiny."

"Great names, Shari! Luckily you picked names that can be a boy or girl's name because we still have to see if they are boys or girls. Well, all except Fred. Let's hope he's a boy."

"I'll look," Shari said, picking Fred up. She looked between his legs and said, "Yup, he's a boy. Oh! We have to name the mom."

"Hum." I looked at the pretty cat. "Let's call her Gina."

The first four days were blissful. Gina's kittens nursed often and Gina carefully licked each kitten clean. We had the easy job of watching them grow and handling the tiny kittens. They were fascinating to watch. They slept curled up together and when they woke up they stretched their tiny arms and yawned. When they nursed their paws kneaded as they sucked. When we held them they purred and blinked their tiny eyes curiously at us. As I sat on the floor holding Jet I decided that cats were far easier than dogs, really a no-brainer. But I spoke too soon.

On the fifth day Shari came racing down the stairs. "Mom!" she hollered, panic in her voice. Hearing the urgency in her voice I raced over to her. "Look." She held out a limp kitten in her hand. "Something is wrong with this kitten." It was Jet. I carefully took Jet from Shari and looked down at him. His mouth was opening and closing like he was trying to catch his breath. His head was swaying from side to side and bending backwards. As I tried to think of what to do I walked over to a clean basket of clothes on the dining room table, grabbed a towel and wrapped Jet up in it. Within minutes he was dead. I stood there looking at the kitten's tiny, lifeless body with sadness in my heart.

Shari peered into the towel. I said, "Oh, no, he died."

"That's terrible," she said, looking down at Jet. "What do you think happened?"

"I don't know." I walked upstairs and into Shari's room. One at a time I picked up each kitten and looked it over. They were all alert, bright eyed and appeared perfectly healthy. I looked at Gina. She blinked at me and began to clean her babies. Nothing looked unusual. No one seemed sick. But even so I wasn't taking any chances. *I'll take them to the vet tomorrow to be sure everything is okay.*

The next morning at the animal hospital the doctor examined all of the cats. Afterwards he said, "Gina is anorexic–not uncommon in shelter cats. Because of that she isn't producing milk. That's probably why the other kitten died. He wasn't getting milk. I hate to tell you this, but you're going to have to feed the kittens every 2-3 hours around the clock for at least ten days or until they can eat on their own."

The vet tech showed me how to mix kitten formula and put it in a tiny baby bottle. Then she carefully snipped the end of the nipple. She then took a long piece of rubber tubing. "I want you to try and get the kittens to drink from the bottle but it's hard to get such young kittens to take to this type of bottle. If you can't get them to drink you'll have to tube feed them." She showed me the red tube. "I am going to measure the tube so it's long enough to get to the kittens' stomachs." She placed the one end of the tube by Ashley's mouth and ran it down along the outside of her body to her stomach. "I'm going to snip it so it's exactly the right length."

She took a scissors and snipped the end. "If the kittens won't drink then fill a syringe with milk." She took the top off the baby bottle and placed the syringe inside and pulled milk into the syringe. "Attach the syringe onto the end of the tube, like this." She attached the tube to the syringe. "Now gently ease the kitten's mouth open and slowly ease the tube down the kitten's throat." Ashley meowed in protest as the tube went down her throat.

"It's okay if she cries. That actually is a good way to tell it's going towards her stomach and not her lungs. Okay, now it's all the way down. Now slowly push the syringe so the milk goes through the tube and to her stomach. See? Done. Now slowly take the tube out. Do you got it?"

"Yep, got it."

"Now I have to show you how to force-feed Gina since she won't eat on her own." She grabbed a can of cat food and opened it. She turned around towards the sink and ran the water, touching it until it was hot. "Make sure the water is warm. You're gonna add water to the canned food until it's like pea soup." She took a bowl and began mixing the food and water until it was watery. "Now suck some of the mixture in this syringe. No needle of course. It's gotta be thin enough to go into the syringe."

She reached for Gina who was walking around the exam room. "Come here, honey." She placed her on the exam table. "Now open her mouth and shoot the liquid down. Do this often throughout the day. She should eat a half can twice a day."

Getting home I unloaded the cats and placed all my necessary equipment in my room. I had to move Gina and her kittens from Shari's room to my bedroom because the care the cat family would need was far too much for Shari. Because the cats had to be in my bedroom that meant the dogs had to stay downstairs. That was going to be rough on them because they were used to sleeping with me.

I slept in our bedroom with Gina and her kittens and Chuck slept downstairs with our dogs so they didn't have to sleep alone. Our dogs were very spoiled! When I wasn't taking care of the cats I was still taking care of Max, who lived in my office, giving him medicine and keeping a close eye on his progress.

Each day Chuck and I took turns force-feeding Gina and alternately bottle-feeding and tube-feeding each kitten every two hours around the clock. Gina was no longer grooming the kittens or stimulating them to pee and poo so we had to act like a feline mom. After every feeding we rubbed each kitten down with a paper towel and then rubbed their privates to get them to pee and poo. After the first 24 hours I got the hang of playing mom and no longer grimaced when I rubbed at their privates.

The around-the-clock care gave Chuck and me a nervous energy that kept us going. Day three of our nursing care I found Gem, the tortoiseshell, lying dead beside her siblings. I was heartsick. I read everything I could get my hands on about raising kittens and consulted the vet. The overall consensus was that some kittens die for no apparent reason and go quickly and there is nothing you can do.

Day five I was blurry-eyed and cranky. Chuck's back was killing him from sleeping on the couch. It crossed my mind that possibly I had gone overboard taking those kittens when I already had a sick puppy. If I had asked Chuck at that time he would have said absolutely, but I was becoming addicted to rescuing animals.

After a week Gina was eating and we celebrated that victory. Now maybe she would produce milk again. But with that celebration came another crisis. Going into my bedroom at dinnertime preparing to feed the cats, I noticed right away that Ashley, our patchwork quilt calico, was dying.

I picked the tiny kitten up and held her in my arms as she gasped for breath. Seeing her suffering I wrapped her in a T-shirt I had been wearing that day so she could take comfort in my scent, and I held her close. Looking down at her, her mouth opening and closing like a fish out of water, her neck craned backwards in a contorted way, I said to her, "It's okay to go, honey. If you want to go, go. I don't want you to suffer."

I placed Ashley down on the floor of my bedroom near a laundry basket and ran downstairs to share the bad news with Chuck. I told him where I had left her. He immediately hurried upstairs to check on her. He looked in the shirt by the laundry basket where I told him I had left her. Ashley wasn't there. *Where is she?* he thought, puzzled. After looking around the room he found her with Gina and the other kittens, still gasping for air and making those strange, contorted movements. Chuck assumed Gina had picked Ashley up and moved her. He didn't see any harm in her staying with her family so he headed back downstairs.

That night Ashley was still alive but barely hanging on. Chuck and I both tube-fed Ashley a syringe full of milk as a last ditch effort to save her and went to bed around midnight. At 2:00 a.m. I woke up prepared to move Ashley's lifeless body. I snapped on the light and stepped onto the floor and out of the corner of my eye I saw movement by my feet. Walking like an apparition hurrying directly towards my feet was Ashley. It was as if she was saying, "Hey, ma, I'm okay. I really am! Look at me!" I was shocked. I scooped her up and looked in her apricot-colored eyes, and after giving her a kiss said, "Well, you, you are quite the little miracle. I guess you decided you weren't ready to go." From then on we called her our living angel.

All three remaining kittens thrived. Gina gained weight and was nursing and cleaning her children. The kittens were four weeks old, eating canned cat food and going potty in their litter box.

I wrote in my journal: *In two weeks the cats will be ready to find new, forever homes. This was a huge ordeal, very traumatic, but well worth it. Seeing those happy cats and knowing that we saved four significant lives made it all worth it. I'd do it again.*

But the problems with the kittens didn't end there. Shortly after she regained her strength I noticed a crusty spot by Ashley's ear. I decided to bring her to the vet to have her looked at. The doctor looked at the crusty spot and diagnosed her with ringworm, a contagious fungus of the skin. He said, "All the kittens will probably get it. It's contagious to people as well. It's not as big of a deal as people make it out to be. You'll have to wait until all their spots are gone before adopting them out." He told us what ointment to get and sent us on our way.

On the way home I remembered when I was in my early twenties one morning I noticed a bull's eye-looking sore on my upper thigh. I didn't think much of it at the time and after a week it went away. I was pet sitting for a lot of clients' cats and realized that I probably had ringworm.

I was more than ready for the kittens to go. Chuck, still suffering on the couch in the living room, was afraid of an irreversible back injury, so he began sleeping upstairs again. But as we would quickly learn, just because he had relief from the uncomfortable couch didn't mean his bed would provide him sleep.

Our first night with both of us sleeping in the same bed, we settling under the covers, turned on the bedside lamp and opened our books. Minutes later we heard scratching and clawing by the bed. Peering over my novel I looked to see what the noise was. There by my feet was Fred. He bounced along the bed looking for things to swat and pounce on. "Aw, look, Fred climbed up on the bed! Hey, sweetie," I purred, sticking my fingers out to scratch Fred behind the ear. Chuck peeked out from the side of his book and smiled. In short order Ashley and Tiny scrambled up onto the bed. It was like a fiesta for kittens! Gina jumped onto the bed and settled by Chuck's legs. We put down our books and watched the kittens play. Oh, they were so cute!!

After a bit we decided to shut off the light and go to bed. Settling on my side those kittens jumped on my head, attacked me anytime I moved (and I move a lot at night) and bounced around the room like jumping beans. By midnight it was no longer cute or funny.

It was like a wild party in our bedroom from ten at night until sunup, the kittens jumping, bouncing and batting at everything. We tried to determine where to put them at night so we could sleep. We had not a single spare place for them to go in the house. So we learned to stay as still as possible, minimizing the number of pounces that shocked us out of sleep. Even lying still stopped working because they pounced and batted at our heads, faces and necks. We finally resorted to covering our heads with our blankets and curled up in balls, barely sleeping all night. I learned to breathe in long, slow breaths under the covers, reminding myself I had plenty of oxygen.

Mercifully when the sun rose the kittens fell fast asleep in the crook of an arm, a neck, a soft belly or curled side, allowing us to finally drift off into a deep, blessed sleep for an hour before beginning the day. It was impossible to be angry with them because they were so darn adorable.

Chuck was first to see the round bull's eye that indicated ringworm on his stomach. In short order David had a spot on his leg and Shari and I had spots on our arms. All the kittens developed spots, as did our dogs. Every day I examined each one of our animals and dabbed on the medicine and passed it along to be used by my human family. After two more weeks the spots disappeared from everyone and the kittens officially were up for adoption.

All four kittens were adopted out quickly to approved homes and we could sleep again with our dogs around us. The first night was like heaven. Every night the first month Chuck and I would sigh deeply as we nestled under the covers encased by our slew of dogs, the dogs already sound asleep.

Max was finally feeling better and could be put up for adoption. In just a few days a woman who introduced herself as Barb called and said she and her husband Rick were interested in adopting a lab. They had never had a dog before and had a two-year-old son. Rick also had a 12-year-old son and ten-year-old daughter from his first marriage, who lived with them part-time. I almost didn't adopt Max to them because I felt that he might be too much for them. But they pleaded their case, saying that Max would be very well cared for, so I reconsidered.

I drove Max to their split-level home in a nice neighborhood in the suburbs. Max was still getting well from his illness, but I told the family as he continued to feel better to expect that he may have more energy. I spent two hours with them and provided them with written information on housebreaking, behavior problems, basic obedience and more. I gave them his medicine for the mange and showed them how to give it to him.

Just before I was getting ready to leave they decided they would like me to come back for an official dog training session at their home. I was impressed with their willingness to learn and we set a date for the following week for training. Heading towards the door Max followed along as if he was going home with me. I gathered him up in my arms. I put my face against his and told him, "I am so proud to have saved you. You will always be in my heart." I patted his side and added, "I'll see you next week and, oh," then I paused and said my traditional farewell, "I love you and have a wonderful life."

Max looked up at me and tried to push past me out the door, intent on going with me. It broke my heart. We had this invisible connection only the shared experience of being on either side of the gateway of death could cause. Barb held his collar and I opened the door. Max lunged forward trying to follow me. I swallowed my lump and took solace in the fact that I would see him again the following week.

The next week I arrived at their home and was bowled over in greeting by Max. He kept jumping up like I was the big party in town. "Hey, Maxy, how ya doing, buddy?" I asked him. Barb watched Max with her arms crossed as he continued to dance around me. "He never gets that excited with us," she commented.

Week after week I came to their home to work with them on training techniques. They just didn't seem to "get" Max and Max continued to be over-excited to see me and try and leave with me. They continually made comments like, "I don't think Max likes us," or, "We're concerned about how Max is with the baby," "We think maybe he's too big," and "He keeps jumping up." They were not bonding to him and it was more than obvious he wasn't bonded to them.

They never fully invested in him or welcomed him 100%. They had promised me they would finish fencing off their yard so Max could burn off steam in a fenced yard, but each time I came they avoided giving me a reason why the fence wasn't getting done. It was as if Max had one paw out the door from the beginning. So it was no surprise they began talking about giving him back to me.

When I received a message on my voice mail, "Sandy, this is Barb, please call me back," I knew Max was coming back. The next morning I drove to their home to pick him up. Rick was outside with his son Denny. As soon as I got out of the car Denny burst into tears. I felt like a real heel taking this boy's dog from him. But, I reminded myself, this is not my doing, it's theirs. What a rotten thing to teach a kid. Denny learned that dogs are disposable. Poor kid, first his parents divorce and now his dog is taken away right before his eyes. Rick walked over to me with tears in his eyes. "This is the hardest thing I've ever done," he said to me. I knew he didn't want to give up the dog and that it was Barb. I looked over at the front door where Barb was coming out with Max.

Max pulled Barb, causing her to lurch forward, stop and steady herself. She waited on the front step for Rick to come get Max. Her face showed no emotion as she handed Max over to Rick. She lifted her arm in a wave and mouthed "Thanks" and went back inside the house. I wondered if she had any idea the example she was showing Denny, and at that moment I was pretty disgusted with her.

Max hopped into the car without a glance back. Rick said, "Max never stopped loving you." I wanted to say, *Your family never gave him the chance to learn to love you.* But instead I just smiled and said good-bye. I pulled away and looked in the rearview mirror at Denny, who stood by the basketball hoop in their driveway doubled over, his father's arm around him. *What a shame. What a crime,* I thought, shaking my head and rubbing Max's back.

Max stayed with me another three weeks until a new family expressed interest in him. On a rainy Sunday afternoon they came to my house and after just minutes fell head over heels in love with him. Later that evening I drove Max to their home in a neat, middle upper-class subdivision in the town of Wauconda. They had another dog, a Beagle named Bailey, who welcomed Max with open paws, and in short order they were racing around the house after each other.

Finishing the educational program and signing the paperwork I knew Max was home for good. I had to grab Max by the collar as he raced after Bailey so that I could say goodbye. Too big to pick up anymore I got down on my knees and wrapped him in a hug. "I love you, Max. Now you have a wonderful life." As they walked me to the car, Max on leash beside them, I got in and waved goodbye and pulled out of the driveway. Looking in the rearview mirror I noticed Max didn't look at my car as I drove away. Instead he pulled his dad towards the door to get back to his new buddy, Bailey. Max was home, finally home.

Black Pepper

A shelter in Missouri was closing for good. I received a plea via e-mail from their director, asking for help to save the dogs that were still there. They had two weeks to find placement for 45 dogs otherwise they would have to be put to sleep. What a horrific situation for them. I couldn't even imagine the daunting task of placing all 45 dogs.

The crate in my front office was empty so I e-mailed them telling them I could take a dog. That weekend over 15 dogs from the shelter in Missouri were transferred to a no-kill shelter in our area, where they would be distributed to local shelters and rescue organizations. My new dog would be one of the 15 arriving.

The transport arrived at 8:00 p.m. on a Sunday night. It was a perfect summer evening, not hot and not cold, like lukewarm bath water. Chuck and I drove the 20 minutes to the shelter and were there by nine. Entering the building workers pointed us to a back area where all the Missouri dogs were supposed to be staying until they were picked up. Walking past a few medium-sized, enclosed carriers, eyes peering out at us, I looked around the big, empty room wondering where all the other dogs were.

Seeing us looking around a middle-aged woman with butt-length, dishwater blond hair approached us. "Hi, I'm Sue, shelter manager. Can

I help you?"

"We're here to pick out a dog. We're with Animal Education and Rescue."

"Most of the dogs were taken or spoken for." She pointed at the enclosed carriers and said, "They're already spoken for by other rescues. Let me show you the last two dogs. Hold on, I'll get them."

Waiting in the big, vacant room I wondered what purpose the room served. *What I would give for a room this size,* I thought, looking around me. Sue returned with a small shepherd mix. I approached the dog and offered my hand for her to sniff. Crouched down like she was bracing to be hit she looked at me with weary eyes and slowly leaned forward and sniffed my hand. Chuck approached her next. Like a shotgun exploding the dog jumped back and began barking and growling ferociously at Chuck. Chuck straightened up and backed up a step. "Sandy, we can't take a dog that isn't going to like men."

To Sue I said, "Can we please see the other one?"

"Sure." She left with the shepherd mix. Moments later she returned with a black lab mix.

"Hi, sweetie," I crooned, slowly approaching the dog. I put out my hand and scratched her behind her ear. "You're a good girl." She looked at me passively. Chuck followed behind me and also reached out to the dog. She allowed Chuck to pet her. "Okay, we'll take this one," I said.

During the ride home I sat in back of the van holding the dog's leash and petting her. She stood silently indifferent to the attention I was giving her. Rolling names off my tongue I decided on Pepper for the black dog that stood passively beside me. Patting her head I said, "Pepper, that's a good name for you, girl, a good name."

At home I coaxed Pepper out for a short potty break. Afterwards I led her into the crate, where a soft blanket and a few toys waited for her. She curled up and went to sleep. The next day she wearily got out of her crate and we headed outside for her to go potty. Her head hung low and her tail stayed tucked between her legs. She walked ahead, looking side to side as if someone was going to jump out of the bushes at any moment.

After doing her business we headed inside and I put some food in her crate and left. A few hours later, busy handling calls for Pet Sitters, I asked Chuck if he would take Pepper outside to go potty. He came back a few minutes later and said, "I can't get her out. She was growling and showing her teeth."

"What? You're kidding."

"No, I'm not. What do you know about this dog anyway?"

"I don't know," I answered defensively.

"Well, maybe you ought to find out," he said with a see-you-shouldn't-have-taken-that-dog-you're-in-over-your-head tone of voice. To prove his point we went over to Pepper. She backed up in the corner of the crate, crouched low, gave him an evil stare, growled and bared her surprisingly white teeth menacingly. What did I get myself into now?

In the rescue and shelter world there is a saying, "It takes a day or two or sometimes a week for a dog to unpack their bags." What that means is that when you first meet a dog sometimes they are on their best behavior, in shock or shut down and only later do you see some behavior problems. It took only 24 hours for us to see some serious behavior problems that were worrisome at best.

Looking through my piles of paperwork way overdue for filing I found the paperwork that came with Pepper. It said she was a five-year-old lab mix. At first I saw nothing important and then I looked at the intake day at the shelter in Missouri. *No, it couldn't be. That dog lived in that shelter for two years and ten months. Oh my God, that poor baby.*

My mission was to turn Pepper from a terrified convict to a good member of society. Luckily Pepper liked me. But I had to make sure everyone else was safe from those sharp teeth. I took some precautions and told everyone that came into my office not to go near Pepper unless I was there. I loaded myself up with yummy dog cookies and put some in a jar on top of her crate.

My first goal was to get Pepper comfortable around Chuck. I asked Chuck to offer her dog biscuits whenever he passed her cage. When Pepper was out of her crate and with me I asked him to give her dog cookies while I lavished her with praise. Every day Chuck would spend time talking softly to Pepper and throwing her biscuits. He bent down to her level and talked to her in a soft voice. When she would lift her lip or growl he stepped back and said in a soft voice, "Oh now, Pepper, that doesn't look very nice." Over the course of the next two weeks Pepper slowly warmed up to Chuck and he was able to pet her. She no longer growled at him and would go to him for attention.

Meanwhile I took Pepper for walks to downtown Liberty, a convenient four blocks from my home. I carried a pocketful of dog biscuits and every time we would pass someone on the sidewalk I would give her a dog biscuit and praise her like crazy, as long as she didn't growl. I kept a safe distance from people and made sure I had a good grasp on her leash.

I introduced Pepper to fire hydrants, statues, playground equipment, alleyways, store windows and walkways, park benches and more, the whole time praising her and giving her treats. We took different routes so she would get comfortable with different environments, all in an effort to reintroduce her to things she had been secluded from for almost three years. After repeating these objects and routes to her over and over she began to see them as good places because she was always rewarded with treats and praise. Over time she'd see something that used to cause her fear, touch it with her nose and look at me waiting for a treat. Positive reinforcement training was working.

Pepper was beginning to warm up to my female staff and volunteers. She now wagged her tail for my son, who she learned was a treat dispenser, and was more relaxed on our walks. I knew I had to get her to the point where she could go to an adoption event at our local pet store. I began driving her to the pet store and walked her around the store getting her used to the sights, sounds and smells of the store. I still kept a tight lead on the leash when people passed us but utilized some of the helpful staff to offer Pepper dog biscuits.

By week four I believed Pepper was ready for an adoption event. I knew she would not approach people, nor would she "show" well because she was still holding her head low and tucking it between her legs, but I was confident she would mind her own business and not growl or snap at people. I was pretty confident no one would show interest in her because of her passive and shy personality, but it would be a good trial run.

Another thing I learned after taking Pepper is that it is a known fact that black dogs are the most passed-over dogs at shelters, especially big, hairy black dogs. Pepper had many strikes against her. But I was committed to this sad soul and bound and determined that there was someone out there for her.

We set up our table in our designated corner, foster dogs and volunteers standing around waiting for visitors. I was alert and aware, making sure I was closely watching Pepper's behavior. My motto has always been to be extra safe and not to take any chances.

Pepper and I were sitting on the floor. I was stroking her back, telling her what a good girl she was when a short, stout, dark-haired lady with hip eyeglasses walked by us. She abruptly stopped right in front of us and turned to face us. A big grin filled her face as she bent down to see Pepper. She was so animated and excited it felt surreal. "Who's this pretty girl?" she asked.

"This is Pepper," I answered, continuing to pet Pepper.

The woman plunked down on the ground and gently reached

out and began petting Pepper's head. Pepper instantly relaxed. "You wouldn't believe this. I can't believe this," she said excitingly but in a whisper, instinctively knowing to be quiet for Pepper. "I dreamed about this dog last night. This is my dog," she told me. Looking at Pepper she said, "I knew I'd find you here. We were driving by and I told my husband to stop the car. I told him that my dog from my dreams is in here. Oh, honey, I knew I'd find you."

I sat there not believing my ears. All my worries for this dog may have been unnecessary. But I didn't want to get my hopes up. I just could not believe this was happening. I sat there stunned and blinking back tears.

"I have to go get my husband. He's not going to believe this," she said to me. She jumped up and strode off. As she disappeared through the sliding glass doors I thought I had hallucinated the woman. The air around me was thick like it is if you get in a fender bender and can't believe it just happened. The minutes ticked by as Pepper and I kept our eyes on where we had seen the woman. As the woman had promised she was back with her husband in tow.

"This is my honey, Marty," the woman said, motioning towards a round, balding, kind-faced man. He waved and smiled at me. I smiled back. "I'm Melody. Our Basset Hound Sammy would love his big sister. I just spent $3,000 on surgery Sammy had to correct a back problem. But we don't care about the money. Our dogs are our babies." *She has a Basset Hound named Sammy, just like my neighbor's Basset Hound growing up–ironic.* I loved this woman.

Melody filled out the adoption application right then and there and said, "So, when are you going to come over with Pepper?"

Stammering because I couldn't process this as fast as it was coming at me I said, "I'll check your references. How's um, uh…" I mentally checked my schedule for the next two days. "Tomorrow evening? As long as I can get ahold of your references."

"Marty, will you be home?" She looked over at her husband. It was clear he would do anything for his wife.

"I'll be home, sure. Tomorrow's good."

Having checked their references Pepper and I were all set to go to our home visit. Driving into their subdivision I looked around at the wide sidewalks, beautiful homes, plush, green grass, trees whose arms reached out in happiness as birds and squirrels played with their long limbs. Pepper sat quietly in the passenger seat looking around.

In my mind's eye I pictured Pepper at that rural shelter for close to three years. I imagined the cold cement, the deafening barking, the sterile chain link and bars and the matter-of-fact, over-worked, small staff that came in to clean her cage. The months after months the black dog was looked over for younger, cuter, non-black dogs. I imagined how she must have shut down into herself, day by day trusting people less and less and going into a deep depression, wanting it all to be over already. As the months and years passed she began to show aggression, backing off and baring her teeth at all but her familiar, emotionally distant caretakers. Her life was a living nightmare.

I snapped back to the rolling scenery and gave Pepper a pat on the head. "You've come a long way, baby," I told her. Then I started singing the song from *The Jeffersons*, "Well, we're movin' on up, to the east side, to a deluxe apartment in the sky. Movin' on up, to the east side. We finally got a piece of the pie!"

Two hours later, after a successful home visit, I gave Pepper my signature goodbye, knowing full well that she would be just fine because an angel was watching over her.

Sadie's Sorrow

All my successes rescuing animals and placing them in new homes were joyous, but not all rescues had happy endings. The first year was very hard and I learned to toughen up. But while I continue to learn to accept the tragedies that inevitably will happen there are some experiences that I will never, ever forget.

It was the sweltering heart of the summer of '04. I received an e-mail about a one-year-old, tri-colored sheltie mix named Sadie, who was being housed in a rural shelter in southern Illinois. Sadie was listed as "extra urgent," a term used for dogs that were first on the list to be euthanized. The shelter representative told us she had breathing problems due to scarring in her lungs. They said she was found as a stray so one could only guess what happened. A veterinarian examined Sadie and told the shelter that over time Sadie would recover. The shelter didn't have air conditioning, which made the heat so thick it was as if hot steam sat like mud in the air. Consequently this caused Sadie's breathing to be more labored. She was extremely uncomfortable and they didn't want to see her suffer any longer. I could visualize that poor dog gasping for air in the stifling heat and I wanted to help her, relieve her suffering. So I e-mailed back and agreed to take her.

I had open foster homes and since we were having one dog transported the seven-hour drive I decided to take two other dogs from the same shelter. AEAR volunteers Ellen and Rod drove the last hour and delivered the trio safely to my house, the pick-up point for the foster families. A few volunteers who wanted to see our new charges came to my house to wait.

When Ellen and Rod arrived we all greeted the dogs with excitement and commented on their individual, unique beauty and sweetness. There was Lars, a large lab mix and Wilbur, a small, scruffy terrier type.

Seeing Sadie in person and how she was struggling to breathe shocked me. The poor baby was breathing deep, raspy breaths in and out, her chest rising and falling with the exertion. But I tried to ease my mind with the fact that she had already been seen by a veterinarian and with our love and care she would heal.

Sheryl, a volunteer who agreed to foster Sadie, arrived first. Sheryl looked like a child getting a special gift as she knelt down and gently petted Sadie. "She's beautiful!" Sheryl exclaimed, looking lovingly in Sadie's eyes. I wasn't feeling so cheerful. I looked at Sadie, her chest still heaving in and out, in and out and suggested to Sheryl that she only take Sadie out for potty breaks and just let her rest in her air-conditioned condo. With that I gave Sheryl a hug goodbye, patted Sadie on the head and Sadie climbed into Sheryl's air-conditioned car.

After Sadie and Sheryl left we gave Lars and Wilbur baths, a request from their foster mom Kristie, before she picked them up. Fresh, clean and looking invigorated the dogs shook their wet coats, coating my bathroom walls with wet dog hair. Kristie arrived and we helped her load the dogs into her car. All dogs accounted for and safely in loving arms I sighed a sigh of relief and thanked the volunteers for their help before they left. But as I cleaned up the hair on my bathroom walls I thought of Sadie and a sinking feeling was in the pit of my stomach.

The next day, Sunday, was our usual meet-and-greet dog and cat adoption event. Before the event I contacted Sheryl and asked her to keep Sadie home and to make an appointment for the vet to see her the next day. The event was busy and hectic, as usual. When it was over I drove back to the office to review applications of potential adoptive families. An hour into my work the phone rang. "Sandy, Sheryl."

"Hi, Sheryl."

"Sadie is on the bathroom floor and isn't moving." She was crying.

"Oh, Sheryl, okay, well..." My mind raced. "Are you with her now?"

"Yes."

"Do you know if she is breathing?"

She paused, obviously checking, and in a shocked voice cried out, "No! She's not."

"Oh, Sheryl, I'm so sorry. She's gone. Poor baby, oh, that poor dog." I couldn't believe this was happening.

"I took her out this morning for a walk and she was in the bathroom with me when I was getting dressed. I left the room for just a minute, just a minute. When I came back she was lying there. I can't believe it. I just took her for a walk this morning."

"I'll be right over," I assured her. "Just give me a half an hour or so."

It was a Sunday so the vet's office wasn't open. *Why did bad things always happen on Sundays?* I contacted a volunteer named Laura, who had been a veterinarian technician. She agreed to go with me. Her eight-year-old daughter Brandi wanted to come as well. Brandi regularly went with her mom when she worked for the veterinarian and from very early on wanted to be a vet herself. She saw this as a good way to get experience. I picked them up and by 5:00 p.m. we were at Sheryl's place.

We entered the building and walked up the stairs to her condo.

Sheryl opened the door, her face red and puffy from crying. I smiled at Sheryl and patted her back. She held the door open and without a word let us pass through. I had been to her home numerous times so I knew where the bathroom was. I led Laura and Brandi to the bathroom opposite the bedroom. I opened the door and moved aside, allowing Laura and Brandi to go in first. I stood behind them at the threshold. Looking past their shoulders I saw Sadie's body, quiet and lifeless, lying on her side. The stillness was like a heavy and dark night, deafeningly quiet just before a storm. *Poor, poor baby.*

Laura and Brandi efficiently and gently wrapped Sadie up in a blanket. Laura carried Sadie's body while I opened doors ahead for her. Sheryl was sitting on the steps leading downstairs. She had her face in her hands as we passed by. There was no way I could make Sheryl feel better, and I felt horrible that she had experienced this. I told her I would call her later. Laura and I headed out to the car to put Sadie in the back seat while Brandi took a minute to console Sheryl.

Brandi got in the back of the car a minute later and said, "Sheryl's just sitting on the steps crying. I feel so bad for her."

"I feel so bad for her, too," I said.

"Poor Sheryl," Brandi said shaking her head.

During the ride home Brandi lovingly patted the blanket Sadie was wrapped in. This child, I kid you not, was by far the most profoundly wise and compassionate child I had ever met. I couldn't believe how she had stepped up and helped.

How do I make sense of it all? I thought, watching the scenery pass. Sadie's sorrow was she was obviously hurt by someone or something that caused her to have scarred lungs. We knew she was alone, without a family. She took a long trip far away to live with someone that she didn't know, only to die the next day, never having found that forever family. But I couldn't think that way.

Instead I had to think that each guardian angel that touched Sadie on her journey to us showed her compassion that was profoundly deep. The volunteer drivers no doubt talked to her in soothing voices and handled her with gentle arms. At Sheryl's home she went for a few leisurely walks, enjoying the bright and sunny day. She slept in an air-conditioned home, comfortable for the first time in a long time. I was confident she felt everyone's love.

In my journal I wrote:

When we have our new facility there will be a marker with Sadie's name somewhere–maybe a stone on the walkway to our educational facility, maybe above the doorway to our offices. She had a home with Animal Education and Rescue and I promised her on that day her body was being lovingly stroked by an eight-year-old girl that she will never be forgotten.

A Long Road for Robin

Pane County Humane Society sent an e-mail about a black lab/ German Shepherd mix that was pregnant and needed to be rescued quickly. She was due to have her puppies any day and the shelter didn't have room for her and her puppies. Molly, a foster mom who preferred fostering puppies, came to mind. I gave her a call. "Hey, Molly, it's Sandy. How are you?"

"Fine, Sandy. What's up?"

"Well…" *How would I broach this?* "Um…" *Okay, just say it.* "How would you like to foster a pregnant dog? (I didn't tell her it was a big, black dog, thinking the size may deter her.)

There was a pregnant pause. I held my breath.

"Sure."

"Sure?"

"Okay, I'll do it," she said. Then, as an afterthought, "What kind of dog?"

"She's a lab/shepherd mix."

"When's she coming?"

"Saturday."

"Alright…."

"Okay, well," I interrupted, now excited about this new venture, "we should read up on pregnant dogs and the birth and all. Do you know anything about it?"

"No, but we'll figure it out," she said with confidence.

"I'll do research, you do, too, and then we'll share the info, okay? This is going to be so interesting. Don't worry, I'll help." Saying this I knew she wasn't the one who was worried, I was. "This will be so cool, so fun." I was like a kid looking forward to a trip to Disneyland.

On a late Saturday night the transport arrived at my house. Molly met me in my driveway prepared to take her dog home. Neither one of us had even been up close to a pregnant dog. Seeing her bow-shaped midsection, she seemed more like a horse than a dog. Even though she was black it was quite apparent she was absolutely filthy because of the strong smell that wafted off her. She stood still, swaying back and forth, as I held her leash and Molly opened her car door. We heaved the dog into the car where she settled herself uncomfortably in a sitting position. It was obvious by the look on the dog's face and her slumped body that she did not like what was happening to her.

It took me back to my own pregnancies. I was a natural at carrying a child. I went through my entire pregnancy without any complications and was comfortable throughout. I walked clients' dogs up to the day before my first child, Shari, was born. Then eight months later I was pregnant again. As my pregnancy progressed I worked, walking dogs, feeding cats, manning the office and toting Shari around with me, big belly merely an inconvenience, up until Christmas evening, when David was born. After his birth I was up and moving within a half an hour. That pregnant dog, we would learn shortly, did not share my sentiments or my natural ability to multi-task.

Fifteen minutes after Molly left my driveway I received a call. "Sandy," it was Molly, "she won't come inside. I've pushed and pulled for ten minutes. Can you send Chuck?"

"Sure, I'll send him over." That should have been a clue we were in for a long road ahead.

Molly fashioned a whelping box by using a plastic baby pool and lining it with blankets. Her son named the dog Robin. Robin received a long wash and scrub. Molly told me later she had never seen water rinse off so black. She had to wash Robin three times. She dried her off and settled her in for the evening. Exhausted, Robin curled up on the floor outside the whelping box and fell asleep.

The next day Molly discovered that Robin was not housebroken. She was pooping and peeing anywhere she saw fit, and to make matters worse she had disgusting, white, spaghetti-looking worms in her poop. She was still acting listless. We decided she needed to see the vet.

The veterinarian examined Robin and took x-rays of her abdomen. He estimated that the puppies would be born in a week and that there were at least five pups. We asked for some advice on the whole birthing process and his response was, "Just have the whelping box ready and she'll know when to go in it." Seemed easy enough, so we went to our respective homes and waited.

There were two other volunteers who wanted to be part of the whole birthing process, Mary and Geri. We devised a plan that when Molly thought it was time then she would call me and I in turn would call Mary and Geri. It was a very exciting time and we were anxious to share the experience.

The following week I received a call from Molly after dinner. "Sandy, I think this is it. She's in the whelping box and is being very quiet."

"I'll be right over!" I hung up without saying goodbye. I picked up the phone again and called Geri first. "Geri, it's time!" I burst out. "I'm going now!"

"On my way, bye." Click.

I picked up the phone again. "Mary, it's time."

"Really? Great! Should I go there now or wait a while? What do you think?"

"I'm going now," I clipped. "Come now if you want. Gotta go, bye." I hung up.

I grabbed my car keys and jumped in the car and drove the three minutes to Molly's house. Quietly but swiftly I entered the house, feeling like a paramedic on a call. I walked up to the kitchen and around to the dining room where I knew Robin was staying. "Hey, Sandy," Molly said, looking up at me from where she sat beside the whelping box.

"How's she doing?" I whispered, joining her.

"Nothing yet, but she's a good girl."

I began stroking her soft, black coat. "Hi, sweetheart. How you doing?"

Her eyes said, *This sucks.*

"Aw, you don't feel good, huh, baby? It'll be over soon."

Ten minutes later Geri and then Mary blew through the door, grinning from ear to ear. We all took positions around the whelping box.

"Okay, now Mary, you take the video. I'll take the pictures with the regular camera."

We all sat around, the anticipation heavy in the room. We took turns reassuring Robin and waited.

And waited.

And waited.

By midnight we were all extra tired and emotionally depleted and realized that nothing was happening. Disappointed we headed to our homes.

In the next few days two more false alarms occurred and by the third time we entered Molly's living room with a here-we-are-again "Hey there" and plunked ourselves down for another round. I am sure Robin was enjoying all this special attention. Well, that last time was different, and Robin began pacing in and out of the whelping pool. By midnight (why does it always have to be at night?) Robin lay down and began panting. But another hour passed and nothing. So once again we all headed home. Going through my kitchen door the phone rang. "Sandy, there's a purple bubble."

"A purple bubble?"

"Yes, a purple bubble."

"I'm on my way."

Next, "Geri, there's a purple bubble."

"Purple bubble, okay, I'm on my way."

Next, "Mary, there's a purple bubble."

"You're kidding, really? What do you think it is? Should I come over? Do you think it's time?"

"It's time. There's a purple bubble. Gotta go." Click.

I was the first to arrive back at Molly's house and flew into the dining room, fully expecting to see some puppies, but there was Robin, in the whelping pool without puppies. She looked up at me like, *Oh, God, you AGAIN! I'd just like some peace. What exactly is the problem?*

"Anything else happen?" I asked Molly.

"No, but look at this, Sandy." She lifted Robin's tail and sure enough there was a purple bubble.

"Ew," I said, scrunching up my face. "What the heck is that?"

"Maybe the sack comes out first."

"Should I pull it?"

"Well…" she trailed off.

"Maybe I ought to pull. Maybe it's stuck." I grabbed a dishtowel that was on the chair and taking a deep breath grabbed ahold of the object. Molly watched with interest. "Ew!" I whined. "It feels just like a bubble." I gently pulled. Nothing happened. Robin looked at me disinterested. "Okay, let's not pull," I decided. I also realized we had no clue what we were doing. Just then Geri and Mary flew in the room.

There we were again, watching a dog watch us. I instructed

Mary to start filming. Taking her job quite seriously she began filming Robin and the bubble. After a bit I suggested we call the vet. The doctor returned our page with a tired and annoyed-sounding "Yes?"

"Yes, doctor, I'm sorry to bother you this late, but do you remember that pregnant dog you saw? We think she's in labor because there is a purple bubble down there."

"Then she should start having the puppies soon."

"About how long?"

"It shouldn't be more than a couple hours."

"Okay, thank you for your time." He hung up. He was not Mr. Personality, that was for sure.

Two excruciating, long hours later, nothing, so once again we all went home and to bed.

The next morning Molly and I touched base at 8:00 a.m. Molly told me there still weren't any puppies. We agreed the best thing to do was to call the vet's office. After speaking to the office they told us to come in immediately. Molly loaded Robin in her van and picked me up and we raced to the animal hospital. We entered the hospital with Robin and her purple bubble. That animal hospital's front office person, Beatrice, had a reputation of being incredibly rude. She was the kind of person that when you looked at her, you were sure she needed prune juice. Then when she started talking to you like you were lower than dirt, you wanted to pour the prune juice down her throat to try and get her to loosen up.

Beatrice looked at us passively while she finished up with someone else. Then she stuck her pointer finger up in the air as a way of telling us to wait. Then with a nod of her head she motioned us over to the exam room. The doctor came in and did a quick assessment and told us Robin needed a C-section. We were shocked. I also didn't know how expensive it was going to be, and once again I had the pleasure of worrying about money.

Molly wanted to stay with Robin in the exam room until they

took her in back but Beatrice made it very clear we needed to leave. Then as we stood signing the medical release she made a point of lecturing us about not calling sooner and saying, "It is quite possible because you waited that some or all the puppies are dead. I just want you to know that." A sneer on her lips expressed her disgust further.

"We didn't know that it was an emergency," I answered defensively. "The doctor never told me if she didn't have the puppies in two hours that we needed to come in." We left both insulted and worried. We couldn't believe what was happening. Molly had to work that day so I agreed to check in with the vet later. Two hours later at 12:33 p.m. I looked at my cell phone and realized I had a message. Dialing my voice mail I recognized Beatrice's nasal, monotone voice.

"You have eight puppies," she said. You can come pick them up." I was just leaving an appointment with a client and her dog. It was a sunny, glorious winter day, I decided, smiling ear to ear. I called Molly and told her the good news and headed for the animal hospital.

I was the first to arrive at the animal hospital, where a two-faced, close-mouthed, smiling Beatrice motioned me with a tilt, tilt of her head to follow her. Going into an exam room she said, "Wait here." I stood looking around the small room, hoping Molly would make it in time to share this experience. Moments later Beatrice opened the door carrying a clear plastic drawer, the kind you'd use for closet reorganizing. The drawer was making squealing and frantic weep-weep sounds. With a smile she set the container down. *This woman must be bipolar. Okay, not nice, sorry.*

Peering inside I saw seven, four-inch, squirming, fretting, black and brown, guinea pig-looking puppy dogs. I sucked in my breath and with an open-mouthed, could-catch-flies smile I stared in awe. Beatrice picked one of the pups up and said, "They are all healthy, except for one. One of them, the one that had been stuck, barely made it and isn't doing well at all." She looked at me with an I-told-you-so face. "The doctor will be in in a minute to talk to you." She turned and left the room.

Alone in the room with the puppies, their weep-weeps were strong and frantic. I gingerly picked up a puppy. "It's about time, you cutie." I wished someone were with me. I set him back down and watched them as they squirmed around the plastic box. It was awesome to see those tiny pups. I had never seen newborn pups before and I was taking in the whole experience.

Molly arrived a few minutes later and joined me in the room. The vet tech, Julia, came in to speak to us. She explained that the one pup, a boy, had been stuck and that's why she didn't deliver naturally. "We almost lost him twice," she explained. "But we got him back. But don't be surprised if he doesn't make it the night." She left and came back a minute later with a tiny, black puppy. The poor thing was quiet and still. Julia showed Molly how to tube feed him. "You'll have to feed him every three hours throughout the night. If he makes it we want to see him sometime tomorrow."

After a few more minutes a shaky, groggy Robin was brought into the room. She looked like she had been walking in a desert for miles without water. "Hello, honey," Molly said, bending down to pet Robin. Robin looked up at her with weary eyes. "Let's go home," Molly said to Robin, giving her a reassuring pat. We walked to the front desk and settled our bill (which to my relief was less than I thought) and left. Loading the new family in Molly's van I followed her to her house and helped settle the dogs in.

The doctor said that Robin would naturally know what to do so I left Molly's house and headed home. No more than an hour later I got a call from Molly. "Sandy, Robin won't have anything to do with the puppies. They're screaming and I can't get her to go over to them."

"Pull her over and tell her she has to feed them."

"Hold on." I waited. "She won't go over there."

"I'll be right over."

Arriving at Molly's (making note that I now knew the intricate pattern of her kitchen tiles and the names of each book on her dining room table) I went into the dining room. The puppies were squealing and weeping like crazy. "I can't get her to feed them, Sandy. I can't possibly bottle feed seven puppies plus the sick one."

"Come on, Robin," I ordered, grabbing her collar. I led her to the pool and commanded her down. She reluctantly lay down at which time we hurriedly stuck each pup on a nipple. They began drinking greedily. We were relieved.

Molly named the sick pup Toby. He survived one night but died at the dawn of the following morning. That shook Molly and her family to the core. She decided to bury his little body on the side of her house near the door they always used to go in and out of. They fashioned a cardboard coffin and tenderly laid him to rest.

Day after day Molly had to take Robin to her babies and force her down to nurse. Our theory was that Robin got pregnant during her first heat and was therefore technically a teenage mother. She was probably not mature enough to be a good mother. To make matters worse she was cut open and had seven squalling puppies pulling at her incision and grabbing at her. Poor thing.

Meanwhile Robin was still having potty accidents and to make matters worse still had those nasty worms. When she was pregnant the doctor couldn't give her the medicine to kill the worms. The worms were falling out her butt for two weeks before she had her babies. Molly said that was by far the worst part. Then after the pups were born those stubborn worms just didn't want to die. But finally after numerous deworming treatments she was free and clear of them.

The pups were growing into adorable, roly-poly bundles of energy. Their eyes were open by two and a half weeks and they began walking at three and a half weeks or so. By a little over four weeks they were escaping the pool. When they broke out they would look around, dumbfounded as to how they got where they were and would cry to be put back in with their siblings. By five weeks the puppies were crawling out of the pool consistently, so Molly removed the pool and put down newspapers for the pups to go potty on.

Robin was enjoying her pups much more once they started eating puppy food and milk-mush Molly made in a blender. She learned to associate her pups with the sweet and tasty food because after they finished eating she got to lick their plates clean. Robin was quite agile and learned to jump the gate that blocked the puppies in the dining room, and at will she jumped back and forth, hanging out with Molly's dogs then back with her puppies again.

One day while on the phone with Molly she said to me, "I love coming home to seven wagging tails. It thrills me to see them. They are so excited to see me it makes me feel really important." She never complained about the enormous amount of work and thrived in that element. She said, "This is the best thing I have ever done."

By eight weeks, though, the pups were a handful and Molly gladly handed them over to their new families. "I was glad to see them go but missed the homecoming I always got from them." Molly wouldn't have to wait too long to experience the joy of being a foster mom again to a brood of pups.

Soon after the pups were gone Molly started taking Robin on walks in her neighborhood. One day I decided to join them with one of my foster dogs. Rounding the bend I spotted Molly and Robin at the end of Molly's driveway. When I got 12 feet or so away from them I noticed that Robin became alert, her tail rose high and the hair on her back went up. "Robin," I called out, "it's just me." I kept walking towards them. Robin began lunging towards us barking. I realized her aggressiveness was towards the dog I had (who wasn't paying any attention to Robin), not me. I stopped seven feet away and Molly and I went for our walk on opposite sides of the street from each other. I was very concerned by

Robin's behavior and made a mental note to give Molly some advice on how to handle it.

The following day I taught Molly what she needed to do to correct the behavior. "When Robin lunges and snaps yank her back with the leash and bellow at her, 'Leave it!' and pull back on her leash. Don't allow her to get away with that behavior," I cautioned Molly.

At adoption events I was a nervous wreck. I made sure that only certain people held onto Robin's leash and we kept her a good six feet away from any dog. Even with that I watched her like a hawk. The last thing we needed was another dog getting bit, especially in front of a crowd of people.

Summer arrived and Molly was preparing for her annual summer vacation. She asked me to take Robin for the duration of her trip. I agreed partly because I knew I needed to get her to behave better with other dogs but mostly because there was no one else to take her. In preparation for Robin moving to my house I slowly introduced her to my foster dogs, Julie and Lainey, by bringing her over for short, supervised play visits. After a week of supervised visits I was confident Robin would be fine at my house with my foster dogs.

The night before her departure date Molly dropped Robin off at my house. Robin settled in nicely and enjoyed being able to romp in the yard with the other foster dogs. (Molly didn't have a fence so running free was new to her.) I was growing quite fond of Robin, loving her sweet, regal and loyal German Shepherd-type personality. She reminded me a little of my dog Heidi.

When Molly returned home from her vacation she called me. "Hi, Sandy, I'm back."

"Hey, Molly, how was your trip?"

"It was great. Relaxing. How did Robin do?"

"She was good." I paused. "I was thinking. Maybe Robin should stay with me until she's adopted. I can work on her dog issues and she loves running in the yard."

"That's fine with me." So it was that Robin stayed with me, and offering to keep her would later prove not to have been such a great idea.

My home was an old stucco house built in the early 1930's, with lots of additions that were put on before we moved in. There was an entranceway through the front door that flowed slightly to the left and into a living room, then a dining room and beyond that a kitchen. There was an old-fashioned eating nook off the kitchen, and the stairs to the basement led off the eating nook. That was one side of the main level. Going through the kitchen door was an enclosed porch at the back of the house, and around the other side of the porch was another door that led to the Pet Sitters' office. Past the Pet Sitters' office was a short hallway and a bathroom and then there was my office. Through my other office door you wound back around to the front hallway and front door.

When we moved our offices back home in 1996, after two years in a strip mall, we wanted more privacy. The dining room had a door to the upstairs where there was a staircase leading up to four bedrooms and one shared bathroom. On the other side of the doorway of the dining room was the hallway and bathroom between the two downstairs rooms.

To increase our privacy Chuck built a wall to divide the downstairs by building a wall along the stairway. He also built an entrance to the house on the porch from the side closest to the Pet Sitters' office. Essentially that gave us complete separation between the two downstairs offices and bathroom and our private living quarters.

Shortly after I started Animal Education and Rescue Chuck built a wall and a door separating the front hall from the living room. Enclosing the front hall gave me the small space I needed to bring animals in on an emergency basis as well as inevitably experience raising pups.

Because I had foster dogs in and adopted out so often it was easiest not to have to always introduce my dogs to every foster dog. Additionally it prevented any personality conflicts between dogs. And in the case of Robin, who was still somewhat unpredictable with dogs she met it, having separate quarters for the foster dogs served an additional purpose. When our foster dogs were outside in the backyard going potty or playing, my dogs were inside and vice versa. It worked out wonderfully. Unfortunately there were occasions when one of my dogs was left outside by accident and then the foster dogs were let out, thus a surprise meeting. One dog in particular notoriously was the last of my own crew to trail inside. His name was Rascal, a Chihuahua and Jack Russell mix. Rascal loved to sit outside on top of the picnic table and take in the sights and sounds of the outside world. He loved the fresh air and open space.

One day I let the foster dogs out and went back inside. I never left the dogs out for more than ten minutes so roughly ten minutes later I headed back to the porch to let the dogs in. Opening the screen door my heart leapt when I saw that Rascal was standing with the other dogs. My concern was Robin. She had acted aggressively to all dogs she met outside the home. I scooped up Rascal and examined him for possible wounds. The other dogs looked at me like, *What's the matter, Mom?* Finding no wounds I sighed with relief. I took a moment to experience gratitude that he was okay. I put him on my side of the house and then herded the foster dogs into the offices.

The following week Rascal lagged behind my crew again and was basking in the sun when I let the foster dogs out back five minutes later. Looking out into the yard as the foster dogs ran past me I noticed Rascal. They greeted each other passively so I wasn't worried and let Rascal stay outside with them. A few minutes later I called Rascal and put him in the kitchen.

The following Saturday I was rushing around trying to get ready to pick up a dog I agreed to watch for the afternoon. I let the foster dogs out and yet again Rascal was still outside. That dog was sneaky! I was going to be gone 15 minutes and it was a gorgeous, sunny day so I decided to leave all the dogs outside while I quickly went and got the dog.

I thought briefly of bringing Rascal inside but decided I was being an overprotective mom and reasoned that Rascal was perfectly fine with the foster dogs. I was back home 15 minutes later with a black lab pup in tow. I put the pup in a crate in my office and headed out back to let the dogs inside. Just before I opened the door I thought I heard a strange noise. I opened the door and standing in a row from right to left were Lainey, Robin, Julie and Rascal. As I opened the door I caught the tail end of Julie telling Robin off with a snarl and air-snap. My eyes scanned to my left and to my absolute horror I saw that Rascal's neck had a gaping, bloody wound. He was standing there with a look of shock on his little face.

"Oh, no!" I screamed. I searched my brain frantically for what to do. I was terrible at handling emergencies. I had a tendency to go into hysterics and not know what to do. Thinking it was likely Robin who attacked Rascal I grabbed her and dragged her into the house and put her in her crate. Next I called Julie and Lainey to come in. I was sobbing. I was scared for Rascal and just literally exhausted, mentally and physically. Once again I had a fleeting thought, *I need to quit this rescue business.*

I knew Chuck and the kids weren't home. *Why do I always have to handle things alone?* I thought in frustration. I went back outside and gently lifted Rascal into my arms. "You're okay, baby, we'll fix you up," I said through my tears. I looked down and saw blood staining my shirt. Like an out-of-body experience I saw myself get in my van and drive down the street towards the closest animal hospital.

I have a neurological disorder called essential tremor, which causes my hands to shake. When I am upset my tremor causes me to shake like a washer on an agitated spin. I was forcing myself to breathe. "Sandy, breathe," I said out loud, to try and calm my tremor enough so I could push the little buttons on my cell phone to try and get ahold of Chuck. I was finally able to dial and his voice mail picked up.

Pulling into the animal hospital parking lot I raced to the door with Rascal in my arms. The door was locked. "Oh, no!" I looked at their hours. They wouldn't open for another hour. I got back in my car and called the other animal hospital about ten minutes away. Through my tears I explained that my dog had been bitten and needed emergency care. They told me to come on in. On my way, patting Rascal and telling him he'd be okay, I realized that the black lab pup was still at my house in a crate. I needed someone to get him. Why, I wasn't sure, but that's what I thought at the time.

It took me four tries to finally be able to push the buttons of Molly's number. "Molly," I said, my voice shaking, "Robin bit Rascal. At least I am pretty sure it was Robin. His neck is ripped open. Ripped open." I burst into fresh tears. "I am going to the animal hospital. I can't get ahold of Chuck. Can you please go to my house and pick up a lab pup and bring him to your house?"

"Sure, Sandy, I'll go right over. Do you want me to meet you at the animal hospital?"

"No, it's okay, just take care of the puppy. I'll call you if I need anything. Thanks, Molly."

Pulling into the animal clinic's parking lot I tried to compose myself. I wiped my tears away with my shirt and gently lifted Rascal up and stepped out of the car. The entire ride there Rascal was quietly sitting on the passenger seat beside me. Opening the door to the animal hospital I came face to face with Beatrice, the last person I wanted to see.

To her credit she actually got up right away and told me to follow her into an exam room. The doctor entered immediately afterwards through the other door. "What do we have here?" he asked.

"Rascal got bit by Robin, you know, the dog that had the C-section."

"Um," he said, examining the wound, "and it's a bad one. I can actually see the jugular vein. One centimeter further and we'd have a different story." He opened a drawer and took out some gauze and began wrapping Rascal's neck. Rascal remained quiet and subdued. "He's a nice boy. I can't believe how good he's being," the doctor commented. "He's going to have to have surgery so you can give us a call later to check in." He gently took Rascal from me and left the room. I just won the lottery, I thought. My boy was going to be okay. But now I had another huge problem sitting heavy on my shoulders and it was in the form of a big, black dog named Robin.

On the way home Chuck called and I broke the news to him about Rascal. Rascal was our sweet, little cuddle-bug. He was the one dog we gave to ourselves that didn't have any physical or mental issues. Unlike Scrappy, who was largely my dog, Rascal was a family dog equally loved by everyone. I told him, "We have to make sure it was Robin. I don't know how we're going to do it, but we have to."

We arrived home within minutes of each other and went into the office. He looked down at my blood-soaked shirt and shook his head. We looked from one dog to another, all three looking at us with innocent eyes.

"It can't be Julie," I said, pointing at the pointer mix with the liver-colored nose and matching eyes, "because she is almost all white and there is no blood on her. Besides, when I went outside to get the dogs I swear Julie had just finished scolding Robin. I can only guess to protect Rascal. That would be like Julie, she's very sensitive." I lifted Lainey's chin and examined her white neck. "And Lainey, Lainey wouldn't hurt a fly. She's got a lot of white on her and I don't see any blood." I stood there a moment thinking. "I have an idea. Because Robin's so black we wouldn't see blood anyway. Do me a favor and take a wet paper towel and rub it on her neck and see if the towel turns red."

Chuck went into the bathroom with Robin and after a minute called out, "Yes, it's coming off dark."

My heart was so heavy. I knew that what Robin did was very,

very serious. "What am I going to do?" I asked Chuck. He didn't answer and walked away.

In the afternoon I picked Rascal up at the animal hospital. He had stitches six inches long around his small neck. I looked down at him, his ears held back and his blackish-brown eyes expressing the pain he was feeling. I gently stroked his head and back, being extra careful to avoid his neck, trying to offer reassurance. Back home I brought Rascal up to my bedroom, the quietest room in the house. Holding Rascal I grabbed a small blanket from the trunk at the end of my bed and laid it on top of the bed. Gingerly placing Rascal on the blanket I kissed his yellow muzzle and told him I'd see him later. Before I closed my bedroom door I took one more look at Rascal. He looked so small and fragile lying motionless on my bed that my heart melted.

What was I going to do about Robin? After such a vicious bite how could she ever be trusted again? I imagined in my mind all the times she could potentially see other dogs. At my house we had to check and double check the doors to make sure the foster dogs and my dogs were never out at the same time. To make matters more challenging our door occasionally popped open from the wind so I checked and rechecked that the doors were secured shut. I began to know what it felt like to have obsessive-compulsive disorder.

Molly came over so she could see Rascal. She looked at the severe bite and said, "I think you should put Robin down." I didn't say much then but I was taking what she said to heart and was panicked at even the thought of it. I was the one she loved and trusted. For all she knew I WAS her mom, her family, her protector. Just to think that I would have to kill her was something that might have put me over the edge. My whole life was lived on a foundation of not hurting others, being a peaceful human. My entire family was vegetarian, my children never having had meat touch their lips. And I was to kill a living, breathing animal that loved and trusted me?

The next day I was talking to Molly on the phone and the conversation turned to Robin.

"Have you decided what to do?" Molly asked.

"That's all I've been thinking about. I just don't know. How can I do that?" I couldn't even say *put her to sleep.* "She's so wonderful in every other way, but what she did to Rascal..."

"Sandy, it's really bad."

"I know. Maybe I can adopt her out to someone without dogs, someone that is experienced with difficult dogs and knows to never have her with other dogs. I could offer free dog training lessons."

She was silent. I knew that she thought that my suggestions sounded stupid. I started to feel panic overwhelm me. "I can't take her, I can't. If I have to do that I can't bring her, can't be with her. I'll melt." I began to cry. "I'll melt into the ground and never get up. I'll quit this whole damn thing. This is too much for me."

"I'll take her," Molly said matter-of-factly.

"I can't ask you to do that," I sniffled.

"Really, I don't mind. I know it might sound strange but I can handle it, really."

"Okay, let me think about it."

That whole week I thought of every option I had for Robin. Rascal was healing nicely so the freshness of the attack was fading. Sitting at my desk deep in thought I said, *You are not giving up on her so easily. You don't know what happened to cause them to fight. Rascal can be very snappy with other dogs. He has that little dog I-think-I'm-a-big-dog attitude. She is counting on me to do everything I can for her. I am her guardian, I am her savior and I will not give up on her so easily.*

I have always been a big believer in the fact that knowledge is power, and I was confident that if there were any behavior modification techniques out there I didn't know about I would find them and learn them. I sent my warrior energies out to the universe and began my search for answers.

First I began an Internet search on dog-to-dog aggression. As a dog trainer my experience prior to rescue was limited to simple problem solving with dogs such as housebreaking, chewing and jumping. I had little to no experience with dog-to-dog aggression. Frankly, before rescue I didn't want to deal with aggressive dogs. I didn't need to. There were enough people who needed help with ordinary and typical behavior problems that I didn't need to put myself or another dog at risk by working with an aggressive dog. But with rescue comes dogs with issues much more serious than the average dog, and so I needed to buck up, suck it in and learn to deal with what serious issues came to me. That was my responsibility if I was going to be involved in rescue.

I purchased books and videos that specifically dealt with dog-to-dog aggression. While waiting the five to seven days for them to be shipped to my house I started going through my dog trainer's association member-to-member handbook. Each trainer had a description of their expertise in their short bio under their name. After some searching there was one name that stood out over the hundreds of names in the book. Her bio said that she was involved in rehabilitating homeless dogs as well as handling aggression. So with nothing to lose and much to gain I called her.

On the second ring a woman answered the phone. I asked to speak to Karey Brimmer. "This is she," she said. I told her who I was and my dilemma. I was unsure if she would give me the time of day, after all our advice as trainers is how we make money, but it was obvious from the beginning she was willing to share her advice. She explained to me what might have happened to cause Robin's aggression.

"The way we all trained dogs not to be aggressive with other dogs was to snap back on their leash and tell them 'No!' in a big voice," she told me. "Like what you did when she was acting aggressively. I made the same mistake for a long time until it backfired. It happens to all of us, so don't feel bad."

"What do you mean?" I was perplexed. I didn't know I had done anything wrong.

"Actually doing that yanking on the collar and yelling at the dog when they are acting aggressive can make some dogs more aggressive."

"Really, why?" I was intrigued.

"It makes them think you're joining in with their aggression, kind of like you are saying, 'Come on, let's get 'em.'"

"Really? What do I do instead?" I had no idea.

"The only real way to solve dog-to-dog aggression is through positive reinforcement. Traditional training does more harm than good–time has proved that. When your dog sees another dog, *before* the growling and lunging happens you praise the dog and offer her a really delicious treat. The trick is to find out where your starting point distance is right before the dog's bad reaction, like barking, standing stiff, too alert, and praise the dog for good behavior with a treat. Each day and week the distance at which the dog is reactive should get closer to other dogs. So if you started at, let's say 15 feet, the next time might be 12 then 10 and so on." She paused and then added, "So in other words the dog will begin to realize: see dog, I get good things, dog good. Good behavior, reward."

"Oh, okay, I get it." I was amazed by that theory. It made perfect sense. I felt new hope for Robin on the horizon. "I'll work on it."

"You have to understand it can take hours and hours and weeks and weeks of training. Frankly, I'm sorry to say this, but in my years in rescue the worst dogs I've seen that are the most squirrely are shepherds. I won't even deal with shepherds anymore–too much of a risk. I know you don't want to hear this, but there are so many dogs without issues that need homes and are being killed because they have nowhere to go."

"What are you suggesting?"

"Euthanize the dog and move on. You can devote your time better to dogs that don't have issues. I'm sorry to be bitter that way, but I've seen it all and that's the best advice I can give. Just think, you've done all you could for her."

I thanked her very much for her time and we hung up. I was so very grateful for her advice. I did not agree with her statement that I had done everything I could. I knew logically there were thousands of dogs that were more adoptable waiting to be rescued, but they weren't living with me. While I hold no judgment to someone else who would have chosen to euthanize her I was just not capable at that time. The main thing I needed to be able to say to myself was that I had done everything I could. Then if I had to euthanize her I could live with myself. Training would start the next day.

The following day I got some treats, pocketed them, snapped the leash on Robin and headed off. I purposely walked a direction I knew we would see dogs. I was very nervous and was trying not to show it. I stayed acutely aware as I walked, prepared for dogs we might encounter. I was on a mission and was determined to fix this dog.

The first dog I saw was a Golden Retriever being walked by his owner on the other side of the street. I spotted the dog before Robin, which was an important part of the training. Then I watched Robin, with my treat ready in the palm of my hand. As soon as Robin noticed the dog, and before any bad behavior could start, I said in a very high, happy voice, "Good girl, Robin!" and gave her the treat.

Over and over again I did this. Over the period of two weeks Robin was starting to look at me as soon as she saw a dog, anticipating a treat. That's when I knew the training was working. I had renewed hope and the weight of my burden began to lift. On our walks I began to relax. The weather was perfect. It was a mild, sunny summer–two years since I had walked the same roads with my sweet Heidi. The smells of greenery and freshly cut grass were like nature's perfume. The sounds of lawn mowers, basketballs bouncing on pavement and kids laughing outside made the task ahead of me more than bearable.

Every now and again I would slow to a stop and command Robin to sit and stay, which she did with eager and enthusiastic pleasure. I stroked her long muzzle and soft cheeks, as she looked up at me open-mouthed in a smile, with soft, brown eyes looking at me in love. My chest would swell with love and devotion for her. Sometimes I'd say, "Right back at you, babes."

After at least 25 hours of training that lasted for three months Robin no longer acted aggressively towards other dogs. Then one time I saw a dog coming our way on the sidewalk and Robin looked at the dog, and without me saying a word, she looked at me with her tail wagging. I had successfully programmed her! I began introducing her to new dogs and not once did she act even remotely aggressive. She was finally ready to get adopted.

One day, while sitting in my office working, the phone rang. It was a woman who introduced herself as Helene. She said she was looking for a companion for her dog. She explained one of her dogs recently died and her remaining dog, Cappy, was very depressed. She went on, "He mopes around the house and won't play. I'm worried about his weight because he's not exercising as much and it's like he's aged years."

"Is there a particular dog you are looking for?"

"Not really, I just need one that'll get along with Cappy and is good with kids because I have a seven-year-old."

"Any size?"

"I'd like one that really needs a home, you know a real rescue dog. I'm open to size, mix, whatever."

Was I hearing this right? I thought.

"Well, I have this dog named Robin. She's a big, black lab/shep-herd mix. She's had a rough time. She was a teenage mom, hated it and then came to live with me. She attacked one of my dogs, but to her defense I wasn't there to see what happened. But the attack was severe." I paused, prepared for her to say she was no longer interested. She was silent. I went on, "I've spent hours and hours with her and she is so eager to please. I believe she is much better now. Would you like to meet her?"

Undaunted by what I told her she asked, "Is she good with kids?"

"Fantastic. She's good with all people."

"Then yes, I want to meet her. I'll bring Cappy."

That afternoon Helene and her dog Cappy arrived at my house. Cappy was a big Rottweiler mix with a dopey, jowly face and barrel-shaped middle. He trotted up the stairs to the porch. I walked them through the porch to the backyard. "Why don't you take the leash off of Cappy? It's totally fenced in so he can't get out."

"You sure I should unleash him or should they meet on leash instead?"

"Many times dogs actually do better meeting other dogs off leash. That way they don't feel confined by a leash, feeling it necessary to protect themselves. Besides," I smiled looking over at Cappy, "I am confident that Cappy could hold his own. He's a big boy."

I asked Helene to wait outside in the yard while I got Robin. I was nervous and prayed silently that this would work out. I let Robin outside and she immediately went down the deck stairs and abruptly approached Cappy as he was sniffing the grass, startling him. Looking intently at Cappy she stood tall and erect, her tail high over her back and hackles up. She snapped three times fast at Cappy's face. The poor guy bowed his head in submission.

I grabbed Robin's collar, afraid she would hurt him, and told Helene, "Well I guess this isn't going to work. Let me put her inside." I led her inside totally depleted. Heading back outside Helene seemed unaffected by what had just happened. We started discussing what other dogs we might have that would work when Helene said, "Let's try Robin one more time."

"You sure?" I said, fully aware of the liability risk. But with her relaxed attitude and her permission I felt it was worth another try.

"Yeah, let's try again."

I brought Robin outside again and she immediately went down the stairs towards Cappy, her body confident. I held my breath. She went nose to nose with him. He lowered his face a little. Robin sniffed his face and then, with Cappy quietly standing still, moved around to his back end and sniffed his rear end. That's a dog's way of saying "How do you do!" *Good news!* I thought. "Good girl, Robin!" I said in my ever-so-happy voice. "Good girl!" Robin looked at me, walked over and gazed up waiting for an ear scratch. "You're so good, Robin! What a good girl! This is good," I said to Helene.

Helene seemed unsurprised by it. I knew she had no concept of what I had been through with this dog. Robin went back over to Cappy and gave him a quick nose-to-mouth greeting, a very submissive gesture, and went on her way to explore the yard. After some separate exploring the dogs greeted each other again. Then Robin hopped up and opened her mouth, a clear sign she was giving Cappy that she was cool with him. He bowed and then she bowed. And they were off! Robin was chasing Cappy and then Cappy chased Robin. They dodged each other and then jumped up at each other. They ran more circles around the yard, body slammed each other and then Cappy licked Robin inside her mouth. Yet another sign that they were becoming friends. We spent a good half an hour with them together and everything seemed to be going quite well.

"What do you think?" I smiled, watching them gallop around the yard.

"Well, it's Cappy that I have to think of, and I think they'll be good together. When can you come over?"

"How about this afternoon?"

"Okay, sounds great."

That afternoon I drove to the other end of town where the houses were larger and the properties at least an acre. Fences were not allowed so everything looked spacious and open. I pulled into their driveway and with Robin taking the lead walked up to their traditional colonial's red front door. Robin seemed to know where she was going. Helene opened the door before we had a chance to ring the bell and we were led into a large kitchen and family room area. It was a beautiful house with tiled floors and wide hallways. Cappy greeted Robin like, "Hey, I was wondering when you would get here."

I snapped off Robin's leash and Cappy and Robin immediately engaged in play like long-time buddies. Looking to my right a large, middle-aged man wearing casual clothes and a baseball cap walked into the room. "Hello, I'm Marc, Helene's husband," he said, offering his hand.

"Hi, Marc. Sandy."

Marc looked at Robin, as Cappy and Robin were playing. He called her over. Obediently she trotted over and sat beside him. He petted her head as she looked up at him longingly. "Is she good with kids? We have a son and she has to be good with kids." As if on cue their son came in from another room.

"She's great with kids. She's very loyal and loving."

"We had a bad experience with a dog that attacked our older son. I said I would never get another dog unless my vet got to see the dog first." Robin had walked over to their son to give him a quick sniff of "How do you do?"

I was blindsided by what this man was saying, just as I thought this might be working. "I assure you this dog is outstanding with children." I paused wanting to sound philosophical. "Why do you think your vet, who is a medical doctor, would know about animal behavior?"

"I trust him."

"I have spent more time with this dog than your vet ever will. I am a dog trainer," I said, trying not to sound irritated. "I can assure you this dog would not hurt a human being. My concern is other dogs. I know Helene filled you in. I am more than happy to come to your home and do training sessions to teach you how to work with Robin on getting along with other dogs. But as far as kids go, there is no problem."

We stood around silently while he thought. He had it in his head that because of his bad experience with a dog biting his child he needed his vet to make a decision as to whether a dog was good for his home. I respected that but it made no sense. Vets are trained primarily to handle health issues with animals, not behavioral issues. I would never claim to be an expert in veterinary medicine, just as veterinarians should not claim to have extensive training regarding behavioral issues.

After some time and watching Robin interact with his son he said, "Alright, we'll give it a try."

"Are you sure?"

"Yeah, it's okay."

We had completed the necessary paperwork and educational information. It was time for me to say goodbye to Robin. "Come on, Robin," I called, slapping my thigh. Robin hesitated for a second looking at Cappy and reluctantly followed Helene and me to the door. I wrapped my arms around Robin's neck. I breathed in her unique dog smell and hugged her tight. I thought back to all that we had been through. I could feel her physically pulling away from me. I said, "Now, I love you. Be a good girl and have a wonderful life." She looked at me briefly and trotted off to be with her new doggy brother. "Well," I said with a lump in my throat, "I guess she knows she's home." Slightly hurt but also feeling like I had conquered climbing a mountain, I opened the door and exited the house. It had been eight long, hard months. I drove away, the car still

carrying the scent and silent presence of my canine friend. I had done it.
I had really done it, one more time.

A Trip to Remember

In the fall of 2005 I decided to take an impromptu weekend trip to visit Pane County Humane Society. Pane County was the shelter where we had gotten Daisy, Stretch and many other dogs. I thought it would be interesting as well as educational to actually see the facility. While I was there I also planned on picking two dogs to take back with me and foster until I found them homes. Sally, an active volunteer, agreed to go with me.

We left on a wet and dreary Friday. The weather didn't squelch the excitement I felt for our adventure. I decided moments before we left to bring my video camera along and put together a film of our trip. We loaded the car with two crates, two leashes and two collars.

Before we left I showed Sally how to use the video camera (she wanted to film, not be filmed) and we headed out. Our seven-hour ride turned into nine because of the lousy weather and roads that were lined with bumper-to-bumper traffic. The time moved quickly, though, as we passed fields and more fields of grassy, muddy, cornstalk oceans. Plunked down here and there like islands were farmhouses, tractors, buildings and barns of all shapes and sizes. I let my mind wander to my childhood dreams of owning land with a big farmhouse and lots of animals. I could picture the big vegetable garden, the dogs running the big fields, their spirits soaring, chickens pecking the ground and a goat or two.

We finally arrived in the town where Pane shelter was and pulled into the only hotel, a Best Western. Right away I noticed that the parking lot was packed with manly, well-worn trucks and Blazers any testosterone-driven male would grunt at in approval. "Boy, there's a lot of people staying here," I commented to Sally. As she combed the parking lot for a single open parking space I added, "Look at all those man-cars! Not a single mini van, compact or sedan in the bunch." We found a spot on the side of the building and parked. Getting out of the car my aching butt and hips reminded me of our long ride. I stretched, moaned and like a cowboy moseyed stiff-legged inside the hotel lobby.

Checking in I asked the woman behind the desk, "Is there a business conference or something? The lot's full of cars."

The woman looked at me like I was an alien and said, "Ma'am, see here it's huntin' season. They come from all parts to hunt here. Lots of deer."

"You're kidding," I said not missing the ironic situation.

"No, Ma'am, Pane County is known for its huntin'."

"We're here to save dogs," I told her, wanting her to know at least two people in this building cared about animals. The woman handed me my credit card without comment. With eyelids at half mast and a forced smile she said, "Thank ye, Ma'am, ye jus go right 'round the corner and up the stairs to yer room."

As we walked towards the stairs I looked over at Sally, my eyes wide. "And we're sleeping around hunters, with guns." We giggled nervously.

By the time we got to our room we were exhausted. Neither one of us could get over the fact that we were sleeping under the same roof as dozens of hunters. Each man was packing a soon-to-be critter-killing firearm. It was slightly creepy not to mention very sad for me. I hated thinking of those beautiful animals dying. After we ate some breakfast bars and mixed nuts for dinner we set the alarm for 6:00 a.m. and went to sleep.

The next morning we woke up and after a quick breakfast at the local restaurant we headed for the shelter. Pulling into the gravel drive I was surprised at how small the shelter looked from the outside. They had more than 100 dogs and cats listed on their web site. I couldn't imagine how they stuffed all those animals inside that small cement building. Walking up the gravel drive towards the front door the sign on the building in big, cheerful letters said: Pane Humane Society.

Opening the door we walked in. Just inside was a reception area. A pretty, middle-aged woman was behind the desk shuffling through some paperwork. She looked up and said, "You must be Sandy." She smiled a tired, weary smile. "I'm Michelle." She offered her hand.

"Michelle, nice to meet you." I shook her hand. Motioning towards Sally I said, "Michelle, this is Sally."

"Hello, Sally," she said, shaking her hand.

"Come on in," Michelle said, her gentle, syrupy, southern accent making me feel instantly comforted. She took a red bandana out of her shirt pocket and folded it into a long strip and wrapped it around her fluffy, blond hair. "Now we just got here so I apologize for the mess. We do the best we can. We just started doing our mornin' cleaning."

"We are planning on documenting this experience. Would you mind if we filmed?" I asked her.

"Sure, honey, whatever you'd like." Every facial feature looked fallen in exhaustion and the day had just begun.

Following her into the small front lobby I had no clue what she was apologizing for. I had seen and smelled animal hospitals that were worse. Frankly, my house smelled worse. We followed her through a door to a room with concrete floors and walls and dog runs in a group in the center. As soon as we walked through the door dogs erupted in a barking frenzy, the noise bouncing loudly from cement wall to cement wall. My ears instantly hurt. The smell of urine and feces hit my nostrils. I noticed small vents on the walls and wide, high windows that were propped open. Ventilation was obviously an issue. Again, she apologized and said they were still cleaning up.

Each dog run housed two or three medium or large-sized dogs. Michelle stopped in front of each cage and spoke loudly over the barking, telling us each dog's story while the camera rolled. One dog in particular still burns in my memory. It was a hound dog, maybe a tree walker, curled up in a ball. Michelle said he was at the shelter because "he won't hunt." As if he knew he had failed he lifted his head up and looked at us for a fraction of a second before he laid it, far too heavy for him, on the concrete floor.

"You're telling me that they gave up their dog because he wouldn't hunt?" I hollered to her.

"Things are different here." I looked at the dog that had lost all hope.

"He looks so incredibly sad and defeated," I said. Briefly it crossed my mind that I should take him home, but I knew hounds, especially larger hounds, weren't popular in our area, making him hard to adopt out. To this day I wonder what happened to him and regret not taking him.

Michelle led us around to the other side of the room with four identical dog runs and more dogs looking sad and stressed out. After brief introductions to those dogs we followed her out of the room and outside the back of the building. I was grateful for the reprieve from the sharp stink inside the building and the barking so loud it actually was painful to my ears. I breathed in the fresher air, tainted with the faint odor of dogs, hay, fresh grass and gritty dirt.

Just past some outdoor dog runs that were lining the back wall of the building was a large 20 x 20 dog pen with a cement floor. There were a dozen dogs under 30 pounds walking around inside it, many of them barking and most of them looking like they couldn't believe they were there, their eyes bugged out and their ears sitting back on their heads. Michelle said loudly, "This is the outdoor play area for the small dogs. I have picked out a few dogs here that I think you will like." She pointed to a tiny, scruffy, yappy dog she said was named Scooby and a purebred black and white Cocker Spaniel named Oreo.

"Okay," I said, thinking, *Those two could be very adoptable in our area.* "Can we take them for a walk?" I wanted to assess their temperaments.

"Of course, honey. I'll bring you to where the leashes are and you just take them on up front in that grassy area and you spend as much time as you'd like. Let me show you everything else first, hon, and then you can take care of what you need to do." She had a way of shouting and still sounding feminine.

She showed us the six other dog runs under an overhang attached to the back of the building. Each dog run was about five feet long by three feet wide and six feet tall. They were furnished with a well-used doghouse. There was a hound mix, two Border Collie mixes, a huge, Mastiff-looking dog and two black lab mixes. The number of dogs was staggering. Afterwards we continued our tour through a walkway and back into the building. We passed a primitively built bathtub on a plywood platform used for bathing and then arrived at the room that housed the cats. The 12 x 12 room was lined with cages on every wall, one on top of the other all the way to the ceiling, as well as cages in the center of the room that were stacked floor to ceiling. Each small cage housed one to three cats with just enough extra space for a litter box, food and water.

Stopping inside the much quieter room an eerie feeling emerged. "This is a far worse problem than anything else," she said, looking around her, profound dismay clear on her face. "There is just no place for these cats to go." She shook her head and shrugged her shoulders. Then in a voice little bigger than a whisper, "Coming here is a death sentence."

"Don't any rescue groups step up to help?" I asked.

"Very, very unusual." She paused, slowly looking around the room. "No, nowhere for them to go," she said as if reminding herself.

"Why do you have so many cats?"

"People around here just don't understand. It's…" She paused, searching for the right words. "We're just country folks here. Changing the way people think is a long, long road."

"What do you mean?" I asked.

"People come in with litters of kittens and don't think anything of it. I just say, 'alright then,' and take the kittens, and they leave and we now have more kittens we have to stuff in cages. People let their cats run loose and don't spay and neuter and then give us the kittens…the ones that get here anyway. The ones that don't, well…we usually get them anyway, when they're grown at some time or another."

"Why don't people spay and neuter here?" I asked.

"It's hard to explain." She paused and smiled at me with a sweet, tired, red lipstick smile. "They're farmers here, set in their ways. They just, well, just don't do it. Many of the animals live outside and run the area and then they make babies." Sally panned the camera around the room.

I looked around at the 80 or so cats and kittens in the room. Their faces were sad, stressed and tired. *This was no way to live. But there is no place for these cats and this is their small cell before death by lethal injection,* I thought. *Like a holocaust that doesn't have to be, if only people would be responsible pet owners… The problem is much bigger and more complicated than I ever thought possible.*

We stood there silently for a few more minutes just taking it all in. I could feel heaviness sitting on my chest like a weight. Breaking the silence Michelle said, "Anyone that gets into this kind of work has to realize that it is going to be very, very hard. They have to prepare themselves for it and expect to get their hands dirty. This work is only for some people."

I nodded and a large pause ensued. Then, "Do you choose who is euthanized?"

"Yes, I have to."

"How do you pick who to euthanize?"

"Well, honey, I pick by who's old or maybe sick or who won't like to be cuddled. 'Cause if they won't be cuddled and loved on no one will want them."

"How do you emotionally handle it?"

"I cry, a lot. I know it has to be done. I have to make room for other animals that come in." She blinked back tears. "I cry a lot, hon. I cry a lot." She paused. "I'm sorry." She wiped away a tear. "I also think of how things were before I came. You don't want to know how they got rid of animals then." She shook her head. "At least they don't suffer and they die with some dignity. But sometimes I wonder how I got into this."

I felt so bad for this woman. She was so brave but she was a soldier destined to lose a war, knowing full well most of her troops would die. "How did you get into this?" I asked her softly. Sally stood quietly filming.

"I knew the way they handled things here in the past and I wanted it to be better. I thought nobody else would do this so I might as well."

"Do you think of quitting?"

"I have given up everything for this place and yeah, I think of quitting. I know if I leave it'll go back to the way it was before. At least with the help of rescue groups like yours," she paused and smiled my way, "we are savin' some. We're doing a little better each day, hon, a bit better anyway. It's just very, very hard."

As I listened to Michelle I imagined for her invisible glowing arms holding her up, giving her the strength to go on day after day. I prayed for her strength, her happiness and her soul. I knew her heart and soul were large and raw with passion and heartache like an invisible pull that kept her going. She was and is an amazing, awesome human being, and a true animal warrior.

"And you still manage to put on makeup and lipstick and look so good," I half joked trying to lighten the mood. (I was impressed with that because I didn't take the time to put on makeup or do my hair much anymore. I didn't make looking good a priority anymore.)

She laughed. "A girl's gotta make herself feel a little good, even if it's just a bit of lipstick."

By 3:00 p.m. Sally and I were back at the hotel and relaxing before our scheduled dinner date with Michelle and her husband. That evening Sally and I met up with Michelle and her husband Jay at the pizza and pasta joint in town. During our meal, just making small talk and relaxing, numerous people stopped at our table to say hello to Michelle. She smiled at each person in greeting, making a point to ask them how they and their family were doing. All the while I was with her I sensed her exhaustion. I also felt her muted passion for what she did, I was sure with a bit of regret and feelings of being trapped mixed in.

While I would never compare what I was doing to being nearly as difficult as what she was doing, I could relate to the passion for animals and the desperate need to save them combined with the hours and hours of very difficult work necessary to just save some. There were many days when I was fed up and felt in over my head, especially when tragedy struck. I wrote imaginary letters in my head at those times to my volunteers. It went something like this:

Dear Volunteers:

It has been a pleasure beyond measure to work with you. I value all your hard work and devotion to Animal Education and Rescue. It is with deep regret I inform you that Animal Education and Rescue is officially closed.

It gives me great pain to do this but I cannot bear the burden and worry anymore. I worry constantly about running out of money and never having enough of what we need. I worry that some animal we take in will become sick and need surgery and I will have to decide whether to spend the thousands necessary to save the animal or think of all the animals and euthanize the one. I also worry constantly that I will have to euthanize an animal because of severe behavior problems.

My house is a disaster, always in a state of disrepair and clutter. Every single room in my home shows signs of destruction by one or many of the dozens of dogs I have fostered. My husband Chuck is so upset about that. Our home has become a shelter and I feel closed in on and stifled. Even my porch and my garage are stuffed full of Animal Education and Rescue things. My kids are resentful and in turn I am so disappointed by their attitudes.

I have put my writing, my public speaking and all my other projects on hold because there is simply not enough time. My precious books I've worked so hard on writing sit unfinished in my computer. I have set aside my job as marketing person of Pet Sitters of America, and therefore our company that pays my salary is suffering.

I wish with all my heart I were wealthy because then I could make this work, but I'm just a middle-class girl with a dream too big for her to handle.

Thank you again and bless you for your work.
Sandy Kamen Wisniewski
Founder, Animal Education and Rescue

But just like Michelle told me she did each day, I pictured all the animals waiting to be rescued. I also thought of all the people we visited every month in the nursing homes whose one thing they looked forward to each month was visiting with the animals. I saw the young, idealistic and moldable children that I could teach about how to live in harmony with animals. But most importantly, as Michelle said when we met, "Who else would be crazy enough to do this?" Then I'd say to myself after I wrote the imaginary letter: *Okay, I may be crazy, maybe not, but I can handle this one more day.*

In Pane the following morning Sally and I headed to the shelter at dawn in preparation to load up the car with our selected dogs so we could be home by dinner. Originally I was going to take only two dogs because I was the only open foster home. But after seeing all those needy eyes staring at me I buckled and ended up taking five. My stomach was heavy with worry. *How could I manage five dogs along with my six dogs? What did I get myself into?*

Michelle gave us a few crates since we had only brought two. Dogs all loaded and Scooby sitting in my lap, we were ready to head home. But before we left I set Scooby down on the seat and told Sally I would be right back. I went back into the shelter to seek out Michelle. Finding her in her small, cluttered office she greeted me warmly. "Michelle," I said, looking into her wise, ocean-blue eyes, "thank you so much for your hospitality." She smiled warmly. My heart swelled for her. "I'll make it one of my missions to tell people about you, try to educate, try to get you support. You are an amazing woman and I really admire you."

"Aw, honey, just tryin' to do something. Well, then..." She paused, searching for words. "Thank you for coming." I gave her a hug and walked out to the car.

I tried not to show Sally how worried I was about taking the five dogs and remained cheerful during the uneventful ride home. When Sally pulled into the driveway Chuck appeared by the SUV and stood in horror as Sally and I unloaded dog after dog from the car. I tried to shrug off his look but with my own self-inflicted worrying he was like a finger poking a wound. After a few minutes to my relief he walked back into the house and out of sight.

Sally and I set up crates for the dogs in my offices. Stressed out from the long car ride the dogs were antsy, pacing about and barking. I let the dogs out in my yard for a little romp time and then put them all in their respective crates. Scooby instantaneously hated his crate and was barking his head off, setting me on edge. I shut the doors to my office, the ear-piercing yap of Scooby still audible but thankfully slightly muffled. *Oh, no, how long will I have these dogs? How will I manage? I am such an idiot!* I scolded myself as I headed outside with my own dogs in tow.

The next day after the chaos of letting 11 dogs out to go potty and feeding them I got to thinking about my thoughts the night before. Knowing full well it did me no good to have such negative self-talk about my predicament I summoned up my positive inner voice and was determined to make it work. I focused on creating a routine for the dogs and reminded myself that this wasn't forever. I envisioned patting myself on the back for rescuing the dogs. I imagined the dogs living in new, loving homes.

Within two weeks three of the five dogs were adopted to loving families. I was so grateful it all happened so quickly. The two remaining dogs were a Beagle mix named Buddy, and Scooby. They were settled in nicely into our daily routine and I was enjoying getting to know them. I worked with them on housebreaking and correcting minor behavior problems.

One afternoon I received a call from a woman named Lydia, who saw Scooby on our web site and wanted to meet him. We set up a date for the following evening at my house. That evening the doorbell rang, which set off Scooby's high-pitched, little-dog bark. "Shhh!" I hissed at Scooby, thinking he was blowing his chances for a new home. To no avail he kept on yapping even after Lydia and her friend were in the office. Bending down to pet Scooby he was still barking little yips of excitement, causing my ears to ring. Lydia's facial expression suggested to me she was a bit taken aback by the barking. As Lydia was leaning over petting Scooby, Buddy came trotting in the room and looked at them.

"Who's this?" Lydia asked, looking over at Buddy standing in the doorway observing.

"This is Buddy. He's Scooby's best friend. He's looking for a home too." As if on cue Scooby stopped barking and went over to Buddy and they touched noses.

"Does he pull a lot on leash?"

"Not at all," I replied. "He's actually really calm for a Beagle."

She walked over to Buddy and scratched him behind the ear. "Can I take him for a walk?"

"Sure, I'll get you a leash."

Lydia and her friend left with Buddy and I picked up Scooby. "Well, Scoob, you may have competition. Don't worry, we'll find you a home." I kissed his scruffy muzzle. "But you gotta let up on that barking!"

Lydia came back with Buddy a short while later. "So how'd it go?" I asked.

"Good, you're right, he doesn't pull at all. I had back surgery, and I can't have a dog that pulls. I think I might be interested in him." She ran her hand through her hair in thought. "Did you say they're best buddies?"

"Yes, they really like being together."

"Okay, well, I'd like to take them both."

"What?"

"I'd like to adopt both." She pointed at them.

I got goose bumps. "Are you sure?"

"I'm sure."

We scheduled a time for me to go to her house with the canines I had affectionately nicknamed "the boys."

Lydia lived in a sweet, middle-class suburban neighborhood with mature trees, the roads winding around two small lakes. I pulled into her long drive and helped the dogs out of the car. We walked up to the cottage-style home's front porch door. In seconds Lydia appeared at the door and opened it, her face beaming. (I always loved the home visit because I got to play Santa Claus.)

After a quick tour of her quaint home I began the educational segment of the home visit. The whole time I was speaking and pointing out important information on the handouts Buddy and Scooby explored their new home. Every now and again the dogs leapt onto the couch to check in with us and then jumped back down to continue their adventure. Lydia didn't mind the couch leaping and never stopped smiling. She was one adoptive mom that I really connected to. She seemed like such a kind-hearted person. My analysis of her good character and kind heart would be confirmed in the coming few days.

Saying a tearful goodbye to the boys I walked out of the house and to my car. I could hear Buddy leaping up on the door and barking, trying to go with me. We had really bonded. Buddy and I were intensely close and had spent many hours quietly cuddling. Before Buddy I wasn't a huge fan of Beagles, mostly because they tended to follow their nose and therefore run away, much more interested in their surroundings. But Buddy's sweet and cuddly personality and expressive face converted me to a major Beagle lover.

Two days later I received a phone call from Lydia. I could tell immediately from her tone of voice something was wrong. She explained that over the course of a few days Buddy didn't seem well. She didn't like the way he would all of a sudden get very quiet and close his eyes. I had seen Buddy do that with me but I had taken him to the vet and since the vet found nothing wrong I assumed it was just his personality. On a hunch Lydia took Buddy to her veterinarian. After the examination her vet said he thought something was wrong but that Buddy needed further testing from a specialty clinic. He suggested she make an appointment the following morning. I asked Lydia to phone me after the appointment.

We hung up and I sat there with a deep feeling of dread. The following afternoon Lydia called and said, "The doctor ran some tests and found that Buddy had previously been injured by a blow to his abdomen possibly by being struck or being hit by a car. This injury caused all his organs to shift. If it is not corrected Buddy won't have long to live."

"Oh, no, Lydia." I put my hand on my forehead, my elbow on the desk. The only thing I could think was, *Lydia is going to give Buddy back and how will we afford the surgery? Poor Buddy. Do I risk having to close the whole organization by spending all our money on saving one dog or do I put him to sleep for the good of many? How much money do we have...$2,000-3,000? This WAS always one of my biggest worries.* Not sharing my concerns I asked, "What will you do?" I held my breath.

"He's going in for surgery tomorrow morning," she answered, the heavy sadness in her voice far different from the joyful woman I had come to know. I let out a deep breath, grateful beyond measure.

"Do I dare ask," I paused, "how much will this cost?"

"Thousands. I don't have the total yet but over two thousand."

"Can you swing that?"

"That's what plastic is for."

"Will you keep me posted?"

"I'll call you after surgery."

"Please call me if you need anything."

"Thanks, Sandy."

"You take care. I'll talk to you later. Will you give Buddy a kiss from me?" I choked out.

"Of course."

We hung up and I sat in my chair stunned. I was scared for Buddy. He had to make it. I thought of the chain of events that brought

Buddy to Lydia. Lydia came to my house to meet Scooby, intent on adopting him. Then Buddy caught her eye. Buddy and Scooby were best friends. Lydia didn't want to separate them so she adopted both.

Had Buddy still been in our care we never would have known that he had this terrible injury and he would have likely died. Even if we had known how could I possibly have paid that kind of money to save him? It would have put me in a huge dilemma. If he had been adopted by someone else I am sure that many people, even the most well-meaning people, would not spend thousands of dollars on a rescue dog they had adopted only two weeks earlier. Buddy had a guardian angel in Lydia and we had a guardian angel that brought Lydia to us. All in all it was a miracle and Buddy just had to survive.

As miracles happen Buddy's surgery was successful. The doctor said that the injury was worse than he had anticipated and Buddy was lucky that he survived. *Luck?* I thought. *No. It was an intervention, a deliberate saving grace.* The doctor instructed Lydia that Buddy would have to be kept quiet while he recovered.

I received regular reports from Lydia as she cared for Buddy at home. She told me that Scooby had taken on the role of junior caretaker to his best friend. He checked in on him as he slept and when he was awake gently offered Buddy toys by placing them near him. Their relationship was very special.

The week after Buddy's surgery I put together an e-mail to all my Internet animal rescue circles. I explained what happened to Buddy and asked for donations. In short order many kind-hearted rescuers from all over the country sent money to help with Buddy's costs. I raised over $700. I knew it wasn't the whole amount but I was sure it would help and Lydia would appreciate the gesture.

The following week I visited Buddy. Approaching him slowly I softly cooed his name. I got down on the floor and gently enveloped him in an embrace. Lydia showed me his incision, which went up the length of his abdomen, a scary reminder of what Buddy went through. I gave Lydia the cards and donations I received on Buddy's behalf. She was touched to tears. I told her, "Lydia, you are a very special person to have done this for Buddy."

To this day, on occasion, I have the pleasure of seeing my boys. Buddy changed a lot after he recovered from surgery. The quiet, gentle Beagle turned into a rambunctious, tenacious, happy dog. Ironically, Buddy has turned into the dog Lydia never would have wanted, but like I had to experience Buddy to love Beagles, Lydia needed to experience the old Buddy to appreciate the new.

Two months later over 50 people filed into a meeting room at our local civic center to watch our new documentary, *Saving Dogs,* which chronicled the trip to Pane County Humane Society. After the film and applause, five dogs with five families entered the room and took center stage. "And here," I announced as the families and dogs stood up front, "are Sylvester, Oreo, Champ, Buddy and Scooby. And these are their families." There wasn't a dry eye in the house.

Love Stuck

Every so often when we had some open foster homes we visited the Kind Hearts City Shelter where they, just like rural shelters, needed rescue organizations to take their dogs, cats or other critters. But in their case we were restricted to one shelter room (where dogs had yet to be evaluated) and the medical ward. Dogs and cats on the adoption floor were available to take but at a fee. One Saturday Geri, Linda, another volunteer, and I decided to visit the city shelter because we had a couple open foster homes.

After our arrival, inspection and selection of the two dogs we were to take, we were on our way to the front desk to arrange the paperwork when a vet tech that recognized me from past visits stopped me. "Hey, would you see this little dog in the medical ward?" Dogs in the medical ward were there either for physical or emotional reasons. In the past we had taken dogs from the medical ward that were emaciated, handicapped or terrified. Because of the dogs' issues they were not put on the adoption floor.

"Sure." Looking at my companions I said, "I'll meet you in a few minutes. Can you see about the paperwork on the dogs?" We were short on time. We all had things to do afterwards.

"Sure," Geri said.

Following the vet tech towards the medical ward she filled me in on the dog. "She's just petrified here but she's really sweet. She needs a good grooming but with some attention she should get better quickly." We walked through double doors and to a room with a group of stainless steel cages stacked on top of each other. In the bottom cage was a small dog. Peering into her cage I noticed she was the spitting image of a dirty mop. She was so heavily matted it was impossible to tell what breed she was. She had tan, brown and chocolate-colored hair and milk chocolate-colored, round eyes and a nose that matched her eye color. Other than that she was a complete mess.

The vet tech lifted the shaking dog out of the cage and handed her to me. I was surprised by how light she felt. "She's so matted. I have never seen a dog so matted."

"Yeah, someone brought her in."

"Don't people notice when their dog looks like this? Don't they get it that the dog can't be happy, let alone can this be sanitary or healthy?"

"I know," she said. She added, "People can be real idiots."

"Poor thing," I said to the little dog. As she looked up at me with sad eyes, shaking, I assured her she would be just fine. (All it takes is for a dog to look at me in the face and me to look back and I'm hooked.) "Okay, I'll take her."

Where will I put her? I thought as I walked down the corridor looking for Linda and Geri, the little dog in my arms. I didn't have any other open foster homes (besides Geri and Linda's homes and they had just selected their dogs) and my offices were filled with dogs already. *I'll keep her in my living quarters with my family and my own dogs,* I said to myself.

During the ride home Geri drove, Linda sat in back and I sat in the front passenger seat with the little dog on my lap. She was so filthy, smelly and gross that I had to keep reminding myself that clothes and skin could be washed. I tried not to think of what could be hidden in her hair. I also went through name options and due to her current condition I came up with the name Moppett. She was warming up to me quickly. By the time we pulled into my driveway she was no longer shaking and was responding positively to my ongoing baby talk with tail wags and smiles.

At home it didn't take long to introduce Moppett to my crew. I was convinced that because of her physical state, with the immeasurable smells on her, my dogs thought that anybody with that many smells must be someone to be admired. In short order she settled into the rhythm of our house. But of all my dogs Moppett took a special liking to my Chihuahua mix Rascal. Little did I know but that friendship would leave both of them love stuck and me learning far more than I ever wanted to know about dogs' natural instincts.

Moppett's first night was spent smack in between Chuck and me in our bed. Looking back at that it was an absolutely disgusting decision because of the state of her hair. But often times I think from the heart not the head, and I couldn't see Moppett sleeping by herself, especially after all that she had been through. Rascal slept below Moppett and Scrappy, and my Basset Hound mix was curled up below Rascal. Sophie, my Rhodesian Ridgeback mix, and Shrek, my Rottweiler, were at the foot of the bed. A queen-sized bed not nearly big enough, Chuck and I curled ourselves up in fetal positions taking up the two slivers of space left for us. Both our butts were hovering past our respective ends of the bed.

Every night from the time I had my own home I always at least one dog that slept with me. With as many dogs as I had while Moppett was living with me it was getting rather ridiculous, but I would squeeze into a space the size of a Christmas tree box if I had to in order to be able to sleep with my dogs. Besides being unable to pick who would be banished from the bed I had other selfish reasons for having my dogs sleep with me. I loved the feel of their warmth and the rhythm of their bodies breathing against my body. They made me feel safe and protected. Plus, just the act of slumbering together was like no other kind of bonding. As an extra bonus when I woke up in the middle of the night, not at all sleepy and maybe with worries on my mind, all I needed to do was sit up and pet my dogs or give them hugs and like a sleeping pill I fell back into a restful sleep.

The next day Moppett went to a dog groomer where she was shaved down. Without her thick mop of hair I realized how small she actually was. She was no more than ten pounds and underweight by a pound or two. Shaved down it was still hard to tell what breed she was but a good guess was a Shih Tzu and poodle mix. Arriving back at my house all my dogs gave her a once-over, bombarding her with nose sniffs on all parts of her body. She willingly accepted this accosting of her body…maybe too easily. Rascal in particular sniffed her long and hard then ran around her in circles in glee and repeated the process.

After all the inspections Moppett galloped around the house at full speed, thrilled with her lightened load. Rascal decided to join her and ran behind her. Seeing him chasing her she ran faster every now and again, looking back in a flirty kind of way. Around and around they went, tails and ears low, so as not to interfere with speed, mouths open, smiling. Then like a speeding car putting on the brakes Moppett abruptly stopped, which caused Rascal to run smack into her–crash! Unfazed by the body slam he hopped back a step and shook himself off. Moppett shook herself, too, and then invited Rascal to play again with a bow. Delighted, Rascal bowed back. Moppett lunged forward and nipped at Rascal, Rascal nipped back and they began wrestling. I felt like I was watching two people courting.

Later that day I was sitting at my computer and glanced at Moppett as she strutted towards the water dish to get a sip. *Boy, she's all that,* I thought to myself, smiling. *She's come a long way in just a few days.* I was very proud of how quickly the terrified dog turned into a happy dog. Looking after her I noticed she looked a tad swollen between her legs.

I knew what a female dog in heat looked like. Their private area swelled, making "it" obvious where normally it's obscure. I called Moppett over to me and had a look. Yep, she was in heat. I was told from the shelter that Moppett was six months old so I had made an appointment with the vet to have her spayed the following week.

I called the vet to explain the new situation and he told me we would have to wait until her heat cycle was over before spaying her and that the cycle could last six weeks.

Later that day I was working in my office when Chuck came in to talk to me. "I just witnessed something very disturbing," he announced.

"What?" I said, looking at the computer half listening.

"Moppett and Rascal were just stuck together."

"What?" I pulled myself away from the screen and looked at Chuck.

"Yeah, my little boy. Something I never want to see again."

"You mean like making babies stuck together?"

"Yeah," he said in an annoyed tone.

My attention now fully on him I said, "You're kidding?"

"I wouldn't kid about that," he said, shaking his head obviously trying to get the image out of his head.

"What did you do?"

"I pulled them apart."

"Yeah, right."

"I'm NOT kidding," he emphasized. The phone rang by my desk and I picked it up. In moments while on the phone with a business associate the conversation Chuck and I had was nearly forgotten.

The next morning after doing the morning chores I sat back on the couch to relax a minute. Rascal was lying beside me panting heavily. My mom radar went up right away. *Rascal should not be panting like that. That's not normal.* "Rascal," I said with concern, "what's the matter?" I lifted him up preparing to put him on my lap when I noticed something bright red underneath him. I lifted him higher and sure enough Rascal's normally skin-covered penis was fully exposed. I put him on the couch. "Rascal," I scolded, "what are you doing? Put that away." It stayed exposed. *Strange.* I waited five minutes and looked again and sure enough it was still exposed. *This is not right.*

I went to the office where Chuck was working and asked him to follow me. Back in the living room I went over to Rascal, still lying on the couch, still mildly panting, lifted him up and turned him to Chuck. "Look at that!" I exclaimed.

"Rascal!" Chuck said in his best shame-on-you voice. "Put that thing away."

"He can't," I said matter-of-factly.

"What are you talking about?"

"I'm telling you it's stuck that way."

"Rascal, put that away," Chuck demanded him. Rascal looked at him with innocent *What, Dad?* eyes.

"I think Moppett has something to do with this." I looked over at Moppett, looking for some admission of guilt. She looked at me with soft eyes and batted her long eyelashes. "I'm going to call the vet," I announced, heading towards the phone.

"Hi, Julie, it's Sandy with Animal Education and Rescue."

"Hi, Sandy."

"This is going to sound really weird but I have this foster dog that is in heat. My dog Rascal, who is neutered, well, his, um, his penis is sticking out and I think that maybe Rascal and Moppett did it."

"Is it sticking out now?" she asked in a serious tone.

"Yeah."

"You need to get him in now. This is an emergency. He could lose his penis because it's exposed."

"What?"

She sounded annoyed. "I *said* he could lose his penis. It could have to be amputated. You need to bring him in now."

What?

I looked over at Rascal sitting on the couch and then Moppett, who continued to bat those gorgeous, long eyelashes. *OH, NO, MY BABY COULD LOSE HIS PENIS!!!* "We'll be right there," I told Julie.

I walked back to the living room and told Chuck, "*You* have to take Rascal to the vet now. Julie said that Rascal could lose his penis."

"Lose his penis...What?"

"Yeah," I said annoyed, "cut off, amputated, no more p-p."

"I don't want to take him, you take him."

"He's your boy, you take him. You have to go now." This was a guy problem and since I had a guy who loved that little dog, he could do it. Besides, I went last time.

"Now?"

"Now."

Chuck left with Rascal, which gave me plenty of time to think through what just happened. I looked at Moppett, who was lying daintily on the couch. She batted her eyes. "I can't believe you, Moppett," I said to her, mildly disgusted. Then as I busied myself scooping dog poop in the backyard I worried that my dog's pecker was going to be chopped off. *How would he pee? Would he have one of those bags strapped to him and a tube up the hole that was his penis that would catch his pee?* I had to admit it was one of the strangest predicaments I had ever been witness to.

Chuck and Rascal came home an hour later. Chuck informed me that Rascal's penis was saved. I took a look at it and it was back in its sleeve. "What did they do?"

"They used oil and put it back."

"What?"

"Yeah."

"GROSS!!"

"They said that any time that it comes out again we have to put it back right away."

"Eewww!!! You mean YOU'LL put it back." He didn't answer.

"They suggested we not leave Moppett and Rascal alone together."

"We'll leave her in the kitchen when we leave the house. And she is NOT sleeping with us."

Less than an hour later I was standing in the kitchen making dinner when I looked down at Rascal and noticed that familiar panting. I bent down to look. "Oh, Rascal!" I cried, seeing red. I turned the water off and ran to the office to get Chuck.

"It's happened again."

"What?"

"Yeah, his lipstick is OUT!"

"No way."

"Yeah way. Come fix it."

"Urghhhh!"

I followed him to the kitchen. "Here," he said, handing me Rascal.

"Eeww! I am *not* doing it."

"No, just hold him." I took Rascal and held him straight out.

"I want that Moppett gone," I announced. Chuck grabbed the vegetable oil out of the cabinet. He poured some over his fingers and then dabbed it on Rascal's penis near the spot the sleeve and the penis meet. "Oh, yuck!" I exclaimed, totally NOT helping matters. Gently Chuck eased the penis back inside its cover. "This is SO GROSS!" I added.

"You can put him down now," Chuck said officially. He was now a certified, expert, penis-fixer. I was impressed and so very grateful *he* had that skill and not me.

Keeping Rascal and Moppett separated proved to be impossible. We tried gating Moppett off, but she was able to scale any and every gate, no matter the size, determined to get to her man. She wanted her love muffin. At all times Rascal's chest was puffed out so far he could have fallen over from the weight of it. We crated Moppett when we left the house or couldn't watch her and supervised them at all times. The extra work was a strain and I wanted that dog adopted!

The following day I was in the kitchen toasting some bread when I looked over and Rascal had mounted Moppett and they were standing there fixed together with a look of complete ecstasy on their faces. I screamed, "OH, NOOOOOO!" Searching my brain for what to do I realized first off that my doctor-of-fixing-penises was out pet sitting. "Oh, help. Oh, jeez! Rascal," I screamed, "GET OFF HER NOW!" He looked at me with distant eyes. "Rascal, I said GET OFF HER!" They both just kept standing there latched together. I grabbed Rascal around his body and pulled. Nothing happened. Then I tried to pull them away from each other. They stayed stuck. Then I tried twisting them apart, and to my horror Rascal was now facing the other way but still attached. "OH, NO! HELP!!" I screamed. My other dogs looked at me placidly. I put Rascal back into doggy position.

Grabbing the oil out of the cabinet I poured oil between the dogs. I tried to pull them apart again. No luck. Then, remembering how Chuck had fixed Rascal's penis, I put some oil on my hand, and hesitating just a moment, rubbed the oil down there, the whole time groaning in a grossed-out voice, my face contorted in disgust. My hand and their bodies now soaked in oil I did the one thing I knew left to do. I called Chuck on his cell phone. As it always seemed to happen to me when I really needed someone, I got voice mail.

"Chuck," I screamed into the phone, "Rascal and Moppett are stuck together and I can't get them apart. COME HOME NOW!!!" I turned to look at the pair again and to my utter relief they were apart, looking at me like I was nuts.

Lucky for us Moppett got adopted a few days later to a lovely family who DID NOT have another dog. As agreed upon in their contract they had her spayed as soon as she was done with her heat cycle. Rascal went back to his old self and played with his buddy Scrappy. But I never could look at my baby boy the same way again. Thanks to a flirty, adorable slip of a thing with long, doe-y eyelashes and an impossible-to-resist, coy tilt to her head, my boy was all grown up.

For months afterwards Chuck and I laughed about the Rascal and Moppett love affair. Chuck kept the message I left him on his cell phone and occasionally played it for a laugh or to use as blackmail if he wanted me to do something for him.

Looking back on that experience I am not sure why I reacted as I did when Rascal and Moppett were stuck together but one fact I did learn was that if two dogs are stuck together don't try to un-stick them. The penis is swollen and essentially stuck until it wants to be unstuck—a fact I never thought I'd need to know.

Hope

In the fall of 2005 five volunteers including me went yet again to the Kind Hearts Animal Shelter to help them out by taking some dogs. This time we had four open foster homes. As it always was when we were on our way to save dogs excitement charged the air.

After entering the building and showing security our IDs we headed back to see the dogs. Opening the door the room erupted in barking, the noise bouncing off of the cement walls, my ears instantly painful. We scattered and began looking in cages.

Geri spotted a tiny, shivering little poodle mix. The dog was cowering in back of her extra-large cage. She stood looking in the cage, her hand over her mouth and her eyes brimming with tears. She pointed and nodded at the little dog. I took the cage card out of the holder on the side of the cage. It read: Poodle, five years old, bad teeth, rescue only. "Go ahead and take her out," I said loudly over the barking, "and be sure she can be handled. Then if she is fine we can take her." Even though she would need her teeth cleaned I knew small poodles were easy to adopt out. Besides I couldn't stand seeing the tiny thing so scared either.

Over my shoulder I spotted Patty, an AEAR volunteer who had adopted dogs from AEAR and planned on fostering, coming up behind me. Turning to face her I noticed standing beside her was an old Golden

Retriever mix that had to be at least eight years old. I gently lifted his lip to look at his teeth and saw brown, plaque-filled teeth. That affirmed to me that he was an older dog. I said, "You know it'll take a while to adopt this one out because of his age." It was obvious by her face she didn't care. I knew it wasn't smart to take that dog but his sweet, brown eyes told me not to discriminate because of his age. I petted the top of the old dog's head and gave her the okay.

I picked out a little, blond corgi mix for a foster family that wasn't with us. His temperament was excellent and I was confident the foster family would be happy with my choice. Lorrie, a new volunteer who was fostering for the first time, pointed at a big, black lab in a cage. I wanted her first experience to be as easy as possible. "This dog is big and black," I explained. She looked at me like "so?" I went on, "Black dogs are very hard to find homes for. She's also big which means two strikes are against her. I know it sounds terrible but it's true. She could be with you quite a while because most people just don't want big, black dogs."

"That's okay," she said, "I don't mind." As if on cue the dog wagged her tail.

"Okay, are you all sure of your choices?" I shouted over the deafening, echoing barking. They all nodded and smiled. "Okay then, let's go." We headed towards the front desk to complete the necessary paperwork with the staff. While checking out, Charlie, the rescue coordinator, asked us for the cards that accompanied the dogs' respective cages. I gave him the card for the dog I was holding, the corgi mix. The rest of the group forgot to take their cards so they headed back to get them. Meanwhile I waited where I stood.

The director of the shelter approached me. I recognized her from when she gave us a guided tour six months before. I remember as we walked down the hallway, following her to one of the rooms that housed the dogs, she said that 100 animals come in a day. I was floored and disgusted.

We exchanged small talk and then she asked me if we could take a special-needs puppy. She went on to explain that the puppy was paralyzed in her back legs.

"How did it happen?"

"We don't know. One day we noticed that the puppy wasn't using her back legs. We took her away from the rest of the litter and brought her to medical. Since then the other puppies have been adopted."

I hesitated saying anything. I knew we were already taking some hard-to-adopt dogs. Who would even think about fostering a paralyzed pup? Further, who would adopt such a dog? Two of the dogs we were taking needed major dental cleaning, which would be costly, the one was old and big and the other was black and big. Then I thought, *Well, it can't hurt to look.* "I'll take a look."

Turning, I followed her through a maze of doors and hallways to the medical ward, the whole way thinking, *What am I doing? I have no one to take the pup anyway. Who am I fooling?* But she kept walking and I kept following until we got to a room that was empty except for some complicated-looking medical equipment. She left me there to wait for the puppy.

Moments later a young woman in a powder blue lab coat blew in carrying a doll-like, adorable puppy in her arms. The director followed behind with a big grin on her face. The dog's button-shaped, dark brown eyes were alert and bright. Her ears stood straight up and flipped over at the tips. She reminded me of a German Shepherd mix. "She's adorable!" I exclaimed.

For a moment I forgot she was paralyzed—that was until the vet tech put her down on the linoleum floor. Placed on the floor the puppy took off like a baseball out of a pitching machine. Jumping and hopping around like a Mexican jumping bean, moving around the room at full speed, she had obviously learned how to work the front end of her body even though her back legs dragged behind her. She was unperturbed by her lifeless back legs swinging around like sticks stuck on at her hips.

My first thought was, *Oh, you poor thing.* But I quickly realized there was no reason to feel sorry for her; she didn't. Her zest for life was obvious. I walked over to the pup still moving in fast motion, and like catching a fast moving baseball scooped her up. She looked up at me with trusting, brown eyes and instantly my heart melted. I began to think seriously about taking her home with me. *But I can't,* I thought. *I have too many dogs already.* It was just killing me. As I stood in that room thinking, I could feel the director's and the tech's eyes burning through me pleadingly. I said, "What's the chance another rescue will take her?"

"No one has and she's rotting away in medical," the director responded sadly.

"Okay, let me take her up front to my friends and see what they think." In my mind I was thinking, *They'll help talk me out of it. They'll get me back to reality. They'd tell me I was crazy to even think about it.*

I carried the pup to the front of the building where my friends stood waiting for me. They saw me carrying the pup and in chorus said, "Ohhhh!"

I said, "Now wait a minute, you have to see this." I gently placed the pup on the floor. Like a battery-operated toy she began hopping and scooting along. They gasped as they noticed her back legs trailing behind her.

Picking the pup back up I asked them, "What do I do? I don't want to leave her." There was a pause, as we all looked at each other and the pup, grief stricken. I was waiting for someone to reason with me. But that just wasn't happening.

Patty looked at me and then at the puppy and said, "I'll take her." We all looked at her, our eyes wide with surprise.

I said, "Are you sure?"

"Oh, yeah, I'm sure." She nodded with conviction.

On the ride back home we were trying to think of a name for the pup. After a bit of name tossing I said, "How about Hope?" They all agreed it was the perfect name. We felt there was indeed hope for this dog. But from the moment we left the building I had a dreaded feeling of worry. *How would we handle a special-needs dog like this? We had so little money. Who would adopt her?* Then I thought of all the other dogs in the car, most of them having issues of one kind or another. *Had I done us in on this one?* I was putting on a brave face for my friends, but inside I was thinking, *Have I gone nuts?*

On the way back we stopped at the vet to have the dogs checked out and to get their shots. As I had suspected two of the dogs needed their teeth cleaned, the poodle had a heart murmur and then there was Hope. My state of worry escalated.

Before Hope's examination I was standing in the lobby with Patty when the vet tech asked us if we knew what happened to Hope's legs. We told her we didn't know. She went on to inform us that we may have to "manually get her to urinate and possibly with bowel movements too. Did we know that?" I felt sick.

"No, I didn't know that," I answered. Patty and I looked at each other panic stricken. After the vet tech went in back we concurred that if that were the case we were going to have to put her down. There was no way we could handle that. I was glad I could see the bathroom from where I stood just in case I really got sick.

"Things happen for a reason, Patty. There's a reason we took this pup. Don't worry," I told her, trying to reassure her as well as myself.

Hope's examination was next. The doctor felt her bladder and said that it was not too full, so that was hopeful. He suggested I call the shelter and find out if she was eliminating on her own. I called the shelter from the vet's office and was relieved to find out that yes, she had eliminated on her own. Other than her back legs she seemed healthy. He couldn't determine what caused her legs to be paralyzed and said if we wanted to know the first step was x-rays. With minimal funds we decided to wait and maybe do that at a later time.

Loaded back into the car we headed back to my house where everyone was parked. Unloading their dogs and placing them in their cars we hugged goodbye. I told Patty, "If you need anything at all, let me know."

"Thanks," she said, "I'll be fine." She was a very brave woman.

At a meeting the following evening I asked Heather, a volunteer and friend, if she could research a cart for a new foster dog that was paralyzed. I had heard about other dogs who didn't have use of their back legs using devices that they would be strapped into in the back, and by using their front legs and wheels for the rear, they were able to walk. Heather enthusiastically agreed to help. To my surprise and delight within 24 hours Heather had personally built a cart with wheels that would work as Hope's back legs.

I sent press releases to all the local newspapers telling them that Hope, a paralyzed puppy, was being fitted for a cart that would help her walk and anyone wishing to watch her try out her new wheels was welcome to come over. Within hours the local paper, *The Daily Herald,* called and said they would be there.

On a sunny fall day, in my driveway, a small group of people stood around as Heather fitted Hope in her cart and strapped her in. Her back legs were resting comfortably behind her on a sling. *The Daily Herald* photographer was lying on the ground, at Hope's level, snapping pictures.

Looking adorable and yet strange in her makeshift contraption Hope looked all around, her brown eyes bright, as if she was seeing the world in a brand new way. Suddenly she backed up ten steps. She opened her eyes wider in surprise and her ears perked up. We all laughed with excitement. Patty bent down towards Hope and said, "Wrong way, baby. Come on." She motioned with her hand and stepped back. "This way."

Hope looked at Patty and with one front leg inched herself forward. We applauded and cheered. Hope had taken her first step.

The next morning Hope was on the front page of *The Daily Herald*. It was exciting to see and my hope was that donations would start coming in. Within days we began receiving money for Hope's care. In short order I would come to realize how vital it would be for the donations to keep coming.

With some money to use for Hope we decided to bring her to see a specialist in case there was something more we could do for her legs. We met with a specialist at a well-known animal hospital. She took x-rays and told us that it appeared as if Hope might benefit from hip surgery. She couldn't promise anything but said that there was a possibility she may be able to walk again. We grabbed ahold of that and were praying for a miracle.

Due to the seriousness of the surgery and the cost that could exceed $2,500 we decided to see another specialist for a second opinion. The exam was short and the prognosis grim. He said, "Put her in a cart and let her enjoy her life as it is. There is nothing that can be done."

By this time I was beginning to notice by what Patty was saying that she was seeing Hope's prognosis with rose-colored glasses. She was grasping on to what the original doctor said and understandably not looking at things as objectively as I was. She was determined that Hope would walk. I was committed to Hope and if Patty wanted another opinion then we would do it. But through it all I never stopped worrying about the money we were spending.

After seeing a third doctor it was determined, and confirmed by the original surgeon, that Hope would benefit from hip surgery on her one hip. The surgery may not get her walking, the surgeon cautioned us, but if she didn't have it then her hipbones would rub bone-on-bone and cause severe pain. We couldn't let that happen so we scheduled surgery. Patty still had it in the back of her mind that Hope would walk.

Meanwhile we had been to a rehabilitation center that examined Hope and agreed to work with her. They took Hope under their wing and with great confidence reinforced Patty's belief that Hope would be able to eventually walk. I was skeptical but willing to go along with it.

Hope's hip surgery went without a hitch and she recovered at home. After some weeks Hope was at the rehabilitation center for treatment. I went with Patty a few times and was simply in awe of the different things they did for Hope. The most amazing was the underwater treadmill, which was meant to strengthen her leg muscles. Throughout that time watching her therapy sessions I never saw any obvious improvements, and hearing about Hope's minimal progress through Patty and Heather I was skeptical that she would ever walk. But I kept my thoughts to myself. I figured it didn't really matter at that point what my thoughts were about her progress because what would be would be, and the last thing I wanted to do was squash Patty's enthusiasm.

Meanwhile I was juggling running an entire organization and 30-plus animals in foster homes at the same time. Eventually all the dogs we took from the shelter when we took Hope were adopted into awesome homes. Money, or lack of it, was always on my mind. I continued to try and raise money to help Hope but also had to think of the dozens of other animals in our care. To top that off I had a momma dog that was having a litter of puppies in my front hall.

On the home front I still struggled daily with my family's attitude towards what I was doing. They were far from enthusiastic and it weighed heavily on me. But I was still determined and continually fed myself positive affirmations. Chuck helped when he felt like it, nothing more. The kids, well, they were teenagers so as was typical everything was a chore and lazy was their middle name.

One day an e-mail came across that someone might like to adopt Hope. I wrote back and forth with the woman, telling her all about what we had done with Hope and what to expect when caring for her. The woman filled out an application and sent it in. She was a nurse and her heart went out to Hope. She was excited about the prospect of adopting her.

I contacted Patty and left her a message. I didn't hear back from her for 24 hours. I had a feeling that Patty was not happy about learning we had an application for Hope. Finally I received a message back saying that she wanted to adopt Hope. Patty had invested so much time, energy and love into Hope that I couldn't blame her, but I was concerned about whether or not she could handle it. By that time she had adopted three other dogs from us and one of them had a clubbed front leg, hopping on three legs. Patty was on disability from work and by no means had endless amounts of cash available to her. After expressing my concerns she said with determination, "I can handle it."

"Okay, Patty, well, of course she's yours." Hope was one lucky girl.

Since that time I have not heard what has happened to Hope. Patty, Geri and Heather cut all ties with me, for reasons I still don't know, and started their own small, charitable organization raising money for Hope. Last time I saw Hope she was a striking, 40-pound, six-month-old dog that resembled a German Shepherd. She was still unable to walk but could stand on all fours, her back legs immobile as she stood up like a car jack. I think about her often and hope she is alive, pain-free and happy.

Would I do something like that again–take a dog with such a severe disability? Unless I had endless funds and resources, no, I wouldn't. We spent more than $4,000 on Hope. It is vital that I think of the organization as a whole, what's best for everyone. Doing what I did had a domino effect of spent money and lost volunteers. It was impractical and drained too much from AEAR. But in any case it was a lesson well learned…at least to an extent.

Lessons in Rabbits

A year and a half after beginning AEAR I received a call from an urban, privately run humane society in Chicago. The woman on the phone introduced herself as Dawn, the intake coordinator. "We regularly have domesticated rabbits dumped at our door and we don't adopt them out; we only deal with dogs and cats. I heard you take rabbits."

"Yes, I've taken a few. What do you have?"

"We have a gorgeous, lop-eared female. We'll get her spayed before you take her, if you'll take her."

Thinking back to my childhood rabbits Princess and Sammy, I had a real soft spot for rabbits. Besides, after what happened to them I felt I owed them. "Okay, sure, I'll take her."

The following week the rabbit was transported to my house. She was black and white with precious, cartoon-length, long, floppy ears. She was simply adorable. I set the rabbit up in a cage on my enclosed three-season porch. In short order more calls came from Dawn at the shelter and soon enough I had three more rabbits. My porch became a regular rabbit sanctuary. I set up a playpen in the center of the room and rotated the rabbits so they each had time to exercise.

Over time word got around that we took rabbits. At one point I had ten rabbits on my porch. Each morning after taking care of the dogs, cats and birds, I headed out to the porch to take care of the rabbits. Although time-consuming and labor-intensive the rabbits calmed me, centered me and rejuvenated me. I loved holding them tightly to my chest and stroking their silky fur and ears. I loved the smell of hay and the soft munching sound the rabbits made when they ate it. I loved the way their noses twitched excitedly, and I appreciated having audibly quiet animals. But two big challenges were that they overtook my porch and they were extremely expensive to take care of with all their necessary fresh veggies, bedding, feed and hay.

With the added work necessary for the rabbits–and rabbits required a lot of care and attention–I was struggling to get it all done on my own. Luckily I was able to find a few teens and young adult volunteers to help. Each day a different volunteer came and cleaned up and played with the rabbits. It was a very special time. I saw the joy those rabbits brought to the volunteers. It gave them a purpose and it was obvious they felt part of something bigger than themselves. Then in turn I felt like I was helping the people as well.

One volunteer in particular named Rochelle, a 19-year-old college student, showed me what a small thing like taking care of rabbits can mean to a girl with special needs. Rochelle's mom Nan heard about us through a friend and contacted me, asking if her daughter could volunteer. "Rochelle has problems with people socially. She has a hard time communicating and you must give her very specific instructions or she gets very frustrated. She's really good at schoolwork because it doesn't involve interacting with people. Do you think you might be willing to let her volunteer?"

"Sure, I'd be happy to have her. The rabbits might be a very good fit for her."

"I think so, too. I really appreciate you giving her a chance."

"Animals do wonders for people. Besides, I could use the help."

So Rochelle began volunteering twice a week. Rarely did I look at any woman at eye level, being that I'm five feet ten inches tall, but Rochelle was just as tall as me. She had long, thick, straight, chestnut hair she put in a ponytail at the nape of her neck and almond shaped eyes the color of her hair.

Rochelle's first day I introduced her to each rabbit. She walked along beside me her hands clasped in front of her and her eyes shy and weary. I knew she was nervous. Trying to make her feel more at ease I suggested that for that day she just get to know each rabbit. "Rabbits don't communicate like dogs or cats," I explained to Rochelle. "They communicate very subtly with grunts, grinding of their teeth, thumping their back feet when they are really mad." I paused for affect. "They could scratch or try and bite you." She looked at me with surprise. "But all these rabbits are nice and don't bite. So don't worry."

"So you want me to pet them?"

"Yes. I'll show you how. And the main thing I want you to learn is each one of their personalities."

"Okay." She seemed unsure. *Specific instructions, her mom had said. I wasn't giving specific instructions.*

"Come on over here." I motioned her over to the large playpen where Simon, a huge, white rabbit, sat chewing on some hay. "Let's make it your goal to pet Simon today."

"Okay," she said, her face very serious. "What do I do?"

"Here, let me have you go inside the pen. Climb on over." She slowly swung one long leg inside and then the other, standing inside with Simon. Simon hopped away from her. She looked down at him her eyebrows furrowed.

"Okay, now go ahead and sit down in there and let Simon just hop around you if he'd like." She slowly sat down. Simon jumped farther away.

"I don't think he likes me." She shook her head and looked like she was about to cry.

"He just doesn't know you. And it's normal for a rabbit to hop away at first. It'll take him time to get to know you."

"Okay…" she trailed off. She wasn't at all sure of this.

"Go ahead and reach over and pet Simon's back." Slowly she did. She stroked him ever-so-lightly, then stopped, hesitated, and petted him again. "Great, Rochelle! So you're just going to sit by him for a little while and let him get to know you. I have some calls to make. I'll be back in ten minutes."

"Okay," she said as she looked at her wristwatch to verify the time.

"I'll be back."

Ten minutes later I came back to the porch and looked at Rochelle still sitting in the pen with Simon. Simon was sitting on the other side of the pen. They looked like two beings just coexisting, both in their own respective corners. "How's it going?"

"He doesn't like me," she announced close to tears.

"Oh, Rochelle, yes he does. Just be patient." She shook her head and blinked back tears. I wasn't sure how to handle Rochelle. This was going to take time. I had never dealt with someone with that kind of disability. In some ways she seemed incredibly smart but emotionally she was like a nine-year-old. But I wasn't giving up. I knew the power of pet therapy and I knew the quiet power of love rabbits could share.

"Come on out now," I said. "We'll spend more time with Simon tomorrow. We don't want to spoil him." I smiled at her. "I'll show you how to clean the litter boxes."

I found that the practical knowledge of cleaning litter boxes was very easy for Rochelle to grasp as long as I told her specifically what to do. After demonstrating the second litter box she was doing them on her own. It was obvious that tasks that did not require any emotional exchanges were a breeze, while the task of Simon getting to know her was daunting. Now I understood what her mom was saying when she told me Rochelle didn't communicate socially like other people. I was determined to help Rochelle become more comfortable with Simon and thus help to build her confidence.

The following four times Rochelle came to take care of the rabbits I had her pet each rabbit and then get in the pen with Simon (I wanted to have her spend the most amount of time with the same rabbit each time to ease her discomfort). After that she cleaned all the litter boxes and swept. Each time she got out of the pen after spending time with Simon her face was in a frown and her eyes looked down to the ground. She told me, "Simon still doesn't like me." Once again I reassured her that she needed to give him time.

During her fifth visit she performed the same tasks with less of my supervision. During her time with Simon I went into my office to get some work done. After ten minutes I returned. Rochelle looked up at me smiling, her face beaming. "What's up?" I smiled back.

"Simon likes me now!" she announced.

"He does?"

"He jumped on my lap and I got to pet him." She touched her lap to show me.

"Oh, yeah?"

"He just needed to get to know me. Now we're friends. He's my favorite rabbit."

"That's great, Rochelle. That's awesome!"

Each day Rochelle came over her confidence grew. She moved around the porch like she owned the place, cleaning the same way each time and being sure to spend time with Simon. Once her relationship with him felt secure she asked to spend time with Carl, a plain, brown-colored, smaller rabbit. "Of course," I told her.

So began her strong bonding with the rabbits on the porch. By summer's end Rochelle was a new girl, sure of herself, confident and happy. She made eye contact with me and we enjoyed small social exchanges. While I still had to be very specific and keep it simple, she communicated back to me if she didn't understand something and even made a joke or two. I knew she would be starting school soon and I wouldn't see her again.

The last time Rochelle came I gave her a hug, which she returned awkwardly but willingly. I told her how proud I was of her and that I would miss her. She nodded her head and said, "I'll miss the rabbits, especially Simon." As she walked down the stairs, her chestnut ponytail swinging behind her, I realized what a profound miracle I had witnessed. A bunch of homeless rabbits, without saying a word, gave confidence and meaning to a very special girl.

Mr. Teacup Poodle

Being Hope's guardian did make me more cautious about taking special-needs dogs, but I still felt this pull towards helping dogs with special problems and challenges. One day I had been at the Kind Hearts Animal Shelter and saw a tiny, black poodle that was in a cage, curled up in a ball, terrified and trying to be invisible. I couldn't get her out of my mind, so a couple of days later Maggie, one of our teen volunteers, and I took the drive to see the poodle, with the idea of possibly taking her and placing her into our foster care system. I arrived and went directly to the cage where I had last seen her. The poodle was in the same cage as she had been in the week before.

I gently picked her up and began looking her over. She was a little underweight but otherwise appeared normal, that was until I took a good look at her face. To my dismay I noticed that her eyes were completely shut and there was grayish-green, slimy stuff oozing from around her eyes. "Oh, Maggie, look at this." I held the poodle out for her to see. "Her eyes look awful. I have never seen anything like it."

"Oh, yeah. I see what you mean, wow," she gasped.

"Let's take her to the medical ward and see if someone can look at her."

So we walked down to the medical ward with the poodle tucked under my arm. There we found a vet tech that was willing to take a look at her. The little dog was cooperative as the vet tech poked and prodded her. Afterwards she said, "She has really bad eyes and a tumor on her stomach." I was so sad for the dog. I knew we couldn't take her. She would be too expensive to treat, if she would even survive.

Knowing she likely wasn't going to make it I kissed her filthy face (I didn't care) and told her I loved her, leaving her with my love energy, the only gift I could give before handing her back to the vet tech.

"There is another poodle," the vet tech told me. "He is in the medical ward if you want to see him."

"Sure," I said. "We're here, might as well."

She put the black poodle in a cage and we walked to the adjacent room. There sitting in a cage was a bitty, apricot poodle that couldn't have weighed more than five pounds, in a cage that, while small, was huge for him. She opened the cage door. The dog wagged his tail in delight. He was as cute as a miniature-sized pastry.

She explained that he had bad teeth and that he would need blood work and x-rays. *Well,* I thought, *we can handle a teeth cleaning and tests.* Once we fixed him up he would be easy to adopt out. The apricot poodle's medical issues were not nearly as bad as the black poodle's medical issues. If I couldn't save one, I reasoned, I'd save the other.

Molly agreed to take the poodle into her home. (She had reached the level of foster mom sainthood, if you asked me.) The very first day he fit in perfectly at Molly's house. He played with Molly's poodle and bichon mix Angel and hung out with Fergie, her Great Dane. When Molly was home he followed her around the house.

By the second day Molly's daughter Theresa took him for a car ride and carried him around in her handbag. That night he slept in bed with Molly. Molly told me that going up stairs was easy for him but going down was not an option. From his vantage point it was a straight down drop to nowhere. So when he followed her up the stairs she had to remember to carry him down otherwise he would stand at the top of the stairs and whimper. She fed him soupy food because of his teeth, which he ate without a problem. By the end of day two Molly's son Sean named the poodle Mr. Teacup Poodle or Tea for short.

I added Tea to our web site and asked for help with funding for his medical problems. I hoped and prayed someone would step up and be willing to help him. I figured if worse came to worst we would do a fundraiser for him. I set up an appointment for the vet to look at him the day after Christmas.

I was sure Tea's medical care wouldn't cost more than $500 and we could raise that if we had to. But within hours of posting our request for donations on our site we had two people e-mail us saying they were interested in adopting Tea. Leonard and Sharon, a Chicago couple, also agreed to pay his medical expenses, as well as adopt him. I was elated. I just hoped that their application looked good otherwise it could get awkward. They sent their application in and I reviewed it. To my relief they were a wonderful couple. We set up a time for them to meet Tea after Christmas.

Christmas Day arrived. Typically, Christmas Day the office phones don't ring and we already have our pet sitting scheduled. We spend Christmas quietly, just the four of us. I don't do quiet and slow well so I thought I would take a dog to the nursing home we visited each month to spread some holiday cheer. I thought Tea would be the perfect pooch to take with me.

Arriving at Molly's to pick up Tea she handed him over with a red ribbon around his collar and a gold bell fastened onto the collar at the back of his neck. He looked like a stuffed toy come to life. I chatted with him on the way to the nursing home. "Tea," I began, "you and me are going to make some people happy today." I patted his tiny, puffy head with two fingers. "You are a good boy, you know that." He looked up at me with curious eyes. "Cutie pie." I smiled, bringing his peanut body towards my face where I snuggled his head next to mine. He smelled like baby powder.

Arriving at the nursing home we headed up the elevator. The residents and staff couldn't get enough of him. They all wanted to hold him and everyone was smiling from ear to ear. Tea never squirmed or fussed and patiently watched as each person made baby noises in his face, proclaiming him the best Christmas present ever! It was a memorable visit.

The next day Molly took Tea to the vet. Upon examination the doctor said, "Tea's teeth are not the only problem. His jaw is broken as well. He also has puss all over his mouth." She had sadness in her voice when she said, "He is in a lot of pain." Then she added, "He has a type-three heart murmur, too. Overall, he is a very sick dog."

"How did his jaw break?" Molly asked her.

The doctor shrugged her shoulders. "Who knows for sure, but someone wasn't very nice to this little dog. Jaws don't just get broken."

Molly called me with the news and my stomach sank. The phone line was thick with sadness and worry. *That poor, sweet baby*, I thought. *How could we afford treatment for him? What had I gotten us into? When would I ever learn my lesson not to take animals with medical problems? This poor baby! Someone hurt him badly. How could they? And he had sat in the shelter with a broken jaw for almost a month, in pain.* All those thoughts and more rushed through my head. Molly and I hung up, agreeing we would speak later after we thought things through. We had one other dilemma. Leonard and Sharon were on their way to meet Tea and we would have to tell them the bad news.

Just before leaving for Molly's house I updated our web site to let people know about Tea's health conditions. Leonard and Sharon were already at Molly's when I walked into Molly's house. They were sitting in her dining room holding Tea when I broke the news. Surprisingly they handled the news very well.

As Sharon and Leonard observed, Tea strutted around like he owned the place. When Sharon tried to pet one of the other dogs Tea pushed his way between them like "Hey, me, me!" The couple couldn't resist Tea's adorable disposition and his sweet, fighting spirit.

Like angels sent from above they agreed to pay all of Tea's medical expenses. "It would run in the thousands," I told them.

"Okay, when do you need a check?" Leonard asked.

We were thrilled. Before Sharon and Leonard left we took a photo of Tea with his new parents. Their kindness and love for a helpless dog in need touched me to the core. While I often times was disappointed by people and their actions, meeting these people affirmed to me that there are good, kind people in this world. I needed to be reminded of that because I saw so many bad things people did, like whoever hurt Tea. Seeing the good kept me going. I still had a gnawing bad feeling, though, that I couldn't explain, deep in my gut.

The next day we went to a surgical specialist at a well-known specialty veterinary clinic in Buffalo Ridge, Illinois. After the examination the doctor told us she was confident that she could fix him. The jaw would either be wired or a soft muzzle would be put on afterwards to mold the jaw back in place. She said the heart murmur shouldn't be a problem either. She was very optimistic. I still had that worried itch at the back of my neck but I wanted to believe everything was going to be okay. I told myself that I was just a worrywart. Surgery would be the following morning.

Molly opted to take Tea home for the night. She wanted him to have a stress-free evening with her family. We left relieved and so very thankful for these kind people who would love Tea the rest of his life and happy for Tea that that he would have a second chance at life. He deserved it.

The next morning Molly picked me up and we brought Tea to the animal hospital. I had to continually take deep breaths and remind myself everything was going to be okay. *Stop being a baby,* I said to myself. In the waiting room I took Tea in my arms–he was so tiny and fragile–and kissed his black button nose. I looked him in his bitty black eyes. "Tea, dying is not an option," I choked. "You will be fine. We love you, baby." The worker came and took Tea. Before he left I said, "Take good care of him."

He answered, "Don't worry, we will." I still remember Tea's little face looking back at us wondering what was going on.

Hours later I was at the Kind Hearts Animal Shelter helping a foster family pick out a dog when my cell phone rang. It was Molly. She said, "Sandy, it's not good. Tea went into cardiac arrest. He's been gone ten minutes. They want to know if they should keep trying to get him back."

I leaned up against the wall. "Oh, my God. What am I supposed to do?" I searched my scrambled brain. "How should I know if they should stop? I'm not a doctor." Frantically I tried to think. *Think, Sandy, think.* "Will he have brain damage?"

"I don't know," she replied.

"Give me their phone number." *This is crazy.*

I called the veterinarian and she informed me that brain damage was very probable. So I said, "Well, then, you have to let him go." I could not speak anymore; I hung up after saying I would have to talk to her later. It was so incredibly sad. I stood leaning against the side of the brick building tears falling down my face.

Driving home I checked my messages at my office from my cell phone. Seven out of the ten messages were from people all over the country responding to my earlier postings of needing help with Tea's medical expenses. When I returned to the office there were 12 e-mails offering help for Tea. The outpour of love for that little dog was beyond anything I could have imagined. I returned phone calls and e-mails, telling the well-wishers the news and receiving supportive love back–more good people.

Tea was in our lives for a mere week. During his week with us he brought love to Molly and her whole family. Christmas Day he brought love to lonely people at a nursing home. Then he brought dozens of people together. Through him I saw that people CAN be good, CAN be kind.

Tea brought us new friends in his adoptive parents Leonard and Sharon. And no doubt for Tea he HAD A HOME. He really had two homes—one with Animal Education and Rescue and one with Leonard and Sharon. He did not die unloved or unknown or without a family. While I wish with my very being there would have been a happier ending, if we believe in angels Tea was just that, an angel.

Braille the Fully-Charged Canine

I received a call from the manager of Kennedy-Price Animal shelter, a rural shelter in central Illinois. A seven-month-old puppy had been left outside their facility tied to a pole. "Would you be willing to take her?" Before I could answer she added, "Um, uh, also she's deaf and blind in one eye."

"Are you sure?" I asked, instantly feeling a special connection to the dog.

"Yes, positive," she replied. Then she added in a speedy kind of way, "She knows sit and down already, with hand signals. She's really smart. One of the volunteers loves her. Wishes she could take her home but can't." She ran out of speed. "We could drive her halfway to you." Her voice pleaded. "She has no hope here."

"Does she have any medical problems?"

"None, she's healthy."

So, within 24 hours the dog they named Braille was on her way to us and to her new foster mom, Molly. (Months later Chuck would joke with me, "It was the season you took blind, deaf, paralyzed, one-eared, one-legged, purple-haired dogs.") *How hard can it be?* I thought. This should be fun, interesting and a challenge. So on a warm summer day Braille arrived at Molly's house via transport. I was at her house within hours to see our new charge.

She was so much smaller than I imagined, under 30 pounds. She had the whitest hair I had ever seen, like white frosting, with character-creating gray patches (not that she'd need any character creating we'd soon find out) around her eyes. Her eyes looked like oceans you see in postcards. The blind one was deformed, barely visible within pink, fleshy skin. She had a pink nose the color of Bazooka, my favorite bubble gum when I was a kid. All in all she was a beauty.

Within hours Braille settled into her paces at Molly's house. The first night Molly took Braille out, intending to take her for a walk around the block. But Braille was unwilling to walk farther than 20 yards and headed back home. I couldn't blame her. With only one working eye and no hearing it had to be scary.

Shortly after her arrival we discovered Braille had an unusual personality trait. She had this bark that sounded like "woo-woo-woo-woo-woo." She would sound off when she was excited or trying to get her point across, kind of like a trumpet sounding off, an eruption of applause, a train whistle or the woo-woo-woo people do at sports games when something good happens.

With 24 hours we received an application for Braille from Mary and Don, a couple living in a country setting in central Illinois. After checking their references we scheduled a time for them to take the two-hour trip to my house where they would meet Braille. They arrived on time with their 10-year-old Beagle Clancey in tow.

Sniffing around my dog-scented yard the Beagle basically ignored Braille. While Clancey followed his nose, Braille charmed the couple and they fell in love. We were a little concerned about how Clancey would handle a young, rambunctious sister, but they seemed like a sincere couple that would be good to Braille and work it out between the dogs if there were issues. So Molly and I made arrangements to take the long drive to their home to do a home visit.

The trip took a lot longer than we anticipated. Near the destination I told Molly that in the future we just couldn't do home visits that were so far anymore. It was going to be a whole day affair, time neither one of us could spare. Pulling into the driveway of their log cabin-style home at dusk, I was putting the car in park when all the lights in their home went out. "What the heck?" I said.

"Their power must have gone out," Molly commented.

"Just great," I said in a crabby tone, in no mood for power outages. I had driven over two hours, had so much to do back home and now I was in the middle of nowhere and the power was out.

"Let's just wait here," Molly said, looking at the dark house.

I petted Braille's head and kissed her cheek. I was far more nervous about letting go of Braille than was rational. A lump was growing in my throat.

"I don't know why I'm so worried about Braille," I said still petting her.

"She'll be fine," Molly said matter-of-factly.

Staring towards the house, the darkness closing in, a dark figure walked out onto the front porch, a flashlight in hand, and motioned us in with big waves of his arm.

"Here we go," I said, grabbing Braille's leash and opening the door.

Meeting Don on the porch he said, "That's the one bad thing about living out in the country. The electricity goes out sometimes."

"Really?" I commented, knowing that now Braille was not only deaf but with her one working eye she was near blind. I guided her up the stairs and inside the front door. I had an uneasy feeling about this but knew it had nothing to do with the people. It just didn't feel right. But I reasoned that I was just being overprotective of Braille.

Entering the home the glow of candles gave us enough light to maneuver around. In the front room Mary and Clancey greeted us.

Clancey and Braille butt-sniffed greetings to each other, that one greeting the closest Clancey had come to acknowledging Braille. Then Clancey, totally disinterested in Braille, left the room. Braille looked after him like, "Hey? You don't want to play?"

Don and Mary gave us a tour of their home in the shadowy, flickering light as we discussed where Braille would spend the day and where she would sleep at night. They showed us their big, open yard. Chicken wire surrounded a large-sized area where the dogs would be able to go potty outside. We were reassured that Braille would never be let outside off leash in an unfenced area.

Nearing the end of our visit, standing in the kitchen, I asked them if they were positive they wanted to adopt Braille. I pointed out that Clancey was still less than interested in Braille and getting the two to coexist might be a challenge. They were totally enamored by Braille and assured us they could handle it. We finished up the paperwork and headed for the front room, the electricity still out. We shook their hands, and bending down I wrapped my arms around Braille, kissed her cheek and said, "I love you. Now you have a good life." I was near tears. Molly gave Braille a quick pat on the head and we walked out.

Getting in the car I said, "This was so hard. I don't know why. Maybe because she's so vulnerable." My voice cracked. I looked over at the house. "I hope it works out, and they better not let her outside off leash."

"She'll be fine," Molly said, more than ready to head home.

The following morning I was checking my e-mail and received the following letter:

Dear Sandy:

I'm sorry to tell you this, but last night Braille jumped on Clancey's back to play with him and hurt his back. We had to rush him to the emergency room. Mary and I are too upset to speak by phone but we cannot keep Braille. We'd like to drop her off today.

Sincerely,

Don Hoffner

I wrote him back:

Dear Don:

You can drop Braille off at my house tonight at seven.

Sandy

My letter, far from warm and fuzzy, reflected my frustration at the whole experience. They gave up on Braille too quickly and we wasted a ton of time–at least that's how I felt at that moment. But after a bit of being angry I thought, *Well, it wasn't meant to be.* At least it was only one night and she won't be traumatized because she barely knew the people and to her it was just a sleepover.

I called Molly. When she answered the phone I simply said, "Braille's coming back tonight. She jumped on the Beagle's back. Can you take her?"

"Sure," she said, "no problem."

That evening Mary and Don knocked on my porch door. I opened the door and saw two very sad people. Mary was near tears and Don simply said, "I'm sorry." My anger behind me I felt bad for the couple that really did love Braille.

"We just can't take a chance with Clancey," Mary said, choking back tears. "If it weren't for him…We just have to look out for him. He's our dog."

My first less forgiving thought was, *What, and Braille isn't your dog?* But then the more compassionate me said, "I understand." I took Braille's leash. Noticing me finally Braille jumped up on me in greeting. She was no worse for the wear. "Braille will go back to Molly's. For all she knew it was a sleepover."

"Okay," Mary sniffled. "Sorry."

They left, shutting the door quietly behind them. Braille, not skipping a beat, went about exploring my porch. Molly showed up moments later and took Braille home.

Often when I spoke to Molly on the phone I could hear Braille's trademark woo-woo-woo-woo in the background. I could just picture her standing still and tall, tail held high and curved over her back, excited about something and trumpeting woo-woo-woo-woo in a raspy bark-howl. It happened often and randomly, cutting up our conversations with pauses when she went off.

Months passed and animals got adopted. New dogs came in and Braille remained a fixture at Molly's and a humorous diversion at adoption events. Braille was enthusiastic about everything. Each new (or not so new) thing she explored brought her the joy and the enthusiasm of a child opening gifts Christmas morning. She woo-woo'd often during adoption events, which would have volunteers and visitors laughing. People often commented on her bubble gum-pink nose and her crystal blue eye, surprised by her beauty. Then when they learned of her handicaps they would say a sympathetic, "Aw, poor dog."

I always made a point to say, "You don't have to feel sorry for her; she doesn't. She knows no different and is completely happy in her little Brailley world."

A few months went by and at an adoption event a woman named Bonnie showed interest in Braille. By that time Braille was 11 months old. Bonnie kept saying, "I fell in love with her pink nose." I found that strange but tried looking past that. She filled out an application and we checked references. Bonnie was married, had two cats and previously had worked in a dog grooming shop. Her husband Michael worked full time. She was between jobs. She did not have a fenced yard. I was uneasy about it but was reassured by Molly that it would be okay. I figured, as usual, I was just oversensitive so we scheduled the home visit.

Their home was located much closer than the last home, just 30 minutes away. They lived on a dead-end block in a middle-class neighborhood with large yards and modest but well-kept homes. This time Molly drove and I kept Braille on my lap the whole time. Again, like an overprotective momma bear my heart felt heavy with worry.

Molly pulled into the drive and I said, "Here we go again," as I petted Braille's chest. Happy-go-lucky Braille led the way out of the car and up to the door. Bonnie and Michael opened the door and invited us inside. The home was a tri-level with old carpeting and comfortably worn furniture. Braille, thrilled with this new adventure, sniffed her way around the house.

Near the stairs a cat peeked its head around the corner, saw Braille and bolted away. "I am worried about how my cats will react," Bonnie commented, seeing her cat run away.

"Braille lives with seven cats," Molly explained. "She'll be fine."

We went to the lower level and sat down to talk. We kept Braille on leash and settled back on the couch. "What do we do if Braille goes after the cats?" Bonnie asked.

"What you want to do is get Braille to see the cats as a good thing. So let's say a cat walks past. As soon as Braille spots the cat, pet her and offer her a treat. Over time Braille will make the connection that when she sees a cat good things happen. But you shouldn't have a problem. She lives with cats now."

I went through their educational program emphasizing that Braille could not be tied outside in back and she would need a lot of exercise because she was very active. I told them they could never let Braille loose in an unfenced area and that I was available at any time for questions or concerns. I was still very leery about this couple. She was in-between jobs, they didn't have a fenced yard and this was their first dog. But hearing Molly's reassuring voice in my head I reminded myself not to worry.

We left after once again I hugged Braille goodbye and Braille began her new life with her new family. Weeks went by and we did not hear from the couple. Many times when Molly and I spoke we joked about Braille's family saying, "I didn't hear from the people who adopted Braille. Well I guess this one stuck." But by the third week Bonnie called.

"I'm having a problem with Braille," Bonnie began. My heart jumped. *Would we get her back again? If we did where would she go? Molly couldn't take her.* "I think she tried to bite one of my cats. I'm not sure if she was playing or serious."

"What happened?"

"My cat was walking by Braille towards her litter box and Braille bit at her."

"I am sure she was just trying to play."

"She's really a handful. I am not sure she's happy here. I have to watch her all the time or she's into something."

"Is she getting enough exercise?"

"It's just too cold to take her for really long walks and when I put her out on the tie out she just jumps at the door to come in."

My blood instantly boiled. I had talked to them about NOT using a tie out for Braille because she was vulnerable being left outside tied up, PLUS it is stressful on dogs. They feel they can't protect themselves. Also, Braille's handicaps and the fact that she was tied to a pole when her original owner dumped her at the shelter were more reasons why tying her up outside was a bad idea.

I tried to remain calm. I said, "We talked about Braille not being tied up outside when I came to your home. I also told you she needs a lot of exercise."

"But I didn't realize… Well, I'll give it a try." There was silence on the phone as we both uncomfortably waited for the other to talk.

"Okay, well, I'll give it a try. Thanks, Sandy."

We hung up. I was sure Bonnie heard the disappointment in my voice. Two weeks later Bonnie called. "I got a job and I'm sorry, Sandy, but Braille is just too much. She takes up all my time, and what am I going to do with her when I go to work? She just exhausts me. I think she needs a fenced yard and another dog."

"Bring her back."

That night Bonnie brought Braille to my house. I was stuffed full of dogs myself and Molly didn't have space at her home either. Carrie, a foster mom who had only fostered a few times before, agreed to foster Braille. I had reservations because no matter how many times and ways I would explain to Carrie that there were certain ways we did things, she chose to always do things her own way. The worst thing she did was letting her foster dogs outside off leash in her yard, which wasn't fenced.

But with no other option I explained to Carrie that in all seriousness she could not let Braille outside off leash. Then I shared other particulars about her care so that her transition and lodging would run smoothly. I handed Braille off to Carrie and her children and hoped for the best.

The following morning Carrie called and said, "I can't do this, Sandy." She was crying. "My husband is going to kill me. Braille is having accidents in the house and I don't know what to do."

"I thought we talked about that, Carrie. You need to watch her all the time or crate her."

"I can't do it. I'm sorry." *What is the deal with people?* I thought. *Here I am with ten dogs at a time, not to mention all the other animals and other things I am doing and this stay-at-home mom has a big, fancy house and no other job and she can't handle it?* I just didn't get it and still don't get why more people can't just buck up and deal with stuff. People are spoiled and fast to dump anything on others if it isn't easy. It's a constant source of disappointment to me. But I tried to focus on the few people I knew who did follow through, who owned up to what they agreed to do, and I reminded myself that not all people can handle a lot. That was something I would have to remind myself of over and over and over again.

"Okay, you can drop her off." I wasn't going to argue with her and if I said much more I would open my big, fat mouth and tell her what I really thought.

An hour later Carrie was at my door. By then Braille must have thought this was some sort of fun game. *Here I am at Sandy's again. This is way too fun.* I was glad she was so unaffected.

Carrie was crying (which seemed to be a theme with Braille), saying, "I'm really sorry." I didn't feel bad for Carrie. I thought she was wimpy for not trying to stick it out. I also heard time and time again, "My husband is going to kill me" or "My husband won't let me" or "My husband said no." What year was it anyway? 1950? I hoped I was faking my sympathy for her well enough for her not to see what I really thought. Frankly, overall I was just plain burnt out, felt dumped on and wanted to kick Carrie in the butt. But I didn't. I just took Braille's leash and closed the door behind Carrie. "Braille," I told her, "you're just going to have to get squeezed in here."

I felt sorry for Braille from the first day that she moved in with me. All the times I had told others not to feel sorry for her, and here I was not following my own advice. I refused to put her in a crate when I couldn't watch her. I reasoned that it would limit her already limited senses.

One dilemma I had was that Braille still wasn't housebroken. At a little over a year old I was beginning to think she would never be housebroken. She seemed to have no concept of where she should eliminate and would pee and poo everywhere in the house, like our house was an outdoor park. She even peed right in front of me while looking up at me. Unable to scold her (scolding a dog when they eliminate has been proven ill-effective anyway) I would grab her collar and try and pull her outside. But by the time she got outside she had left a trail of pee or poo behind her and was completely empty. Outside, she looked up at me momentarily bewildered and then scampered off to play. She was lucky she was so cute.

When she did go strutting outside with all of my dogs it was as if she was the center of a rowdy party. She was too distracted playing with my dogs to even think about going potty. When she did occasionally go potty outside it was always when I was nowhere near enough to be able to seize the moment and praise her by petting her or by giving her a treat. Besides, giving her a treat with all my dogs outside with her, she surely would be bombarded by seven other dogs wanting treats and therefore confusing her. In a home with just one other dog and with a family that had more time to devote to Braille, I knew she could be housebroken. But with my situation as it was I thought I'd be more able to win a triathlon than housebreak that dog.

Meanwhile Braille was proving to be a fantastic chewer. She chewed bones, toys and dogs...when she was behaving. She constantly needed something in her mouth. Being a family of clutterers, keeping stuff away from Braille was impossible. Over time (months I have to admit) she had destroyed countless apparently delicious TV controllers and broken plates, cups, etc., by pulling them off the kitchen counters where they smashed to the ground and she proceeded to chew them.

Later she found my cell phone a tasty treat and no matter where I left my cell phone, on counters, in my pocket, on a shelf, she would find it and in one crunch it would be history. I must have gone through seven cell phones in one year. My son David called Braille "The Goat" because not only did she chew up expensive and plastic items, she would eat scraps of paper, pens, chips of our kitchen tile, our wood floors and anything else she could get her mouth around.

As Braille matured she developed this tortured animal sound–

kind of like a cow, duck or sheep, pumped up on steroids, being shocked by a cattle prod–when playing with another dog. I had to make sure any visitors or people I was speaking to on the phone knew no one was dying. Bottom line, she was draining me of all my positive energy, and my family resented me for bringing her home.

The light bulb began to brighten in my brain–feeling sorry for her wasn't good for anyone. I began crating her when I couldn't watch her (which in the beginning made me feel awful) and was diligent about supervising her when she was out of her crate. I reinforced her basic commands and taught her to come, only possible when her one working eye was watching me. She went to agility class where, to my delight, she excelled. She learned that a wag of my finger and my face set in a grimace meant she was being naughty.

When I punished her with a wag and grimace wrinkles would form around her muzzle as if she was saying, *Come on, Mom, I'm just having fun.* She responded well to everything I taught her. I was amazed by her smarts and ability. She followed cues from my dogs such as when I called my dogs inside she watched them go in and followed behind them.

Some nights as I sat watching television I watched Braille as she interacted with my dogs. She knew which dog would play with her and who to avoid. Somehow she knew when a dog was growling at her, possibly by how still they became, their eyes fixed. Somehow she could tell when someone's bark was friendly or angry.

Stepping up on Braille's training I purchased a vibrating collar. My idea was to teach Braille that when the collar vibrated she was cued to come to wherever I was. I wanted to take her to the dog park so she could blow off some steam. I invested in the collar and began training her. Because she was so easily distracted it was a challenge.

Taking her outside in the backyard on leash she looked around wondering why she was outside by herself. Armed with treats and the remote I put the collar around Braille's neck. I pushed the button, which caused the box on the collar to vibrate and then fed her a treat. I did this over and over. She showed no sign she was feeling anything around her neck so I tested it with my hand. It was working. Again I tried over and over but she didn't seem to feel it. After a few more times with the collar I figured it was a bust but wanted to try her one time at the dog park anyway.

The day I decided to take Braille to the dog park it was a gorgeous spring day, the kind of day I always thought heaven must be like. Chuck and I loaded the van up with Scrappy, Sophie, Shrek and Braille. My theory was that now that Braille was bonded to my dogs she would stick with us as we walked the seven-acre park. My dogs always stayed fairly close and always checked back with us often. It was completely fenced in so I didn't worry about her safety, only the time and energy it would take to find her if she were to run off.

As we approached the park, my dogs recognized where we were and began barking and yelping in glee. But Braille had never been there before so she looked from dog to dog, ears perked up, eye wide, wondering what all the commotion was about. We parked, and as I held onto Braille's leash I opened the door and the dogs tumbled out of the van, falling all over each other. I held tight to Braille's leash as she dragged me after the other dogs.

Like pool balls colliding we spilled into the gated park, and my dogs burst out for a quick run before coming back to Chuck and me to check in. Braille pulled me forward, watching my dogs run off, wanting to do the same. "Should I take her off leash?" I asked Chuck.

"Go ahead."

"But if she takes off you'll have to run after her, okay?"

(Grunt)

"Okay, here you go, Braille." I snapped off her leash. She took off like a rocket, running faster than I had ever seen her run before. Heading towards my dogs in an open field 25 feet ahead, she began bouncing up and down as she ran like a jackrabbit. *What a goof.* Reaching the dogs she stopped abruptly, stood erect, her tail curled over her back. Excited she proceeded to hop up and down like a pogo stick, lifting her pink-topped muzzle to the blue sky and trumpeting her woo-woo-woo. I smiled and shook my head.

Running her heart out no dog could have been happier. She ran ahead many times to follow other people with their dogs, joining each group as if she belonged. She played enthusiastically with every dog she met. It was a joy to watch.

Having rounded the fringe of the seven-acre field, nearing the area where we parked our car, Braille took off with a family that was headed for the trail-lined woods. I knew if she got there we would be there for hours looking for her.

Chuck was able to run much faster and longer so I said, "Quick, Chuck, go get her before she heads into the woods." I yelled to the people some 50 feet ahead, "Stop that white dog! She's deaf!" But they didn't hear me.

Seeing my short, stocky husband trotting after Braille I laughed and laughed. Chuck finally caught up to her and grabbed her collar. Surprised she looked up at Chuck as if to say, "Hey, Dad, having fun? This is a BLAST, too way cool!" With a grin on his face Chuck led her to me. Not wanting to have poor Chuck have to chase her again I hitched her up to her leash. She was barely winded and probably could have run for hours. "Let's go home," I announced. "We don't need to lose her again." I was giggling all the way to the car, thinking about Braille running with those strangers and Chuck trotting behind.

Braille routinely set Chuck's temper on edge. Every time he found something chewed up he grumbled or cursed. The worst, though, was when Braille ruined his handmade trim that he painstakingly created himself in our garage and installed in our kitchen. He had been so proud of it. His handiwork was gnawed at, scraped up and basically ruined, and he never let her live it down.

To make matters worse, while sleeping in our bed with us she peed a lake where we slept. Chuck dragged out the hand-held cleaning machine and between strokes wished Braille would disappear. The mattress had just dried and Braille hopped onto the bed, lay down and moments later got up and it was wet again. This time I tried hiding it from Chuck, cleaning it myself, but unable to ever hide anything from Chuck, he found out and said, "That dog is not allowed in this bed ever again!"

Braille was lying on the floor during her rare downtime the following night, and I looked down and noticed a wet spot by her rear. Braille sniffed down there, wondering why the heck she had pee between her legs. That would explain the pee on the bed. To make matters more concerning, Braille had been itching a lot and her skin was becoming raw and she was losing hair on her legs and belly, exposing red skin underneath.

The following day I brought Braille to the vet. She had skin allergies with a secondary infection that had given her an ear infection. She was also likely incontinent, which would explain the uncontrollable leaking. Armed with three different medications I looked down at the medications in my hands and then at the doctor. "Now we have one adoptable dog," I said sarcastically. "A deaf, blind-in-one-eye, incontinent, hyperactive dog with skin allergies." He looked at me with a glad-it's-you-and-not-me look.

Thankfully after a month of medications and daily baths Braille's seasonal summer allergies cleared up. The medication for the incontinence worked like a charm. But there was no getting around it that Braille was difficult. My family still barely tolerated her, my son calling her "it" or yelling at her to "Shut up!" when she did her woo-woo-woo. It was a constant strain and frustration for our family. I continued to be the main caretaker for Braille (and of course all the other animals) and worked on her basic commands and gave her attention. My family didn't understand how I could love her so much.

Over time Braille was nearly housebroken and we had become expert in keeping things off the floor and off countertops where she could destroy them. Braille started to wiggle her way into Chuck's heart as he began to see her unusual behavior as endearing and humorous. At night the now 45-pound mutt would crawl into Chuck's lap and lie down for a rubdown and face lick combined with love nips. She was getting under his skin. After the first two families adopted Braille, no one showed interest in her. Then on a snowy day, a year after obtaining Braille by default, something terrible happened.

The winter of 2008 was long and harsh with record snowstorms. By January I was sick and tired of the winter, the snow and the dank dreariness that went with it. But there were some positives about snowy weather. The dogs could romp and stomp in the backyard without tearing up the grass or getting muddy. So on a Sunday afternoon at dusk, when the snow was inches thick on the ground and the falling snow like confetti on New Year's Eve, I let the dogs outside in the backyard to blow off some steam.

Fifteen minutes later I opened the porch door and called the dogs inside. One by one my snow-covered dogs ran inside and shook themselves off. Someone was missing. It was Braille. I went out the porch door and stood on the deck scanning the snowy yard for a snow-colored dog. Unable to see her I ran down the deck stairs and began looking all over the yard. She was nowhere to be found. I began to panic. *Oh no, she got out!*

Running inside I dodged the dogs saying, "Move, move," and headed for the stairs and Chuck upstairs. I cracked open the door so as not to let all the dogs race upstairs and yelled up, "Braille got out!"

"What?" Chuck yelled back.

Louder, panic clear in my voice, "Braille got out!"

"What? Damn. How did that happen?" I could hear him getting up and coming towards the stairs.

"I don't know, but she's not out back."

"Are you sure?"

"Yes, I am sure. We have to go find her. God, there's a snow-storm and she's a white dog. She could be dead. The traffic…"

"That dog," he said, stomping down the stairs.

"Hurry up. I'll go around back by the church and you go up the road and look in the street."

We grabbed our coats and headed out into a snowstorm look-ing for a deaf and blind-in-one-eye dog, the last flicker of sunlight gone. Stepping out on my driveway I zipped my jacket under my chin and headed towards the church parking lot behind my house. Chuck walked towards the busy road in front of our house. "Call me if you find her, and keep in touch," I hollered to Chuck.

My gym shoes were soaking wet within minutes as I trudged through the snow. *Where the heck are my snow boots?* I thought to my-self. I was always losing everything, shoes, keys, cell phones, my purse, anything I needed regularly. Rounding the corner I squinted and shielded my eyes from the large snowflakes falling rapidly and looked all around the parking lot and by the trail beyond it for a white dog that wasn't able to hear me even if I called her. *I must prepare myself that she could die tonight, after everything we've been through.* I struggled over a snow-drift and onto the trail and began walking west. Braille was nowhere to be found. I didn't see any paw print tracks either, but with the snow com-ing down so fast they would quickly disappear anyway.

I flipped open my cell phone, grateful to have not lost that today, and called Chuck.

"Any luck?" I asked him.

"No." He sounded winded and very unhappy.

"I was thinking. We need to stop people and ask them if they saw her. That's the only way we'll find her if someone catches her or spots her, and we can get within close enough range to either grab her or have her see us and motion her to us."

"Okay. Well, I've been all the way up the road. I think I saw tracks crossing 176."

"You think she crossed 176?" 176 was a busy highway right in front of our house. While traffic was moving slow due to the weather the cars were lined up out front all along the road.

"It looks like it."

"And you don't see her in a ditch?"

"No. Maybe by some miracle she made it across."

"Beautiful," I said with anger in my voice. "A white dog, deaf and blind in one eye, in a snowstorm crossing a busy highway. If she makes it she's one lucky dog."

"Let me know if you see her."

"Okay, bye." Hanging up with Chuck I started making phone calls. First I called the animal hospital to notify them in case someone brought Braille in. Then I called some local volunteers, none of whom could come out to help due to the weather. Then I called Molly.

"I'll pick you up in 20 minutes," she told me. I could always count on Molly during a crisis.

I ran back home and got on the computer and sent out an e-mail to all our volunteers. It said: Braille, my deaf and blind-in-one-eye foster dog dug out of my yard and is loose in Liberty. If anyone can help, please drive around looking for her. My cell phone number is: 555-4540. Please pray for her safe return.

Heading back outside Molly picked me up and we began driving slowly from one street to the next, stopping anyone we saw outside, asking them if they saw a white dog running loose. I called the police and gave them a description of Braille and my cell phone number in case anyone called in that they found a dog. I had no idea how Braille would behave if someone tried to grab her, being that she was probably disoriented. Block after block I feared the worst would happen.

Then my cell phone began to ring. Mothers of kids from our youth club were heading out to help look for Braille. Two cars loaded with kids were going to park at my house and spread out on foot looking for Braille. Then I got a call from another youth club member's mom. "I think I saw Braille cross 176 an hour ago when I was heading home. I just got home and got your e-mail. The dog was white and crossing the street right by the light."

"Oh no, she did cross the busy street. Did you see where she went?"

"She went by the blue house, the one with the small fence in front. Do you want me to knock on their door and see if they have her?"

"That would be great. Thank you." She told me she'd call if she found out anything and we hung up. To Molly I said, "We have youth club members and their moms coming over to help. Wow, isn't that awesome?" It made me feel like crying I was so grateful.

"Yeah, it is. Let's try by my house." Molly lived five blocks from me and we thought maybe Braille would remember where Molly lived. It was a long shot but worth a try. "Let's go through the high school parking lot first." I lived kitty corner from the high school.

Slowly creeping through the parking lot looking out into the blinding snow I said, "Molly, I don't know what I'll do if she gets killed."

"We'll find her."

My cell phone rang. "Hello."

"Is this the person who reported you were missing a white dog?"

"Yes," I said and held my breath, hoping she wouldn't say someone had hit Braille with their car.

"I got a call from a man at 1244 Maple. He said a white dog is outside his door barking."

"That's her! Tell him we're on our way. Thank you so much." I hung up. To Molly I said, "They found her." A sob escaped my throat and I began to cry.

"Sandy," Molly said with authority, "she's fine. Hold it together."

"I know. I'm just so relieved." I took a deep breath and wiped away my tears. "Do you know where 1244 Maple is?"

"That's my neighbor."

"Braille went to your neighbors? I wonder if she was looking for your house?"

"Could be."

We pulled into the driveway of the biggest mansion in the entire town. "Braille has good taste," I said. "Oh, look, Chuck's here," I said, noticing our Honda Element. "How'd he know she was here?" Chuck had Braille flung over his shoulder and was opening the car door. I rolled down my window and waved. He put Braille inside and we all backed out and Molly took me home.

Heading into the house Braille greeted me with a very vocal and agitated-sounding woo-woo-woo. I bent down and wrapped my arms around her. "You little poop head. I am so glad you are okay." I looked at Chuck leaning against the kitchen counter. "How did you know she was at that house? The police only had my number."

"On a gut instinct I thought maybe she'd go by Molly's house. I had the windows rolled down so if she woo-woo'd I'd hear her. I was driving near that mansion and thought I heard her. I stopped the car and listened and knew Braille's woo-woo and knew she was somewhere around there. I just followed her voice to the mansion. I guess the guy who lives there said he saw her outside his window and when he opened his door she growled at him so he shut it and called the police. He said she was looking at him through the window."

"You're kidding!"

"When I pulled up Braille didn't see me at first. She was by his door and he opened it a crack for me. She was in front of me looking at him growling."

"How'd you get her then?"

"I knew she was pissed off so I didn't want to scare her and get bit so I tapped her back. That startled her and she turned. Then I motioned for her to come. She paused for a minute and then must have realized it was me and walked over to me. Then I picked her up and put her in the car."

"I'll tell you, she's something."

"Then when I got back the kids from the youth club were in the driveway. They had been out looking. They wanted to pet Braille but she was really crabby and growling at them. So I thanked them and told them they could pet her some other day."

"It's a miracle. She's lucky to be alive. Happy ending to the day."

As of this writing Braille still lives with me. Having Braille has been very difficult but I do not regret saving her from death. All her faults don't outweigh what she brings to my life and what I hope someday she will share with her forever family. She has a silly, confident, I'm-all-that attitude about everything in life. She accepts everyone (canine and human alike) without hesitation. Further, if she can live her life to the fullest, with her limitations, shouldn't we all stop complaining about our lives? I am intensely touched by her enthusiasm, her energy and her uniqueness. There is not, nor will there ever be, another Braille.

At the end of a long, exhausting day nothing feels better than when Braille crawls into my lap and leans flush against me as I stroke her ever-so-soft coat. She looks at me with that one working, sweet, icy blue eye and I know she is saying from her heart to mine, "Hey, thanks, Mom. You're pretty great, too." (Because of course she already knew she was great.) I am her protector for as long as she needs me.

Relationships and Humans

A year and a half into my work for Animal Education and Rescue my marriage crashed, burned and experienced, by some miracle, a rebirth. It took a bottoming out and giving up to get both of us to realize that our marriage was worth saving, and we grappled with how to go about doing it.

Chuck's negative attitude about AEAR, I told him, had to stop. I had found something I was very passionate about and driven by, and Chuck had to be on board. If he had a passion I would have supported him. (He didn't at that time.) I couldn't run both Pet Sitters and AEAR, and he needed to take a leadership role with Pet Sitters so I could concentrate on AEAR. In return I agreed to start consulting him when it came to AEAR and ask for his input. And I would try to balance all of my roles better. It was a slow, creaky start.

Today I can tell you our relationship is better than in the 20 years we have been together, and we now share the same passion and mission, helping animals in our own ways and making a difference in the lives of others. He is now my partner and my best friend. He has grown to love the work of AEAR. He attempts to keep me grounded and I attempt to get him to just go with the flow more often.

My children, as of this writing, finally stopped complaining about

AEAR and what comes with it. They gave up in a way, I suppose, knowing that all the complaining wasn't going to change the fact that I was doing what I was doing with or without their support. Someday I hope they look back on this time in their lives and are proud of what a unique and colorful home they grew up in.

Unusual Rescues

Maggie, a dedicated teen volunteer, was accompanying me to a foster home where Missy, a Schnauzer mix, was waiting to have her infected ears cleaned. Just before passing the YMCA in Vernon Hills, we both noticed a rabbit lying on the road. We said in unison, "Poor bunny!" Then we saw its head move.

"It's alive!" Maggie exclaimed. I put my hazard lights on and stopped the van. "There's a blanket in the back," Maggie barked.

"Get the blanket," I barked back. She rushed to get the blanket as I headed to the middle of the road to stop traffic from hitting the rabbit again. I slowly approached. More often than not I got really panicky about seeing sick or dead animals. My first thought as I stood over the rabbit was, *Wow, I don't have to throw up.*

Observing the rabbit I noted that he could move his head but the rest of him was still. He had blood by his nose. Most likely the rabbit was run over by a car. I thought, *He's probably a goner,* but not wanting him to be in the middle of the road awaiting his impending death by car, I took the blanket that Maggie handed me and gently wrapped up the bunny. Maggie opened up the back of the van and I placed the rabbit gently on the floor.

Missy would have to wait; we had to tend to the rabbit. On the ride back to my place I warned Maggie that this rabbit could die. He was breathing rapidly through his nose. "He could be paralyzed or have internal injuries," I informed her. "Let's just get him in a crate and make him comfortable. It's cars that did this to him. The least we can do is make his last moments comfortable," I said.

Arriving at my place we jumped out of the van and went to look for a crate. Crate in hand we headed back to the van. Maggie got in first and I told her to take one end of the blanket while I took the other, and we would slide the rabbit in the crate.

Just then without warning the rabbit sprung up into a sitting position. "He's up!" Maggie exclaimed.

"Hurry, let's get him in the crate," I said, my voice rising. He began to slip out of the blanket. "Uh oh, oh, no. Grab him! He's getting away!" I yelled. I was imagining this wild rabbit loose in the van. I grabbed ahold of the blanket, rabbit half inside and half out, and shoved him towards the crate. Obliging, the rabbit hopped in. We both rejoiced at his unlikely recovery and sighed with relief he wasn't loose in the van.

One hour later, after resting in the crate, the rabbit was released and hopped away.

The Racecar Turtle

Driving north I was heading home. The car just ahead of me drove over what looked like a round object in the road. Passing over the object, I looked in the rearview mirror. It was spinning like a top. It took my mind about 3 seconds to register that it looked like a turtle. *Should I stop, should I not?* Who was I kidding? Would I ever pass up an animal in need? Never.

I swung into a driveway and pulled around and headed back. I pulled over on the gravel shoulder and when there was a break in traffic ran across the street and stood next to the turtle, who was the size of an appetizer plate. Its head and legs were tucked deep inside its shell.

Quickly I snatched it up and ran back across to my car. I put the little guy on the passenger seat and thought about what to do with him. I pulled onto the road and headed to the forest preserve across the street. Halfway to my destination–a little pond on forest preserve land–the turtle popped his head out.

Next thing I knew it was running around my car like a giant spider with a shell. I am not ashamed to say I was saying a lot of "Oh, nos" and "Uh ohs" and other nondescript guttural nonsense as I drove along, trying to get that creepy-crawly thing under control at the same time as using the stick shift of my Geo Tracker (a tent on wheels).

Mustering some courage I snatched him up around his shell so he would stop crawling around my car and began talking to him like I would a dog. "Now you stay. Be a good turtle," etc. Sweat trickled down my brow as I juggled the turtle, a winding forest preserve road and a sticky stick shift. I sat the turtle down on the seat for a moment so I could turn into the parking lot and reminded him to "stay" until I could stop.

I jerked the car to a halt, put it in neutral, yanked the parking brake up and grabbed the turtle. As much as I loved animals I just wanted this creepy-crawly thing out of my car and back in nature where he would be far more appreciated.

Arm fully outstretched in front of me (as if he would turn and attack) I went straight for the little pond and gently set the turtle down. Placing my hands on my hips I watched him slowly ease his way into the water. "Have a nice life, little guy," I told him, wiping the sweat from my forehead. I turned back towards my car and said out loud, "Good save, good save."

A Little Brown Rabbit

Every month AEAR volunteers and their dogs flooded the halls and rooms of a local nursing home in my hometown of Liberty, visiting with the residents. This monthly practice had been going on for years. In the ten-plus years we had been going to not only that nursing home but also many, many others, 99% of the animals we brought with us were dogs. On a rare occasion a cat would come along. So it was an unusual evening when Carl, a little brown rabbit–the fifth foster rabbit AEAR saved from being put to sleep–came with us to visit people at the nursing home.

Jennifer, a young volunteer with a contagious smile and warm, brown eyes, wrapped Carl in a warm blanket and held him as we waited in the lobby before the event started. His nose twitched with excitement. He was a friendly, calm rabbit with no phobias or aggression, perfect for a program such as pet therapy.

That Tuesday evening Carl was quite obviously the lone bunny in a sea of wagging tails. He sat quietly, snug in the blanket, like a newborn babe, his little, dark brown eyes looking around curiously. As more and more dogs entered the building Carl continued to be undaunted by the wet noses that sniffed him in greeting and the human hands that tickled him behind the ear or petted his soft fur.

After our usual introductions and announcements in the lobby, we strolled down the hall and to the elevator and landed on the third floor. We spread out and began moving from room to room, visiting residents. It being Jen's and Carl's first time volunteering I tagged along in case they needed any help or Carl got antsy.

Our first stop, at the end of the hall, was Pam's room. In her 40's, Pam was a long-term resident. She had advanced Parkinson's disease (and I'm not sure what else), causing her body to make involuntary, jerky movements and rendering her nearly speechless. As it always was when I saw her she was lying in bed, her eyes alert and her face eager, telling me she was ready for our visit. Pam was a huge animal lover.

After a warm hello Jen placed Carl on Pam's chest. As if he knew what to do he sat very still waiting to be touched, which was very unusual for a rabbit to do. Pam looked at Carl and laughed, surprised to see a rabbit six inches from her face. We laughed back and said, "You thought it was a dog, huh?" She smiled widely and nodded her head. She began touching Carl's silky coat. Her hand wasn't gentle at first because of its jerky movements. Even so Carl remained calm and still. With each stroke her arm seemed to have more control, the movements smaller and more deliberate. I could visibly see her breathing slow down. She had a peaceful look on her face.

After visiting Pam, Jen and Carl went to another room where he received enthusiastic attention. Room after room and person after person Carl sat on laps, in arms and on beds. The interactions of the residents with Carl were sights to be seen.

You could hear residents catching wind of the rabbit being there and saying, "Where's the bunny? I want to see the bunny." He was stroked, cuddled and kissed all over, including on his nose that was twitching nonstop. Not once did he try to squirm away, scratch or bite. It was as if he knew he had a job to do and was glad to do it. That entire evening Carl worked his magic, showing up all the dogs by practically having to be pried out of people's arms. The dogs were second best to Carl.

So thus began a new mission for Animal Education and Rescue, to bring foster rabbits to the nursing home. The amazing and remarkable impact Carl made on those people was profound. It never ceases to amaze me how when saving a life you can help not only the life you saved but another as well–and in this case dozens.

Say a Prayer for a Black Lab

In the summer of 2004 I started writing columns I titled Pet Wise for two local publications. The purpose of the columns was to educate, inform and entertain. I varied the columns so that if you read a serious column one time it might be sad, but then the next column would be either humorous or lighthearted. I have included a sprinkling of some of my most memorable columns here.

Oh, was I livid. I don't get angry easily and try to be forgiving of people's ignorance, but this was just too much. About two weeks ago I was stopped at a garage sale in my hometown with my husband Chuck. The house was a nice split-level in a desirable part of town.

We walked up the drive and into the garage where a variety of objects sat on tables. I noticed a small child crouched on the floor playing with a toy. I heard the toy make noise so I zoned in on it. It was one of those cute, electronic dogs that when put by its water or food dish made chewing and slurping noises. I laughed as I watched the little girl make the dog drink water.

The girl's mom–whose home I was at, was standing nearby so I jokingly said, "So is this your daughter's only dog or does she have another?"

"Oh, that's it," she answered. I thought to myself, boy this must be a parent's way of pacifying a child who wants a dog–pretty sorry substitute. I continued to browse the sale items.

It was then I heard a low growl and looking noticed a small, black lab in the back of the garage behind a makeshift wire and wood cage. The cage obviously led to some sort of run on the side of the property. The dog seemed nervous and agitated. Surprised I said to the homeowner, "Oh, I thought you said you didn't have a dog."

She said, "Oh, that's just our hunting dog. My husband takes the dog hunting. He's gotta clean that pen, though. I'm not doing it."

I peered at the area she was indicating. The pen was about five feet by three feet, with dog feces scattered about the floor of the small area. I said, "You mean the dog lives out there?"

"Yeah, he hates it inside, freaks him out. I tried bringing him in once and he just bolted for the door." I could feel my blood beginning to boil.

"If you leave a dog in a small, enclosed area without human contact and without running and playing room, of course they are going to be terrified if, after a long time, you bring them in the house for a minute or two." I went on to tell her that dogs are meant to be with people and do not fair well not having daily human contact. They can become aggressive, scared and unmanageable. I went on, "How would you like to be stuck in a small area by yourself all the time?" I told her that it was very cruel what they were doing. My voice was not raised nor was I confrontational. I made a point to force myself to remain calm. Shouting would only have made her think I was a nut.

Her response, "Well, my husband would debate you on that." The whole time she never appeared remorseful, worried or at the very least questioning. Instead she seemed indifferent, as if the dog was an object rather than a living, breathing soul. From my short observation of the dog and how the dog owner described him, he had been ruined by this treatment and only extensive rehabilitation could save him.

Had I thought to ask her I would have said, "What will happen to the dog when he becomes too old to hunt? And really, how often does your husband take him hunting?" Having a small child I doubted the man went hunting several times a week.

People like that should have their dogs taken away from them. But unfortunately, as long as the dog has food, water and shelter there is little that can be done. I left the garage sale with a heavy heart and a strong dislike for this unfeeling family and ashamed that such people lived in my town, which was known for its educated people and progressive ways of thinking. Then I said a prayer that somehow the dog would get out of its jail and find a new life full of love.

Even though I knew that I had done all I could and the woman was not breaking any laws, I felt obligated to follow up on the dog some day, somehow.

After writing the above column for the first and only time I received hate mail. People accused me of not doing enough, of contributing to the dog's suffering. It would be a year and a half later but I would revisit the woman and her dog.

Reflections on Walking Dogs

Following are two humorous columns I wrote that reflected my experiences walking my dogs.

Today the weather was beautiful. The sun was shining and the temperature was in the mid 70's. It was a stressful day and part of me wanted to just relax in front of the television, but I knew my dogs would not forgive me if I didn't take them for a walk, so I forced myself to grab a coat and head for the door.

Sophie, my shepherd mix, was first to go for a walk. She danced around me, clearly excited, making it challenging as I snapped the leash on her collar. Yanking me down the stairs and dragging me down the driveway to the sidewalk, heading east, she clearly was in charge of which way we were going. "Slow down!" I commanded, with no success. Being a dog trainer I hoped that none of my clients were driving by and seeing my dog nearly pulling my arm out of its socket as I surged forward like a robot in high speed. My dogs are without a doubt grossly untrained and spoiled. I admit I am the equivalent of the shoemaker whose own shoes have huge holes in them.

Sophie was on a mission and I was a just along for the ride. First, she piddled on the neighbor's grass, warning all other dogs that she had been there, and next, a good, quick sniff on a nearby tree. All this was accomplished in record speed. Around the bend she abruptly stopped, looked up towards the sky and with a whiff took note of the fresh, crisp air. I followed suit. Just then out of the corner of her eye Sophie saw a rabbit nibbling the grass 15 paces ahead. Her body tensed, my cue to hang on tight. She lunged forward; I pulled back on the leash. The rabbit, spotting Sophie, hopped into the bushes. Sophie, proud of her ability to make the rabbit disappear, pressed onward.

A block down Sophie spotted a purebred, cream-colored Standard Poodle trotting daintily towards us, keeping perfect pace with his owner. As the poodle and his owner came nearer to us they both held their noses up like some sour smell hung heavy in the air. Sophie attempted to sneak a quick sniff of the poodle's butt. Most dogs and their owners know this is a common "howdy do." But the poodle, totally indignant to such moves by a mix breed, moved out of reach of the butt-sniff. Pulling Sophie back I apologized to the owner. His response was a curt nod. I suppressed a giggle.

Sophie finally calmed down enough to stop pulling me so we walked along more slowly, enjoying the scenery. A butterfly, a bird, another squirrel, some passersby, all helped me unwind and through Sophie's eyes share her journey. Each new moving object or smell brought her unrestrained joy. Twenty-five minutes into our walk she left me a present to clean up with a grocery bag. This marked the time to turn around.

Nearing the house I got to thinking about what I found so relaxing about walking my dogs. What I concluded is that my dogs force me to slow down and look at the world around me, well, at least once they calm down. Just being able see things through my dog's eyes I can see the beauty in the small things and enjoy life's simple pleasures. Oh, and do they make me laugh. I'm still laughing about that cream puff poodle and his owner.

Reflections on Walking Dogs 2

Following is a follow-up on the Walking Dogs column:

A while back I wrote a column about why I like to walk my dogs. I talked about how on walks my dogs helped me to appreciate the small things like fresh air, a rabbit, a squirrel or another dog coming our way. I also confessed that my dogs are unruly and pull like crazy on leash. As a dog trainer I readily admitted that it looks bad but as the shoemaker's shoes need repair, yet he never gets around to it, I suffer the same dilemma.

Well, tonight, while Chuck and I were walking (or honestly being dragged) by our two biggest dogs, Shrek, a Rottweiler, and Charlie, a German Shepherd and wolfhound mix, my husband thought of some clever ways to explain our dogs surging ahead with us in tow. For those of you who have dogs that drag you, you are welcome to steal these ideas.

He suggested that we wear a blue jacket, blue pants and dark glasses and with an air of confidence give the impression that we are on a serious hunt for bad guys and our dogs are "on the scent of the perpetrator." Seeing a neighbor trimming their lawn we would yell out, "They've got the scent! Keep at it, boys! Good dogs, good dogs! Go get 'em!"

Being slightly illogical because you'd need to purchase a uniform for such a ruse, he also suggested that we tell people that our dogs are being trained to pull a sled and therefore we are encouraging them to pull. Every now and again as people gave us a puzzled or disgusted look as we walk/run behind our dogs we would yell out, "Mush, boys, mush!"

Then there is always the we're-in-a-huge-hurry-because-we-are-such-busy-people excuse. As we pass neighbors, going the speed of a moped, we would wave at them and say, "We have to get home. We have an important meeting." Then Chuck would flip open his cell phone and speak loudly (so the neighbor could hear) to an imaginary person, "We're on our way. We'll be there momentarily."

He also made a brilliant suggestion that was really thinking outside the box. Why not tell people that we purposely trained them to pull as a new and dynamic approach to working out? I could explain that with each step you take you are using your biceps, shoulders and back muscles. I'd go on, "As you surge forward you are walking at brakeneck speed, far faster than you could walk if you weren't being pulled by your dog, thus all this strength training and power walking burning more calories." We'd make a video and sell it on the home shopping network. We'd title it: Burn Fat While Being Pulled By Your Dog.

Journal Entry March 10, 2005:

Today I visited with a family interested in adopting my foster dog, Holly. Holly had been with me longer than any other foster dog. We couldn't understand why the perfect home hadn't come along. Then finally a promising application came in from a couple living in Hickory Hills.

Holly and I were bonded. She followed me around the house, jumped up on me for love and snuggled up by my feet at night. But I knew I couldn't keep her. There were dogs waiting to be rescued just behind her. Thus is the burden of a foster mom–to give them up.

After spending an hour with the couple I knew this was the perfect family for Holly. Saying goodbye to her was incredibly hard. I cried part of the way home, sad to be apart from my dear friend. I still get choked up when I think about it. It's always hardest on the foster family. The dogs forget us soon enough.

When I tell people I foster some have said, "I don't know how you do it. I could never do what you do. I'd keep every dog." I would say if it wasn't rude, "How can you not save a life? It's not about you it's about them, the animals." An estimated 4-6 million dogs are killed every year just because they don't have homes. That's enough motivation for me.

Have a wonderful life, sweet Holly. New beginnings for you!

On to the next dog to rescue,
Sandy

A Light That Guided Me

On a sweltering summer day in 2005, during one of our regular lunch dates, my girlfriend Liz told me a disturbing story about a dog in her neighborhood that was chained up outside 24 hours a day. She said that on nights when there were thunderstorms and the rain was coming down fiercely he would howl and cry in fear. During winter storms she would also hear the forlorn cry of a sad and pained animal. This happened year after year. I was mortified to hear about the dog's horrible situation and told her I would look into it. At that time I knew very little about the laws that pertained to animals and who had jurisdiction where.

I knew an animal control officer and humane investigator named Beth, so I gave her a call and asked for her help. Shortly thereafter Beth went to investigate the situation. According to Beth when she arrived at the residence she noticed the dog lying by an igloo doghouse out front beside an industrial-sized garbage container near the driveway. She could smell a foul decaying odor even before she approached the dog. Going up to the dog she saw a prong color around his neck, dark red blood around it. On closer examination she saw that the collar was embedded in his neck. She knocked on the door. No one answered so she left a notice and took the dog to the animal hospital where he received emergency surgery.

That was my first personal experience with helping a dog out of a neglectful situation. That's when the taste of it began churning in my system. I wanted to save more animals that really needed saving. A slow burn began inside of me, which would one day light like a bonfire. Meanwhile I wanted to get that dog, whom we named Duke, to a place where he could start a new life.

Here is what I wrote to my e-mail animal friends:

Duke The Malamute
I have a very sad story to tell but one I hope you can help me make a happy ending. Please read this, don't not. Duke deserves all of us animal lovers' attentions!

There is a 4-year-old malamute dog named Duke that I met just recently. When I met him I had never seen such sad eyes. The eyes told me that he had given up hope that anyone would come and help him. Duke had been chained up outside to a small igloo doghouse for three and a half years. The bare minimum was done–food and water–but he was NEVER touched by human hands, never, ever taken for a walk or allowed to run around a yard. There he sat with no one for 3 and a half long, dreadful years. The ground around him was nothing but mud. There was animal fat and old, dried-up food for him to eat and a bucket of water.

His owners would have to walk past him to get to and from their expensive, north-suburban home to their Hummer or one of their other wildly expensive cars in their spacious, 3-car garage. He would cry and cry, lunging towards them saying, "Please pet me, please." They saw right through him, not a word or a glance in his direction, as if he didn't even exist.

On freezing cold winter nights or during the pouring rain or heat of the summer, his howling could be heard throughout the entire neighborhood, a forlorn cry and moan that would make the hair on your neck stand straight up.

A friend of mine witnessed this firsthand–she is a neighbor. She called the animal control office numerous times but their response was, "If he has food, water and shelter then there is nothing we can do." Her husband tried speaking to the people who owned Duke, only to be driven off their property by threats.

I became involved only recently when my friend, knowing I was involved in rescue, begged me for help. That's when I went to see Duke. When I saw the haunted eyes looking at me as if to say, "I know you won't help me. I've tried to get help for years. I know no one will come," I knew we had to do something.

I was warned that the owners could be dangerous so I kept a distance. I gave my friend ideas of what to do to free Duke.

It was YESTERDAY MORNING when an animal control officer finally arrived to check out the situation. Duke was taken from those horrible people because he had a prong/pinch collar embedded in his neck. The officer said the "stench from the decay around his neck was sickening."

Now, if I was Duke I'd be mad at humans. I'd hate them, really. Not Duke. My friend and the vet's office staff said, "He is sweet, loving and extremely friendly." The animal hospital treated his wound yesterday and he sits there waiting to see what his future holds. The officer assures us that the owners will not get him back. Further, she will prosecute them for their abuse and neglect.

But we still have a dilemma: what to do with Duke?

If all goes as planned he would end up at the county's animal shelter. That's not the worst place and since he is so friendly he would probably eventually be adopted. BUT why should Duke spend one more day of his life living without the love of a family? The officer told me that it is possible for us to adopt him out through a rescue group and bypass the county shelter.

Can anyone find it in their heart to take Duke, either as a foster or forever home? I would help with his adjustment period. He is so very sweet. I don't want to see him spend one more day than necessary behind any kind of bars.

Please pass this along and help if you can or ask around and tell his story. Let's work together to make the rest of his life so good it'll make up for the horrible first years of his life.

Thanks,
Sandy Kamen Wisniewski
Animal Education and Rescue

I sent the e-mail off and within hours a woman affiliated with malamute rescue called. She would do whatever she could to help Duke. I was thrilled. She accompanied us to the court dates and was a huge help because of the connections she had. It took a month for the man to get prosecuted, and the judge ordered that the dog be given to animal control. He was fined and told he was not to own a dog for 12 months.

Duke was finally free. He was sent to a foster home where he got to sleep beside his foster dad's bed at night, curl up on the couch with him in the evenings and romp in the huge, fenced yard with his malamute brother. His foster dad eventually adopted Duke.

Months later I received a photo of Duke and his doggy brother. In it, Duke, a vibrant, magnificent, wolf-looking canine, unrecognizable from the former Duke I had seen before, was comfortably lying on the snow-sprinkled ground outside. He was looking up at the sky, his eyes soft and wise. It was as if he was saying, *life is good, life is good.*

That was my first experience dealing with a case of neglect, and I wanted to find out how I could do more. I contacted my friend Beth, who had helped save Duke, and asked her, "What do I need to do to become a humane investigator?" She explained that a humane investigator is licensed by the Department of Agriculture. Having that license allows us to legally investigate people who are suspected of abusing or neglecting animals. She said I have to be sponsored by a humane society and the next testing was in eight months.

Thanking Beth I hung up and looked up the phone number of the Department of Agriculture. The Department of Agriculture representative said she would send me an application. Waiting for the paperwork all I could think of was being a humane investigator and helping animals on a much bigger scale. But little did I know what I was getting myself into.

Hands-on Education

The summer of 2005 seven volunteers and I arranged to take a trip to Pane County Humane Society for an educational field trip. Three of the volunteers were teenagers who wanted careers working with animals. Bryan, a sixteen-year-old, wanted to be a veterinarian. Maggie, the teen volunteer who helped me save the rabbit that had been injured, also wanted to be a veterinarian. Fifteen-year-old Lori wanted to work for a humane society or other animal-related non-profit. All three kids had spent a year or more volunteering for AEAR. They helped take care of the rabbits on my porch, the dogs I was fostering, as well as helped me during special events. In addition to the three teens, there was Molly, the foster mom extraordinaire, and Sheryl, the volunteer that had fostered Sadie, the dog that sadly died in her home.

This trip was the first one where I was the driver. Before AEAR I never would have driven for seven hours on highways–no way, no how. I hated the speed the cars drove and the close proximity they were to my car. The highway signs confused me and I always imagined myself getting in a horrible car accident. But with this very important mission, the drive was a piece of cake. I noted that small feat as one more little, unexpected blessing AEAR bestowed on me.

Arriving at the hotel we found our rooms and got ready for bed.

I was sharing a room with Molly and Sheryl while the kids had their own room. Molly and Sheryl promptly fell asleep. Unable to sleep I tiptoed out of the room and knocked on the kids' door. I spent a while with them just hanging out and enjoying their young-persons energy.

The following morning we woke up at 5:00 a.m. Bleary-eyed we shuffled out of the hotel and to a restaurant in town where we shoved down some food before heading to the shelter. Arriving at 6:30 a.m. we were greeted warmly by Executive Director Michelle. It was nice seeing her again.

The shelter's staff was sending some dogs to other rescues and shelters where they would have a better chance for adoption and were furiously preparing dogs for their transport. Crate after crate was crammed into an old, rusty, was-white-once cargo van. Dogs loaded inside it was amazing to see what small spaces the dogs could fit in. At first I thought it was cruel to put the dogs in such small crates, but after thinking about it I rationalized that the alternative of not going was far worse and besides it was just a day in the rest of their lives.

After the van was loaded with dogs and headed off Michelle turned her attention to us. Our first job, she told us, was going to be to clean all the cat cages. We followed her to the cat room, lined from floor to ceiling with cats, in addition to cats in the center of the room. The top and face-level cages had one to three adult cats in them. The chest-level cages had moms and kittens, and the lower-level cages had dozens of kittens crammed in them. The number of cats was no different than last time I was there.

Michelle tied her fluffy, blond hair back with a red bandana, her trademark red lipstick freshly applied, and she turned her attention to the room at hand. She demonstrated how we would empty out the litter boxes in the oversized garbage can, soak the litter box in the water-filled, raised bathtub, wipe down each cage from top to bottom, including the bars, fill up a clean litter box with litter and add fresh, dry food and fresh water. "Please make sure you all wipe down the cages good. The cages must be very clean and tidy," she explained. "Here are extra rags." She pointed at shelves stocked from floor to ceiling with tattered rags and towels of all shapes and sizes. The day had just begun and Michelle already seemed stressed out and frazzled. With a brief smile she left us to get to work.

We split up and began cleaning cages. It was a daunting task. As we scrubbed and dumped and filled I felt as if we were going in warp speed. Michelle periodically checked in and more than once pointed out our less than perfect cleaning job. She was furiously busy getting ready for when the shelter doors would open at noon. She wanted everything perfect before the first person walked in. I quickly realized what a perfectionist Michelle was and that it was necessary we adhere to her expectations.

All the adult cats, while in small cages and many doubled up, seemed healthy enough. It was obvious they were used to the tight quarters and seemed as adjusted as they could be, considering. Most of the kittens on the other hand were in awful shape. There was a cage that was two and a half feet by one and a half feet filled with sick kittens. Their eyes had whitish-gray gook oozing from them and their noses were thick with mucus. They were all between six and eight weeks old and were hanging their heads low and meowing desperately and painfully to us, each other, and to the universe itself. It was beyond heartbreaking.

Very concerned, I found Michelle scrubbing down a countertop and told her about the sick kittens. Shaking her head slowly she sadly said, "Honey, I know they're sick. There really isn't much we can do."

"The volunteers are pretty upset about it. Is there anything at all we can do to help?"

"Well, honey" she said, looking slowly away. She paused in thought. "You all could give them this medication we have and you never know, it could bring one or two around." I followed her over to beat-up, makeshift kitchen cabinets where she pulled a bottle of medicine out. She found a box of injection needles. "Have you given injections before?" I had because we do our own vaccinations for our foster animals.

"Can you show our teen volunteers, though? A couple of them would like to be veterinarians and it would be a good experience."

"Sure, honey," she answered. She took a sick kitten out of the cage. I quickly gathered the kids together and around Michelle and told them to watch her give the injection. Michelle patiently showed them how to give an injection and then handed me the bottle of medication. She whispered to me, "Please only use it on the ones that look like they might make it. It's very expensive." I nodded my head and mouthed "thank you."

I knew then and there that Michelle was allowing us to give the kittens medication to make us feel like we were doing something to help, not because it would likely help them. Later that day when I caught her alone and thanked her for allowing us to give medication to some of the kittens she said to me, "Okay, hon', that's okay. But you know..." She paused. "There is no place for those kittens. They come here in bucket loads, just dumped. And really it's a death sentence." She shook her head in sadness. "The folks that bring us these kittens, they think, *I'll just drop these kittens off and my cats will just breed some more and then when those kittens are born I'll just drop them off again.* It never ends. I'm sorry, I really am. I don't mean to complain." She paused. "But you know we must keep going." She breathed in and let her breath out slowly. "I'm sorry, hon. It's just hard. I don't mean to dump on you."

"You're not," I replied. "I don't know how you do this. I couldn't. You are very brave."

She laughed. "I don't know about brave. Stupid maybe, but who else will do it if I don't?" She was running on a flicker of light close to burning out. My heart went out to her.

Of the three teens Bryan felt the most confident about giving the injections. He injected one kitten after another, gaining confidence as he worked. He wiped each kitten's eyes and nose and tenderly worked with them. I saw a future veterinarian blossom. I was so proud to be part of his learning experience. He handled his task with a soft, gentle, professional dignity. I knew someday I would see him handle himself in the same manner with his patients when he became a veterinarian.

There was one kitten in particular that makes my whole body ache when I think of her. She was a smoky gray kitten, maybe seven or eight weeks old. She sat in the cage gasping for air, her mouth opened and closed like a fish caught and lying in a boat. Her eyes showed little else other than pain and fear as her chest heaved in and out. I picked her up and brought her over to Molly. "Molly, look at this kitten. She is suffering. There is nothing we can do for her. I feel horrible."

"Here, I'll take her," she said, taking her from my hand. Standing there she talked to and stroked the sick kitten. Watching her do this for over 15 minutes, as I kept busy working, I knew what she was doing was something the small staff here never could have done. I knew, too, that we were seeing the true impact of the reality of not spaying and neutering.

As I watched Molly give attention to the kitten part of me wanted to tell her that she needed to put the kitten back, that we didn't have time for that, that we had to think about the ones who could be saved and that there was too much work to do. I wanted to tell her that to truly understand what these people in this rural shelter go through on a daily basis we must experience it as it is, not how we wish it to be. But I didn't. Instead after some time I approached Molly and said I was taking the kitten to Michelle.

"This kitten is very sick, Michelle. I think she's suffering," I told Michelle after finding her in her office.

"I'll take her," she said, taking her from me. She quickly went into the back. I knew what she was doing and it was for the best. That kitten suffered enough. If only people who dump their kittens could be forced to spend a week at the shelter maybe they'd be more responsible.

Nearing 11:30 a.m. we were close to finishing our cleaning of the cat area when Michelle came to me and said, "You all need to hurry along with this. We have to open by noon and there are still all the dogs to tend to."

"We're working as fast as we can. I'm sorry." I felt like we were more of a nuisance than a help. "How do you do this with just two people?"

"We have a routine that we do every day so it goes by quickly. You just don't know our routine. It's fine. You're all doing great, hon', great. Just finish up and we have to get the dog cages cleaned."

After finishing up cleaning the cat area we all felt pretty awful about the situation with the kittens. Further, we didn't have any time to play with or exercise the cats so they stayed in their small cages. The volunteers all looked exhausted and it was only 12:30. And to think Michelle and only one other worker did what we did plus everything else every day.

We began taking dogs out of carriers and for short walks on the grass out front. Many of the dogs had urine or feces in their cages because they were only walked twice a day. Most of the dogs seemed shell shocked, confused and stressed.

Bryan took a little, white dog with brown patches out of her cage. She looked like a Chihuahua mix. The first thing he noticed was small bumps on her skin. Under closer examination the small, tack-like, black bumps looked like ticks. Michelle confirmed that–notably unfazed by the blood-sucking buggers, and showed Bryan how to pull the ticks out of the dog with a tweezers. "Grab the head of the tick around either side of it, the part that sticks out, and pull straight out. Here," she said grabbing a small plastic container, "Fill this with a bit of dish soap and water and put the ticks there. They'll die. Then when you're done just dump the water down the sink."

So for a full hour Bryan, with the assistance of one volunteer or another, pulled one tick out after another from the small dog. During the whole procedure the dog remained listless and unfazed. Between short naps she looked up slowly at Bryan, eyes at half mast, soulful and sad. Bryan reassured her when she gazed at him. "Good, girl, good girl," he crooned. More than 100 accounted-for ticks later, Bryan bathed and toweled off the dog.

Checking in I asked him how she was doing. He informed me of the number of ticks and added, "I am supposed to save this dog. I know it. I HAVE to take her home."

"Bryan, your parents won't let you foster."

"I'm gonna convince them. She needs me."

"Okay, well you better work some magic because we are leaving tomorrow morning."

Meanwhile Maggie had fallen head over heels for a bright, multicolored, female calico cat. Maggie recognized the cat's feisty and confident attitude and couldn't get enough of her. She snuck many extra minutes with the cat and even brought me over to meet her. "I wish I could adopt her, but my parents will never let me," she said.

"Why don't you call them and ask? It can't hurt."

"Yeah," she pondered, crinkling up her freckled nose in thought. "I don't know, though." She pulled her red hair back in a ponytail, giving her something to do while she thought things through. "I guess it can't hurt. But we have to make sure she's okay with dogs because of my dog."

"Don't worry about that. We have plenty of dogs to introduce her to here."

It wasn't a busy day at the shelter as far as visitors were concerned, unless you consider the people who came to give up their animal or drop off one that they said they found. I wondered what the hurry was in getting ready for the public because only a half of a dozen people stopped in at all. I understood even more why rural shelters needed the help of rescue groups and shelters in more heavily populated areas–there were simply more people to adopt animals. But that was only one logical reason why there were more adoptions in urban and suburban areas. As Michelle told me on my first trip to Pane, "People just don't neuter and spay here. They just don't see the point."

That night we met Michelle and her husband at the local Italian restaurant. Scanning the menu I noticed there wasn't much for us vegetarians. It made me think of my last trip to the area and all the deer hunters we shared a hotel with. This was not an area that catered to vegetarians. We settled on spaghetti with pizza sauce and waited for our food, tired from our long day. Once again I wondered how Michelle did this day after day.

The spaghetti was watery and bland but we ate it, along with a tasteless iceberg lettuce salad that went with the meal. The red-checkered tablecloth was sticky and the smell of the musty carpet combined with a flowery air freshener was strong in the room. Silently observing those things I momentarily wondered if I was a snob or just an urbanized person, living in suburbia and used to more choices of restaurants and thus the businesses competing to make their food better. I could understand why the place I was eating at fed us tasteless pasta; there was nowhere else to go to eat pasta or pizza, so what did they care? Besides, this was obviously a meat-eating town and they were catering to the needs of those in their community.

That night we returned to our hotel room tired but having learned so much. Seeing everyone's wheels turn, especially the teens, I was glad to be the one to show them what a rural shelter was like. They are our next generation and teaching them about the overall plight of animals was one of my life's goals. I was confident that I had opened their eyes and given them an experience they would take with them and would learn from and apply to their future.

Maggie and Bryan were both on their cell phones, trying to convince their parents to let them take the animals of their choice home. I was in my room on my phone, checking in with Chuck and sharing with him our day. Afterwards I checked in with the kids, and both Bryan and Maggie had big grins on their faces. Bryan was going to be allowed to foster his little dog and Maggie was allowed to adopt the cat she picked out. I was so happy for them and grateful that their parents saw how important this was to them.

The following morning we left for the shelter early. We spent the morning picking out which dogs and cats we would take with us. I picked out two dogs and two cats that I would foster. We bathed all the animals, loaded the SUV, stuffed ourselves inside and headed home.

We stopped midway so we could all stretch and take potty breaks. Looking around at the volunteers, I saw the depth of the experience reflected on their faces. I felt a surge of strength as I thought of how these newly deepened people would spread the word of the epidemic of the pet overpopulation. I knew that showing by example and spreading the word from one person to another was the only way to explain to others how horrible the problem was.

· · · · ·

Each new day brought me increased challenges. One of the ongoing tasks that I was finding mind stifling was the growing paperwork, office work and phone calls. Nothing made me feel more like a caged animal than being stuck in an office shuffling papers and making routine calls. I was getting 25-30 calls a day. Following are dialogues of some typical phone calls I received daily:

"Hello, Animal Education and Rescue, may I help you?"

"Yes, um, I was calling because I can't keep my cat."

"Okay…"

"Would you take it?"

"Why are you giving up your cat?"

"We're moving and I can't take him with. The apartment we rented doesn't accept cats."

"How old is the cat?"

"He's 12. I had him since he was a kitten."

"We can't take your cat. A 12-year-old cat likely won't get adopted."

"I've tried everywhere else."

"Did you check with family, friends, co-workers or neighbors?"

"Everyone. I also have called every shelter. No one can take him."

"I am not surprised. There are over 6 million homeless cats. There are perfectly healthy cats and kittens put to sleep every day because there are no homes for them. That makes the chances for a 12-year-old cat in a shelter getting adopted far more unlikely."

"What do I do?" the man asked angry and exasperated.

"I don't know. Find an apartment that accepts cats."

"I can't do that."

"Okay. Well, we can't take your cat."

"Goodbye," he said in a tone that said I-am-angry-with-you-not-myself.

"Goodbye."

Here's another call:

"Hello, I am interested in adopting a puppy from you. His name is Tyson."

"Okay."

"Can you tell me how I go about adopting him?"

"Sure…"

Next:

"Hello, I found a baby rabbit in my yard. I picked it up and put it in a box with grass and carrots. I don't want it to die. Can you take it?"

"How big is it?"

"It's about six inches."

"Are its eyes open?"

"Yes."

"It's old enough to be on its own. Let it loose near where you found it."

"I don't want it to die."

"It's a wild rabbit, you need to let it loose."

"Okay."

Then:

"Hi, I have two cats I can't keep anymore because I am moving."

"We don't have room for two cats. They are too difficult to adopt out for us."

"They're really nice cats. I love them so much."

"Then you should try and keep them."

"I wish I could," she said, trying to sound sincere.

"Are they spayed or neutered?"

"No, but they never go outside. They can't get pregnant. Well, actually one did once when it escaped my house. She had six kittens. We found homes for all of them. But we're more careful now."

"Are they up to date on their shots?"

"Well, I was going to take them in, but then I found out I was moving."

"Sorry, we can't take your cats."

And:

"Hi, I saw your web site and I'd like to volunteer."

"Great! We'd love to have you."

"What kind of things do you have that I can do?"

"We have lots of different things. We have adoption events where you can come and help with the animals. We have a pet therapy program where we bring animals to the nursing home in the area. You can join a committee."

"That all sounds good. Where would you suggest I start?"

"Why don't you join us at an adoption event to start with?"

"Sounds great!"

Next:

"Hello, I have a dog I need to give up. Do you take dogs?"

"What kind of dog is it?"

"It's a black lab. She's five years old and we just had a baby and it's just not fair to the dog. She doesn't get enough attention now."

"I understand that but I am sure the dog will adjust to the change."

"It's really not fair to her."

"I would suggest trying to work it out. It would be far more traumatic for her to be given up, plus there are millions of homeless dogs already and you would just be adding to that."

"It's not going to work. I understand what you're saying, but my wife is just overwhelmed and can't handle the dog and the baby."

I paused and took a deep breath. "Okay, well, we'd need to meet the dog and then we can tell you if we could take her." *Poor dog.*

And:

"Hello, we'd like to adopt a kitten. Do you have any baby kittens?"

"What age are you looking for?"

"No more than eight weeks."

"No, we don't. But we do have two cats under a year, about eight months. They are very deserving and older kittens and cats really need homes. The very young kittens everyone wants. Would you consider an older kitten?"

"No, sorry, I feel bad, but I can't. I promised my children a tiny kitten that could grow with them."

"An older kitten would be less rambunctious and would be less destructive."

"No, sorry, I feel bad, but no. Thanks anyway."

"Okay. Good luck."

The majority of calls we received on a weekly basis were from people wanting to give up their cats. Secondly, were calls asking about animals we had for adoption. A close third were wildlife calls, such as injured animals and baby animals. Then there were calls from people wanting to volunteer. After that were a variety of calls from people asking questions about what we do, requests for speaking engagements and other miscellaneous calls.

Between the office work and everything else I was doing for AEAR I was putting in 12 hours a day. I just kept reminding myself that some day someone else that likes doing office work would take that over. Until then I would keep sight of the vision and deal with the tasks that needed doing.

Meanwhile a sore spot remained for Chuck as the state of distress our house was in continued to escalate. We bought the house as a fixer-upper and during a span of eight years Chuck had remodeled each room with love and care. Quite quickly all the years of work Chuck had put into repairing our old home were being destroyed by foster animals or our own animals because I was too busy running AEAR and didn't have the time to train them.

In every room there was evidence of destruction. Ninety-nine percent of the foster dogs I took in had some kind of behavior problem I needed to fix. Further, I always had to take the foster dogs that other foster people couldn't handle anymore. I was the last stop. They had nowhere else to go.

More often than not the dogs weren't housebroken, so our antique, refinished wood floors lost their luster due to heavy mopping and bleaching. That progressed to discoloration, scuffs, splinters and deep scratches. Then, thanks to Braille, chunks of floor in our living room were eaten away as we sat watching TV and Braille was bored. Ultimately the floors would have to be replaced. But when I broached the subject of laying down new flooring Chuck would say, "What's the point?" I had to agree with him.

The doorways and baseboards throughout the house were chewed and thus ruined. The kitchen baseboards Chuck had lovingly hand sculpted and nailed on the walls had beaver-like marks. Their demise made Chuck feel like a masterpiece he had sculpted was destroyed.

Chuck had refinished the front hall the year before starting AEAR, creating a cheerful and welcoming entranceway. By 2005, due to the litters of puppies raised in that room, along with the many, temporary foster dogs, the linoleum floor was coming up in sections and the sponge-painted walls that Chuck and I painted together that looked like a cloudy, blue sky were filthy and needed repainting.

Chuck's despair watching his lovely lady fall to pieces around him made me sad for him. But for me I saw all those animal faces in my mind, ones looking at me, waiting for me to save them. I admit it was an obsession, but I reasoned that I'd rather have an obsession saving animals than be cold, uncaring, selfish and superficial. I was changing lives, bringing animals and people together. I was saving souls in need, fixing them and sending them off to a glorious life, all the while meeting like-minded people who may not have shared my obsession, but they did share my vision.

The Animal Warrior Born

After eight months of waiting, Rita, Jillian, Cory, Molly and I, all volunteers at AEAR, left our homes to take a test to become licensed humane investigators. After the test it was a long six-week wait, but one by one we got letters in the mail saying we had passed. We were now licensed humane investigators.

And So It Began

In the late February winter of 2006 I received my first official call requesting our services for an investigation. The caller, a canine police officer by the name of Patricia Kelly, said that she recently saw a dog that looked like it was in terrible pain. She said it was hunched over and appeared to be leaking urine. She asked if we would investigate. She added that the owner of the dog was Mexican and didn't speak any English, so she suggested we take a Spanish-speaking person with us. Rita, age 27, was our Spanish-speaking investigator, so I asked her to go with me.

The town we were heading to was known for its run-down trailer homes, gangs and drug houses. Growing up in middle upper-class suburbia I lived in a safe and protected environment. In my neighborhood people didn't lock their doors. The biggest crime was a kid shoplifting a candy bar or teenagers driving their cars too fast. Kids as young as five rode their bikes and played outside well out of the eye and earshot of adults. I had absolutely no street smarts and was completely naive when it came to real crime, let alone how to spot potential danger. That day in February I was going to get a rude awakening–I would realize that becoming a humane investigator only had a little to do with saving animals.

Rita was driving and we couldn't find the address. I called Officer Kelly on my cell and she redirected me to the location. Before hanging up I asked her, "Do you think its safe or should you meet us there?"

"You should be fine. It's not too bad of an area."

Following the directions we drove to an industrial area where there were big, low, brick buildings with hard-to-read names of businesses on the buildings. We searched for numbers, spotted one, called it out loud and slowly continued driving down the deserted-looking area. There was an eerie quiet as we drove along. Finally we came upon the only house in the many blocks we had crept down, tucked in among the buildings. It was an old, small, two-story with a big window in the front and peeling, pale yellow paint. Rita pulled alongside the house and parked.

"This is strange. A house among all these buildings," I said.

"Yeah," she agreed.

We got out of the SUV and walked up the broken sidewalk to the front door. I noticed on the big window a sign saying that the house was condemned and the residents had seven days to vacate the premises. *That's strange,* I thought to myself.

Rita and I stood on the small cement stoop and knocked on the door. We looked at each other and then the door and waited. It was cold and windy and I was shaking uncontrollably both from the cold, nerves, and my inherited neurological tremor. After a minute or so we heard rustling at the door and it opened and standing opposite us was a very tall white man with no shirt on and low-slung, faded blue jeans. *This is not a short Mexican man.*

Rita said, "Hello, we are humane investigators and we received a complaint about the condition of a dog…" Just then an old, white dog hobbled into view by the door and lay down on an old blanket on the filthy, carpeted floor.

"My dog is just old," he answered defensively. "I can't believe someone would call and say I don't take care of my dog. This is nuts."

"Well, sir," Rita said in a businesslike voice, "we have to follow up if we get the complaint."

"There's nothing wrong with my dog."

"This is your dog?" I asked. "We were told it was someone else's. Does a Jose Ramirez live here?"

"No, he lives down the block," he said pointing. He was getting increasingly agitated. His eyes were glassy and a film of smoke seemed to surround him. The smell of musty smoke and dust hung heavy in the air.

"Hold on one minute, please." I took out my cell phone, turned away from him so he couldn't see my hands and concentrated my shaky fingers on the buttons. I dialed the officer.

"Yes," Officer Kelly said into the phone.

"I'm with a man right now that is not the man you were describing," I said, looking at the shirtless man. "He said that other person doesn't live here."

"Tell him you need to see his driver's license."

"Sir," I said, addressing the man, "I need to see your driver's license."

"This is ridiculous," he said, becoming increasingly annoyed. He pulled a credit card out of his pocket and handed it to me.

"He gave me a credit card," I said into the phone.

"No," she said firmly, "you tell him you need a photo ID."

"Sir, I need a photo ID."

"This is fuckin' stupid. Hold on." He closed the door in our faces.

"He's getting an ID," I told the officer, "but he is not happy."

"Too bad," she said not feeling bad at all.

"Something doesn't seem right," I told her. Just then he opened the door and handed me a driver's license. I read her the information.

"I'll call you back," she said and hung up. The man mumbled something to us I couldn't understand and again closed the door on us. I could feel this creepy feeling growing in my chest and rising up the back of my neck.

"Rita, I don't feel good about this." I looked up and down the deserted street. "Let's go back to the car."

"Okay," she said unaffected.

We walked to the car and got in and closed the doors behind us. I was starting to get very nervous. "That guy's creepy. I'm gonna try and call the cop back." I dialed her number and it went straight to voice mail. Thirty seconds later the phone rang.

"Hello?"

"Where are you?" Kelly barked.

"Well, he said something and closed the door and it was creeping me out so we went back to the car." Just then the door to the house opened and the man began walking towards us. "Uh oh, he's coming towards us."

"Get out of there!" she screamed into my ear.

"What?"

"Go! Go! Go!" she yelled.

I looked over at Rita and ordered her, "Go! Go! Drive!"

She looked at me like duh-you-are-a-complete-idiot and said, "What?"

Like slow motion the man walked to my side of the car and around to the front. Being frozen in place, I thought right then and there my life was going to be over. I was speechless and terrified. Appearing around the bend, with lights and sirens on, came the canine cop. She slammed on her brakes, flung open her door and her canine partner jumped into the front seat. She began walking towards our car with her hand on her gun. The man stopped and stared at her.

"Sir, take your hands out of your pockets and step away from the car," she ordered him firmly.

"This is so cool," Rita whispered to me. I looked at her and thought, *I do NOT think this is cool.*

"What's the matter officer? I just wanted to talk to them." He slipped his hands back in his pockets.

"Take your hands out of your pockets." He did. "I need to pat you down. Please turn around." The whole time I was watching this it was in slow motion and it felt like I had little needles pricking me all over. After she patted him down and found nothing she said, "You remember me?"

"Yeah, you were here last week."

"Your friend Ramirez, where's he?"

"He's down the block at 204," he said, cocking his head to the left.

"What's going on with the dog, Hank?" she asked.

"He's just old. Come on, I'll show you. I've had him since he was eight weeks old. He's 15, can't hold his urine. I love him; he's my best friend. I just want to share a few more star-filled nights with him."

Getting out of the car we all headed back to the house to look at the dog. The whole time I was still in shock. This could have gone a totally different way. I was so angry at Rita. She risked my life when she didn't drive away when I told her to. I was beginning to question whether doing this was a good idea at all. My kids flashed through my head.

As he had indicated the dog was just very old. He showed us the food and water and by no means was the dog abused or neglected. We thanked him for his time and the three of us headed back to our cars.

"Meet me in the parking lot over there," the spunky, blond-haired cop said getting into her car.

"That was so frickin' cool," Rita said to me as we drove towards the parking lot. "I just love this. How cool is this? Isn't that cop just so awesome?" As she kept going on, obviously pumped up, she pulled in opposite the police car and put the car in park. We rolled down our windows.

"That was awesome!" Rita exclaimed. She was like a cheer-leader after her football team won a game.

"That guy's a real loser," the officer said. "You know why I told you to get out of there?"

"No, why?" Rita said, totally enjoying this exchange.

"He had two aliases and had been caught on gun possession be-fore."

"You are kidding!" Rita exclaimed.

"No, I'm not. Hey, don't you guys have uniforms or badges or anything?" she asked, changing subjects.

"You think we should?" I asked.

"Yeah, they'll take you more seriously."

"Where would we get badges?"

"I'll get you a catalog." We wrapped things up with her and said our goodbyes.

Driving away I was mulling over how I would talk to Rita about this. I took a deep breath and began, "Rita, why didn't you drive when I told you to drive away?"

"I didn't think there was a problem."

"Rita, it was the police officer that was telling us to go. I need to trust my partner. Things could have gone drastically wrong."

"It was really cool."

"I don't think it was cool at all. I have a family, kids that count on me. I can't risk my life." I paused, reflected. "I don't know if this is something I should be doing."

"I understand what you're saying," she said instantly sober.

"You don't have kids and maybe you're willing to take big risks but I just can't. Once you have kids you have to think beyond you."

"Yeah," she agreed sullenly.

I had taken the wind out of her sails. But I wasn't sure whether she fully understood how much of a mistake she made when she didn't go when I told her to go. It made me wonder if I could trust her the next time. I also thought her fantasy attitude that we were in some kind of action movie was just plain immature and stupid. We were silent in our own thoughts as we drove.

Finally I said, "I have to know I can trust you next time." We remained silent the rest of the ride home. I felt like I had just crashed a party and told everyone to go home. *But*, I reminded myself, *this ISN'T a party.*

Finally home, I walked inside depleted and sad. My dream of saving dogs from neglect and abuse seemed too dangerous and nothing like what I thought it would be. It was dusk and I walked into the safe haven of my home, went upstairs and changed into my nightgown. I slipped under the cool covers of my bed, savoring the softness. Quiet and protected, I slept.

That first case slapped me in the face sharply with reality. My safe and secure upbringing did nothing to prepare me for what I was to face if I was to continue as a humane investigator. I needed to become street-smart and fast. In time I would become a new and tougher girl because even though that evening as I slept I chose to escape, I still saw the eyes of those animals in need, and my fear of what could happen wouldn't stop me from saving one animal at a time.

Lessons and Lainey

Lainey was 35 pounds, colored white with black cow-like patches, with some smaller, brown splotches thrown in for good measure. She had black ears with tips that rested very neatly at her temples and a black mask around her always-curious eyes. She looked like the kind of dog who'd be in a scenic landscape picture, over a cabin's fireplace, running through a field of tall grasses with her rifle-clad owner and ducks flying overhead.

Joyce–the woman whose mission it was to take dogs and cats from shelters where their days were numbered and transport them to the safety of no-kill shelters and rescues–asked me to do her a favor. "Would you be able to take a dog for just a day? The dog will be going to a foster home tomorrow with another rescue group. Her name's Lainey and she's a beagle mix."

"No problem," was my answer. Joyce did so much for us, taking the dog overnight was the least I could do. As I led Lainey into my house I had no clue that six months down the road Lainey and life lessons would collide.

The following day Joyce called and told me that the foster home that was lined up for Lainey fell through. Lainey wasn't too much trouble the night before so I agreed to keep fostering her. After a few days Lainey began to settle in and began to change.

Much to my frustration Lainey was completely clueless when it came to housebreaking. Instead of peeing in the backyard she watered my wooden floors over and over again, often times looking at me happily as she squatted. Each day she was more hyperactive than the day before. I questioned her hearing ability because she never listened when I called her, until I realized it was merely selective hearing.

By the following week, fully settled in, she was more obnoxious than ever. She greeted visitors with a two-pawed punch on their chest, *POW*, like a kangaroo boxing. This caused unsuspecting visitors to stumble back or be knocked down. In addition, her attention span was equivalent to that of a happy drunk after too many shots of tequila. Me, the major dog lover, was finding it very hard to love the exasperating, high-voltage, firecracker of a hound dog.

By the third week Lainey began to climb the five-foot, chain-link fence that separated one area of my yard from the other. After the first success she made a habit of climbing the fence each time she went outside, mostly to amuse herself, because as soon as her paws touched the ground on one side she was climbing the fence back to the other side. Luckily a 6-foot, wood fence bordered my yard–that she was unable to climb–but it wouldn't be long before she figured out that if she couldn't go up she would go under.

One morning I let her out for a five-minute potty break and returned to find she was no longer in the backyard. Running down the driveway I began searching the neighborhood on foot, then by car. I was terrified I would find her lying dead or injured in the road. Finally, driving slowly around the neighborhood the second time I noticed two young girls holding a dog by the collar. It was Lainey. When I pulled over and approached them, Lainey looked happy to see me, but just as happy to be with them. This made me wonder if she realized who her caretaker was or if she even cared. *I WILL love this dog,* I said to myself as I led her by the collar to the car, *even if it kills me.*

After getting her home and with her safe in her crate in my office, I went out back and found logs, big rocks and any other big item I could find in the yard and garage and lined the fence in an attempt to prevent her from digging out. Now without being able to escape, Lainey found the next best thing to keep herself occupied. Over the course of a few days she dug giant-sized holes all over my yard. (If digging to the other side of the world had been an option she would have found a way to hop with the kangaroos in Australia.) It took her mere moments outside alone for me to come back to another crater-sized hole replacing an area where nice, smooth, green grass had been. Not wanting my yard completely destroyed, I resorted to staying outside with her, which cramped my already hectic schedule even further. Meanwhile each day I chanted to myself, *I love Lainey, I love Lainey, I love Lainey.*

Each day I checked my voice mail and my e-mail in the hopes somebody would express interest in adopting her. No such luck. Around that same time was when "Looney" was added as her first name and Lainey her middle name by my ever-creative spouse. It was also at that time I resolved to the fact that Looney Lainey wasn't going anywhere fast. So with no other choice I decided I needed to help Lainey become a better-behaved dog. I had to come up with a game plan.

I researched dog breeds and learned that Lainey, a "Beagle mix," was actually likely a Tree Walker Coon Hound. They were described as dogs that were bred to flush raccoons up trees. They are fun loving, high energy and stubborn. I read: "Give them a job and they'll thrive, but if you don't they'll find a job you don't like." Lainey was in a suburban home completely out of place and with a temporary mom who didn't have the time to assign Lainey a job. So without a job Lainey kept quite busy finding things to keep her always-alert self amused. I realized I could get her more under control if I took the time to set stricter rules in the house. I was going to have to work on some basic obedience with her and make sure she got more exercise. Hopefully those things would give her the constructive jobs she so badly needed.

Along with her new training regime, I decided to look at Lainey through new eyes. I noticed the way she bounced up and down instead of simply walking, as if she were a child skipping down the block. Periodically she sprang up in the air mid-hop as if to say, "Whoopee, life's grand!" I noticed the sweet relationship she shared with Timmy, a four-year-old volunteer who regularly visited the dogs with his mother. When Timmy came over he sat on the floor cross-legged and Lainey climbed onto his lap–far too big for him–which caused him to fall backwards, giggling. As if giggling was Lainey's cue to take action she pinned Timmy down and stood above him and bathed him in big, slurp-y kisses all over his face, which caused him to laugh bigger and louder 'til his belly shook. That, in turn, made all us adults watching laugh and laugh. This routine became a regular event during Timmy's visits.

Watching her play in the yard along with my other dogs I noticed Lainey's mouth was almost always open with lips tipped up at the corners in a smile. Her golden-brown eyes sparkled at every new object she discovered and sniffed in inspection. Each new person (or one she hadn't seen for five minutes) was greeted with a rejoicing usually meant for long-lost friends. She was about the happiest dog I had ever known, without a care in the world, and always, I mean always, looking at the world in a positive way. *I could learn a thing or two from her.*

With my new action plan and mind-set in place it didn't take long for Lainey to be much easier to live with. Still no one showed interest in adopting her. In our area Tree Walker Coon Hounds were not the most desired of dogs at that time. Most people wanted lab mixes, Golden Retrievers, poodles and little lap dogs.

It was six long months when finally one day I received an application for Lainey from a family that, on paper, seemed like the perfect fit for my girl. They had two active, young boys, a six-foot fenced yard and mom only worked part-time.

The day arrived when the family met her at my house. They were enamored with Lainey's free spirit and happy-go-lucky nature and thought she was "just beautiful." I was thrilled to meet people who saw the beauty in my Looney Lainey. I also knew my hard work was paying off. A date was set for me to bring Lainey to their home the following weekend.

As we traveled towards (hopefully) Lainey's new home I reflected on our time together. As I stroked her soft coat memories flashed in my head. Smiling, I remembered Lainey's unique skip-hop-walk. I thought about the holes she dug in my yard, still there where she had left them. I remembered her jumping up on everyone with unbridled excitement and her gentle but many licks showered on Timmy. I remembered her love of everyone and anyone who crossed her path. I cleared my throat and gave her a squeeze. She turned towards me and looked at me with love.

Arriving at their home the family greeted us with boundless joy and excitement. The mother particularly reminded me a little of a human version of Lainey with her enthusiastic energy and her endless optimistic observations. After spending a few hours with the family Lainey was settling in and it was time for me to go home. I gave Lainey a big hug and kiss goodbye. I looked into her mischievous brown eyes filled with happy light and ordered her, "No digging under fences, no climbing over them, no running away, no big holes in your yard, no jumping on people and be good to your family. I love you and you have a good life." As I walked out of the door Lainey tried following after me. Stopping her I said, "No, baby, you stay here. This is your home now."

Lainey's new mom grabbed hold of her collar and said, "Thank you, thanks for everything. She'll be in good hands, I promise. She's so wonderful, so great! We just love her!" Leaving their subdivision I wiped a tear from my cheek and sighed. *Life serves you lessons in unexpected ways.*

Breeders and Hoarders

Following is a column I wrote that was published August 23, 2005:

In the past ten years or so there have been many cases of neglect at the hands of puppy mill breeders and animal hoarders. The media loves to report those cases because they make a good news story. The public is understandably shocked by it. Animal lovers regularly ask me, "What is going on?" First, to answer that we have to understand who these people are.

The National Companion Animal Coalition defines a puppy mill as a high-volume, substandard dog breeding operation, which sells purebred or mixed-breed dogs to unsuspecting buyers. Characteristics common to puppy mills include: substandard health and/or environment issues; substandard animal care, treatment and/or socialization; substandard breeding practices that lead to genetic defects or hereditary disorders; and erroneous or falsified certificates of registration, pedigree, and/or genetic background.

Pet stores receive the highest number of puppies from puppy mills. This makes perfect sense because reputable breeders would not sell their puppies to a pet store because they want to know who buys each of their dogs. The puppy mill breeders consider the animals as objects–not living, breathing, and feeling animals. They couldn't care less where their dogs go or if they are bred as long as they are paid.

Sadly the breeding females are housed in poor quality and small quarters often times never or rarely leaving their cages. The idea is to mass-produce puppies. The more dogs they can fit per square foot of space the more money ultimately they will make. When the puppies are six to eight weeks old they are sold to pet stores and the females are bred again. These places are literally factories for canines.

According to Illinois law an animal hoarder is defined as someone who has more than the typical number of companion animals, has an inability to provide even minimal standards of nutrition, sanitation, shelter and veterinary care, with this neglect often resulting in starvation, illness and death. They are in denial of the inability to provide this minimum care and the impact of that failure on the animals, the household, and human occupants of the dwelling. Hoarders are people who keep too many animals and the conditions of the animals deteriorate because their caretakers do not have the ability or the means to care for their increasing number of animals.

Hoarders become hoarders for various reasons. Some never get their animals fixed–maybe they thought it would be neat to see puppies or kittens born or maybe they couldn't afford to sterilize their pet and the numbers increased. Maybe they don't get their animals spayed or neutered and the animal runs away or is allowed to roam the neighborhood and mate with another unaltered pet, thus producing more animals over and over. Maybe they get animals that are being given away in the newspaper or by people they know. Some people are even able to convince shelters or rescue organizations to let them adopt animals.

Hoarders develop an unhealthy attachment to their animals and largely are oblivious to the lack of care they are able to give their increasing number of animals. People who hoard animals are obviously mentally unstable. We had a case where a woman had 23 cats at her house. After we developed a positive relationship with her she confided in us that her daughter had died a few years back from cancer and she was filling that void with cats. Upon that realization she was able to seek help and is now assisting us in rounding up and spaying and neutering stray cats in her area. That case is not typical though.

There was a case not long ago in a town neighboring mine where it was reported that a woman and her two teenage children had over 150 cats living in their home. When the police and animal control were called to deal with the problem they found dozens of sick and injured cats. To make matters worse they found dead cats in couch cushions and underneath couches and tables. That woman was obviously mentally ill. Should she be jailed? How would jail help her to never do something like that again? Mandatory counseling, educational classes and fines, along with ongoing checks of her property would make more sense to me.

Both hoarders and puppy mill breeders have way too many animals, in poor conditions. The animals are suffering and there are often violations of many ordinances and laws. BUT the difference between them to me is clear. The hoarder wants to keep the animals because, though sick as it is, they love them, while the puppy mill breeder has the animals strictly for the money.

Puppy mill breeders are greedy, cruel and sick. Their motivation is to make money, no matter the cost to the animals. Someone like that lacks a moral conscience. Someone like that should spend some time in jail. They should know what it feels like to be caged. A judge should also order that they couldn't breed dogs anymore. They too should receive mandatory counseling, educational programs and be fined.

Whether a puppy mill breeder or a hoarder, animals are suffering because of human greed, sickness and ignorance. It is vital that we educate the general pubic, create stricter laws to protect animals, and as human beings with a higher brainpower, use what was given us by saying we insist on change and we will not tolerate abuse and neglect of animals.

Saving Grace

Constance, a 66-year-old dog rescuer who lived in rural Missouri, contacted Joyce about an urgent situation. There was a dog hoarder in her area that was threatening to shoot the 49 dogs she had in the head. That was unusual for a hoarder but a threat taken very seriously. Constance had arranged a way to get the dogs out of the situation but needed somewhere for them to go.

Joyce contacted all the shelters and rescue groups she knew and by some miracle found placement for all 49 dogs. But the miracle wouldn't end there. In time a bigger miracle would happen, one that would change the life of a little boy and his family forever, and that miracle would come in the form of Grace.

The day of the transport seemed to go without a hitch and all the dogs were safe. Joyce went home relieved it went well. But the next morning she received a call from the humane society in Chicago that took 11 of the dogs. All of the dogs had mange, a contagious skin condition. They told Joyce she could either, "Pick the dogs up and find another place for them to go or we will euthanize them." Joyce called me for help.

I was furious that the humane society would put Joyce in that kind of position. She was just the transporter and now she would have to make the decision whether those dogs would live or die. "Don't worry,"

I told a panicked Joyce, "let me see what I can do." I called the animal hospital we were affiliated with and they agreed to allow us to board the dogs until foster homes could be found. It would cost $10.00 per dog per day, plus whatever medical treatment they needed. It was the best I could do.

Joyce was relieved to find a place for the dogs to go but that did not come without a price. We could not afford to pay for their boarding or care so Joyce was prepared to cover the expenses. I felt horrible for her but admired her intense moral obligation to make sure the dogs she transported were safe.

All 11 dogs made it safely to the animal hospital and started treatment for their skin condition immediately. Within a month Joyce found placement for eight of the dogs at other shelters and rescue organizations. That left us with Tara, a shepherd mix, Kelly, a five-month-old black lab mix and finally Grace, an eight-month-old, leggy black lab mix.

After a little over a month I had an opening, so I took Tara. The following week Joyce took in Kelly. Try as I might I couldn't find anywhere for Grace to go. The poor dog was living at a boarding facility for over two months. That wasn't good for any dog.

Occasionally I got reports about Gracie from the staff at the animal hospital. It usually started out nice. "She's a sweet dog." I learned to wait for the "but she pees and poos all over her cage." They said it didn't matter whether they had her in a small crate or a full run, she always walked, lay in or played in her waste. I just *KNEW* I would end up being the one to have to foster that dog. It seemed to always happen that way.

Finally Tara and Jessie, my two foster dogs, got adopted and I could no longer avoid the inevitable. Besides, I felt horrible that she had spent so much time in a kennel, in a stressful environment, with limited attention. So on a sunny, windy, spring day I picked up Gracie and brought her home.

Gracie settled into my office and the routine I had set up for all my foster dogs. She was an adorable and sweet, young lab mix with legs that looked like they belonged on a Greyhound or Great Dane, instead of a lab. But as I was warned she regularly shared her crate with smeared, loose poop and pee. That was NOT going to continue.

I figured out that Gracie needed to pee and poo immediately after she ate a meal. Because I had so many animals to feed at a time I couldn't possibly make it back in time to rush her outside directly after she ate. So I began feeding Gracie outside on the deck and it worked like a charm. After a week of that routine Gracie could be fed inside and no longer went potty in her crate.

A few weeks passed and I received a call from a woman who wanted to adopt a dog for her family. She had ten-year-old twin boys and a teenage daughter. I suggested Gracie. They came to meet Gracie and fell in love with her. Finally Gracie was going home.

Gracie had been in her new home two weeks when I received a call from her mom, Ruth. She wanted me to come out and work with her and Gracie on some training. I came by the next day and was met at the door by Ruth, a tiny woman who wore impressively high heels and a warm and friendly smile. "Gracie is the best thing we have ever done."

"Oh, yeah?" I said, following her into the living room.

"Make yourself comfortable," she said, motioning to the couch. "Matthew," she shouted up the stairs, "bring Gracie down. Sandy's here."

"Okay," a boy shouted back.

Matthew, a small and frail looking boy with curling, dark brown hair came running down the stairs with Gracie at his heels. "Come on, Gracie. Sandy's here."

"Hi, Matthew," I said.

"Hi," he said as he wrapped his arms around Gracie. Gracie's tail was wagging in slow, relaxed motion, calm and contentment in her eyes.

"Gracie looks great, Matthew."

"I know," he said, wrapping his arms tighter around her.

Ruth and I looked at each other and then at Matthew and Grace. They were quite a pair.

I spent the next hour going over training techniques and giving advice. Matthew had long gone up the stairs and back to play. Getting ready to leave I said, "Call me any time if you need me to come back or if you have a quick question."

"Thank you, Sandy," Ruth said sincerely. "You know Gracie is the best thing that ever happened to Matthew."

"Oh, yeah?"

"If you only knew what we have gone through with that boy. You know he's got a twin."

"I know, I met Josh when we originally met."

"Matthew and Josh may be twins but they are very different. Matthew has had a lot of, well, let's say, emotional stuff. Do you know he hasn't slept all night long his whole life?"

"You're kidding."

"No, and that means we haven't gotten a full night's sleep since then either. That's nine-plus years."

"Wow, what causes it?"

"We've been to every doctor you can imagine. They can't figure it out. It's been very hard. That is until Gracie."

"What do you mean?"

"Since the day Gracie came home Matthew sleeps all night long."

"Really?"

"Gracie's crate is in Matthew's room. At 8:30 every night Matthew says, 'Gracie, it's time for bed,' and then Gracie follows Matthew into his room and goes directly into her crate and lies down. Then Matthew pulls up his blanket and pillow right beside the crate and falls asleep and sleeps all night long. For the first time in his whole life."

"That's beautiful," I said choked up.

"Yeah, it is. We even sneak in around ten to take Gracie out one more time to go potty and Matthew doesn't wake up. Then we put her right back afterwards and he just keeps sleeping."

"That's remarkable," I commented, thinking back to all Gracie had been through. She had an invisible string from her heart to that boy's heart. "She spent so much time waiting because she was waiting for her boy," I said in awe.

Ruth's eyes filled with tears. She cleared her throat and said softly, "Yes, she was." Then she paused in thought and added, "Gracie is our saving Grace."

A Barn and Pit Bull

In the heat of the summer of 2005 I received a call from a man concerned about a dog. He explained that while working on a farm repairing a roof on a house he heard a dog barking at an adjacent vacant property. Following the sound of the barking it lead him to an abandoned barn where inside it he discovered a dog tied to a pole. "I fed the dog my sandwich. I didn't know what else to do." For three days he checked on the dog always hoping the owner would show up. Each day he found the dog the same way and each day he gave him his lunch. By the fourth day he realized the owner wasn't coming back so he called us asking for help.

Unable to reach any of our other investigators, as a last resort I asked Chuck to go with me. Following the man's directions we headed out to the barn. The weather that day was sweltering, with the sun beating down, big, looming and unbearable. Arriving at the location we pulled off the road onto the gravel shoulder, parked and were met by the man who called about the dog.

"Hello, I'm Jerry. Thanks so much for coming."

"No problem," I answered. "I'm Sandy and this is Chuck."

"Hi," Chuck nodded.

"Hey," Jerry nodded back. "He's this way." Jerry motioned for us to follow him. Walking over uneven, patchy grass we followed Jerry to an imposing, run-down barn some 50 feet off the road. Walking inside I blinked and squinted, adjusting my eyes to the dim light. "There's the dog," Jerry pointed. Tied to a pole by a short chain was a blond-colored pit bull terrier.

"How has this dog survived?" I said, hearing my voice swallowed up in the large space. "It's obvious the only thing he's gotten is the sandwich once a day."

"Yeah, I know. It's crazy," Jerry commented.

Chuck and I slowly approached the dog. "I haven't touched him. No clue how he is. Just threw the sandwiches towards him. Seems nice though," Jerry said.

"What a good boy," I said sweetly to the dog. "You are a good boy. What are you doing here anyway?" He reacted to my voice with a fast and excited tail wag, the kind where the butt sways back and forth, too. Standing beside the dog my heart dropped. "Oh, Chuck, look. He has bite marks all over his face. He was probably fought." Chuck unhitched the dog from the chain and slipped a leash around his neck.

Inspecting the dog's head Chuck said, "Yeah, he has a lot of scars. Poor dog." He patted the dog on the head.

"I'll tell ya, people. I'd like to get my hands on the idiot who had this dog," Jerry said shaking his head. "Listen, I gotta get back to work. Thanks for taking the dog. I know at least now he won't suffer or die of thirst in this heat."

"Thanks, Jerry. Nice meeting you," I said. Chuck waved and Jerry waved back and walked out.

Toppled over within reach of where the dog had been chained was a can with some sort of oil or grease lining the inside of it. "I hope that wasn't what he was drinking out of," I said, kicking the can away. Looking around the barn garbage was piled up two feet high along the sides; empty liquor bottles and beer cans littered the dirt floor like confetti. "I can't believe this dog has been living like this. We better get out of here; we don't want his owners to show up now. With what we know they are probably very bad people. With dog fighting comes gangs and drugs. Let's go."

The dog practically dragged Chuck back to the car and when we opened the door he leaped right in. Once in the car the dog continued to wag his tail nonstop. We got licks and more licks as he tried to jump on our laps. I was so sad because I knew we couldn't take him into our rescue system. At that time we didn't adopt out pit bulls through our organization because they were hard to place. Besides that, because of the dozens of scars he had from probable dog fighting he was likely be very dog aggressive.

Making call after call on my cell phone as we drove I exhausted all of my resources to find him placement and as a last ditch effort we drove to a local animal shelter that was well established and regularly took in pit bulls. I knew some of the people who worked there, as well as some of the board members, so I figured I had a shot.

Chuck waited in the van with the dog while I raced in to talk to someone. Both the intake coordinator and the president of the board were in the front lobby. They both knew me. I explained what had happened and asked, "Can you possibly take him?"

"We can't, I'm sorry. We have too many pits already," the intake coordinator said.

"You sure?" I pleaded.

"Sorry." They shook their heads sadly.

Leaving the shelter Chuck and I drove to animal control knowing full well the dog would be euthanized as soon as they saw the scars. I didn't blame them; I couldn't take him either. They were just doing the dirty work, what they had to do. As I was dragged to the door of animal control by the dog I forced myself to close my heart just a bit. I had to otherwise I couldn't keep doing what I was doing. I handed the dog over without saying goodbye. I couldn't. No way. On the drive home I said to Chuck, "Even though that dog won't make it we saved him from ongoing suffering and that's something. Yeah, that's something."

Following is an excerpt from a journal entry dated September 22, 2005:

Nine months ago I was licensed by the Illinois Department of Agriculture to be a Humane Investigator. Most people were unclear what a Humane Investigator was so I had to come up with an easy way to describe it. I tell people: I do the same thing as the people on Animal Planet's television show, Animal Cops, but without a gun, without a bulletproof vest, with limited resources and without pay. We are kind of like DCFS for animals.

For me, these past months, doing investigations can be described as exciting, heartbreaking, frustrating and gut wrenching. One of our first cases was in McKain, Illinois, where we received a complaint about a boxer owner and amateur breeder neglecting her dogs. The complainant went to the suspect's home to see a litter of puppies she was selling. She told us she was shocked at the puppies' condition. She told us that they were "emaciated" and looked "near death." Animal control was the first on the scene and seized the three remaining puppies that were in very poor condition. The woman was charged with animal cruelty and would face court. Animal control also noted that there were complaints about the five adult boxers living outside during the frigid winter, without shelter. We agreed to work with the owner to improve conditions for the dogs.

Boxers are never supposed to live outdoors because their coats are way too short. After hours and hours of talking to the owner we were able to convince her to relinquish one adult dog to us. He was re-homed to a fabulous boxer-loving couple that I knew personally. We worked with the woman to improve the living situation for the remaining three dogs, and equally as important, convinced her to get the dogs spayed and neutered. We did this on our dime. While the boxers are still not treated the way I would ever treat my dogs they are in a much better living situation. I am very proud of what we were able to do for those animals.

Our most recent case was a situation where two dogs and two horses were living in a barn. A neighbor told us that the dogs were living in cages in the barn and were only let out of the cages once a day. It seemed impossible, but upon investigation the caretaker of the animals admitted that indeed he was only letting the dogs out once a day. He also admitted that the dogs did not receive water, except for the one hour of the 23 he let them out. The heat in the barn exceeded 100 degrees for over five days during our investigation. How those dogs survived is beyond me.

When we spoke to the owner by phone she was annoyed and did not see anything wrong with the situation the animals were living in. The dogs were filthy, starved for attention and panting nonstop. Their cages were rusty and the barn had absolutely no ventilation. The barn was dark as mud with only faint light coming through a tiny, dirt-covered window high up near the roof of the barn.

Illinois state law says it is not against the law to leave a dog crated for 23 hours, or horses in their stalls for the same amount of time. The law states as long as they have food, water, shelter, humane care and medical care then a pet owner is not breaking the law. But the laws are subject to some interpretation.

After over a week of dealing with both local and state authorities our local animal control spoke to the woman and demanded change in the way she was caring for the animals or they would be taken away. The following day all the animals were secretly moved and the woman was unable to be reached. The dogs' crates were taken as well, which leads me to believe they would suffer the same situation elsewhere.

It's extremely frustrating to work within the laws of our state because frankly our laws do not protect our animals well enough. We need stricter laws, ones that will end the suffering of animals. Personally, it can be very depressing and I spend some time crying in the privacy of my bedroom when it gets to be too much, but I believe I am making a difference.

I am proud to say we have been able to take many animals out of deplorable conditions and place them into new, loving homes. I try and focus on that and not the ones that suffered a sad fate like the horses and dogs in the barn or the pit bull tied to a pole. Every animal's face is etched in my memory; many of them we still get to hear about through their new families. We have not been able to save them all–those still haunt me–but the ones we did save keep me moving forward.

When I wrote that journal entry I meant every word I said. But what I didn't write much about was the toll that going on so many investigations was taking on me. When I became a licensed humane investigator I didn't factor in the amount of hours that would be necessary to properly conduct investigations. Naively I thought, okay, you go on an investigation, fix the problem and then go home.

In all reality it's not that simple. Each investigation takes hours of time. If you are lucky you catch the suspect the first time you knock on their door. But more often you are going to the house numerous times before you catch the person at home. Then you likely have to follow up on the investigation, making sure they comply with what they need to do to be within the law. Then finally I have the dreaded paperwork, which is essential to complete for each investigation.

Also, although there were five humane investigators, the other investigators were rarely available and if they were they went to a home once with me, sticking me with doing the follow ups and often times the paperwork. Because there were always two of us doing an investigation (for safety reasons) I went on almost every single investigation.

Meanwhile I was still trying to juggle raising two teenagers, running a full-time non-profit and caring for my personal animals. My house was in constant disarray and in need of cleaning. But the floors never cried, begged or whined when they weren't washed, the laundry lay quietly waiting and the dust balls could be ignored, so my house cleaning was the lowest priority. But that didn't stop any of us from wishing our house was cleaner and better organized.

I stopped exercising because of lack of time (except for walks with my dogs) and was beginning to see the dreaded flap, flap, flap of the granny skin under my arms. My muscles, which I had so diligently worked on building up by attending group exercise classes three times a week, were turned to mush. My clothes, well, they sat in my closet waiting for me to lose enough weight to fit in them again. One revelation I had: I figured out I was an emotional eater. Always priding myself in looking good I now felt like a middle-aged, frumpy old lady that always smelled like dog pee. (Or so I imagined.)

The most frustrating and upsetting thing of all was not having time to write. Writing was my love affair with words. I adored putting words on paper and making them come to life in color and depth. But with everything else going on my computer sat sadly waiting for me to come to my senses and create some balance so we could begin our relationship again.

To complicate things further I was always being stuck with foster dogs that had behavior issues. Let's be frank, when the going got tough for another foster home, the dog could get pawned off on me. The buck stopped at my door. I had the dogs that were the most hyper, most destructive, and to Chuck's constant dismay, the most un-housebroken. Our poor house, as Chuck proclaimed nearly every time a foster dog peed a lake that dripped through the floorboards, was going to fall down with pee saturation.

My children, ages 15 and 16, hated everything about Animal Education and Rescue. They were constantly complaining about the foster dogs. They hated the fact that the porch, once possibly considered being converted to a sitting room, was now home to dog and cat food, crates, litter, dog towels and more. Each room of the house had evidence of AEAR supplies. I tried over and over to explain to them why we were doing what we were doing. I pointed out the lives we were saving and the positive changes we were making. They weren't buying it. To try and appease them and to share time with them I spent one-on-one time with them away from the house, at the mall, out to eat, wherever. But no matter what I did they were very negative about the non-profit and what it was doing to our home.

I didn't think I was a bad mother for continuing to do what I did. I would not stop my work with AEAR because of my kids. *What kind of example would I be to them in the long run if I give up what means so much to me just because someone else wants me to?* I continuously spent time with them and they were always my number one priority. But I had a life of my own, too, and I hoped (and still do as of this writing) that some day my kids would look back on what I had done with pride and respect.

But during moments of weakness and exhaustion I would write that letter to the volunteers, giving them my resignation. That imaginary act made me feel better, like I had a way out anytime I wanted it. But in all reality my attitude remained steadfast that I would do what I was doing until the passion left me or my work was complete.

Labs and Phobias

It was the summer of 2006 and exactly one year since the last time I had seen the black lab in the wire cage inside the garage of a homeowner's sale I was browsing. I had written about the dog in one of my columns, the only time I ever got negative mail because I "did nothing to help that dog." That comment made me feel awful and that I was judged unjustly.

So in the spring, after I received my license as a humane investigator, I decided to check on the dog's living conditions. I wanted to be sure the dog had food, water, proper shelter and that his pen was clean. The words "you did nothing to help that dog" wouldn't haunt me anymore. But revisiting that lab would bring another fear knocking on my door.

On a bright and sunny day Molly and I drove out to see the lab again. Our intention was just to be sure the dog's living conditions were okay. We pulled up to the residence and walked up to the six-foot fence next to the house. I peeked over the fence and looked in at the dog's pen. It was ten feet by two and a half feet with a very small dog door that led into the garage where I first saw the dog. "How can a big black lab fit through that dog door?" I asked Molly.

Molly, much shorter that I, looked through the slats in the fence boards and stated, "It can't."

"It must because I saw the dog in a small, caged area inside the garage when I was here last summer."

"I don't know." She shook her head.

We headed for the front door and I knocked. Molly hung back behind me while I stood on the stoop. A slim, 30-something-year-old woman with shoulder-length, brown hair–the same woman I recalled from the garage sale–came to the door. "Yes," she said, looking suspiciously from Molly to me.

"Hello, my name is Sandy Wisniewski. I am a humane investigator. This is Molly." I motioned to Molly.

"Hello," Molly said.

"We need to speak to you about your dog."

"What about my dog?"

"We need to make sure that your dog has the proper care according to the law."

"Why?" she snapped defensively.

"Because we received a complaint."

"Who complained?" she demanded, looking around at her neighbors' houses.

"Sorry, I can't say. It'll only take a few minutes."

Silently and seething with anger she walked out of the house and in a huff walked towards the fence. She swung the gate open and snapped, "Here. What else do you want?"

"Where is the dog?" I asked.

"In the garage," she stated. "Gunner," she called. A big black lab appeared in the tiny dog door and squeezed through. He looked at us with dull eyes.

The pen had three piles of poo and a silver pail in it with an inch of water on the bottom. That was it. There were no toys, food or a doghouse. Making mental checks I went over in my head the different laws.

The dog had shelter in the garage. The pen was relatively clean if she cleaned up the piles of poo. The dog looked like he was in good weight as well. The water was low in the pail and dirty. I would point that out, but there was nothing by law I could do, as I suspected a year ago when I wrote the column. At least I could try and educate her.

"The dog looks like he's in good weight. That's great," I said, trying to develop rapport with her. She crossed her arms tightly over her chest, her lips set in a fine line. I wasn't getting anywhere. "How old is he?" I asked, trying to make conversation.

"Ten," she answered flatly, the underlying anger still very obvious.

"Oh, wow, he's older. You wouldn't know. He doesn't have a lot of gray hair."

She was silent.

"You'll just have to keep the feces picked up here. And he'll need fresh water." I paused. "Why does your dog live outside?"

As she shifted from one foot to another the steam might as well have been coming out of her head. *This woman has a serious underlying anger problem,* I thought. *What a piece of work.*

"My husband uses him for hunting. He's an outdoor dog because he is. We don't want the dog in the house and he doesn't want to be there."

"Really? Huh." I paused. In a soft voice I began, "Did you know dogs are pack animals and really need to be with their pack? Your dog would be much hap..."

"This conversation is done. I have nothing else to say to you. You can leave. What I do with my dog is my business."

"As long as you keep obeying the laws," I stated.

"This conversation is done. I am going inside to my child."

"Okay..."

She walked away. Molly and I looked at each other in surprise and walked to the car. I was visibly shaken. She was just about the coldest person I had ever met. I didn't often get angry but this time I was furious at her arrogant I-know-everything-I-will-dismiss-you attitude. "That was one of the nastiest people I've ever dealt with. She oozed anger. I can't pinpoint exactly why but she does. It's almost creepy," I commented. I started the car and drove away. A fleeting picture of the black lab coming out of the dog door, his eyes dull, brought me sadness.

"Yeah," Molly agreed. "You couldn't get anywhere with her. She was very, very cold. Poor dog."

"I can't believe she wouldn't listen at all. That's so aggravating that she wouldn't even hear me out about her dog. She just cut me off, didn't care, didn't want to hear it."

"Yeah. It's too bad."

We rode the rest of the way to Molly's house in silence. I dropped her off and then went home.

Moments after returning home the doorbell rang. I opened the porch door and standing on the stoop was a police officer. Without introducing himself he abruptly asked, "Did you go to a house on Greenwood today?"

"What?" I asked, trying to take in what was happening.

"Did you go to a house on Greenwood?" he barked accusatorily.

I thought back, confused as to why this police officer was at my door. It hit me, the nasty lady we just investigated, the one with the black lab. "Yes, we were making sure her dog was being cared for properly."

"What right do you have to tell people how to care for their dogs?"

"Hold on a minute," I said, completely surprised by his attitude. I wasn't some animal rights nut. "I am a humane investigator."

"I don't care what you call yourself."

"No, it's not what I call myself. I am licensed by the Department of Agriculture..."

"What?" he interrupted.

"Let me get my ID. I can explain what our job is also."

"I don't need you to explain anything to me."

I could feel myself become short of breath.

Let me give you some history before I go on with this story so you will see my perspective and how it relates to what happened with this officer. When I was 19 years old I had a traumatic experience involving a police officer. I do not want to tell you exactly what happened but I will tell you it changed my view of police officers in regards to how they deal with the public. What I learned from that experience was that the police could have all the power they wanted, whether legal or not, and they could do anything they wanted to you and get away with it.

Before becoming a humane investigator I did not realize that I would have to rely on police officers over and over again to protect me, if necessary, when I was investigating a complaint, or that I would have to collaborate with them on cases. Had I known that, I would have paused before going forward with the process necessary to be a humane investigator. But I am sure that my need to help animals would have superseded my fear of the police anyway, even if I had known.

After the incident when I was a teenager I developed an intense fear of the police. Whenever I was driving and a police officer was in his squad car behind me I would nearly have a panic attack. I would drive completely out of my way to have the police car stop following behind me. On the rare occasions I saw a police officer in public my heart would race. I felt completely and utterly helpless around them. The few times I spoke to police as an adult I found them to be cold, curt and rude. I often said to my husband that I was glad we had dogs to protect us because I would never trust the police.

So anyway, the police officer said he "knew everything and I didn't need to explain anything" to him. I felt like an enemy was invading my home. My knees were knocking.

But I held it together on the outside and said in a non-confrontational way, "I'll go get the ID." I raced into my office, wanting this man with the bad karma off my property. I felt my whole house becoming contaminated with him. I grabbed my ID and the booklet *Humane Care For Animal Act* and went back to the door. "Here's my ID." He took it and stared at it in a half-hearted way. "And here is the laws we go by." I tried handing him the booklet.

"What's this?"

"It's the animal laws. It might help for you to understand." This was my big mistake. Since then I have learned you NEVER tell a police officer they need to learn anything. He ignored the book so I held onto it.

"You could make up your uniform," he said, motioning with his head, looking at my T-shirt with the AEAR logo and "Humane Investigator" on it. "And you can make up an ID. This doesn't prove anything."

Now he was making me mad. *I can't stand police. Arrogant, pompous bullies in the playground,* I thought to myself. "You can call the Department of Agriculture and verify who I am," I said in a neutral tone.

"I'm not calling anyone. You could be a gypsy for all I know."

I had NO CLUE what the gypsy reference meant but it sure sounded prejudiced to me. "You mean I would take the time to forge an ID, make up T-shirts, create a web site, business cards, a phone line with voice mail, all so we can go to a woman's house to see how she takes care of her dog? And for no money? Now that wouldn't make sense." *I want this IDIOT off my property.*

"Next time you go anywhere in this town, to any resident's home, I want you to call the police so we know where you are," he said, wanting the ultimate control.

"Okay, will do." I tried not to sound angry. Without another word he walked down the stairs and back to his patrol car.

Furious, I stomped into my office and feverishly wrote an e-mail to the other humane investigators. Two of the investigators worked at police departments. Within hours I got responses from most of them. They were all just as angry at the police officer and felt an injustice had occurred. The two investigators that worked at police departments in the area said that I MUST write a letter to the Chief of Police. They said that the chief would "care how a police officer in my community treated me." They were right, I thought. I had lived in that town for more than 15 years, was active in the community and was a law-abiding taxpayer. So, taking their advice, I wrote a letter.

After writing the letter I felt better just getting it off my chest. While I was nervous about sending it I kept reminding myself of what the other investigators said. I hand-delivered the letter to the clerk at the police department. Two weeks passed and to my disappointment the chief did not contact me. Then one day I got a letter in the mail from the village I lived in, essentially saying that I was running an "illegal animal boarding facility." I knew this had come because of the letter I wrote to the chief. There would be no other reason, and the timing was more than a coincidence. This set me off in a panic. Could they force me to close my offices?

Keep in mind I had this irrational fear of the power of the police, and I was convinced this letter from the village was an extension of the police. I knew rationally that we were not doing anything illegal. Our pet sitting clients hired us to go into THEIR homes to care for their pets. We had been doing it that way for nearly 20 years. And as far as Animal Education and Rescue, we were licensed by the Department of Agriculture as a shelter, I was a licensed foster home and our other animals were all in licensed foster homes as well. BUT the paranoid side of me was terrified I would lose everything.

I spent two weeks jumping every time the doorbell rang, fearful a police officer or the village would be at my door. I wrote letters back to the village explaining what we did. Not convinced they asked in writing for more details. I wrote back explaining what we did in more detail. The harassment of the village took time away from doing good work and made me incapable of feeling safe and secure in my own home. I felt completely invaded, under a microscope and betrayed. I was sickened that I was the center of some vendetta the police department had against me because of some nasty, rude, unprofessional cop who came to my door and claimed to be king.

Finally after almost a month of back and forth communication with the village representatives they decided we needed to fill out a home business license. In the 15 years I had run a home business in the village not once had I needed a "home business license." *Come on now, how many people run businesses out of their homes without a business license?* I said to myself as I filled out their two-page application.

Shortly thereafter I received an official-looking home business license certificate in the mail. That whole ordeal was over. But I will never forget how it all started, with wanting to just make sure a dog was being treated properly. What it ended up costing me was more than a month of harassment from the people who should have been glad to have us in their community, doing something they didn't do themselves, making sure animals were being treated humanely.

I have learned a lot about police officers and about myself. Most police officers know little about the animal laws of Illinois. Learning the animal laws is not a priority of most departments because they prefer to concentrate on people-related laws. I know not to try and educate the police directly but to passively and in a round-about way point out breaches in the laws so as not to bruise their egos.

Since then I have dealt with many police officers. Some of the officers were indifferent, some were jerks and some were incredibly helpful and friendly to us. Some officers even treated us with respect and as professionals. But I'll never forget the officer who came to my door accusing me of possibly being a gypsy. He provided me a crash course on how to learn to manage my phobias.

I also learned a lot from revisiting Gunner the black lab and what came of it. I learned that I couldn't change people unless they themselves wanted to change. (Many times in the future I would have to be reminded of that.) And Gunner's owner didn't want to learn anything, or even open her mind to a different way of thinking. Coming to terms with the fact that many people are just like Gunner's owner would lower my expectations of people and cause me to just get on with what I needed to do–try and protect animals.

Here We Go Again!

The miracle of birth evaded us when Robin teased us during the long, drawn-out and emotional process of waiting for a natural birth that ended in a C-section. Fortunately it wasn't too long before we had the opportunity to try it again.

Beth, my humane investigator friend, called and said she heard about three dogs that were left alone for weeks at a time while their owner went on long, alcoholic binges. During those times the dogs were left in the basement with loaves of bread and boxes of donuts, a bizarre choice for dog food. Beth said, "One of the dogs is very pregnant. I'm planning to go to the man's home to investigate tomorrow. Should he give up the dogs would you be able to take in any?"

Without hesitation I said, "I'll take the pregnant dog."

The following evening Beth called from her car. "I have the dogs with me. The pregnant dog looks like she's due any time. Could you take her tonight?"

"Sure, no problem."

Hanging up I hurried to the garage and pulled out the baby pool, which would act as the whelping box. I rinsed it out with water and wiped it down. I dragged it through my front door and laid it down in the front hall, the dog's temporary home. I lined the pool with papers and filled a bowl with dog food and another with water and set in near the pool. I grabbed some clean towels from the porch and stacked them beside the pool. There was enough room for two chairs on either side of the pool. It was cramped but warm and clean. I doubted the dog would complain after the way she had been living.

I called Molly and told her my plans. She was as excited as I was. We agreed that I would keep the dog and her puppies until the puppies were two weeks old. By then the dogs that Molly was currently fostering would hopefully be adopted and then the mom and puppies could move to Molly's house until they were adopted. Molly loved the experience she had raising Robin's pups and looked forward to it again. Her most favorite memory was coming home and being greeted by all those wiggly bodies whining and crying out in joy because she was there.

Pulling my coat's collar up to shield my face from the cold wind I waited outside for Beth and the dog she told me was named Princess. Shortly, Beth pulled up in her big, the-only-reason-I-have-this-giant-beast-of-a-boat-is-to-save-animals SUV.

Getting out of her car, looking exhausted, she mustered a unconvincingly enthusiastic, "Hey, how ya doing?"

"Good, thanks, you?" I answered, jumping up and down trying to keep warm.

"Yeah, fine, fine," she said tiredly. I could tell how tired she was. That girl lived, breathed and gave her heart and soul to animals. I was sure she spent the whole day in the city, her only day off, to get those dogs.

She walked around to the back of her SUV. "She's really pregnant. I'm surprised we made it in time before the puppies were born."

"Really?" I said excited to meet my new charge.

"Yeah, I thought she might have them in my car," she laughed, opening the back. She unlatched a large crate. Looking inside, the dog, a hairy, tri-colored Collie mix, regarded us with spent eyes.

"Here, let me help you," I said, reaching inside the crate to help Beth. We lifted the dog out of the car and onto the driveway. I walked her to the front of the house where the light shined down on the sidewalk. "Wow," I said, stepping back to take a look at her sagging belly, "she is really pregnant."

"Let me help get you situated."

We walked slowly to the front door as Princess trailed behind, and we stepped into the warmth of the front hall. "Princess, sweetheart, this is your home for now," I told her. I closed the door behind us, unhooked her leash and coaxed her to get into the pool. "Go on in," I said, patting the blanket in the pool. Obeying, Princess gratefully climbed into the pool and lay down on the blanket. "Go home," I lovingly commanded Beth. "Get some sleep."

"Do you need anything else?"

"Nope, I'm all set. Thanks for dropping her off, Beth," I said as I guided her to the door, gently pushing her along between the shoulder blades. "I'll keep you posted." I opened the door.

On the steps she turned and said, "If you need anything…"

"I'll call. Thanks."

"Thanks, Sandy, thanks."

"Sure." I closed the door from the cold wind and turned to Princess. "Okay, babes, now you're safe to have your kids."

That night, Princess was comfortably situated in the front hall so I headed for bed. I set my alarm for 5:00 a.m. so I could go down and check on Princess. Falling into a deep sleep it seemed like just minutes passed when the insistent buzz, buzz, buzz of the alarm pulled me out of a dream that had something to do with animals but instantly was foggy. I stumbled out of bed and headed downstairs to check on Princess. Opening the door to the front hall I fumbled and bumbled in the dark, arms outstretched for guidance, carefully avoiding tripping over the pool, to the light switch on the wall near the front door. The light flooded the room and I stood there momentarily blinded. Blinking I looked down at Princess. Blinking a few more times my eyes cleared and I saw Princess lying comfortably in the pool looking up at me. "Hey, sweetie." Then I heard a squeaking noise coming from the pool. I bent closer and buried in her fur were two tiny puppies. I gasped with delight.

"You had puppies!" I whispered excitedly, bending down to take a closer look. She looked up at me with those sad puppy eyes. I petted her head. "What a good girl! Two babies. I'm going to call Molly. I'll be back." I raced to the kitchen phone thrilled that finally we would be part of seeing a mom dog have pups!

"Hello," Molly answered groggily.

"I went downstairs to check on Princess and I couldn't believe it she had two puppies already, all by herself. They're so tiny. I don't know when the next ones are coming but I'm sure soon," I was rambling. "So if she had the puppies recently then we could have an hour, otherwise it could be any time." *This is so cool!* There was a pregnant pause over the phone line. *I better shut my mouth.*

"Okay, well I'll be there when I can," Molly said grumpily.

Oh well, I thought, slightly disappointed, *I'll just watch by myself.* "Okay, bye," I said, deciding I didn't need her anyway.

"Bye."

I went back to Princess and sat in a chair and waited. The house was so quiet, my family and my animals still sound asleep. It felt somewhat surreal, like I was floating in the center of a cushy cloud with Princess beside me. Relishing in our cloud we whooshed back to reality when Molly quietly turned the knob to the office door and slowly peeked her head in. "Any more puppies?"

"Not yet," I answered instantly thrilled for the company. No need for apologies either way, we accepted our early morning exchange as just that, an exchange. The main thing was we were experiencing this awesome process together.

Molly tiptoed in and gently closed the door behind her. She bent down and first acknowledged Princess by patting her on the head. "Hey, sweetie, so you had two puppies?" She picked one up and brought it to eye level. "So cuuuute!" she sing-songed. "Do you know if it's a boy or girl?" she asked, turning the tiny thing over as it squirmed in slow motion in her hand.

"No, I haven't looked."

"It's a boy." She put that one down and picked up the other. "Another boy."

I looked at my watch. "Well, it shouldn't be much longer. They should come about every 30 minutes or so."

Minutes passed and all of a sudden Princess had a far-off look in her eyes and she held very still. "I think another one's coming," I said. It was very hard to see anything because Princess's hair was so long and shaggy.

Molly gently lifted Princess's tail. "Yep, it's coming," she said matter-of-factly.

I bent down to look. Sure enough through Princess's thick hair between her legs something was coming out. It was the famous "purple bubble" reminiscent of Robin's purple bubble. The purple "blob" fell out and Princess bit and tore off the layer of filmy, rubber-like substance that surrounded the lump, and as she broke away the cover out spilled a puppy. She proceeded to lick the puppy clean. "Wow!" I exclaimed, amazed. The puppy squeaked and cried and searched the air with his nose.

"Hand me a towel," Molly said with authority. I did as I was told. She picked up the puppy and began rubbing it cleaner. Princess looked on, totally trusting Molly with her baby. Molly turned the pup over and declared, "It's another boy!"

Just a half an hour later another puppy emerged. Puppy after puppy arrived, with mom cleaning up first and Molly cleaning and examining afterwards, announcing yet again, "It's another boy." By the afternoon we had eight suckling, noisy, healthy puppies.

Molly and I were both tired but thrilled with what we had witnessed. I felt Princess's abdomen to see if I could feel another puppy. "I hope she's done," I said with a sigh. "Eight puppies are enough." Just then another puppy slipped out of Princess. She barely gave it a second look.

Molly took the limp sack and tore it open. A lifeless puppy slipped out. "Oh, no," I moaned, "I think it's dead." Then I thought back to a show I had seen on *Animal Planet* about a mom dog that had puppies. I remembered what they did when a puppy was struggling to survive. "I think we need to try and stimulate the puppy and then get the stuff out of its lungs so we can get it to breathe." I picked the puppy up and wrapped it in a towel. Princess looked at me with bland eyes. I began rubbing the puppy vigorously. After a minute of that the puppy remained lifeless. I then proceeded to gently rock the puppy upside down and back up again over and over, trying to get stuff from his lungs out. Liquid spilled on the floor. "Oh, look!" I said hopefully. "Stuff came out." Stopping to see if the puppy was breathing I held my own breath hoping for the best. I looked at the puppy's lips and gums, which were white. "He's really white," I stated. I then put my lips over his mouth and nose and blew gently in is mouth. Nothing. "Oh, Molly, this puppy is dead."

"Here, let me try." Molly took the puppy and rubbed and rubbed. Then she swung it slowly upside down again and again. "He didn't make it." She looked underneath. "Another boy."

"That's so sad," I said, looking at the tiny puppy. "I want to name him. Let's see, um, how about we name him after one of the nicest men I knew, my grandfather, Nate."

"Sounds good."

"Okay, little guy," I said. "Nate, I'm so sorry you didn't get to live with your brothers, but you will see them again some day." I picked up a towel and gingerly began wrapping him up in it. "You now were officially adopted by Animal Education and Rescue." I set him down on the side. Later that night Chuck took Nate to our backyard, where he was buried.

The puppies settled in to a simple routine of sleeping, eating and crying. They used their tiny legs to swim to get towards their mother. With their noses they sought out teats, the whole while making grunting and squeaking noises. Then they would latch on. With a loud sucking sound and deep gulps, combined with puppy-content noises, they enjoyed their meal. Visitors came to see them and many people held the puppies between feedings. Mom cleaned up their poop, which was gross, but I was ever so grateful for it. After two weeks we transferred mom and pups to Molly's house for her to finish raising the pups.

Just a week later I received an e-mail asking us if we could take a yellow lab mix that was pregnant and living at a rural shelter in Indiana. She was in danger of being put to sleep. Hooked on puppy caretaking I contacted the shelter and told them I'd take the dog.

The dog arrived on a Saturday. She was an adorable, yellow lab mix with a faint white blaze going from her forehead to her nose, and a slight spray of freckles on her muzzle. Her hair was short and her belly enormous. "Poor thing," I crooned as I petted her head and looked into her tired, dark brown eyes. "You're safe, baby girl." She looked at me with a sad puppy-dog look like, *Ugh! This is no fun.* "Hum, what should I name you?" I said to her. "How about Hunnie? You're honey colored but we'll spell it a unique way so that it's different. How about H-u-n-n-i-e?" She licked my forearm gently. "Yeah, girl, that's it. Hunnie."

I settled Hunnie into her pool where she collapsed down into it and sighed gratefully, laying her head down to take a nap. I left her to rest and was excited about my new charge. Molly arrived and immediately took on the auntie role, making sure she was comfy with her blankets and offered her water and food. Before she left I agreed to contact her as soon as anything changed.

Days went by without puppies. I was starting to worry we might have another Robin situation. Hunnie was so big she was like Jiffy Pop popcorn after all the kernels were popped. I called our new veterinarian to ask for his advice. The doctor assured me that when Hunnie was ready to have the puppies she would. "Labs rarely have trouble giving birth," he told me. So I went about my days and checked on Hunnie a lot. I took her outside for short potty breaks but other than that she stayed in the front hall getting bigger and bigger.

Finally, on a Friday evening around dinnertime Hunnie was acting differently. She was restless and kept trying to get comfortable by digging at the blanket and newspapers in her pool. I called Molly and told her I thought it was time. Then I called Rita, our reformed-to-more-caution humane investigator, who desperately wanted to see Hunnie have her puppies.

I warmed my hands with a cup of coffee and Molly sipped on a soda pop as we settled in to watch Hunnie. In short order Rita blew in, and with exaggerated movements like she was walking on hot coals, tiptoed over to Hunnie and in a syrupy voice whispered, "Hunnie, baby, how are you?" She petted her head and squeezed in the tight space between the pool and my office door and sat down on the floor.

I decided I wanted to document the whole thing for a future film. My shaky hands always made any filming I did cause the viewers to be nauseous from the earthquake-like footage so Rita agreed to be the cameraperson. I showed her how to use the camera and she put it on her lap in preparation to film. Chatting casually the excitement hung in the air like a crowd waiting for a band to take the stage. Chuck threw some frozen pizzas into the oven and I declared it a puppy-making party.

An hour later we were munching on our pizza and Rita took Hunnie's muzzle, cupped it in her hands and looked into her eyes. "Hunnie, sweetie, I expect you to have your first puppy in fifteen minutes." We laughed at her command of Hunnie–as if she could be commanded–but to our astonishment all of a sudden Hunnie really started fussing and moving around.

We stopped talking and fixed our eyes on her. Rita exclaimed, "Oh! I think they might be coming!" Just then Hunnie plunked back down and stretched her back legs out and lifted her tail. Her abdomen contracted in a big push. As she pushed we looked down between her legs and a dark purplish-blue bubble started coming out.

"Ooohhh!" we all chorused at once. She continued to strain until the bubble was completely out, followed by what looked like a miniature-sized placenta-glob of goop.

Hunnie immediately went to work licking and biting at the bubble. We cringed, worried about the pup inside and, only speaking for myself, slightly grossed out. With efficiency she worked the pup out of its first home and the pup spilled out into our world. She licked it clean and then ate the placenta, a normal but nonetheless disgusting thing to watch. The pup, fully exposed and clean, looked like a little guinea pig with a tail. Hunnie nudged the pup with her nose, which caused the pup to stretch, squirm and open its mouth in a yawn. "Aw," I said, marveling at what I was witnessing.

"This is amazing! Awesome!" Rita cried. This was the first time Rita had seen puppies being born.

"Sandy," Molly commanded, all business, "hand me that towel over there." She reached out her arm in the direction of the pile of towels by my hip. "Hunnie-girl," Molly said, patting Hunnie on the head, "let me take a quick look at your baby." She picked up the little one as Rita continued filming. Molly rubbed the pup with the towel and looked at its parts. "It's a girl!" she announced.

"Aw!" we said in unison.

We went to task sitting with Hunnie and helping her have one puppy after another. I am sure we didn't even need to be there; this mom was fully capable. Frankly, we may have been even a bit annoying to Hunnie as she went about what nature told her to do. But Hunnie was soon going to show us she did need us after all.

By puppy number nine I was beginning to hope that she was done. I knew the undertaking it would be to care for nine pups and to also find them quality homes. After pup number nine we tracked the time yet again. It was well after dinner and the puppies were arriving every half an hour. Hunnie was starting to look tired and I was sure she was ready to call it a day. Twenty-five minutes later Hunnie got up, causing her nursing pups that were latched on her teats to lose their grip and let go. Like crickets singing on a summer night the pups began crying like their lives were in jeopardy. "What is she doing?" Rita asked.

"I don't know," I answered. "Hunnie," I asked the dog, "what are you doing?" Standing there with a worried look on her face all of a sudden she began straining. "Oh, no! She's having the pup standing up!" I cried.

"OOOHHH! Should I catch it?" Rita asked her arms yearning to reach under Hunnie.

"Yes! Sure!" I said urgently, and glad I didn't have to do it. Rita put both hands between Hunnie's legs like a quarterback grabbing a football. Her whole body and face was bursting with excitement. Just then the puppy began to emerge. "Catch it, Rita!" I coached.

Like a pipe clogged and being released the puppy plopped into Rita's hands and a rush of liquid flooded her hands. "Oh, my God!" Rita exclaimed. "This is so beautiful!" Holding firmly to the slimy bundle Rita asked, "Can I take the sack off?"

"Sure," I laughed, thrilled to see Rita so excited.

Gingerly Rita began taking the sack off the puppy, Hunnie nudging her nose in to help. We had read that after the first five or six puppies we should try and take the sack and placenta away from the mom because she could get sick from eating so many of them. Rita moved away from Hunnie's grappling nose and finished up the job of releasing the puppy. I held open a plastic grocery bag getting ready to take the goop from Rita. Just as Rita was transferring the stuff to the bag Hunnie grabbed it before we could get it in the bag and in one slurp sucked it down. We chorused, "Ewww! Yuck!"

Puppy number 11 happened half standing and half squatting some 30 minutes later. *Okay,* I thought, *enough is enough. No more puppies!* We wagered bets on whether there were any more pups. By then it was close to midnight and we were exhausted. All the pups were healthy looking and strong, all vying for positions to suckle from mom.

Molly pressed on Hunnie's abdomen and said, "I feel another puppy. Here," she said feeling a certain spot.

I placed my hand by hers and sure enough I felt a lump. "Oh, yeah, I feel it." By then there were bloody towels on newspapers and half-full cups of cold, stale coffee and empty soda cans. Discarded plates that had contained pizza sat in a tumble on the tiny table in the corner. The room smelled of blood and sweaty dog.

Puppy number 12 made his debut exactly 43 minutes after number 11. The tiny puppy slipped out of Hunnie seemingly unnoticed. He was limp and quiet, far different from the others. We were able to steal the goop from Hunnie and place it in a bag. The puppy was breathing shallowly, opening his mouth in slow motion over and over and his color around the mouth pale. Molly picked up the tiny puppy and began rubbing him to stimulate him. He moved his head around with great effort.

"He's grabbing on," Molly said. "He's grabbing on."

"Molly, he's having a hard time breathing," I said.

"How do you know that?" Rita asked, camera rolling.

"See how his mouth is opening and closing. That's not good." I grabbed an infant booger sucker I had gotten for such an occasion. "Here, let's try this," I said, holding up the booger sucker. I placed the tip in the puppy's mouth and squeezing the rubber hoped to get some gook out of the puppy's lungs. Not designed for dogs it didn't help at all. "Try giving him some air," I told Molly. She blew into the pup's mouth and nose, her lips a few centimeters from the pup's mouth. He was still gasping for air.

"Here," I said, reaching my hands out to the pup, "let me try." I took the tiny pup and rubbed him assertively and then gently put him upside down and then back up again, hoping to dislodge what might be in his lungs. He was still gasping for air so I tried breathing in his mouth as Molly had.

Chuck had come in moments before and he finally said, "Here," and took the puppy from me. He placed his lips over the puppy's mouth and nose and ever so gently blew his breath into the puppy twice. Then he looked at the puppy that was now breathing comfortably and handed him to me. "Put him with the rest," he told me.

I took the puppy from Chuck and put him down by Hunnie, who had been watching the whole thing. "Here, clean this," I commanded her. She nudged the pup's butt and then began licking him. Perking up even more he began crying. Smelling his mother's milk he swam towards the smell, his tail acting as a rudder. He pushed his way between half a dozen of his siblings, found a teat and latched on. He was half the size of his siblings so Molly decided to name him Junior.

Looking at the crew, 12 puppies all making grunting, squealing, sucking and crying noises, we looked in amazement at what we had experienced. The puppies were all shades of yellow and yellowish red, near impossible to tell apart. Molly instinctively kept placing any puppy that had wandered away from their food source back to a nipple. She laughed, "This is crazy. I am so overwhelmed." We laughed along with her as she kept placing puppies on nipples.

Reacting to our laughter Hunnie looked up at us with worried eyes. "You're scaring the dog," I teased her.

Molly patted Hunnie's head. "It's okay, Hunnie. I'm sorry. You're fine. What a good girl." It felt so good to just laugh. The tension was gone as audible sighs of relief passed through the room.

Cleaning up the dirty plates and cups I thought about the next eight weeks ahead of me. Through experiencing Molly's caretaking of Robin's litter and Princess's puppies I had a decent idea what I was in for. I just had no clue the big difference there was between Robin's eight puppies, Princess's nine and my 12. Not to mention the small-sized area I had the big family living in.

The first two weeks were blissful. Every time I entered the little nursery I enjoyed the natural music of the hum and squeal of the puppies. Hunnie enjoyed the company and she readily let me or anyone else pick up and snuggle her puppies. I looked down on the crew they were like a small island of yellow-dog, squirming with life. But by the end of week number two they were beginning to half toddle, half swim, which meant that the time of peace and quiet was soon to end.

The third week the puppies' eyes were open and at times when I walked into the room a puppy or two would be outside the pool, having climbed up and over the lip of it. The wailing and wailing alerted me to the dilemma and I would scoop the pup back up and put it back in with mom. Hunnie was doing a great job caring for her babies, but when they escaped the pool she just looked at the screaming pup like, *You got yourself out. Get yourself back in.* I am sure she realized with 12 puppies she had enough to do.

The puppies were becoming these adorable, yellow fluff-balls with wagging tails, the perfect commercial-making subjects. Applications for the puppies came pouring in when they were just two weeks old. Four volunteers agreed to take on the daunting task of screening the applications. Prescreened and approved families began visiting the puppies and picking out which puppy they wanted to adopt. By the fourth week the puppies were no longer staying in the pool, so I took it away and lined the room with newspapers.

By that time most of the puppies had collars on, indicating that they were adopted, and Hunnie was absolutely exhausted. She didn't clean up after their stinky poop anymore, so that job was left to me. I took Hunnie for walks to give her a break from her demanding family. She ate huge amounts of food because nursing 12 puppies took so many nutrients from her. What went in must come out, and I must say I hadn't ever seen dog poop so huge, more like the size of horse poo and over six times a day to boot. Also, the poor girl's underside was so heavy with milk that walking was a chore as her engorged teats swung back and forth. But lucky for Hunnie, when the pups were just three weeks old one of our humane investigators, Tina, and her family fell in love with her and decided to adopt her. She had a home to go to when she was done nursing.

Hunnie wasn't the only one feeling like they were trudging uphill both ways in the snow. Chuck and I were working on empty. Besides handling the everyday of all the businesses we ran, our household tasks and our children, we were taking care of 12 puppies four times a day. By four and a half weeks old they needed dry food soaked with warm water, fresh water numerous times a day and their newspapers cleaned. Plus they needed attention, and lots of it. The cleaning of the newspapers proved the most challenging–they pooped EVERYWHERE.

To make matters worse when we came in to visit they were so excited to see us that 12 wagging tails would bound towards us, jumping all over us after trampling through dozens of piles of poop and pee. We frantically rolled up the newspapers as they bit, clawed and jumped their poopy selves all over us.

The garbage bags were filled with dirty newspapers overflowing our garbage cans each week. Mornings were the worst. Waking up after eight hours of soft serve poo-poo being deposited all over the newspapers was not a great way to wake up. Oh, and the smell, well, I'm sure you can imagine.

The vinyl tiles in the front hall were coming up and the walls were smeared with poop. Poor Chuck was so upset. He had spent many hours sponge painting the walls in that room and laying down the tile. No matter how well we cleaned there was no mistaking it; the room was officially destroyed. We had to get a handle on things and fast. Meanwhile Hunnie continued to get more and more exhausted. She had no way to get away from the puppies so they were constantly on her.

One day, when the puppies were five weeks old, Tina came to visit Hunnie. I was working at my computer when Tina came out of the room and said, "Hunnie is so tired. I feel so bad for her."

"I know, me, too. There's no way for her to get away from her puppies." I paused and turned from the computer to look at her. "Tina, take her home."

"What?"

"Yeah, take her home."

"What about the puppies?"

"They're eating on their own. They don't need her."

"You sure?" A big grin spread on her face.

"She needs to be a puppy herself now. Take her home. Love her."

"My kids are going to flip out. What a surprise!" Hunnie was their first family dog. It had taken years for her husband Tim to agree to a dog and they had fallen head over heels when they met Hunnie. They had been visiting Hunnie on occasion and the family thought it would be two more weeks before Hunnie could come home.

After taking a picture with Hunnie and me, Tina led a grateful Hunnie out the door and to her car. I waved to them from the driveway, a lump in my throat. That night I called Tina to see how Hunnie was doing. "She came into the house, found my daughter Alexie's bed, jumped up, curled in a ball and fell asleep. She's been sleeping ever since."

Now that Hunnie was gone I had to find a way to clean the newspapers without the puppies jumping all over me. I also needed to be able to let them run around in a bigger area. The front hall was way too small now. I had three dogs in my offices, Tara, a shepherd mix, Josie, a spaniel mix, and Jessie, a Boxer. I decided to introduce the puppies to the foster dogs so the puppies could run around my offices while I cleaned their papers.

First, I let one adult dog at a time into the front hall to meet the puppies. Tara was thrilled and immediately took on the role of surrogate mama. But when they tried to nurse she growled and nipped. In no time the puppies learned the rules and loved having Tara as a playmate.

Next, Jessie came in to visit. She looked around at the mass of yellow fur like, *What the heck?* But in moments, after sniffing out the food, she was far more interested with their food than them. I lifted the food up and put it away and Jessie sniffed around for kernels left behind. Indifferent to the puppies I knew she would be fine with them in the offices.

Finally, Josie took a peek in the room and eyes huge and terrified ran the other direction and under my desk. She was a scared and oversensitive dog so I decided I would simply crate her when I let the puppies out of their room and into the offices.

Everyone introduced and situated I opened the door from my office to the front hall and chanted, "Puppies, puppies, puppies. Puppies, puppies, puppies." At the sound of my voice they bounded out of the front hall and flooded my two offices, their little legs like tiny drums on the hard wood floors. The adult dogs looked at them like, *What the...* as the puppies went running past them. It was a sight to be seen. It was like a sea of puppies bursting through a dam.

Going into the front hall and quickly closing my office door so no puppies turned around to follow me, I cleaned up all the newspapers and laid down new papers. How wonderful not to have to contend with the puppies! Meanwhile the puppies were busy exploring the offices. But quickly the puppies learned that they had a "cleaner" place to poop and pee and proceeded to do so all over my offices. It made sense. Dogs don't like to eliminate where they live so knowing they lived in the front hall they were more than happy to poop and pee outside of it.

So the four times a day routine was, let puppies out of hallway and into offices, let Tara and Jessie play with them, hurry and clean the papers, put new papers down, put down fresh food and water, go into the offices and clean up all the poop and pee and then call the puppies into their room. In no time the puppies would come barreling towards me whenever I called, "Puppy, puppy, puppy, puppy, puppy, puppy!" There was nothing like it–12 eager, wagging, happy puppies running full blast at you. When that happened it reminded me how lucky I was to have that experience and I totally understood why Molly had missed it after Robin's puppies were adopted.

As approved families came to meet and pick out their puppies I got to know some of the people who were adopting. The Duffy family consisted of a 50-something-year-old couple and their young adult kids. They were the first to pick out their puppy, the tiniest of the females. Collette Duffy, the mother, rubbed me wrong in the beginning. She would say things like, "Boy, they look like blobs. They have no character." (At that time the puppies were two weeks old.) Her husband Donald looked down at the puppies expressionless, with almost slight disgust. He wouldn't pick up the puppies and just stood there with his arms crossed. When I questioned Collette about her husband's disinterest that's when she said, "My husband doesn't get it. He doesn't see what people see in puppies that age. They don't have personality."

Concerned about the family's commitment I contacted Diana, the volunteer who screened their application. Diana was surprised by what Collette had said to me and said Collette didn't talk that way with her at all. "Maybe she's trying to get a rise out of you."

"Well, that wouldn't be good."

"I assure you they really are good people. Wait and see."

"Okay," I said, wanting to believe her.

The Duffys came to visit their puppy numerous times and over time Collette stopped saying things that made me uncomfortable and the family was growing on me. Collette and one daughter or another would come, find their puppy and stand and hold her. They also called me periodically to check in and see how their puppy was doing. While Collette's choice of words hadn't been the best her actions spoke volumes and I knew that dog would be in good hands.

I encouraged all the families to come and visit as often as possible so their puppies could get to know them, which would ease the transition when it was time for them to go home. Adrianne Carthy and her kids adopted Sammy, the largest pup in the litter. They regularly drove the 45 minutes from their home to visit him. I loved Adrianne and her kids from the beginning.

Adrianne had a smile that lit the room and a warm and loving heart. They loved the routine of letting the puppies out of their room and giggled and giggled as the herd stampeded past them only to run into the porch door, tumble over each other, realize they had visitors and come stampeding back to mug attention from them. They helped me clean the poop and pee without my having to ask, just digging in and helping, and once the dogs had settled down to exploring, they plopped themselves in the center of my cramped office and let the puppies climb all over them, biting their limbs, jumping up and licking them. I knew Sammy would be so loved.

The third family I will never forget is the Smyths, a family with three children. One of their children, Steven, had cerebral palsy. Steven had a hard time walking and needed help as he walked stiff-legged. Junior was still the smallest in the litter and had a bow-legged walk that made him look like a cowboy with chaps on. When the Smyth family came over to meet the puppies the whole family fell in love with a medium-sized, female, reddish-yellow puppy. But Steven's eyes were for Junior from the second he spotted him. He saw a pup that walked a lot like him and he felt something special for the tiny dog.

The family was in a quandary. They were compassionate to Steven, who could relate to the not-so-perfect underdog, but they had to think of the whole family. They left my house to think about it. They came back two more times to see the puppies going back and forth, unable to make a decision.

Meanwhile I took Junior to the vet for an examination and an x-ray. I wanted to be sure that Junior's bow-legged cowboy walk wasn't serious. The doctor took x-rays and said, "This puppy has as much of a chance to develop hip dysplasia as any other puppy. He looks fine." I was thrilled for Junior and confident that should this family–or any other –choose Junior, he was as healthy as any of the other pups.

The following day I received a call from Bea Smyth. "We just can't decide which dog to adopt. This is torture." She paused. "Do you, um, is there anything wrong, do you think, with Junior? He walks kind of funny." I could tell she felt bad even asking because I was sure she was thinking of the similarity between Junior and Steven.

"I took Junior to the vet and the doctor said that he is as healthy as any other dog."

"Oh, okay, well, let me talk to my family one more time. Can we come this afternoon to see the puppies?"

"Sure. How's 3:00?"

"Okay, see you then."

That afternoon seven people, the whole family plus Bea's sister Jane, squeezed into the offices to see the puppies. Standing very still so as not to step on any puppies they bent down, picking up one puppy after another. "Does anyone see the girl puppy?" someone called out.

"I got her!" someone else called.

"Where's Junior?"

Steven pointed, his face lit up. "There he is." His dad, John, bent down and scooped Junior up, looked him over and then cradled him in his arms.

After a while Bea motioned to John to come beside her. "We'll be right back," Bea announced. John put Junior down and they left and went outside. Five minutes later they came back inside. Everyone stared at them. Bea announced, "We'll take them both."

"Woopee!!!" everyone shouted.

"I hope we're making the right decision," Bea said nervously.

"We've had another couple who adopted two puppies from another litter and they said it was the best thing they ever did. Here," I said, looking through my database for their number. Finding it I found a scrap piece of paper and wrote it down. "Take their number and call them. They'll share advice and hopefully ease your mind."

She took the paper and handed me a check deposit to hold the two dogs. "You'll be fine," I assured her. "If I didn't think you could handle it I wouldn't adopt both of them to you." I thought what they were doing for their son was profoundly moving. The not-so-perfect-looking puppy was not the last to be adopted and the therapy that dog would provide the boy I knew would be beyond measure.

Finally, there was only one golden-colored male puppy left. A local couple came by a few days later and after only a few minutes decided to adopt him. They named him Caribou. The last step in the adoption process was for all 11 families to attend a mandatory educational program. I spent the next week preparing for it.

The following Saturday I arrived at the animal hospital to teach the first round of classes for Hunnie's puppies' families. Five of the 11 families crammed themselves into the lobby of the animal hospital. Eager faces looked at me, prepared to take notes and ask questions. The excitement was evident and pulsated in the room.

"Congratulations, everyone, on your new puppy." I smiled around the room. "You chose to adopt verses purchase a puppy so therefore you saved two lives." I looked around at their puzzled looks. "You saved two lives because by saving your dog we can now save another. Isn't that wonderful?" They nodded, understanding. I noticed at the corner of my eye a boy around ten years old fidgeting. Looking over I saw the boy's mom, Sondra–who was adopting a boy puppy they named Lucky–trying to get her son to stop moving around.

"Let's talk about housebreaking first. That's going to be one of your biggest challenges in the beginning." I went on to explain housebreaking in detail. Sondra's son continued to fidget, distracting me. I was beginning to worry about the puppy they were taking home.

Throughout the program the boy became more and more disobedient and obnoxious, whispering to his younger sister and scooting around on the floor, disrupting not only me but also everyone else. The parents were unable to control him. I kept thinking of the tiny puppy and worried that if they couldn't handle their son, how were they going to handle the puppy? But I assured myself that the family had been interviewed and prescreened by a fully capable volunteer and everything would be fine. After the program the families followed me to my home.

The families formed a line outside my house, and one by one they went inside and picked up their puppy and their medical records. Then afterwards they stopped outside on the grass, where Molly took a snapshot of them with their new dog. By the time we were done I was exhausted but relieved. Six more puppies to go. The following weekend the remaining families attended the educational program and our house finally was free of destruct-o puppies. We could now begin clean-up efforts.

Four and a half months passed and I received glowing reports about the puppies. Junior was now 60 pounds and surpassed his sister. Sondra, the woman with the unruly boy, kept in touch, sent photos and expressed their love for their dog. I was glad my fears about them were unfounded. But during a conversation with Annie, an adoptive mom who was hosting our adoptive families' reunion, I learned that Sondra was struggling with the dog she adopted.

"Sondra called and said she was coming to the reunion but she joked around saying when she came maybe someone would want to adopt Lucky."

"What?" I said alarmed.

"Yeah, she said that Lucky jumps all over her daughter and she has to keep them separate."

"That doesn't make sense," I said bracing my forehead with my fingertips, leaning over my desk with worry. "She said everything was great. I even have pictures of Lucky with the daughter."

"I don't know."

"Well, I'll talk to her at the reunion." *Darn. I knew that family was no good,* I said to myself. I was very worried.

The whole Carthy family came to our adoption reunion. Sammy had turned into an adorable, 80-pound oaf-of-a-lab that tripped over his own gangly legs. To Adrianne's embarrassment Sammy was also the only dog who stole food from one of the kids at the party. "He's a lab after all," I assured her. She laughed and shook her head.

At the adoption reunion I brought my foster dog Sadie, a hound mix with an independent spirit and long hound ears. She was six months old, the same age as Sammy and his littermates. Sadie spent the entire party hanging out with Sammy and Adrianne's kids. Adrianne and her children fell head over heels for the goofy mutt and within 24 hours were at my house picking up their second adopted dog. I was thrilled beyond belief!

Collette and her daughters came to our adoption reunion. The dog they named Nika was happy, well adjusted and spoiled and they all gave me hugs and took pictures of me with 40-pound Nika. I was glad to have not judged them too quickly.

Sondra and her family never showed up for the reunion. She never called to say they weren't coming, so I was even more worried. I called her the following day.

"Hi, Sondra, it's Sandy from Animal Education and Rescue. We missed you at the reunion."

"Oh, hi, Sandy. Yeah, we couldn't make it after all. I meant to call Annie but didn't get around to it."

"How's things going with Lucky?"

"It's been kind of hard but we have a trainer coming in that works with Plains Humane Society. Her name is Patty. She's coming over tomorrow."

"Okay, I'll check in with you in a few days. Meanwhile don't hesitate to call me about anything."

"Okay," she said.

I got the impression she wasn't telling me everything and I was worried. We had not yet made it a requirement that all of our dogs leave micro chipped–a tiny chip injected under the skin that, with a hand-held scanner, carries an ID number that tracks the dog's whereabouts. So if she gave Lucky away I might never know it. We required in our contract that any dog that was adopted to a family be returned to us if the owners could no longer keep them.

Looking up the phone number of the dog trainer I gave her a call and told her who I was and my concern about the people who adopted Lucky. She told me that they didn't seem to have any idea what they were doing and did not have the dog on any schedule.

"They are supposed to call me to schedule a training next week," she told me.

"They told me they already had a training scheduled."

"Nope, I just went out for an evaluation."

"Great, so they lied. They are hiding something. Can you call me if they call you or you hear they are giving the dog away?"

"Sure." I gave her my number.

A few days later I received a message on my voice mail. "Hey, Sandy, this is Patty. You know those people who have Lucky the dog? They gave the dog to some niece of theirs or something like that. I told you I'd call you. Call me if you need anything else." I was sick to my stomach. I had no idea where one of our puppies was and statistically dogs that are given away move many times and often end up at a shelter. The main reason that happens is because the dogs are often placed in inappropriate homes. I could have kicked myself for not micro chipping those dogs–or any of our dogs for that matter. (From that day forward each one of our dogs was micro chipped.)

Taking some deep breaths to calm my anger at that family I called Sondra. She answered the phone. "Sondra, this is Sandy with Animal Education and Rescue. Did you give Lucky away?"

"It wasn't working out. I gave him to my niece."

"You cannot do that. He needs to come back to us."

"Why?" she said, sounding annoyed.

"Because you signed a contract stating the dog would come back to us."

"But why?" she snipped.

Knowing full well I wasn't going to be able to reason with this liar (and I despise liars) I said, "Because that is how we work. That's how all rescue groups work."

"Fine. I'll take him back."

I knew she was lying. "No, you won't. I want him back."

"Fax over the contract we signed," she ordered.

"Fine, I'll send it right over," I said between clenched teeth, trying hard to stay professional and calm. "I want to pick up Lucky tomorrow."

Click. She hung up on me. "I can't believe she hung up on me,"

I said out loud. I was worried sick about Lucky but prepared to fight to get him back. I faxed the contract and called back. The husband answered the phone. I told him who I was and he said, "We'll bring Lucky back to our house and you can pick him up there tomorrow."

"I'll be there," I assured him.

He hung up.

The following evening Connie, an AEAR volunteer, and I drove the hour-long trip to pick up Lucky. The whole drive there I worried that Lucky wouldn't be there after all. Pulling into their subdivision I rounded a corner and recognized that boy from the educational program. "That's their obnoxious son," I told Connie. We pulled into the drive at the same time as the son ran into the house. He was going to tell his parents we were there. "Did you notice that the kid doesn't seem upset at all?" I asked Connie.

"I know. I really wonder what happened. Hopefully they won't give us a hard time," she said, getting out of the car.

Just as I got around the side of my car the father had just come out of the house with Lucky, who had turned into a beautiful, 65-pound lab with ears that were a bit more hound dog than lab, but otherwise he looked like a purebred yellow lab. The man gave Lucky's leash to Connie and turned and walked back to the house. Lucky hopped into my van without looking back and Connie closed the door behind him. I was so relieved to get him back.

Because I hadn't planned on having another dog in our foster care system I didn't have an open foster home for him, so he went back to the place he was first born, the front hall. I tried crating him but he put on the brakes and refused to get in. It left me with the impression that he had never been crated. So I left him with a dog bed and food and water.

The following day I introduced him to my other foster dogs and Lucky moved to my office. It was obvious from the start he wasn't housebroken. He would walk and pee, without even seeming to be aware of it. So starting from scratch I began teaching him about where it was appropriate to go potty.

Lucky turned into a real love with a tad bit of separation anxiety. He cried when I left him and at adoption days wouldn't be satisfied with anyone but me holding his leash. He attended my dog training class, where he got to see Caribou again, one of his littermates. Lucky and Caribou looked and acted very similar but because of Lucky's early childhood he wasn't as advanced as Caribou with either housebreaking or obedience training.

We thought we'd never find Lucky a home; his luck seemed so awful. Lucky lived with me for months. Having Lucky was a challenge because he lived in my offices, a perfect playground for a young and energetic lab to get into things. I loved him dearly but he often times tried my patience. He was a big galoof in a space too small for him. Volunteers regularly commented how shocked they were that no one had come along to adopt him. "He's the perfect family dog," they'd say.

Lucky's luck was about to change. A wonderful couple with a college-age daughter fell in love with Lucky's picture on our web site. They filled out an application and we spoke at length on the phone. After checking their references I scheduled a home visit where they could meet Lucky, and if everything worked out he would stay.

The home visit went as well as I expected. It was a difficult goodbye for me, more because I felt bad for Lucky, not because of me. Lucky was so attached to me I wished I could have told him that I was just the go-between, the one who took his paw and found the hand who would take his paw from me.

I said goodbye to Lucky by my car. I hugged him tight and said, "I love you. Now you have a good life." Lucky's new dad walked him down the block in an attempt to distract him from my leaving. I could see Lucky looking after me through my rearview mirror. I cleared my throat and reminded myself he would be fine, just fine.

So concluded a six-month project of puppy raising that had a happy ending. At first when people asked me if I'd do it again I told them no way because it was incredibly time-consuming and hard. But with time past and memories faded I have been thinking. I kind of miss having puppies.

Journal entry September 2006:

I can't believe I have been running AEAR for three years. I am exhausted and frustrated. I am really not sure how long I can do this thing. I have met so many wonderful people, saved so many lives, made such a difference, but who am I kidding? I'm just a middle-class, self-employed, hard-working girl giving away all her time and money.

Other people that start non-profits are wealthy to begin with and don't have to worry about working, too. I am so tired of worrying about money. I so badly want to keep doing this. We are doing GREAT things, but how long can I last going at the rate I am going and with the stress and hardship I am putting on my family? Am I nuts? If only one wealthy person would see what we are doing and donate money for a real shelter or I would win the lottery. But I'm not that lucky, at least I don't think.

I have these fantasies that someone has been watching what we are doing, the difference we are making, and calls me and says, "I want to donate two million dollars. I want you to hire staff so you don't have to rely completely on volunteers. I trust you and love your work."

Yeah, right. I just hope I don't regret what I have done. My kids keep reminding me how they hate what I do. Am I a bad mother? I just have to let it go into the universe and hope and pray that what is meant to be will be and I will keep moving forward.

Deliah

Deliah was at Pane County Humane Society and needed a place to go. She was very pregnant, heartworm positive, and rescue was vital. I called the veterinarian and he said that she could safely deliver the puppies, nurse them and when she was done nursing she could have heartworm treatment. Heartworm is where worms actually grow in the dog's heart. If left untreated eventually the dog can die from an infestation of the worms.

I contacted Molly and she agreed once again to take in a mother dog. Deliah arrived on transport and was settled into the finished basement at Molly's home. The baby pool was put in front of their three-foot-tall television. But rather than spend her time in the pool Deliah relaxed on the couch, just a few feet from the pool.

Within a week of her arrival Molly came downstairs one morning to find Deliah had given birth to five puppies on her couch. She called me and I headed over. By now both Molly and I were on puppy burnout and because the newness of experiencing the process was gone our enthusiasm was replaced with just going about the task of getting this all over and done with. We were both aware of the work ahead and summoned all our energy to just keep our eyes on the end result, saving lives and providing them good homes.

"Hello," I called out as I walked down Molly's basement stairs.

"Hey," Molly called back from the laundry room. I walked over to where Deliah was, still on the couch, but this time with five puppies suckling hungrily.

"Don't we have to get her in the pool?" I called out to Molly. "I'm worried she'll squash the puppies."

"I already tried once but she refused."

"Great, just great," I said wearily. "Maybe if we both try we can get her in."

Molly walked into the room carrying a basket of clothes. "I put the pups in first and she freaked out and picked up each puppy and put it back on the couch."

"You are kidding. With her mouth?"

"Yep."

"Great," I said sarcastically.

"Yeah, I know."

With an I-am-trying-very-hard-to-be-optimistic tone I said, "Well, let's give it a try again. We'll just tell her 'no' if she tries to pick them up and put them back on the couch."

"Okay," Molly answered, not convinced by my false enthusiasm.

So we each took a puppy and gently placed it in the pool. Just as quickly Deliah ran over to the pool, picked up the puppy and put it back on the couch. "No, Deliah," I scolded. "Don't pick up that baby." So it went, one by one we moved the puppies and with great assertiveness Deliah moved them back. "This is not working," I said to Molly. So, for the time being we let her care for the puppies on the couch.

In short order we could see that Deliah, who was lying on the couch, was straining. "Molly, another puppy is coming, I think."

I took the position on the couch by Delia's head and Molly was near her rear. As the puppy began to emerge I said, "EWWWW!" Molly started laughing at me. "I've seen this a dozen times and I guess I've really hit burnout when it grosses me out," I laughed with Molly.

Seeing things easily through my eyes Molly grimaced and looked away. Now we were laughing so hard we were trying to muffle our laughs with our hands. Puppy number six was born, the sack opened and eaten by Deliah and after she cleaned it up from head to toe it squirmed to a teat and started to suck. We sat there looking at it passively still trying not to laugh.

"Okay, after this mom and pups we need a break," I concluded.

"You're not kidding."

I wiped my eyes clear of laughter tears. "But we have to get serious. We have to get this dog into the pool. She'll end up suffocating these puppies. Should we try again?"

Molly looked at the dog with skepticism. "Okay." So we tried again. It was like hot potato with home base being the couch. After a while we gave up afraid to stress Deliah out. "It's lucky I was going to throw this couch out anyway," Molly said after we gave up trying.

"I think we should call the vet." So we called the vet and they were as perplexed as we were. Just as I was hanging up Deliah got up off the couch, walked over to the other side of the room and delivered a puppy. "What the heck!" I exclaimed, running over and trying to catch the puppy as it came out. I wasn't fast enough. The pup plopped onto the floor. As Molly and I in unison were "ohhing" and "oh, no-ing," Deliah proficiently picked up the puppy in her mouth and brought it over to the couch with the other puppies. Safe and squirming on the couch she proceeded to lick it clean.

"This is not going to work any more. We have to get her into the pool," I said annoyed.

So again we played hot potato until finally Deliah got tired of the game and gave in to the not-so-comfy pool. She lay down and her puppies wiggled over to her, found nipples and began sucking loudly.

"Molly, I hate to do this but I have to go for a little while. I have an appointment. I'll be back as soon as I can."

"Okay, go, no problem."

"You sure you're okay?"

"Yeah, go."

While I was gone I learned later that Deliah delivered a puppy at the feet of Molly's son as he was lifting weights in the basement. She told me, "He looked down and there was a puppy. He yelled over to me, 'Mom, Deliah had a puppy here.'"

Then Deliah proceeded to try and move all the puppies back onto the couch and then began burying them in the cushions. Molly had been going back and forth from the laundry room when she saw what Deliah was doing. "I couldn't believe that dog. She is so strange," she told me later.

"What did you do?"

"I was really mad and I grabbed those puppies and yelled at her. Yeah, I yelled at her. Then I put the puppies in the pool and told her to quit it."

"What did she do?"

"She went into the pool."

I came back in time to help with the last four puppies. There were 13 puppies in all by the time she was done—a record for Animal Education and Rescue. But one little girl didn't make it, as much as we tried to save her. I named her Twilight and later buried her with other small animals that had died, in my yard.

Two days later Molly called. Her voice was panicked. "Sandy, one of the puppies died. I just went out for a short time and came back and I noticed that one wasn't moving. When I picked it up it was cold." She was obviously shaken. "I'll bring her over now."

"Okay, I'll wait outside."

I told Chuck what happened and we met her five minutes later in the driveway. She handed us the puppy wrapped in a towel through her car window. "I don't understand what happened," Molly said obviously shaken.

I took the puppy and looked at the still form. "Poor thing."

"Now I'm afraid they are all going to die. Maybe Deliah laid on her."

"Sometimes a puppy just doesn't thrive. I am sure the others are fine," I tried reassuring her. "They'll be fine. Let's name this one. How about Star?"

"Sounds good," Molly said sadly.

Chuck took the puppy from me and proceeded to walk to the backyard to bury the dog.

Later that day we had a small scare when Molly had a neighbor and her two children visit. Deliah snapped at the seven-year-old child in the face, giving her a scratch. When she told me about it she said, "It's my fault. I shouldn't have assumed she'd want people around her puppies. The girl is fine but she won't come back to visit."

I was very concerned about Deliah's reaction to the girl so I taught Molly what she needed to do to get Deliah to see visitors as good instead of bad. Any time a visitor came over they should make a big deal about getting a treat from the closet at the top of the stairs and then offer it to Deliah. They should not lean down towards her or approach her and instead wait for her to approach them.

Within a few weeks to my relief Deliah was no longer protective of her pups and visitors came and went, holding the puppies and giving Deliah attention. But for poor Molly she continued to have one big problem. Deliah was completely and totally not housebroken and was having too many accidents to count. We were counting the days until we could wean the pups.

Molly had planned her yearly summer family vacation before taking Deliah in so we were prepared to step up and take care of the big brood while she relaxed in sunny Florida. We had a meeting at Molly's house with a half dozen volunteers and were prepared to take care of the dogs in shifts. The plan was that at four weeks the puppies could eat softened food and Deliah would be crated when the volunteers were gone. The idea was that we could work on housebreaking while Molly was away.

Molly left with her family for a much-needed family vacation. The volunteers began caring for the canine family, and on day one Deliah decided she hated the crate. She was tormented hearing her puppies crying in the next room, and with her human family gone she went bonkers. Each visit the volunteers came into a destroyed and dismantled crate and an anxious mama dog.

The third day of this, Lynn, one of the people helping with Deliah, called and said, "Sandy, this is not working. This is very upsetting to see Deliah so anxious."

"Okay, I'll call the vet and get some advice."

So I called the vet and he said it was safe to separate Deliah completely from her puppies and begin heartworm treatment. He said she could stay at the animal hospital until Molly returned home. So that afternoon I brought Deliah to the animal hospital and she began treatment.

By eight weeks old only a few of the puppies were adopted but by 16 weeks all of the puppies had new and loving homes. Deliah was living with Kari and Rich, a young foster couple in the area. A week after the last puppy, Heidi, was adopted, Kari e-mailed me saying that they would like to adopt Deliah.

I wrote back: Yay for Deliah!!!! I am so happy for her and you!!!!

The Little Engine That Could

When I first started Animal Education and Rescue I thought back to what it was like working with volunteers in the past. For more than 15 years I had taken leadership roles with non-profits. I headed committees for our local chamber of commerce and was the president for two years. I headed a committee at our local civic center and founded and ran an adoption support and information organization. I remembered full well the challenges of having volunteers.

Typically volunteers lasted a year, if I was lucky, and only a small handful of people were consistently reliable. I remembered it being hard for me not to regularly feel let down and disappointed by people who didn't follow through on what they said they would do. Working with volunteers was the one challenge of Animal Education and Rescue that I was not looking forward to. I learned a long time ago that I didn't like managing people. I'd just as soon leave that up to someone else. But because the greater good was so important I decided I would just have to remain positive about managing volunteers, at least until I could hire someone else to do that for me.

When I started AEAR I quickly had new, enthusiastic volunteers. I worked hard at pleasing them by giving them tasks they would enjoy, and I was careful not to overload them with responsibilities. I believed strongly in thanking people and verbally expressed my appreciation regularly and often. I sent handwritten thank you notes, each one with a personal message. Inwardly I continued to challenge myself to appreciate the things people did and not expect too much.

From the beginning I was aware that I needed to choose volunteers carefully. From past experience I knew that one bad volunteer could taint other volunteers. Rumors and gossip could be vicious and create significant damage. I thought I was being careful, but I still had a lot to learn. By nature I tended to be very trusting and loving, wanting to be surrounded by harmony and peace. Unconsciously I suppose I always thought everyone else was like that, too. But that was not the case when a few volunteers who were with me the first year turned out to be great disappointments.

Behind my back my closest circle of volunteers banned together and started their own non-profit, mimicking everything I was doing. After burying my pride at being dumped I would have learned to accept it as flattery had they not stolen volunteers as well as a portion of our mailing list and pleas for money to the people on those lists.

What made it worse was that I thought those people were my friends. They spent many, many hours at my home and knew more about me than I should have told them. I opened up to them as if they were my friends. I felt used, abused and kicked to the ground. I was embarrassed that they knew so much about me personally and wished that I hadn't opened up my heart to them. They never told me why they left. They just left.

Running a business, whether non-profit or for profit, can be very lonely at the top. I knew this from running Pet Sitters of America for close to 20 years. Whenever you have to instruct people what to do, make decisions and lead you will not make everyone happy nor will everyone agree with you. Plus, if you have the authority to fire someone that can put a real damper on a potential friendship.

Slightly wounded I dusted my muddy-pawed blue jeans off. I have one of those persistent personalities. When I decide to do something I am like a locomotive going full speed. When I feel like quitting I think of *The Little Engine That Could* and visualize myself going up that mountain, using all my strength and saying, "I think I can, I think I can, I think I can." But with Animal Education and Rescue my obsession and determination was like a marathon runner dead set on winning the race. No one would get in my way.

Over time I sought out new volunteers. I tried to remind myself over and over again to keep a distance emotionally from the people who volunteered, yet to still be caring and compassionate. It is for me a fine line that I still struggle with. Meanwhile I continued to stay focused on the main goal, saving animals and educating people about them.

Toto and the Yellow Brick Road

In the legendary movie *The Wizard of Oz* Dorothy and Toto were trying desperately to find their way home. They followed the yellow brick road, meeting friends and foes along the way, the whole journey yearning to go home. They were terribly homesick. Well, I know a Toto who, by no fault of her own, found herself on that yellow brick road, looking for home.

Toto, a Cairn Terrier, had a family since she was a pup. In her 13th year she found herself homeless. Her parents went to our local animal hospital and wanted her put to sleep because "she was messing in the house sometimes." (It was my understanding that she was being left alone 12 hours a day.)

A compassionate vet tech asked, "If we could find a home for her would that be okay?"

Their response: "Well, we didn't think anyone would want an old dog, but if you want to." So with that they handed over their dog, turned and left the building, their dog looking after them. Upon the animal hospital's request we became Toto's guardian.

Toto stayed at the animal hospital for the first week. Each time she was walked outside to go potty she kept looking around as if looking for her family, confusion clearly written on her face. Her dark brown eyes looked sadly around, perking up every time a new person walked by her, only to be disappointed when she realized it wasn't her family. I couldn't imagine ever doing that to my dog, ever. To experience all their milestones, and them to be part of mine; they are family until the quality of their life is no longer. Being old didn't mean that she was not worth anything.

At that time I wrote about Toto on our web site. Here is some of what I wrote: Toto is in good health and very sweet, but understandably confused and sad right now. She tucks her tail between her legs a lot, but after a few minutes of sweet talk she belly crawls for some scratches. She would be best in a home with no kids or older kids so it's a bit quieter. She would do okay with another dog, as long as it's older like her and maybe small like her, too.

It took just a few days to find her a temporary home where she could stay while she waited for her forever home. At the same time we had numerous small dogs. Two of the dogs were Chihuahua mixes named Molly and Monday, which we rescued from Pane County Humane Society. Small dogs notoriously got adopted quickly so after six weeks I was surprised that Molly and Monday–adorable young dogs with snow-white hair and brown patches–were still with us.

Toto settled in nicely at her foster home. Her Cairn Terrier strut came back after just a few days of love by her dedicated foster parents, Debby and Harold. She acted far younger than her 13 years. Debby took Toto to the groomer where she received an adorable haircut that accentuated her black button nose and her dark brown eyes framed in black as if eyeliner was applied around her eyes.

I was worried about my decision to take Toto into our care. Who would want an old dog? But I resolved to remain positive and be proactive in finding the old girl a home. A month passed and the few inquiries we received never amounted to anything.

Then on a cool fall day, when the sun shone bright and the Midwestern autumn gave us the gift of colorful leaves, we had an adoption event at our animal hospital. Toto arrived with Sheryl, a foster mom who was caring for Toto while Debby and Harold were out of town. Other dogs arrived as well with their foster families, including Molly and Monday.

Molly and Monday were so similar in looks that the only way you could tell them apart was by Monday's prominent under bite giving her an only-a-mother-could-love smile. In typical small-dog style she strutted around the room like she owned the place, wagging her stumpy little tail at everyone. Toto sat beside Sheryl, her ears tucked back and looking a tad forlorn. Sheryl kept reassuring her with a soft voice and gentle pats.

It was a slow day, hardly any visitors the first hour. While I was chatting with Connie, a regular volunteer, a couple came in the building and asked to see Toto. I turned my attention to them as I saw them being led to the little dog. The couple, in their late 50's or early 60's, introduced themselves as Pat and Fred.

Sitting side by side they bent down and petted and talked to Toto. Toto looked up at them and responded to them with a slow tail wag and a content look. Busy helping others, I stole glances occasionally and was praying that this would be a match. It was during one of my times spying on them that I noticed little Monday bugging Fred by first putting her front paws on his legs and then after numerous acts of refusal by him she proceeded to jump in his lap.

So began a game of Monday jumping up on his lap and Fred setting her back down over and over again. Oh, maybe they'll take Monday instead, I thought. She's trying to steal the show. I really wanted them to consider Toto because she was so much harder to adopt out.

Heading to the water bowls to fill and offer to dogs I nearly ran into Fred. "Excuse me," he said, "I was told you're the person to answer questions."

"Sure, what can I do for you?"

"Would I have to fill out another application if I wanted that little dog Monday, too?" He pointed at the little dog that had followed him and was sitting at his feet.

"You mean you want Toto AND Monday?"

"Yes, I do."

"Well," I smiled broadly, "no you do not. I will add her to your application."

"Thank you," he said. "You know this dog wouldn't leave me alone."

"I noticed."

"She picked me."

"She sure did."

So that day, after completing an educational program, Toto and Monday followed their new parents to their car, their tails swinging back and forth confidently and a spring in their step. They jumped one then the other into the back seat and settled in. As Fred pulled away they were both looking out the window perfectly content. Some things are just meant to be, and as I saw the car turn the corner I knew that destiny played a part in this pairing.

Six months later I received a call from Pat. "You know, Sandy, I don't know what would have happened if we only got Toto. Toto relies on Tess for everything. They follow each other around the house and will refuse to go anywhere, including the vet, without the other. Tess keeps Toto young. They just adore each other."

"That's wonderful," I said, happy tears in my eyes.

"You know, we thought Tess picked my husband, but really she picked him because Toto needed her, and she went through him to get to stay with her. They are a joy, a real joy."

Four Kittens in a Plastic Bag

Sitting in my office working on much-dreaded paperwork I received a call. The caller said in a slurred voice, "I found four kittens in a plastic bag. They were in an alley behind the building. I need you to come get them." I wasn't sure if I was victim of a horrible prank. (I'd had people play jokes on me before.) The man sounded drunk, and unsure whether I would be getting myself into a dangerous situation if I went to get the cats, I asked if I could speak to someone else.

The man handed the phone over to someone else. The second caller sounded lucid and was clearly not drunk. By some gentle prodding I discovered that the other man I spoke to was mentally handicapped and the current caller was a social worker at a public facility for the mentally handicapped. He confirmed that they had the four kittens. He went on to say that they couldn't have them in the building and "if you don't come and get them I am going to put them back in the alley. We can't have them here."

Leaving me no other option I agreed to go get the kittens immediately, as long as he agreed to take them out of the plastic bag and put them somewhere safe. He agreed. Secretly I was glad to have been relieved of my never-ending, dreaded paperwork and headed out. Pulling out of the driveway I called Molly and asked if she wanted to ride along.

The town I was heading to, north of Chicago, was a diverse city that had consistently struggled to redeem itself. There were more badly depressed and dangerous areas than there were nice areas, so going with someone else was the smart thing to do.

I picked up Molly and headed for the location. We arrived and entered the building. We were led to the office with the social worker that we had spoken to on the phone. Approaching the desk a plastic container held four tiny kittens, barely 3 weeks old, dirty, flea infested and very unhappy. The kittens meowed sadly, their eyes far wiser than they should have been. We put them in a small pet carrier and headed back.

Quickly coming to the conclusion they would not eat cat food we purchased kitten milk and bottles. Molly and her family agreed to foster the kittens, and with encouragement they were drinking the milk from the little bottle. Forty-eight hours later they were plump, flea treated and happily purring baby cats. In short order all four kittens found suitable homes.

A Cat's Cries Fall on Deaf Ears

For weeks, maybe months, a gray tabby cat with white paws and a white patch on his underbelly begged to be let inside. Door after door, home after home in the upper-class, suburban neighborhood the cat meowed to be let in, to be fed, to be cared for. Face after face silhouetted in the doorframes and in windows looked out at the cat, but no one came out to help. With each passing day the cat got weaker and thinner, losing his fight and losing hope.

Even though thousands of cats find themselves homeless or are born homeless–strays roaming neighborhoods, slinking in alleyways, under porches and in bushes–few beg for humane companionship like that tabby cat did. To add to that unique quality it was obvious that Tabby Cat didn't know how to hunt for food because he was starving to death and saw people as his means for nourishment. That could only lead to the sad fact that likely he was dumped, let loose, or set "free" by his owners. He was completely and totally incapable of caring for himself. Tabby Cat was in trouble.

One morning a woman called the office saying a cat was hanging around her neighborhood for the past week. She went on to explain that the entire neighborhood was talking about the cat and even brought up the situation at their homeowner's association meeting. "I don't know much about cats but one of my neighbors thinks that the cat's a tabby cat. He's gray striped and I think has some white on him, but I've only seen him from far away. He keeps trying to get into everyone's houses and garages."

As we were talking I kept hearing a cat meowing frantically in the background. "Is that the cat I hear?" I asked.

"Yes, that's him."

"Is he in your house?"

"Oh, no, outside. I have my door open and he's by my screen door."

"Oh, my, that sounds just pathetic. Poor baby."

"What would happen if I called Animal Control?" she asked.

"If you call Animal Control it is a possibility he will be put to sleep. It's not certain but a possibility." I could still hear the urgent and insistent "meow, meow" and my heart hurt more with each passing second. "Won't anyone take this cat in, even temporarily?" I asked in frustration.

"No. I've talked to everyone and no one wants to deal with it. I'm afraid of cats but I can't stand this animal suffering."

"*Meow, meow, meow,*" he carried on.

"He looks really skinny, at least from where I can see him."

"I am surprised he's so skinny," I commented. "It's spring and there should be lots of rodents to catch," I said perplexed.

"I know, I don't get it either."

"*Meow, meow, meow, meow.*"

"Cats are so hard to find homes for," I told her. "We have no-where for a cat to go."

"I understand. Do you have any other suggestions for me?"

"I am sure everywhere is full. There isn't a shelter anywhere that isn't loaded with cats."

"*Meow, meow, meow, meow.*"

I couldn't stand it anymore. "I can't stand that meowing anymore. It's killing me." Then I blurted out, "I'll be right over. How do I get to your house?"

After getting directions I called volunteer and humane investigator Rita and asked her if she'd go with me. Always up for a new adventure she agreed and we headed out. "I can't believe NOBODY would open his or her home to him, even temporarily," I said to Rita on the way there. "What a bunch of heartless people." I pulled into the woman's driveway and we got out.

Walking up to the house the woman peeked her head out of the door. "Thanks for coming," she said. "He's at the neighbor's near that cardboard box," she said through the crack in the screen door.

"Okay, thanks," I said. We walked towards the neighbor's side yard and saw the cat sitting beside a cardboard box. Without a second thought Rita approached the tabby cat and scooped him up. He did not struggle or try and get away.

"God, this cat is skin and bones," Rita said. I led the way to the van where we placed him in a cat carrier and closed the door.

The cat safe in the car, the woman came out of her home and said, "To be totally honest I am *terrified* of cats. Thank you so much for taking him."

"You're welcome. We'll get him well and figure out where he will go." A fleeting thought that I might be stuck with him instantly made my stomach turn. *I cannot have another cat myself. I already have four*, I thought.

As we drove back the cat was quiet. I said to Rita, "The one person that spoke up on the cat's behalf was a woman who was terrified of cats. Isn't that ironic," I shook my head in disgust. "Those people should be ashamed of themselves." But in the back of my mind sat a dread. Where would the cat go? The cat was very skinny so I decided the first order of business was to get him examined by the vet. At least that would buy me some time until I could hopefully find him a foster home. I dialed from my cell and told the animal hospital I was on my way with a sick cat.

While driving to the vet I began calling foster homes begging for a place for the cat. Donny and Linda were the third call and the third volunteer foster family who said no. I had a sinking feeling, not knowing what I was going to do with an animal I had taken responsibility for. With cats particularly, there are so few homes and there are just thousands upon thousands of cats needing homes. It was even a far bigger problem finding placement for them than for dogs.

The animal hospital agreed to keep the cat overnight and neuter him the next morning. After a complete examination they confirmed that the cat was emaciated and they set him up immediately with high-calorie food. I spent a little while with him before I left and assured him that he would never be alone again. The look of relief on his face made all my worries about where he would go worth it. As I stroked his bony head one more time his green eyes closed in contentment. He curled in a ball and fell asleep. I closed the cage door quietly and left.

At my office I sent out a plea via e-mail for someone to foster the cat. I included a photo that I had taken at the animal hospital of the cat. Shortly afterwards I got a call from Donny. He said that he and Linda were "suckers for a cute face" and would foster the cat. *Yes!* I thought. *How wonderful!* My shoulder's burden was lifted.

Donny and Linda picked up the cat the following evening. They were enthusiastic and I was so grateful for their help. I knew the cat was in good hands. Later that evening they e-mailed me: "The cat is settling into our spare bedroom. He is very sweet and friendly. We named him Marvin. He was so tired he fell asleep in Donny's arms," Linda wrote.

The following week as I had predicted no one had inquired about adopting Marvin. I knew it could be a long time before Marvin found a forever home. At times foster families became impatient when the animal they were fostering didn't get adopted quickly. Some families actually said they couldn't foster anymore for one reason or another and left me in the lurch scrambling to find a new foster family. I just hoped Donny and Linda would be patient and willing to keep Marvin until he got adopted.

The fourth week, on a bright and sultry summer day, I opened my e-mails and recognized Donny and Linda's e-mail address. With trepidation I opened it, hoping it wasn't saying that they couldn't foster Marvin any longer. Linda's e-mail said: Marvin is such a dear cat and we would just fall to pieces if we have to give him up. Donny is madly in love with him as am I. We would like to adopt him and have him live with us forever if you'd let us.

I wrote back: Of course! Yay for Marvin!

Today Marvin is a big, meaty lap cat with a loving family. I get regular updates on Marvin's life and remain eternally grateful that I rescued him from what certainly would have been death. There are two things I will never forget about saving Marvin. One was how an entire subdivision of hundreds of people, with the means to help that cat, could turn their back on an animal in need, and how one, single person, a woman who had a deep fear of cats, stepped up to help. But mostly I will never forget the look on that cat's face when we saved him. That look was priceless and stays with me, urging me on day after day.

Wishful Thinking

As Animal Education and Rescue experienced growing pains we were rapidly being squeezed out of our home. Every room in our house had evidence of AEAR. Our offices had dogs, dog and cat carriers, office supplies, desks and more. Our living space had supplies, paperwork, dogs, cats and an occasional bird or rodent. Our porch was stacked to the ceiling with donated supplies. Our garage was loaded up with extra dog and cat carriers, birdcages, little critter cages and miscellaneous supplies. I felt like the walls were closing in on me. The summer of '06 Chuck and I began kicking around the idea of moving.

Ever since I first had my vision of running a humane society more than a decade earlier, I always thought the second step was to purchase property so we could have more space and the ability to expand AEAR. It seemed to me that we were at that stage and it was time to start looking around.

We were willing to use the money from the sale of our house to purchase property. I wasn't paid for running AEAR. Pet Sitters continued to pay me a modest salary even though most of my time was spent with AEAR. In our area property was expensive and finding something affordable would be difficult, especially considering our income.

A church that also ran a school, preschool through eighth grade, located right next door, owned about three acres or so of property all around us. We were the only piece of property, smack in the center of all their property, that they didn't own. I often explained to people that we were the island and the church was our mote. They needed to buy our piece in order to expand their church and school. When we moved to our home in 1993 we learned that we had outbid the church because they made a "lowball bid." Since moving in the church board members knocked on our door or called us almost yearly asking us if we would sell our property. We always told them, "No, we aren't interested" and "We are happy where we are." But now that we were considering moving we thought maybe we could come to a reasonable selling price for our house that would benefit all of us.

We contacted the church representatives and after some negotiations they finally made us an offer that was considered the market value of our property. But the price did not take into consideration that we were the key piece of property they needed in order for them to expand. Chuck had taken a real estate course a few years earlier, and after he explained to his instructor our unique situation the instructor cautioned, "Don't you dare sell that piece of property for less than a million." So Chuck never forgot that and felt strongly that the church was "ripping us off," and he spent many nights ranting about it. Even so I felt strongly that we needed to move to live out our dreams, even if we didn't get a million. I convinced Chuck that we should just look around and see what we could find.

After hours and hours of house hunting we found a few properties that might have worked, but they were an hour away in Wisconsin. We decided that an hour away was too far from the areas we serviced for pet sitting and dog training, not to mention that all our volunteers and our connections for the non-profit were where we were currently living. After Chuck and I discussed the location further we agreed to narrow our search to within 30 minutes of where we currently lived. Finally, after months of searching, we found what I had envisioned as our dream property in Antioch, Illinois, just 30 minutes north of our current house.

Meanwhile during the months of house hunting Chuck and the kids and I began to feel like our lives were in limbo. Anything we wanted to buy for the house or do for the house we stopped ourselves and said we'd have to wait and see if we were moving. I was due to purchase new business cards and brochures for our business. I opted to wait until we knew what address would be put on the literature. It was not fun for any of us having our lives on hold.

One more property and one more let down, was my fleeting thought as we followed our real estate agent Mary Lou's SUV into the driveway of the five-acre parcel. I picked up the listing off the console of the car and began reading. "There can't possibly be two houses on the property," I said after reading that there was a main house and a cottage. I looked up and out the window and saw a cute, cottage-style house on the left. "This must be the cottage," I said out loud. It had a wraparound deck I immediately envisioned sitting out on, sharing a meal with friends.

We parked our car next to Mary Lou's and followed her into the small house. Entering the tiny back porch and then the galley kitchen a musty odor sat heavy in the air. There was one bedroom downstairs and two small bedrooms upstairs. There was one bathroom and a quaint living room. "This is adorable!" I exclaimed, as we walked through the house.

Chuck looked at it with a critical eye. He had been a licensed home inspector and said, "This place needs a lot of work. I am not even sure if the foundation is good."

The undying optimist, I told him, "Let's look at the potential. It has lots of potential. We can fix it up."

It was cold and rainy outside so we hurried back into the car. Looking up the long driveway I counted three more buildings. I was getting more excited by the minute. I scanned the property and first noticed the trees. Gorgeous, mature oaks and pine trees dotted the property, creating umbrella shading, and trees and shrubbery lined the perimeter, which created privacy and seclusion. Privacy was top on my list. I didn't want the dogs disturbing the neighbors, nor did I want to deal with neighbors that were going to get into our business.

We drove further up and stopped at an L-shaped building. We got out and hurried to it to look in the windows. The building needed some serious repairs. It had peeling paint on the outside and the inside had been gutted. It looked like it was the perfect size for our offices as well as a place for a small kennel. We got back into the car and drove past a three-car garage on the left. "That would be great for storage," I said to Chuck, pointing at the building.

"I don't know," he replied. "This place looks like it needs a ton of work."

"We could do it though. You're handy and I can help."

Twenty feet up on the right was a small building that must have housed farm animals. "Look, Chuck! You could have a goat finally!" I said, pointing at the building. He didn't reply.

At the far end of the driveway was the main house, a 1970's-style house with a six-car garage behind it. We parked our car by the main house and got out. I said to Chuck, "This feels like where I grew up. This feels like home." I was way too excited for my own good. I saw huge potential in that land both for our personal businesses as well as Animal Education and Rescue. *We don't have to wait years for enough donations to expand Animal Education and Rescue!* I thought to myself. *We could do it on our own.* Mary Lou parked alongside us and we followed her into the main home. After walking through the house we stood in the kitchen to talk. We agreed that the size and layout would work but as Chuck pointed out, "Nothing has been updated since they moved in 30 years ago."

"Paint isn't expensive. We could live with it until we slowly fix it up," I said.

"Maybe," he said not convinced. He looked around himself and added, "I suppose if we got it for the right price. But we need money to fix it up. The asking price is too high."

I tried hard not to be furious with what I perceived as his negative attitude. "It's been on the market for a year. I am sure they would take a lower offer."

"Maybe," he replied, not convinced by any of this.

"Let's just try. It can't hurt. This place is perfect."

We headed out back and walked into the heated, six-car garage. Standing in the center of the garage I said, "I could teach dog training in here. And I could have educational programs in here."

"It's heated," Mary Lou added.

Chuck rubbed his chin, scanning the room and thinking.

"Yeah, see," I said, "we could make money if I have training classes. Where I teach now I have to pay rent. Doing it here would be no overhead."

"This is the only building that doesn't need anything," Chuck commented. "It's actually nice."

We walked out the side door of the garage. "Look." I pointed at the vast space on the side of the garage and behind the house. "We can fence this off for the dogs and put agility equipment in there."

"But we'd need to get it for a really good price and the church would have to give us more for our house," Chuck said.

I left high on dreams while Chuck left feeling shouldered with burden. "Okay, well, lets talk to them," I said.

It was three months of back and forth talk with the church while my dreams among the trees sat waiting for me. The whole while I waited I created the perfect life there in my head. I imagined the cottage used for get-togethers with volunteers, a place where we could house homeless cats and kittens upstairs. I loved to bake and Chuck loved to cook so we could sell homemade food, the ingredients largely from our garden, to raise money for Animal Education and Rescue. The L-shaped building where we would have our offices would give us the much-needed separation of work and home life that we hadn't had before. The kennels on the other side of the building would be perfect for housing animals on an emergency basis. If I went on an investigation and ended up having an animal in the car with me I could just take the animal to the kennel. What a load of worry that would take off my mind.

The three-car garage would provide ample storage space for all our animal-related items. I saw myself teaching dog training classes in the six-car garage. I imagined the room filled with chairs, auditorium style, with me giving educational programs to the public. I saw meetings for our youth club there. I fantasized my whole new way of life in full color, my mind vivid with imaginary potential of making a huge difference.

One morning, being yanked along by my foster dog Braille on a three-mile jaunt, I had plenty of time to think. As was typical of my waking hours during that time my mind drifted to the property in Antioch. Chuck always wanted a goat or two, because he said he admired their sassy, I'm-all-that attitude, so we would have a rescue goat. I saw that goat, even could imagine the sharp, gritty smell of him.

Chuck loved gardening so I knew he would take great joy in growing an impressive vegetable garden on the property. The vegetables would provide us and those we loved and cared about healthy nourishment. We could can fruits, vegetables and soups and sell garden fresh organic vegetables in the summer.

Passing our local playground, I watched as a little girl swung on a swing, her skirt billowing around her. A group of pre-teens were playing basketball. In the summer, I thought, we would offer field trips to youth groups. We would give older teens that wanted to learn about our organization a hands-on experience by allowing them to stay in the cottage on weekends and work alongside us. I would be away from the congestion of traffic and the people. My dogs could run and play without the worry of disturbing neighbors or escaping out of the yard and into traffic. I could sit outside and smell the grass, trees and hear the birds sing.

We stopped all repairs at our house, which was a big deal considering our old home was in a constant state of needing repair. There was no reason to do anything at that point, we reasoned, because it would be time and money wasted. The church would tear down our house if they purchased it.

We were still trying to get the church to buy our house for more than the asking price, but the church kept stringing us along, saying they'd call us back after they spoke to this person or that person or asking to meet us in person again. We were well aware that they had sold numerous properties in the area. One five-acre parcel sold for three million. We were asking for $100,000 over the market value of our property. Weeks passed and the same game played out.

We tried reasoning with them that after 14 years we would finally be out of their way and they could expand their school. The kids would no longer have to play in the parking lot. We told them about our plans to expand our non-profit humane society and that while they helped their people we would also be servicing the community in a positive way. We told them that this could be a win-win situation.

After many long and slow-moving months of trying to work out a deal with the church, wondering if the Antioch property would still be available and putting our lives on hold they finally gave us a solid and definite "no." They would not budge on the selling price of our place. It was a big blow for all of us. But at least the waiting game was over.

For 24 hours I was deeply sad and discouraged. I spent time wondering what I was doing and why. I was mentally and physically exhausted from the high hopes I had created and the ultimate letdown that followed. But after I spent some time recovering from the emotional upheaval I reasoned that it just wasn't meant to be. The universe had something else in store for me. So until or if we moved I decided I would make do with where we were and what we could do with what we had. I reminded myself often that I was blessed now.

No Two Dogs Are Exactly Alike

Following are some of my columns that were published in 2005-2006. (They have been revised to fit this format.)

Often times I'll be at a dog-training client's house and the frustrated dog owner will say to me, "I don't understand. My sister also has a black lab and her dog's not nuts like mine." Or "I got this poodle from a rescue. I thought I was doing the right thing, rescuing a dog, but the dog's not housebroken and is terrified of new people. I had a poodle growing up and she was nothing like this one." What people don't understand is that no two dogs are alike, even within the same breed. Besides breeding you have to consider the dog's current and past experiences, as well as training and socialization.

Within each breed there are certain inherited physical and behavioral attributes common in the breed. That combined with the pup's early socialization and environment make up the dog's unique qualities. Then you add in how the dog perceives the *new* home environment they move into, as well as how their new guardians and others outside their immediate family interact with them–all of which plays a role in the dog's behavior. While a dog at any age can learn, the longer the dog's life, the more experiences that can impact their behavior.

But within every breed there are dogs that have issues. Even the best of breeders could produce a dog with behavior or physical problems. Most bad behavior is changeable, except on very rare occasions. What new dog owners have to understand is that while labs, for example, are known to be "good family dogs," there are laid-back labs, hyper labs, even temperamental labs and a few with a screw loose.

If you rescue a dog from a shelter have someone go with you so you can choose the right dog for you, or go through a rescue group where dogs are kept in private homes and the foster families know the dogs well and can provide all the information on the dog that you need to know to make the right decision. If you decide to go through a breeder find one through a recommendation and/or check their references. Ask to meet the parents of the pup and the facility where the puppy lived. Or you could choose a mix-breed dog. Often times mix breeds don't have the health problems of the purebreds.

So when deciding to add a new member to your family it's important to weigh all the options and consider consulting with a professional before making that final decision. You may need professional training help regardless of what dog you choose. Your choice of dog may depend on how much effort you will have to put into training him or her. But going into it informed and prepared is key, because the dog you pick could be with you for 10-15 years.

Animals Aren't Sweaters or Televisions

Holiday time can be joyous when families create warm memories to last a lifetime. It is also a time of year when puppies are purchased at pet stores in large numbers to give as gifts to their families. I cringe when I hear someone say they are "surprising their family" with a new dog. Dogs are not sweaters, televisions or CDs. They are living, breathing, complicated animals that need a lot of ongoing attention. The decision to get a dog should be the whole family's decision, especially when they are considering one during the holiday season.

Pet stores make a ton of money during the December holidays. They rely heavily on people walking into their store to just "look at the puppies" and impulsively purchase one, which is the wrong way to get a dog. Often times those dogs purchased on a whim are given up later because they realize it was a bad decision and they hadn't thought it through. That only hurts the people and the dog.

Rescue groups and shelters, on the other hand, are more careful about making sure that a dog is not adopted without serious thought because they receive the consequences (dogs) from quick decisions every day. Most shelters/rescues will not adopt out a dog as a surprise but instead require the whole family's involvement.

Careful planning is vital to success with a new pup. An eight-week-old pup has to go outside to eliminate every two hours or so. She'll likely be chewing, jumping, nipping and biting on all family members and guests–not to mention newly acquired gifts. Early on, sleep for the new pet owners will be limited, because likely the pup will need to go outside to go potty in the middle of the night.

If you live in an area where winters get cold having a puppy in the winter could bring additional challenges. Each potty break the owner must bundle up to take the pup out. Quite possibly in the first week or so the pup will sit outside shivering from the cold, looking up at their owner clueless about what outside potty means and instead they just want to go back inside.

So, for those of you who want to add a new pup to your home during the winter holiday just make sure you understand what challenges you will face in advance so the experience can be a positive one as you stand in the cold and say to your new pup, "Go potty!"

Ask Sandy Q&A

Q: Why do shelters and rescue groups charge to adopt a pet? Personally, I think it should be free. I'm saving a life, isn't that enough? David P., Antioch, IL.

A: There are many reasons why charging to adopt is both necessary and smart. The first reason is that the adoption fee helps to defer costs incurred during the animal's stay at the shelter/rescue. One of the biggest expenses is medical care for the animals. Each animal a shelter or rescue takes into their care needs vaccinations, de-worming, neutering or spaying. Some shelters also provide flea and tick preventative, heartworm testing and heartworm protection. All that preventative care costs a lot of money. Those shelter/rescues that offer free or discounted spay/ neuters are getting their funding from private donations or grants to pay for the surgery. Vets most often do not provide free medical care. Understandably, they have to make a living, just like the rest of us.

Shelter costs also include housing, food, water, electricity, repairs, staff and more. Rescue groups, on the other hand, rely on volunteer foster families that open up their home to a homeless animal. In that case the volunteer foster family is paying for their mortgage, electricity, water, etc., which saves the rescue group hundreds of dollars a month. My vet told me that the shelter he works with pays on average $900 per dog that stays there. That's way more than the nominal fee of $100-$300 charged to adopt.

For smaller rescue groups like ourselves we rely on the adoption donations just to continue doing what we are doing. Our veterinarian expenses are the highest bills we have. If an animal is sick when it arrives we have them treated by our vet for their illness. And being that many of the animals that come into our care come from bad situations often times the animal needs medical treatment. Just last year we had two puppies we took in that ended up stricken with parvo–an often-fatal stomach virus. The vet bills were more than $2,000 and only one dog survived! Enough dogs coming in with parvo would financial drive us to close our doors.

Last but not least, if you do not charge a fee for a pet the impression is that the pet has no value. Without a value the perception could be that the animal is worthless. So as you can see now, there are valid reasons why paying a fee for adopting an animal makes sense.

Lowering the Overpopulation

Six to 12 million dogs and cats are euthanized each year. (An exact number has been impossible to calculate.) This is no joke; I have seen the bodies of the dead animals after they were euthanized stacked one on top of the other. It is not the fault of the shelters that they have to euthanize animals; it is society's fault. There are shelters all over the country that are run by their local municipality or contracted by towns/cities to accept any animal that comes through their doors. When space runs out and if the shelter cannot find placement for some animals, someone has to make the grim decision of who lives and who dies. The shelter's actions are just a result of what society has done, and it is the shelter staff that has to deal with the problem.

That's why we must stop buying from pet stores, which only supports puppy mills. We must limit breeding because there are already too many animals. (*We must first and foremost adopt and save what we can* and LOWER the overpopulation.) Finally, we all must spay and neuter our pets. It's not cool for people to let their dog or cat have puppies or kittens. Just think of the dog or cat, perfectly healthy, the ideal pet, its life cut short because there is no home for him.

The Rising Star

Beth, my friend and a fellow humane investigator, received a call from a veterinarian saying that someone had brought in their dog to be euthanized. The vet said that the dog was in such bad shape he had "never seen anything like it." Upon examination of the dog it was obvious the dog had suffered years of neglect. "The dog was severely emaciated and had no hair on its body." The vet knew the owner had another dog and was concerned about its welfare.

The following day Beth asked me if I would go with her to check on the other dog. We were told the owners may be emotionally unstable and it was possible they had physical limitations as well. So, with that knowledge we decided the best approach was to try and befriend them by offering assistance, with the goal being to be able to see the dog and see what condition it was in.

The house matched the town–run-down and depressing. It was a ranch-style home with cheap paneling and big, dirty, thin windows. All the windows were covered with what looked like sheets or cardboard. We followed the short walkway to the front door. To the right of the door was an air conditioner that had half fallen out the window, and a rusty metal chair was toppled on its side on the stoop beside the door.

Beth knocked on the door. We looked at each other and then the closed door. A rustling could be heard inside but no one came to the door. Beth knocked again, louder. Tapping my foot and shifting from side to side I took some deep breaths. Investigations made me nervous. I never knew what was on the other side of the door. The door opened a crack and a middle-aged man looked through. "Yeah?" he asked gruffly.

"Hello, sir, my name is Beth. This is Sandy." She motioned to me. "We're with the humane society. We are checking with some residents to see if they need assistance with their animals in any way."

"No," he barked, "we're fine."

"Sir," she paused to think, "we really would like to help you. You have a dog?"

"Yeah, what about it."

"We can tell you where to get low-cost neutering or even free neutering for your dog. And we have other ways we can help."

"What for?"

"That's what we do," I cut in. "We help people who might need it. We want to help you."

"Yeah?" He opened the door a little wider.

"Dave, Dave," a woman shouted in the background. "Who is it?" A dog started barking. "What do they want?" she bellowed out at us.

He looked back inside the dark interior. "Shut up, will you!" he shouted at the voice. He opened the door a bit further. The smell of musty dirt wafted out the door, like a basement that was in desperate need of dusting and airing out.

"They're not taking my dog," she shouted.

"Sir," Beth said, "we don't want to take your dog. We'd just like to have a look at him. What's your dog's name?" she asked soothingly, the dog barking insistently somewhere inside.

"It's Barkley. What do you want? I'm busy." He was becoming increasingly more agitated.

"Tell them to go away!" the woman screamed.

The man squeezed through the door and came out on the stoop. "I'm sick of dealing with you people. You people have no business here." He began flailing his arms around and towards us. He may have been grungy looking but he was tall and if he felt like it he could have clocked either one of us.

"Mister," I said stepping forward, "you are not acting appropriately and I don't appreciate how you are acting." I gave him my best don't-mess-with-me body stance and voice. "You are acting threatening and all we are trying to do is help you."

"Okay, okay." He raised his arms in a gesture of surrender. "You're just trying to help."

"That's right."

"Sorry, sorry."

"How old is your dog?" I asked.

"He's eight."

"Have you had him since he was a puppy?" I asked, trying to make conversation in order to gain his trust.

"Oh, he's an older guy, huh?" Beth commented. She paused and then added, "Can we just take a peek at your dog?"

"Yeah, I guess, but just a for a second. He doesn't like people. He's very protective of my wife."

"He's protective of me," the woman shouted at us from inside. "He could bite. Go away!"

"They ain't gonna do anything so just shut up already," the man shouted at the woman. He opened the door a bit more so we could see the dog.

Through the darkness my eyes groped around the interior trying to adjust to the lack of light. Beth was standing closer to the door and was first to see inside. I peered around her and saw the dog. The first thing I noticed were the dog's nails, curled around his toes. Then I looked at his body and it looked like hair was missing from the middle of his back all the way down his back legs. He was hunched over slightly and looked at us with weary, painful eyes. It took all my willpower not to gasp at the sight.

"Why is your dog missing all that hair?" Beth asked.

"He has fleas. We can't get rid of 'em. Tried. But he's fine, he's not sick or nothing," the man said defensively.

"Go away!" the woman screamed. "You are not taking my dog!"

"Sir," Beth said, "I think this is upsetting your wife. Why don't we talk outside." The man stepped outside and closed the door behind him. "It looks like your dog needs help and we want to help you. But we don't want to upset your wife. Sandy and I are going to see what we can do and get back to you."

"Yeah, okay, but you know that dog's protective of my wife. We done everything for that dog. He's fine."

"Okay, sir," Beth said. "We'll stop back."

He stepped back inside, grunted, and closed the door without another word.

Walking to the car Beth said, "They haven't done anything for that dog. Did you see the skin and the nails? God, that animal is suffering."

"I know. It's awful. They aren't going to get treatment for that dog. That dog needs to get out of there."

"Yeah. I gotta come up with a plan. Let's go to the next house we have to check and we'll come back maybe tomorrow."

After discussing how to handle the situation with Barkley we decided we would offer to take him to the vet for them and get a quote on what the cost would be to treat him. We decided we would offer to pay for the initial exam.

Arriving at the home Beth knocked on the door. Moments later the door opened and the man squeezed out of the door. The woman began her rant from inside about not taking her dog. I figured this would be a tough battle. After a half an hour of pleading our case the man finally said he'd allow us to take the dog to have him looked at.

Opening the door wide the man yelled at the dog to come to him. We asked if he had a leash. "No, I don't have a leash," he answered gruffly.

"I'll get one from the car," I offered and hurried to the car to get it. Rushing back I handed the leash to the man. He went inside the dark house and we could hear, "Come here! Get over here!" Beth and I exchanged brief glances. The door opened further and the man dragged Barkley out the door and onto the stoop.

Now in full view we saw the true extent of Barkley's neglect. What must have once been a handsome Border Collie mix, Barkley was missing all his hair on half his body and down his back legs. His skin was red, raw and looked tough, almost like a pig's skin. His nails were so curled over he was tiptoeing on them, obviously to try and minimize the pain. Barkley's eyes were wide with fear as he tried desperately not to have to move farther.

"I'll get a crate out of the car," Beth said. "Then we'll just put him in the crate from ground level and then lift the crate into the car. That may be easier."

"You'll give us the dog back, right? You're not stealing our dog."

"No, we're not stealing your dog," Beth answered. "We just want to help."

Beth opened the back of the SUV and pulled a crate out. With some major pulling and shoving along with some words of encouragement we were able to get Barkley near the crate. "Okay, now let's push him inside," Beth instructed. We both grabbed a hind side of Barkley and the side of the crate. I looked down at his raw skin and saw hundreds of fleas skittering and jumping around. It was a sight I had never seen before. The hair on the back of my neck stood up. Once Barkley was finally in the crate Beth quickly closed the door and latched the lock.

"We'll call you after he is seen by the vet," Beth told the man.

"Yeah, yeah," the man said, "alright."

We got into the car and pulled away. "Did you see the fleas crawling all over?" Beth asked.

"Yeah, wow, that was nasty. Poor dog. And he's nine years old. To think he lived like that for who knows how long."

"Yeah, I know. We have to figure out what vet we're going to take him to."

"I can call my vet if you want."

"Sure, that would be great."

So after calling my animal hospital they gave us the okay to bring the dog in.

After a thorough exam by the doctor it was determined that the dog had a severe allergic reaction to the fleas that then caused a secondary infection. It would be months of oral medication as well as medicated baths every other day. The medical expenses would be in the hundreds. Beth contacted the owner with the news and to our relief he decided he couldn't afford the medical expenses, so he signed the dog over. We were well aware that had he wanted to keep the dog, the dog would never receive the treatment he sorely needed.

After Barkley's first medicated bath and with his nails freshly clipped, he needed a foster home. I contacted a doggy day care owner who sometimes would foster dogs for us and asked her if she could take him. She agreed to keep him there and picked him up that afternoon. I always sighed with relief when I was able to find a place for an animal to go, and Barkley was no exception.

The following day I received an e-mail report from Barkley's foster mom, Merle:

I've decided to rename my new foster dog and it is with pleasure I announce PHOENIX because he is like the rising sun. My boy is doing SO GOOD! He is HAPPY now. But he STINKS FROM HIS SKIN and this foster mom DOESN'T LIKE bathing him but he had his first bath and WAS GOOD ABOUT IT. Merle.

So it began, regular reports via e-mail came from Merle. Mostly she gave me news about Phoenix's recovery.

My boy is now PLAYING with Chico. (See photo attached.) His skin is LOOKING BETTER but still stinks. I think he needs his TEETH CLEANED. His mouth looks like it's ROTTING. Can we do that? I can try and help *raise the money for it.*

So we raised the money to get his teeth cleaned and he had regular vet appointments to check on his skin. Weeks turned into a month and then two as Phoenix slowly healed from his years of neglect. But as he healed his behavior began to change.

Merle wrote: Phoenix is starting to GET NERVOUS here and like ALL THE DOGS that stay here for a LONG TIME he is getting anxious a lot. He is SNAPPING at some dogs and seems UNHAPPY. Do you have ANYONE ELSE who will take him? He got his teeth cleaned and THIS BOY ONLY HAS A FEW TEETH. They had to PULL most of them. Merle.

I wrote back: No, I don't have any open foster homes. No one has expressed interest in him. It's going to be hard to place him. He's an old dog with probably permanent skin damage. Try and be patient, I am doing all I can. Sandy.

The boy is REALLY GETTING SQUIRRELY. Any leads on someone to take him? Merle.

No, I wish there was. Can you crate him sometimes so he's away from all the commotion? Sandy

He SNAPPED at Herb today. NO BIG DEAL. I DIDN'T SEE IT and you *know a lot of dogs don't like my husband but* gotta try and get him out. Merle.

Thanks for the update. I hope Herb is okay. Sandy

MY BOY had a GOOD DAY TODAY. Look at him playing with Pepper and Sampson. The OLD BOY still has spunk. BUT he's starting to NOT LIKE HIS CRATE and pace sometimes. It's going on THREE MONTHS. Merle.

What a cute picture! I am glad he had a good day. I can't get anyone to commit to take Phoenix. I am trying my best. Sandy

The dog is OFFICIALLY UNHAPPY. I think he needs DOGGY DOWNERS. I'd like permission to get some. Merle.

I knew medication for depression and anxiety for dogs took a while to begin working, and I had yet to experience some seriously positive results, but to pacify Merle I gave her permission. All the medical care and medication for Phoenix at that point exceeded $900. Beth had given us a very generous $500 donation and the coin jar at Merle's raised a little over $100. My bigger concern was finding someone who would adopt an older, toothless dog with anxiety issues.

A few days later I was at the animal hospital when Merle walked in with Phoenix. I was surprised to see them there because I knew that I had not okayed any appointments for that day. Looking in Merle's face

I saw her heavily applied eye makeup was running down her face and pooling underneath her eyes. "What's wrong?" I asked.

"I can't do it anymore."

"Let's go in a room and talk." I led her into an open exam room, Phoenix trailing behind.

"I came here to leave him at the kennel. This morning I came into work and there was coffee all over my office. I left him loose in my office overnight because he doesn't like his crate anymore and I came in this morning to a huge mess." She began sobbing.

"Of coffee?" I was perplexed as to how that could upset her so much. My dogs were destructive almost daily. Coffee was nothing–how about walls chewed on?

"Yes. I just can't do it. I came to drop him off to have him boarded here."

I knew that to put Phoenix in a kennel would be disastrous. The dog had been through so much and in a dark, dreary kennel with tons of barking dogs he would crumble. "Okay..." I didn't know what to say. I was stunned that she would just dump him here. *She ran a doggy day care. She couldn't handle one old dog?* I didn't get it. *Now what?* I thought to myself.

I put on my best professional, compassionate face and said, "Okay. I understand." Meanwhile my mind was screaming, *Oh, no, now you're stuck with another dog. Another dog dumped on you. How will this dog ever get adopted? A dog that is old, has skin issues, nearly no teeth and is on antidepressants. Another dog at my house. Arghghgh!!*

"Here's his medicine and what's left of his food." She sniffed and fumbled inside a bag hooked to her forearm. She then handed me the bag of supplies. I took it.

"Okay."

"He gets his medicine once a day at night. You can tell them here."

"Okay." I knew he wouldn't be staying at the kennel.

"I've gotta go," she told me, avoiding my eyes and handing me Phoenix's leash. I took it and she walked out. Phoenix looked after her, tugging on the leash.

I put the bag of his things down and bent down to give Phoenix a reassuring pat. "What are we going to do with you, boy? Well, I guess you go home with me."

Phoenix settled into my offices with the other foster dogs. He showed minimal anxiety so I began weaning him off his medication. I resolved to the fact the dog might be with me forever and just decided it wasn't worth being upset about. What would be would be. I was still perplexed by what Merle did but reminded myself that I should never be too surprised by what people did, because you never really know how much people can take.

Within a couple of weeks Phoenix had bonded to me and I was enjoying our blossoming friendship. He was a sweet, old dog whose loyalty was touching and sweet. He occasionally got into stuff like the garbage or papers on my desk, but those things were easily forgiven. I took him on walks, which reminded me very much of the walks my old dog Heidi and I took the last nine months of her life.

One cool, crisp day as I was taking off my fall coat and laying it on top of a crate in my office, the phone rang. It was a woman I knew who owned a dog bakery. She also knew Merle, and Phoenix had spent some days hanging out at her bakery when he lived at Merle's day care. She had a soft spot for Phoenix and I knew she had been keeping a look out for a good home for Phoenix. She said she had some customers that were older folks and were interested in adopting Phoenix.

"Great!" I said enthusiastically. "Can you ask them to fill out an application and then I will call them?"

"Sure. They're very nice. They even met Phoenix once when he was at my place. I think they'd be perfect for him. I have been bugging them for a long time, ever since their dog died, to get another dog."

"Thanks for thinking of Phoenix," I said warmly. "I'll look for the application."

The following afternoon I received their application. It looked great. They were both retired and their last dog had lived to a ripe old age of 16. I checked their references and called them to set up a home visit. After scheduling it for the next day I hung up and looked at Phoenix, always right beside me, patted his head and said, "Well, kid, this may be it. You may actually get a family after all. What do you think?" He looked up at me longingly with a near toothless grin. I realized how in love I was with that dog. He had been through so much and still had room for love. As I gazed in his face my heart happy-hurt.

The following day was as crisp and cold as the three before and it was dreary on top of it. I zipped my winter coat and briefly thought of the long winter ahead. I snapped the leash on Phoenix's collar and he willingly followed me out of the offices and into the car. Riding alongside me I kept my hand on his back or stroking his head the short ten-minute ride to the people's home.

Parking the car in the drive I noted the pretty house Phoenix would be living in. It was in a nice suburban neighborhood and the yard was fully fenced in. "Come on, babes, let's go," I said, leading him out of the car and to the door.

An elderly woman answered the doorbell and introduced herself as Mary. "Hi, I'm Sandy," I said stepping inside. "And this is Phoenix," I said with pride as he followed me inside.

"Sandy. Come in and sit down." She glanced down at Phoenix. I had expected Mary to be happy to see Phoenix but instead it was a lukewarm reception, which puzzled me. "He's bigger than his picture on the computer."

"Oh, yeah?" I said. *Something doesn't seem right. And where is her husband?*

I settled myself onto a couch covered with a blanket. Scanning the room I noted the wall-to-wall carpeting and older but neat and clean furniture.

"My husband will be here in a minute," she said, settling into the wingback chair opposite me. "He's not as keen on getting another dog. But we want to maybe help the dog since no one seems to want him. Kellie, at the bakery, kept telling us about the dog," she glanced at Phoenix sitting quietly beside me, "and thought maybe we could give it a try considering his situation."

"I see," I said not getting a good feeling at all.

"There he is," Mary said as her husband walked into the room. "This is Phillip. Sandy. And this is Phoenix."

"Sandy," I stood up and we shook hands.

"He's bigger than I thought," Phillip commented looking at Phoenix. Phoenix leaned in closer to me. I stroked his back.

"So," I paused, trying to think of what to say. "You're ready for another dog?"

"I don't know," Mary said. "I just felt bad for this dog. You know his story and all. Phillip here would just as soon not get one but he's willing to give it a try. Right, Phillip?"

"If that's what you want."

I felt like I was forcing this dog on them. "If you aren't sure it's no problem," I said. "I could take Phoenix back and you can think about it."

"No, it's okay," Mary said. "Kellie says we'll get along fine. I trust her. We'll give it a try."

I spent the next half an hour explaining to them what they needed to know about Phoenix. The whole time Phoenix stayed beside me, never making a move to meet them. I reasoned that it was just because he was so attached to me. We had seriously bonded, and in time he would bond to them as well. They weren't outwardly loving people, but they did have a dog for a long time that they had said they loved dearly. They had a nice home and Phoenix had no other options now. I couldn't be too picky and I knew he would be cared for properly.

Getting ready to leave I stood up and handed the leash to Mary. Phoenix stayed by my side. I bent down and wrapped my arms around his old frame, the prickly hair on his back where his newly grown-in hair was growing felt uniquely Phoenix. "Okay, sweetheart," I spoke softly, "you be a good boy. I love you and have a wonderful life." Without looking in his face for fear I would start crying I stood up and walked towards the front door. I could sense Phoenix was trying to follow me.

"Thanks for everything," I said, not sure I meant it. I kept trying to shake off my concerns. *He'll be safe. He's fine. They'll learn to love him. I can't keep him forever and his options are limited.*

I headed to the car and drove home melancholy.

The following morning I was in my office when the phone rang. "Sandy, this is Mary. We took Phoenix yesterday. Well, this morning around 6:00 a.m. my husband opened the door to get the newspaper. I told him not to open the door too wide but he wouldn't listen. Phoenix got past him and is gone. He hasn't come back."

I looked at the clock. It was 9:00 a.m. "He's been gone since 6:00?"

"Yes. I've been checking outside every now and then."

"Did you call the police?" I could feel my blood pressure rising.

"No, we didn't know what to do. We called you."

"He's been gone for three hours," I said, trying not to sound angry.

"I know, that's why I called you."

"I'll be right there."

I hung up the phone and composed an e-mail to all our volunteers: Phoenix is missing. He ran away from his new home and has been gone since 6:00 a.m. If you can help find him, please call me.

Seven minutes later I pulled into their driveway. I ran to the door. Ringing the bell I waited way too long for someone who should be concerned their dog was missing, but I reminded myself to keep it cool. Mary answered the door after a minute. "Any news?" I asked her.

"Come in. No. Phillip is really angry. This dog has not been a good idea, I think."

Ignoring that I said, "Did you call the police yet?"

"I didn't know where to call."

Is this woman dense? She is older but not that old. Jeez! Keep your cool.

"Please call the Mundelein police and Lake County Animal Control. Did you check with your neighbors?"

"Well, I saw one neighbor outside around 7:00 a.m. and asked them. They didn't see him."

"Did you ask any other neighbors?"

"No, no one has been out."

"You didn't knock on your neighbors' doors?"

"No."

My cell phone rang. It was Brenda, a volunteer. "I read about Phoenix. I want to help. Where do I meet you?"

I gave her the address and hung up. Looking at Mary I said, "I am going to knock on your neighbors' doors. If Brenda comes to the door just tell her that I'm down the block."

"Okay," she said seemingly put out. I walked out and headed to the house next door. I was choking back tears. *Why did I leave him here?*

By the fourth house Brenda showed up and I received three more calls from volunteers. People were going to come in cars and comb the neighborhood. Carla, one of my foster moms, was going to the printer to make up flyers. Carla, her son and a friend were going to begin posting flyers. The outpouring of love for Phoenix was overwhelming.

The sweat running down my back cooled fast as I continued going door to door with Brenda. It was cold, far too cold for an old dog with thin hair. I was grateful for the company and barely kept it together as I thought the worst thoughts: Phoenix alone shivering somewhere or worse yet, dead in a ditch. *After all we have been through.* By 1:00 we had asked dozens of people within the subdivision, but no one had seen him. The police were all informed and keeping a look out. I was in constant contact with three other cars filled with volunteers, all looking for Phoenix. Another gnawing fear, *Phoenix would likely only come to me.*

By 2:00 Merle had found someone to cover her at work and she was driving around. I knew Phoenix would go to her if she saw him so I was comforted by that thought. Kellie called my cell. "Sandy, I saw the e-mail about Phoenix. Oh, my God, that's horrible. I have been trying to get in touch with a woman who has a dog who is trained to track people. I know if Phoenix is around, her dog may be able to track him. Her husband said she gets off work at five. I know she'll come then."

"Okay, let me know. Thanks, Kellie." *By five it will be getting dark and the temperature will drop. It is 2:15. Phoenix has been gone for eight hours.*

Brenda and I checked in once more at Mary's house. She seemed annoyed already with our presence. Her husband was nowhere in sight any of the times we had checked back. I had decided they weren't getting Phoenix back, if he was found at all. Walking down Mary's driveway I saw a police officer coming down the block. I hurried over and flagged him down.

"Hi. I am with Animal Education and Rescue," I said to the officer. "A dog we adopted out last night got loose and we've been looking for him since this morning. Have you seen a dog that looks like a Border Collie mix around here? He's been through so much and is attached to me. He may not go to anyone else."

"Around 11:00 I did see a dog cross Midlothian and head behind those two houses where they have all those cars. They run that mechanic's shop over there."

"You did?" I said, feeling a glimmer of hope. *Don't cry.*

"Yeah. It was hours ago though. Could be long gone. That's too bad about the dog. I love dogs."

"Yeah, it's been hours since then," I commented.

"Here. Take my card," he said, grabbing a card out of his front breast pocket. "Would you call me and let me know if you find him?"

"Sure."

Brenda and I drove to where the officer said he had last seen Phoenix hours before. We pulled into the driveway between the two homes and drove around in circles yelling, "Phoenix! Phoenix!" By then I was crying. I couldn't help it.

Suddenly a big German Shepherd came out from between some cars and began barking ferociously at us. Startled we gasped and rolled up our windows. "There's no way Phoenix would be here with that dog," I said. "Let's go."

Just then the phone rang. It was Kellie. "Any signs of Phoenix?"

"No."

"Pat, the lady with the search dog is on her way. Can you meet us at Mary's house?"

"Sure."

Parked at Mary's house we waited in the warmth of the car. I watched from the window as the sunset began to fade and the last faint glow hung in the sky. "Pretty soon it'll be totally dark. We'll never find him then," I said. "He could be anywhere."

"I know," Brenda said.

Pulling up alongside us a woman got out of the car. She opened up the back door. A magnificent shepherd jumped down. We approached her. "Hi. You must be Pat. Thank you so much for coming. It means so much."

"Glad to do it. I don't know if we'll be able to help."

"You're helping now. Thank you."

"I need something that has Phoenix's scent."

"Okay, let me knock on Mary's door and see what she has."

A minute later I came back with the blanket that had been on the couch. "He sat next to the couch where you sat when you were here yesterday all night," Mary said as she handed me the blanket. I felt just awful.

Pat showed the blanket to her dog and her dog sniffed it. She gave a command, "Search, Rocket, search." We watched as Rocket led her down the block.

Meanwhile I received numerous calls with other volunteers checking in. No one had seen Phoenix. Lost signs were posted all over town. As 6:00 p.m. rolled around volunteers started heading home for dinner. There wasn't much else to do. It was now pitch dark.

Driving one more loop around the neighborhood with no sign of Phoenix we headed back to Mary's to wait for Pat. A few minutes later she showed up winded. "I'm really sorry but I don't think he's around here. There is no scent. He must be gone for hours." *I don't blame him,* I thought. *He knew those people didn't want him. He's looking for me.*

"Thanks for trying anyway," I said, patting Rocket on the head.

"Wish we could have done more."

"Thanks, really, thanks."

Pat headed to her car and they left. I turned to Brenda. "Do you have to go?"

"No, Tony is watching the kids. I'm here for as long as we need to be." What she didn't say was, *until you're ready to give up.*

"You know where the police officer said they saw him? We can't get out of the car 'cause of that dog. Let's go to the neighbor's house and see if they can help or maybe they know the dog or their neighbor and can secure the dog so at least we can look around."

"Okay."

We drove to the house just east of the mechanic's shop and knocked on the door. A man answered. "Hi, my name is Sandy. I am with Animal Education and Rescue. We're looking for a dog."

"You lookin' for that dog that was lost this morning?"

"Yeah, how'd you know?" I asked excitedly.

"An e-mail has been going around forwarded by people. It's all over the internet."

"You're kidding me." I swallowed down a lump.

"By accident I deleted the e-mail. I can't believe you are here. I was waiting 'til my sister came home. I left a message for her to call me. She works the late shift. Anyway, my son and I saw the dog this morning."

"You did? Where?"

"Next door. We rent a garage from the guy next door. He came into my garage, but as soon as we called to him he took off."

"Did you follow him?"

"Yeah, but he just disappeared. There was no way he was going to come to me."

"He probably would only come to me."

"Too bad. I wish we could help."

"You can. You know that shepherd next door?"

"That's Shep. He's kinda their guard dog."

"I noticed. Could you get them to put him away and show us where you saw him in your garage?"

"Sure," he said, grabbing his coat from a rack in the entranceway.

"But that dog's mean to other dogs. I doubt your dog would stay there. He'd be smart if he were gone."

We waited in the car until Shep was put away. Following the man to his garage he replayed for us what happened. Standing inside the garage he said, "I was workin' on this boat here," he pointed, "and this dog just appeared. My son and I looked up and we called to the dog and the dog took off that way." He pointed into the darkness of the back lot where cars sat parked.

Following where his finger had pointed I began calling out, "Phoenix, Phoenix." *He can't possibly still be here.*

"I don't know if he'd still be here, Sandy." Brenda said my thoughts out loud. "But if he is he'll come to your voice."

"Phoenix! Phoenix! Come here boy!" I stood near the row of cars, the garage light creating shadows in the otherwise pitch-dark area.

"Phoenix! Phoenix!"

I turned to my left and suddenly out of the darkness came a shadowy figure, right towards me. Surprised I gasped. "Phoenix, is that you?" I bent down and opened my arms. The shadowy figure came into full form as Phoenix walked into my waiting arms. I grabbed his collar and wrapped my arms around him. "Oh, Phoenix baby," I began crying. I whispered, "I'm sorry I left you."

The neighbor and Brenda walked over. "You found your dog!" the man said.

"Phoenix!" Brenda said, bending down to pet him.

After we thanked the man over and over Phoenix jumped into the safety of the car. I began making calls. "Phoenix is safe! We got him!" I said over and over. During the ride back to my car parked by Mary's house, Phoenix sat on my lap. He seemed no worse for the wear. Me, I felt every muscle in my body ache. "It's 9:00," I said to Brenda. "Phoenix was gone for 15 hours. Thank you so much, Brenda."

"I'm just glad he's safe. Is he going to Mary's house?"

"No way. They don't want him. Never did. And he knew it. He's going home with me."

Settled back in my offices Phoenix was safe and sound asleep. Mary never called to check on Phoenix and I never called her. I resolved to the fact I might always have him and that was okay. He was happy with me and that's what mattered.

About a month later I received an e-mail from a woman interested in adopting Phoenix. It was the first application ever completed for him willingly and without pressure. I read over the application. It came in from a single 27-year-old woman who lived in a condo in Chicago. *Why would a young, single woman want an old dog?* I was skeptical but willing to speak to her.

"Hi, is Krystine there?"

"This is."

"Hi Krystine, this is Sandy with Animal Education and Rescue. I am calling about the application I received for Phoenix."

"Yes! Great! Thanks for calling."

"Sure. I was reviewing your application and thought maybe we could talk. Is now a good time?"

"Sure, I have time now."

"Great," I paused, scanning the application in front of me. "I guess my first question is, why Phoenix?"

"I thought he was adorable."

"You did?"

"Yeah, he's got this little old man look."

"Yeah?"

"He's so cute. I have a female dog, Melon. She's more like a cat. She's a Shiba Inu. They are cat-like dogs. I love her but I wanted a dog that would be more like a dog, you know, love me, want to be with me. But she's the queen and they'd have to get along."

"Phoenix is good with dogs. I have to ask, are you okay with an older dog? We think Phoenix is nine."

"Oh, yeah, that doesn't bother me."

She's too good to be true. "Let me tell you a little bit about him. First of all, he came from a home where he was severely neglected. He had no hair on half his body and the skin was red and raw. His teeth were terrible and most had to be pulled. His hair has mostly grown back, but it'll always be thin and may need medicated baths." I paused. "Anyway, Phoenix is getting much better, but he has some separation anxiety. He may try and tear up stuff and may be testy with people. He did snap at one person." I paused again, sure that she would step in and say thanks but no thanks.

But instead I heard, "Okay, that's not a problem."

She CAN'T be for real. "The separation anxiety can get pretty bad," I said as I thought of Merle's problems with the coffee and the crating. "And he doesn't like to be crated. He could chew things up."

"He just needs to get along with Melon. She might put him in his place, but if he is good with that everything should be fine. I guess we'd just have to have them meet."

"Alright, well, let me check your references and we'll go from there."

After we hung up I checked her references and everything checked out great. Her condo complex was very dog friendly and they even had a courtyard where all the dogs met and ran and played. I called Krystine back. "Hi, Krystine. Well, everything checked out great so we need to set up a meeting."

"Fantastic! Where and when?"

"How about tomorrow at the animal hospital? And bring Melon. What I was thinking is that since Phoenix has been through so much I thought maybe you could do a weekend sleepover, if the dogs are okay with each other. That way if it doesn't work out it's no big deal. I just don't want him to keep being displaced. Is that okay?"

"Sure. That's fine with me."

"Then if you decide after the weekend you'd like to adopt him then you'd come back for an educational program on Monday night. You'll have a chance to see some photos of how Phoenix looked when we first got him."

"Okay. I can't wait to meet the cutie."

The next day I prepared for the meeting with absolutely no expectations. I had always imagined that Phoenix would get adopted to older folks because he was an older dog. I did not expect a single young woman in a condo in the city. It just didn't match. But I was open minded enough to try, especially since what I thought was an ideal home for him turned out to be a horrible fit.

Phoenix and I walked into the animal hospital and I spotted a Shiba Inu with a pretty, young woman with long, blond hair. She stood up and smiled at Phoenix. "This must be Phoenix. He's even cuter in real life."

A lump instantly grew in my throat. *Something good might be happening.* I took a deep breath, the feelings that had been bottled up about Phoenix stuffed back down. I was so emotionally attached to that vulnerable dog and felt such a deep sense of commitment.

"Hi, Krystine. Your dog's cute, too." We let the dogs sniff each other. After a few sniffs they seemed indifferent to each other. "They seem okay."

"Yep, they do," she grinned. *Was this the family my Phoenix was meant to be with?* "Hey, Phoenix," Krystine cooed and reached out a hand to Phoenix. Phoenix walked over to Krystine and let her pet him.

"He likes you."

"Yeah, I knew he would," she said, not arrogantly but as if a higher power were leading her. She stroked his head. I swallowed down that lump again.

She gently took his leash from me. "Do you mind holding my dog's leash for a minute?"

"Sure." I took her cat-dog who stood there aloofly.

Krystine kneeled down and began stroking Phoenix's face and body. "You are adorable," she said softly as she petted him. After some time I knew that Phoenix would be okay going home with her for the weekend.

"So what do you think? Do you want to take him home for a sleepover?"

"Sure!"

"Okay, sounds good. Now don't be surprised if he gets anxious when you leave your condo. He has a tendency to pace and could tear things up or get into stuff. Go slow with new people, too."

"Sure."

"Will you call me tomorrow and let me know how it's going?"

"Of course."

So I watched as Phoenix willingly followed Krystine and Melon out the door. I couldn't believe it. I stood there stunned.

That evening and the next day even though I was busy my thoughts continued to go back to Phoenix. I didn't call Krystine on Saturday, figuring if things were really bad I'd get a call. Sunday morning I was in the office when the phone rang.

"Hey, Sandy, this is Krystine."

"Hey, Krystine, how's Phoenix?"

"He's been great. He's doing fine with Melon. She growled a little at him, but that didn't surprise me, and he backed off, which is good."

"Did you leave at all and leave him in the condo?"

"Yeah, my boyfriend Mike and I went to the store."

"Did he tear anything up?"

"No, not at all. He's been great. He's even getting to like me, I think."

"Really?" *So quickly?*

"Yeah. I really don't know what you were talking about with the behavior stuff. I haven't seen anything."

"Wow, that's great."

"He's a really sweet guy."

"So what do you think? Do you want to keep him?"

"Yeah, of course I do. I love the guy already."

"Fantastic." I smiled. "Can you come to the educational program tomorrow?"

"Sure, yeah. Do you want me to bring Phoenix?"

"No, you better not. I don't want to confuse him."

"Alright, no problem. See you then."

We hung up and I sat there trying to let it sink in. Flashes of memories flew like a slideshow in my head. Phoenix at his original home, hunched over, in pain, the whites of his eyes as he looked at us. Then shoving him in a crate, the feel of fleas scurrying on my fingertips as I pushed his bare butt. Then Phoenix running around the doggy day care with a big, open grin. Then I remembered a photo on our web site of Phoenix and Merle sitting on a bench outside. Then Phoenix looking up at Merle in the animal hospital as Merle cried her eyes out. Then Phoenix rushing out of hiding in the darkness into my arms after running away. Finally Phoenix walking out of the animal hospital with Krystine and Melon, not looking back at me.

Monday night Krystine came to the animal hospital for an educational program. Half a dozen new dog owners sat in chairs facing me. "Thank you all for coming tonight. Congratulations on adopting your new dog. I'd like to mention one person in particular. Krystine," I motioned towards her, "adopted Phoenix, an older dog who had been severely neglected. Older dogs have such a hard time getting adopted, especially if they don't look or act so perfect. I have to commend Krystine for adopting Phoenix. And as far as Phoenix is concerned it was obvious to me that he knew who his mom was, he just had to wait a long nine-plus years to see her."

"Now when you watch this short movie you'll see photos of Phoenix when we first got him. You'll know it's him because of the missing hair and curled-over nails. Okay, now I'll run the movie."

I went over to the computer and pressed play and stood leaning against the wall as the movie played. When it got to the shocking photos of Phoenix I looked over at Krystine. Even in the darkened room I could see her wipe away a tear. She finally understood the magnitude of Phoenix's history.

Ending the evening I said goodbye to all the new families. Krystine said to me, "I had no idea how bad things were for Phoenix. Those photos, God."

"Yeah, it was bad."

"Don't worry, Sandy, he'll have a great life, spoiled rotten."

"I know. Hey listen, I never got to formally say goodbye. Can you do me a favor?"

"Of course."

I blinked away tears. "Can you wrap your arms around him and tell him I love him, to be good and have a wonderful life?"

"Sure, of course."

I gave Krystine a big hug and said into her ear, "Thank you. Thank you."

To this day I still get periodic e-mails from Krystine: Phoenix is doing great! He's the leader of all the dogs in the courtyard and he loves going to the dog park. Phoenix and Melon are even sort of friends, which is cool. His hair is getting thicker, I think. I have him on this raw food diet that I swear by. I think that's helping him a lot. I really love the old guy and so does everyone else. Thanks for trusting me with him.

Krystine.

One e-mail included a few photos of Phoenix. One was of him lying on the couch looking up at the camera, a big grin on his face. The other was of Phoenix in the courtyard surrounded by some other dogs, his tail obviously wagging and once again that silly, near-toothless grin.

Lessons Through Angels

It was a crisp, bright morning in October when I let my dogs out back after breakfast for a final morning potty break. They trailed outside, one after the other as I reminded each one to "go potty." I stopped on the deck for a moment, appreciating the fine weather, and turned and went back inside.

Five minutes later I was back at the porch door calling my dogs inside. One after another they enthusiastically came running inside, all but Rascal. I was accustomed to Rascal taking his time coming in because he loved to sit on top of the wooden picnic table and sniff the air and enjoy the sunshine. And because it was a particularly gorgeous morning I was not concerned anything was amiss.

"Rascal," I yelled outside, "Rascal, come." He did not come. So I walked onto the deck and kept calling, "Rascal, Rascal." My inner peace closed like a light clicked off and I could feel a heaviness slowly press on my chest. *Something isn't right.*

Standing on the pavement I scanned the enclosed driveway. *Where is he? Did he escape the yard?* My eyes stopped and settled on something small and yellow beside the fence. I ran over to the object and there on the hard ground was Rascal, our precious, sweet, 12-pound, three-year-old Jack Russell Terrier/Chihuahua mix.

I screamed at him, "RASCAL!" as if I expected him to startle awake and jump to attention, but he didn't move. I touched him but still he didn't move. Out loud I said, "Oh, God," my mind racing. *This cannot be happening. What is going on?* I looked at his lifeless body one more time and thought, *I need to get help.* I ran back into the house, through the kitchen and flung open the door to the upstairs and screamed, "Chuck, Rascal is hurt. You have to come NOW!" Then I ran back outside to Rascal.

Bending over my little dog each second seemed like an eternity. But it was only seconds before David, my 15-year-old son, appeared. I felt instant gratitude. "David," I said looking at him, "we have to go now. To the vet." I scooped Rascal up in my arms. He was completely limp, his head flopping over my forearm. Gently I laid him in David's arms. "We have to go now!"

I pulled the car out of the driveway and headed towards the animal hospital. David, holding Rascal, said, "What should I do?" with deep concern in his voice. That poor kid, to have to deal with something so hard. I knew how much he loved that dog.

"Just tell him you love him. Talk to him."

"Okay," he said. He looked down at Rascal. "It's okay Rascal. It's okay." Rascal's head kept flopping over his arm. David kept gently placing Rascal's head back on his forearm. After that David was silent. I felt the shock in the air.

So I took up where David left off, trying to reassure my son. "Rascal, we love you. We love you." I went over a pothole, the bump causing Rascal's head to droop over David's arm again. David once again raised Rascal's head and placed it gently on his arm. "Okay, David, I am going to pull right up to the front of the hospital, by the door, and you get out and run in while I park the car."

"Okay," he said.

I pulled alongside the front and said, "Go! Go!" David jumped out of the car, Rascal secure in his arms and he ran for the door and went inside. I backed the car up and pulled into a parking spot. The whole time thinking, *This cannot be happening to us. This is not real. Not Rascal. This doesn't make sense.* Flashes of Rascal injured by Robin, his neck ripped open, came to my mind. Then I remembered his long recovery from the injury to his neck, the hot packs, the stitches, looking like Frankenstein. *Why this dog again?* I flung open the doors to the animal hospital. David was standing there with Rascal still in his arms. There was no staff out front.

"No one's here," he said, frustration clear in his voice.

"Come on," I commanded. "Follow me." I burst through the door that led to the back. On the other side Dr. Leonard and his assistant were working. "My dog, he's not moving. I think he's...here." I took Rascal, light as a feather pillow, and handed him over to the doctor. "I just found him that way. He was alive. Less than 30 minutes ago. I just let him out for a minute to go potty. I came back and he was, well, like this."

Dr. Leonard took Rascal and gently set him down on a grated, steel table behind him. He put his stethoscope on Rascal's heart and listened. Without a word he picked Rascal up and brought him to the surgery room where he laid him on the table. Wringing my hands I prayed for a miracle. He turned on the ultrasound machine and placed the microphone-shaped probe on Rascal's chest and moved it around slowly while looking at the monitor on the machine. The seconds ticked by as I stood holding my breath. He placed the probe down beside Rascal and faced us. "I'm sorry, he's gone."

Looking behind me I saw David standing by the door. He was blinking his eyes slowly over and over, his face and body frozen in place. *I can't protect my child from this pain.* I walked over to David and put my arms around his shoulders. He stood very still and stiff, not responding to my touch. *Out of all our dogs David adored Rascal the most.*

Chuck arrived and stood outside the surgery room looking in. Rascal looked so tiny lying still on the steel table. This dog was his baby, our baby, and the one dog we gave ourselves that was exactly what we wanted. He was our one indulgence. All the other dogs we had we adopted because they were the hard luck cases, or we owned because no one else wanted them.

Like three trees standing far enough from each other to look alone we stood planted.

"How could this have happened?" I finally said dumbfounded and to no one in particular. "I was gone five minutes. He was fine. He was fine. He was fine." I knew I was repeating myself. It was as if I was speaking above my body. If a needle were to poke me I wouldn't have felt it. Chuck stood there, his face blank, stunned.

Dr. Leonard said he suspected that Rascal might have been poisoned. With that suggestion I thought, *Who might have done this? Would someone want to get back at us?* Before we left the hospital I stroked Rascal's body. *It's not scaring me to touch him when he's dead. A lifeless body feels strange, empty.*

When we arrived home Chuck and I sat in the living room together and tried to think about how Rascal could have been poisoned. Maybe the vacant house next door to us had rat poison in it to kill rats and rodents. We saw squirrels going in and out of the roof daily. We heard through the years they had a mouse problem in their basement. If that were the case could the animal eat the poison and make it outside, die by our fence and then Rascal eat the animal, thus poisoning himself? Or did someone want revenge on us for some reason? With all the investigations I did and the simple fact that I could be easily found because of my years in the public eye, that was a possibility.

That afternoon I went to the church next door to us. I walked into the office and spoke to a woman behind the desk. "Hi, I'm your next door neighbor. My dog just died suddenly and the vet suspects poisoning. Do you know if anyone put out rat poison or some other type of poison either in the abandoned house on the other side of our house or your garage?"

She looked at me in disbelief and said, "You don't think we would poison your dog?"

"No, I wasn't saying that," I said rather annoyed. *I can't believe she didn't even say she was sorry to hear about our dog.* She was far more interested in being defensive. "But," I explained, "you do have an abandoned house next to us and we have seen squirrels and mice go in the house through cracks, and we thought maybe you had used some rat or animal poison." She looked at me like I was a complete idiot. I pushed on, "If the animal ate the poison and died near or in our yard, our dog could have eaten it and that would have poisoned him."

"I'll ask around and get back to you."

"Okay, thank you." And I left.

At home Chuck, David and I were walking around like zombies. Early that evening while Chuck was gone pet sitting David and I, not knowing what to do with our time, went to the nearby mall and walked around aimlessly. He looked around him. "Doesn't everyone look like they have no emotions?"

"Yeah, David," I said and patted his back. *It's strange what grief does to the mind.*

I was aware of the five stages of mourning, and we were in the first, shock. Before going to school the following day David asked me, "Do your muscles hurt?"

"No, they don't. Why, do yours?"

"It's because of Rascal. All my muscles hurt."

For nine days I hibernated in my house. I did not want to say out loud to anyone that our Rascal was dead because then it would be real. Chuck didn't say much except, "He was my baby."

It took three days to get the results from the vet regarding the blood test. It was inconclusive. We opted against an autopsy because it was also probable, according to the vet, that we still might not know what happened to him. Additionally, the cost to do the autopsy was high, and with all the other animals in our care I couldn't justify it.

So we were resolved to the idea that we would never know what killed our dog. From then on we kept a closer eye on what was happening in and around our property.

Here's an excerpt of a column I wrote about Rascal:

Rascal came to us as a foster dog all the way from Pane County Humane Society in southern Illinois. Chuck had always wanted a cuddly little dog. After just a few nights of Rascal sleeping between us, Rascal's head either on my pillow or Chuck's pillow, Chuck was hooked. Gathering Rascal to his chest one night, Rascal closing his eyes in contentment, Chuck said, "I want to adopt this one." It was my decision to adopt all the other dogs we had so of course I had no objection at all to Chuck's decision to keep Rascal. I was thrilled that he finally had his "cuddly little dog."

We are not the only people who have lost a beloved pet in a tragic way. I am sure you can understand how we feel. I thought I would try and do something positive at a time when I don't feel very positive at all. I thought of an idea. I am asking my readers, all of whom I know are animal lovers, to donate money to a charity in memory of Rascal. Then send me a note telling me where you donated the money. I will then have a plaque made up that says where money went in memory of Rascal and present it as a surprise to Chuck and David.

Letters came flooding in. I received heart-felt letters and notes from my readers. Many of the people talked about the pets they had lost and shared with me where they donated money. It was beautiful to think that Rascal was affecting people and animals in a positive way, even in death.

From my personal journal:

The evening of October 9, the night before Rascal died, I had a lot on my mind. When that happens I wake up suddenly in the middle of the night and can't get back to sleep. I spent much of that night cuddling and petting Rascal. I thought to myself how lucky I was to have such a fantastic dog, such a snuggly puppy. I can still feel each curve of his little body, his unique doggy smell, the endless kisses he planted all over my face, his rough black whiskers tickling my lips when I kissed his soft muzzle. I am so grateful for that night.

Rascal had been, by far, the easiest of all our dogs. He was David and Chuck's favorite. He loved to jump in our laps, was so easy to care for and had a little bit of sassy Jack Russell attitude mixed in, which always made us laugh. We just didn't get it why out of all the dogs it would be Rascal who would be taken from us. Not that we want to lose any of our dogs, but frankly many of the dogs we have are here because no one else would want them. Many were not fully housebroken, some have behavioral problems and physical limitations, and a few were just plain old. Rascal was our one single gift we gave to ourselves–a dog without issues.

For over a week I allowed myself to grieve. I questioned myself over and over whether I really wanted to continue to be involved in helping animals. I was very ready to quit. I was tired. I was spent.

Ten days to the day Rascal died Beth called and asked me if I'd go to Robinson with her. Robinson was a depressed town where it was common for pit bulls to be used for fighting and/or protection, dogs were chained up outside protecting property and big, tough stray dogs ran the streets. Beth's mission was to try and clean up their dog problems. I decided it was time to get out of the house and do something productive.

Beth and I worked great together, complementing each other's natural talents. While I was quick about everything, which allowed us to accomplish more, Beth was slower and more organized, which meant everything we did was more complete. We made each other laugh and with our common passion for protecting animals never ran out of things to talk about. Driving into the city limits I decided I was glad I went.

We met up with Beth's friend Shari. Shari, a tough city girl in her 60's, with a growl-y smoker's voice and a heart of gold, was the one who turned Beth on to Robinson and its dog problems. For years Shari spent all her free time getting strays off the streets. She knew every street in Robinson and always knew what animals needed saving.

Pulling up alongside Shari's car, Beth rolled down her window so we could discuss what we were going to do first. "Hey, Shari," Beth said.

"Hi, Beth," she said in her low, monotone voice. She looked at me, "Hey, Sandy, how ya doin'?"

"Hi, Shari," I said cheerfully.

Shari got right to it. "There's a pit I saw tied to a chain-link fence on Seventh. Idiot has a rusty wire crate by it. Why? You got me." Shari was pumped. "There's also this little, yellow Chihuahua mix that I keep seeing in the area. I know the people who own him and they just let him run the neighborhood. Idiots. I hear he lives outside with a big rottie." She lit a cigarette and inhaled.

A yellow Chihuahua mix. That's strange, I thought.

"Where do you want to go first?" Shari asked, raring to go.

Beth thought for a minute. "Let's go to the pit first. Do you know where the Chihuahua is now?"

"No, but probably running the neighborhood."

I doubt we'll see the little dog. What's the likelihood that we'll see the dog running around in this town? It's like a needle in a haystack. But my heart hurt, just thinking and wondering if the dog looked like

Rascal. As it was the past ten days, my mind and body were exhausted.

We arrived at a run-down home, the pit bull allegedly in back. Beth and I walked up to the front door; Shari hung back by the cars. Beth knocked on the door. A young black man wearing a football jersey answered the door. We introduced ourselves and asked if he had a pit bull. He said yes, he did, so we asked to see it. We followed him to the back-yard where a pit bull was tied to a chain-link fence by a four-foot chain. The dog was barking aggressively at us.

The man approached the dog and made a motion as if he was going to take the dog off the chain. "Sir," Beth said firmly, "please don't take that dog off the chain. He doesn't seem too happy to see us." I thought, *How hard could I kick a dog charging at me?* The dog kept barking at us. "Please come over here," Beth shouted over the insistent barking.

The man dropped the lead and slowly meandered towards us. The dog began lunging forward at us, trying to break free to get to us. Beth began, "Why do you have that dog chained up like that?"

"My friends come over and he don't like other people. He's a watchdog." He pointed at the dog as if it was necessary to prove his point.

"Where is his shelter?"

"I bring him in at ten at night and put him in the basement."

"Sir, your dog cannot be outside in all kinds of weather without a dog house," Beth said.

Hearing someone yelling something behind us and towards the street I turned. It was Shari. I walked over to her. "The Chihuahua," she said trying to catch her breath. "It's up the street. It's been hurt. It's bleeding."

"Hold on." I turned and ran back to Beth. *I can't believe she spotted the dog.*

I interrupted the man who was talking to Beth. "Beth, Shari said the Chihuahua is at the end of the block. He's been injured." Beth looked at me and back to the man as if thinking, *what to do?* "How about if we come back here later? I'll begin walking towards the dog," I offered, pointing the way down the block.

"Okay," she said. I walked back to Shari and suggested that she go ahead of us in her car and get some distance ahead of the dog. "You can keep a watch on the dog from ahead and we'll close in from behind."

"Yeah, okay," Shari said and walked to her car.

I took off on foot. I thought, *I must be the strangest sight to anyone watching me right now. We were probably the only white people within the city limits, which would make us different enough, but here was this big, blond, white chick running down their block obviously after something or someone.*

Looking towards the stop sign, I squinted my eyes trying to see ahead of me. *I refuse to get glasses.* I thought I saw a small, yellow dog at the corner. Beth came up beside me in her car. She rolled down her window. I pointed at the corner. "I see the dog! It's at the corner!" I breathed heavily.

"Okay," she said. "I'll go up to the end of the block and turn the corner, hopefully to keep it away from that busy road up there."

"Okay. Shari went ahead and around the corner. I think she's trying to get a few blocks ahead."

Beth drove on and I forged ahead on foot, getting closer. Keeping my eyes on the blurry dog I got within 20 feet and my eyes cleared, and standing slumped over could have been Rascal's brother. My heart leapt. I slowly crept closer and when I was within six feet I noticed a wound on the dog's neck. His eyes were at half mast and his ears were sitting back on his head. The dog was obviously in pain.

Beth rounded the corner in her car and I stepped a little closer. "Hey, Baby," I said in an ever-so-sweet-and-calm voice. "Come here." I slowly reached out my hand. He looked at me and instantly was up and took off down the block. "Darn it!"

I walked to the end of the block, followed the dog right and onto a sidewalk beside a four-lane road, the traffic speed limit 45. *One wrong step for the dog and he's history.* I looked past the dog and noted Beth's SUV was stopped at the end of the block. I looked behind me and saw that Shari was parked a block behind me. I kept walking and the dog kept an even pace away from me.

The dog was trotting straight towards Beth's car. I thought, *Maybe she will get him.* She slowly opened her car door. The dog took off to the right and down the side street. I approached Beth, still standing by her car. "If you can trap him in a fenced yard we might be able to get him," she offered.

"Okay, I'll give it a try." I took off down the side street. Beth jumped back in her car. The dog was a good block away from me down the side street. I could see Shari's maroon van coming out of an alley and turning towards the dog. The dog stopped and looked at Shari's car as she pulled alongside him. She opened her car door. The dog took off back in my direction. I got my leash ready to loop him as he passed, but as soon as he saw me he went down the alley. *Rats!* I followed.

This went on for a good hour with no luck. Each time the dog headed towards the busy road I said a silent prayer to protect him. Then I was standing beside Beth's car, talking to her though the window. We were trying to figure out what else we could do when Shari drove up beside us and said, "I know where the family lives. Should I go get them and have them get their dog?"

"Great idea!" I said. "We'll try and keep him in this area."

"Okay, I'll be back." Shari rolled away.

"I'll just stay behind him," I told Beth.

"You sure you aren't too tired?"

"No, I'm fine. One of us should be on foot. It's easier to follow that way."

It seemed like much longer than it probably was before Shari finally came back. By then I was tired of chasing a dog there was no way I was going to catch, and so Beth and I were both in the car watching the dog as he stood around sniffing the grass ten feet ahead of us next to the four-lane road. Pulling alongside us Shari said, "The owner wasn't home but their kids were. They were going to have a relative take them to meet me. They were following me but I lost them. I told them where to meet me. They better show up."

"It's really our only chance," I told them.

"Yeah," they both agreed solemnly.

Some time passed before finally a small, black sports car pulled alongside Beth's car and parked. I jumped out of the car. A man and two children got out of the car. I pointed at the dog half way down the block and said to the kids, "Is this your dog?"

"Yeah, that's Louie," they answered in unison. *Louie was the name of my childhood dog. Strange,* I thought.

"Okay, we need to get Louie." I looked at the man. "Do you know if the dog will come to you?"

"I don't know the dog," he answered half asleep. *Great,* I thought, *now we have to rely on these kids.*

"Okay, well let's go get him. He's just up the block," I told the girls. I walked fast and they ran beside me, keeping up. "How old are you?" I asked the girls.

Their little legs trying to keep up with me and winded already the older girl said, "I'm eight."

"I'm six."

"Okay, let's stop for a second. I need to tell you what we are going to do." We stopped and I bent down towards them and paused, gathering my thoughts. I began, "Louie is in a very dangerous situation.

A car could kill him so I need you to get him. I am going to walk just behind you with him," I pointed to their driver some ten feet back, "and you walk a little ahead and call Louie's name. When you get close enough to him place this leash around his neck like this." I showed them how to use the noose. "Can you do it?"

"Yeah," the older girl nodded, her heavily decorated and braided hair bouncing up and down. They were simply adorable.

So the girls walked ahead about five paces and I said, "Say, Louie!"

They yelled, "Louie!" Louie turned back and looked at them and stopped for just a second before he moved on. He recognized them, no doubt.

We walked a few more steps. "Say it again," I encouraged.

"Louie!" Louie stopped and waited until the girls were 12 feet from him and then he took off down a side street.

"Call him again," I commanded.

"Louie!" I stopped as they walked quickly towards him. That time they got within six feet of him.

"Stop," I yelled from behind. "Call him to you."

"Louie, Louie come here." Louie began walking towards them. *Please, please, Louie.*

"Okay," I yelled over, "get read to put the leash around him." Louie crept closer to them and just as the older girl was going to put the leash around him he took off across the street and towards a house.

"Darn," I said softly.

Louie walked to the edge of a chain-link fence. "Girls," I called out, "he's going up against the fence. Try and get him." They hurried across the street and slowly approached him and the older girl gently slipped the leash around his neck. I ran over. "Girls! You are fantastic! Good job!"

Slowly I walked closer to the exhausted dog as he leaned heavily against the fence, his nose facing the ground, his eyes slits. I took the leash from the girl and bent down to look at him more closely. Beth came up behind me. "They got him," I stated the obvious.

Looking closer we could see the wound on his neck was actually dripping with a watery, bloody fluid. His eyes were half closed. That was one sick dog. I looked at the man who had brought the little girls and said, "This dog is very ill and needs immediate medical care. I need to speak to the owners."

"They aren't home," he said unaffected by what was happening.

"Do they have a cell phone?"

"I think so."

"Well, can you call it?"

"Yeah." He dialed. "They have your dog," he said into the phone. "They said he's sick and needs to go the doctor."

"I'll talk to her," I ordered. He handed me the phone.

"Yes, this is Sandy Wisniewski. I'm a humane investigator. We have been chasing your dog for over two hours. He was running loose in the neighborhood. We have him but he has a very serious injury to his neck and needs immediate medical care."

"What?" She sounded like she just woke up.

"I said your dog has a wound, an injury to his neck. It is dripping and bloody. You need to take him to the vet now."

"I can't do that."

"Well, it cannot wait."

"Well, what do you want me to do?" By her voice she clearly didn't seem too affected by the news.

"If you can't afford to treat him we will get him treated but you will have to relinquish him to us."

"So I can get him back after you fix him up?"

"No, that means you are giving him up."

"He's my dog."

"Listen," I said, "your dog has been roaming the neighborhood on and off for weeks. Your dog was found over three miles from your house on a busy road. Frankly, you don't take care of your dog."

"Um, well, what do I gotta do?"

"If you give up the dog we will take it in for treatment."

"Okay."

"So you are giving the dog up?"

"Yeah."

"Okay."

"Bye."

"Goodbye." I hung up.

"She gave up the dog," I told Beth. "Let's get him in the car. We have to get him to the vet."

"I'll get a crate." Beth headed for her car.

"You got him!" Shari walked over.

"Yeah, but he's pretty sick. The owner gave him up, but we've got to get him to the vet." I turned to the little girls still standing there. "You two saved your dog." Beth walked towards us dragging a crate. "I am really proud of both of you," I added. They smiled.

Shari went on, "You should be very proud. Here." She dug into her pocket and pulled out a $20. "You two split that for getting the dog." I was surprised by what she did and frankly didn't agree with it. They needed to learn that the way their family cared for the dog was wrong and irresponsible. It was not the time to reward them. But I kept my opinion to myself. What was important was getting the dog to a vet—pronto.

We loaded the dog into the crate and carried the crate into Beth's SUV. We decided we would quickly finish up with the guy with the pit bull and then head to Shari's vet. The whole ride until we arrived at the vet the car reeked of the rotting flesh of Louie's festering wound.

We arrived at the vet's office 30 minutes later. While the doctor was cleaning up Louie's wound I called Chuck. "Chuck, listen, you wouldn't believe it."

"What?" He never knew what to expect from me.

"We saved a little Chihuahua that looks just like Rascal."

"Very funny."

"I wouldn't joke like that."

"You're serious?"

"Yeah, I'm serious."

"We're at the vet. He's got a big wound on his neck. The vet is treating him right now. Listen, do you want to foster him?"

The phone was silent for a few seconds. Then, "Bring him home."

"Tell David so he doesn't freak out. I'm not kidding, he looks like Rascal."

"Okay," he said. I could tell he wasn't sure whether to believe me or not.

An hour later I called Chuck and told him I was five minutes from home. When I arrived home Chuck and David were waiting outside for us. I opened the crate door and Chuck looked inside to see Louie. Silently and ever-so-gently Chuck reached inside and took him out. Holding him close to his chest he looked long and hard at the little dog. David stood beside Chuck and slowly began petting the dog's cheek. I knew their thoughts were about Rascal.

Days followed with doctor's appointments and ultimately the need for the dog to have surgery to repair the damage a severe infection from an animal attack caused. The first week he was shy and in pain and I had to approach him very carefully. Each day I took care of him I was reminded of my sweet Rascal and wondered if Rascal brought this dog to me to remind me that I was needed and not to give up on what I was doing.

We bribed him with treats that were called "Nacho dog treats," which he gobbled up enthusiastically. After a few days of Nacho dog treats and some serious love Louie was coming around. So in honor of his recovery and his favorite treat we renamed him Nacho. After a month his neck was well on its way to recovery and he was settled into my offices.

As Nacho gained his strength and the infection left his body his true personality came shining through. There were many times a certain thing he would do or way he would act would remind us of Rascal. Often times David would tell me that Nacho "may really be Rascal in Nacho's body, he is so much like him." In healing Nacho we healed our hearts, and memories of Rascal became joyous instead of just the memory of losing him.

Chuck told me later that when he first saw Louie he felt angry and sad. He was angry because his dog was dead and sad because he missed Rascal so much. David was excited from the very beginning. I knew in some unique and beautiful way this dog was brought to us for a reason. Ten days to the day Rascal died a dog that looked just like Rascal needed to be rescued. Was it a set of circumstances or was it a miracle?

The months went by and Nacho remained with us. No one seemed interested in adopting him. After six months we thought that maybe Nacho was meant to stay with us, to take Rascal's place. Maybe that is what Rascal wanted? So we tried introducing Nacho to our dogs to see if they would get along, but after many attempts it was determined that Nacho didn't want to live within our crazy pack of canines. He made it clear he wanted a quieter home.

It took one year and seven months for Nacho to finally find a place to call his own. A 30-something-year-old single woman named Melody sent in an application for our little boy. By that time Nacho had been with AEAR longer than any other dog and had quite a following of volunteers who adored him. So when I met up with Melody and her dog at the animal hospital a dozen volunteers came to meet her and say an official goodbye to him.

After an uneventful meeting of the two dogs and the okay that the adoption was going through, everyone began saying their personal good-byes to Nacho. Wanting to be last I watched as one of our young volunteers choked back tears as he said goodbye to Nacho. *He has touched so many people,* I thought. Lastly it was my turn. I picked Nacho up and wrapped my arms around him. I breathed in his unique Nacho smell and breathed out a sigh. I whispered into his ear, "Thank you, baby. Thanks for making me believe I am still needed, that I have to keep doing this. Thanks for helping my family." Then I looked into his little face and said loud enough so others could hear, "Now you be a good boy. I love you and have a wonderful life." Then I planted a loud kiss on his cheek.

As I watched Nacho walk out the door with his new mom I felt like in a way I was saying goodbye to Rascal. It was okay. I was finally ready. I was ready to move on, move forward and keep going.

Ten More Stupid Things People Say About Animals

1. When my dog escapes the house I chase him and scream at him, "Sparky come!" I am angry and mean business. Then when he comes to me I yell at him and say, "You are very bad to run away!" Oh, I am so mad! *So I would ask this seemingly clever man: Now if you were your dog next time you escape the house would YOU come back? Enroll your pooch in training and teach him to come when called.*

2. When my dog runs away and some time later returns home I yell at him so that next time he knows not to run away again. *See number one.*

3. I have an out-of-control dog. I keep him in line by crating him a lot. *If a dog is hyperactive, destructive or difficult then crating him all the time will only make things worse. Work with a trainer and solve the problems.*

4. I believe that children should be able to do anything to a dog and the dog should not growl or snap. My three-year-old stuck a pencil up my dog's butt (*this really happened*) and the dog snapped so I gave him away. *How about I stick a pencil up your butt and see what you do? Everyone, including dogs, has their limits.*

5. I couldn't get my dog to stop peeing in the house, jumping on furniture or stealing food off the counters, so I gave him to an animal shelter. Now it's their problem. *If you take on the responsibility of an animal then you should solve the problems, not make your dog a burden to someone else. You should have hired a trainer, read books, researched on the Internet and done whatever else necessary to help your dog be a well-mannered part of your family.*

6. My cat scratched my toddler. That scared me so I gave him to a shelter. *Did that cat scratch your child on purpose or by accident? Before giving a cat up consider consulting with someone who understands cats. You can also have your cat's front claws removed. (It's better than the cat being in a shelter.) Also, make sure that your child is not terrorizing the cat and the cat can get away from the child when he feels he needs to. Giving up so quickly and without really getting advice to try and solve the problem is not cool. When you give your cat to the shelter you are not only totally stressing out your cat, but you are putting the burden of your cat on a shelter.*

7. My wife is due to have a baby and we felt we couldn't give time to the pet anymore and that someone else will give it more attention, so we gave the dog (or cat) to a shelter. *When I hear that (which I do often) frankly I want to throttle that person. Later what will you tell your child about why you gave the dog away? What will that teach the child? We teach by example, and that is teaching a child that pets are disposable and to not take responsibility seriously. Plus, there are millions of homeless animals in our country; now you've just added to the problem.*

8. I got the dog (cat) for my kids. They would not live up to the responsibility, so I gave the animal away. *Children are children. They cannot take care of themselves completely so how are we to expect them to take care of a pet?*

9. My dog likes to go for rides in the car. I stopped at the store for just ten minutes and some irate lady confronted me in the store and told me I was being cruel to my dog, leaving him in the car. I didn't think it was bad leaving the dog in the car. The windows were rolled down halfway and it was only about 80 degrees outside. *The car gets up to 20 degrees hotter than the outside temperature. It is never a good idea to keep a dog in the car in the warm or hot weather.*

10. If pet stores are selling toys for dogs they must be safe. *Not true. You must be very careful of what you buy your dog. There are many dog toys and chew toys that should be used with caution or not at all. Many toys can be a choking hazard if your dog chews the toy up. Rawhides, edible Nylabones, pig ears and other ingestible chewies can get lodged in the dog's throat or the roof of its mouth and cause intestinal upset or death.*

Chrissy

Chrissy, a Rottweiler mix, lived in Robinson, Illinois. One new thing I learned from going to that town was that most bicycle riders weren't little kids visiting their friends or riding to town to get candy or ice cream. Those bicycle riders most times were older teens or adults riding up and down streets buying and selling drugs. Each time I visited that self-inflicted war-torn town I left feeling deeply appreciative of where I lived.

Chrissy's owners let her run loose in the neighborhood on an ongoing basis. By the time Beth finally got the owners to relinquish her Chrissy had already produced three litters of puppies that were probably scattered around town in people's backyards on chains or in makeshift outdoor pens.

Beth called me and asked if I would take Chrissy in. I was hesitant because she was a Rottweiler mix. They had a reputation for being protective, aggressive guard dogs, which in our area would make them hard to adopt out. But Beth said Chrissy looked like she had some Beagle in her so, hoping people would see she was a mix and not full-blooded rottie, I agreed. Besides, I reasoned, I had a purebred (I assume) Rottweiler myself that I adopted from a nearby shelter that was a great dog.

Molly agreed to foster Chrissy. The first time Molly noticed a problem was a few days after she took Chrissy in and she was walking her in town. Chrissy was strong and difficult for Molly to handle. Beth had said she looked like she had some beagle in her. I found that hard to believe and a stretch to say the least. Chrissy was a 40-pound black canine with brown Rottweiler markings. Her body was impressively muscular, her brown eyes alert, suspicious and weary.

Two weeks after taking Chrissy in Molly called me and said, "Sandy, I just can't foster her anymore. She's just too much for me. She dragged me down the block yesterday when she wanted to kill this little black dog. I had to literally sit down on the ground and she dragged me a good while before she finally stopped."

"Oh, no, that's terrible. Okay, well…" I paused thinking in my head what foster homes I had. "I'll have to take her. I don't have anyone else." I had a sinking feeling about Chrissy.

Always in the back of my mind since I opened the rescue was the fear of not being able to fix a dog. I had been through so many close calls. Pepper, the lab mix from very early on, was a real worry, but now she was living happily in Grayslake, Illinois. Then there was Robin–that was just awful when she attacked Rascal. But somehow I was able to fix that, too, and she was now living in the lap of luxury with a devoted family just a few miles from my house. The thought of having to euthanize a perfectly healthy dog just terrified me. So I was going to use that same determination and dedication to fix Chrissy and help her to find a home.

It was a heavenly day in the spring when Molly dropped Chrissy off at my house. The first step would be to get her used to the other foster dogs I had at that time. I brought Chrissy out in the backyard and then one at a time brought a foster dog outside to greet her. I was fostering a submissive, male, mix-breed dog and a four-and-a-half-month-old, female, mix-breed puppy. After a short meet and greet Chrissy and the two other dogs went inside to their living quarters in my offices and settled in. *So far so good.*

Armed with the knowledge I had learned throughout years of working with dogs I began Chrissy on a training program. The first two goals were: Chrissy and I had to get to know each other; and Chrissy had to learn some rules. For the next few weeks I took her for long walks where we practiced basic obedience. She acted as if she was in the military, looking at me with steel determination and respect. Whenever I said her name and commanded her to do anything she looked at me willing and eager to learn. I was pleased with her progress and we bonded.

But over time I started to see some disturbing behavior emerge. While walking Chrissy she got increasingly more agitated at fast moving objects, her biggest enemy being bicycles. She would lunge forward over and over at the bicycle, barking ferociously. At times when she was super charged she would actually do a complete flip in the air, oblivious to my attempts at redirection or correction, trying to get the bike. She would land on her head or shoulder and get right up again and lunge forward some more until the "enemy" was out of sight.

So I began using a technique of training that would hopefully change her aggression towards bikes by making bikes a good thing instead of bad. Armed with a bag of delicious dog treats we headed outside. We began walking on the trail behind my house. In short order I spotted a bike rider coming our way. Chrissy had not noticed the bike yet. So I put a few treats in my hand and in firm voice said, "Chrissy, sit!" She sat so I gave her a treat. "Stay!" I encouraged. She looked up at me with loving eyes. *Okay, Ma,* she said. I peeked at the bike rider from the corner of my eye and looked back at Chrissy. Her soft, dark brown eyes looked at me with devotion. "Good girl!"

Just then Chrissy spotted the bicycle rider. The idea was to give her a treat BEFORE the bad reaction started but Chrissy went from zero to 100 in the blink of an eye, and she began lunging and barking aggressively at the bike rider that was still 25 feet away. It took all my strength to control her. I knew that technique would not work yet; we would have to tackle her aggression more slowly.

Meanwhile Chrissy was beginning to show some serious aggression to people she didn't know. So I began crating her when I was expecting company and had them give her treats through the bars while not making eye contact. Outside the home I asked people to throw her treats while not making eye contact. Through those techniques there was a small group of volunteers that could come and go from my home with Chrissy loose in the offices. Chrissy was loyal and loving to those people.

In addition to Chrissy's affection towards me she quickly became attached to Chuck, Shari and David. David was crazy about her. She would jump up on him, her tongue hanging goofily out of her mouth, thrilled for his attention. Many times he would say to her, "Chrissy, Rottweiler, good girl," as he petted her and kissed her muzzle. Because Chrissy was good with my family I had high hopes I could turn her around. Failure was NOT an option.

At that point it would have been irresponsible of me to try and get Chrissy adopted. She was evolving over time and changing into a dog that was a real concern for me. Trying to figure out how to tackle her aggression towards bike riders and soon after aggression towards runners, I thought of asking volunteers Lena and Bryan, who knew Chrissy, to help me with some training.

The afternoon Bryan and Lena came over was a perfect day for training. It was sunny and warm, which would no doubt provide us bike riders and runners on the trail.

"Lena, Bryan, I am going to take Chrissy out to the trail. You wait here and in about two minutes go get a bicycle from the garage and walk the bike to the trail."

"Okay, then what?"

"First, I'll have you walk the bike towards us. I'll praise her for good behavior, assuming she is behaving nicely, then we'll let her sniff the bike, praise her some more. I am hoping over time we'll get you on the bike and riding using the same praise and reward technique. If it's you, and she knows you, then I am hoping over time she accepts you riding a bike and then eventually strangers. Does that make sense?"

"Yeah, no problem," Lena said.

I strapped Chrissy into her harness and secured the leash to it and walked Chrissy to the trail out back. As Lena and Bryan began walking with the bike towards us I practiced sit and stay to warm Chrissy up and to get her to concentrate on me. They rounded the corner and headed our way. Chrissy noticed them and did not react so I praised and treated her about every four seconds as they continued to approach us. Without incident they met up with us and Chrissy sniffed the bike. Chrissy appeared very alert but not highly charged up or agitated. I was feeling very hopeful.

After some practice just having Lena walk beside the bicycle I asked Lena to get on the bicycle and ride slowly towards us. Ten feet from us, after having praised and treated her, Chrissy began lunging forward at Lena, snarling and growling. I backed Chrissy up and moved her away. I instructed Lena to turn around and ride away from us. We practiced a few more times and at ten feet the same thing happened.

I decided to experiment. I got on the bike and handed Chrissy over to Bryan. To my dismay Chrissy reacted aggressively to me. I wanted the training sessions short and successful so I said, "Lena, try one more time." This time when Lena was 15 feet away Chrissy began lunging, growling and barking again. She was so charged up that time she jumped in the air, lunged forward and fell smack on her muzzle. Blood began pouring out of her mouth. She looked like she was the main character in a horror flick. Lena got off the bike, set it on its side and walked over.

"Oh, no!" I said very concerned. I examined inside Chrissy's mouth and saw that she had bit her tongue all the way through. The blood was pouring out like a running faucet. "Well, I guess our training session is over."

I called the vet from my cell phone and said I was coming in with Chrissy. But lucky for us (and the vet) the bleeding stopped by the time we got back to my house. Taking Chrissy to the vet, I was afraid, would have been a dangerous ordeal.

It was five long months of daily training. As each day passed Chrissy began to exhibit more aggression. Remember, in the rescue world it is said that it can take weeks or months for a dog to unpack their bags. The reason for this, I surmised, is because a dog needs to feel comfortable and part of their pack in order for them to really be themselves. Makes sense to me. It's kind of like when you move in with your significant other and as you both get comfortable you start seeing things in each other that you didn't know before.

Chrissy was getting comfortable. People with hats and people carrying objects were new targets of her aggression. She was aggressive towards anyone who surprised her, such as when a person rounded a corner and became visible, or someone opening their car door and stepping out. Walking in downtown Liberty I kept a wide birth between us and any other people and when she behaved I would treat and praise her. But frankly, most of the time she was charged up to some degree so the praises were fewer and further between. I also noted that when we passed a shop window where there was a shop cat she would attack the glass ferociously trying to get at the cat. She was getting worse by the day.

One afternoon while I was out Chuck let the foster dogs that lived in our offices onto the porch, prepared to go outside in the fenced backyard with them. On the porch, prepared to open the back door to let them outside, our kitchen door popped open and three of our other dogs, which the office dogs hadn't met before, were now face to face on the porch. Like a bullet shot out of a gun Chrissy began attacking Clyde, a long-term foster dog who lived with my family. Lunge after lunge

Chrissy bit Clyde over and over again as Clyde tried to maneuver around the small space attempting to miss her blows. Chuck was screaming, "Chrissy, NO! STOP," over and over.

Chuck may as well not have been there because she didn't even hear his screams; she was so zoned in on Clyde. It was utter chaos as the dogs wrestled and tumbled, Chrissy biting Clyde over and over, the other dogs standing clear of the crazy dog, items on the porch toppling over and scattering away. After numerous lunges Clyde realized he wasn't getting away so he began fighting back. That just pumped Chrissy up more.

Fearful for Clyde's life Chuck tried to physically break them up by grabbing at their collars and instead got bit in three places on his hands, blood pouring from the punctures. Finally, in desperation Chuck lifted Chrissy up and onto his shoulders and stumbled into the offices with her and slammed the door behind him.

When I got home an hour later I walked onto the porch and noticed that while the room was never neat and tidy it looked like it was in peculiar disarray. I also noticed drops of blood. *What the heck happened here?* I thought. Then I stepped inside into the kitchen and the house was quiet. I looked for Chuck. Finding him in his office he looked up from his computer and told me what happened. "How's your hand?"

He raised a bandaged hand for me to see. "I'll live."

"Do you need stitches?" I asked, concerned.

"Three punctures. I flushed them out and put antibiotic on them. I'll be fine." He opened and closed the damaged hand. "But it hurts anyway."

"I bet. How's Clyde?" I asked, feeling a rock at the pit of my stomach.

"He's got some punctures but I think he's okay."

"I'll go check on him."

Going to the living room I saw Clyde lying on the dog bed looking forlorn. From the door he didn't look bad at all. I approached him and sat down on the ground beside him. "Hi, sweetie. Did you have a tough day?" I asked him, petting him on his head. I looked down his body, decorated not unlike a German Black Pied cow, for injuries. I didn't see any. Then I picked up a front leg. He tried pulling away. "It's okay, babes. Let me see." I looked at the leg and saw at least four puncture wounds. I lifted each leg and each leg had what looked like four or five punctures, although it was hard to tell because of his coarse, short hair.

Reflecting back to the numerous first aid for pets classes I attended, I remembered the veterinarians saying how important it was that wounds get cleaned well and oral antibiotics may be necessary to ensure the wounds didn't get infected. Without proper treatment, infection could set in and cause serious problems. To be safe I took Clyde to the vet that day.

Dr. Leonard took Clyde in back and cleaned up all of his wounds. When he came back with Clyde, the poor dog looked like he had been in a war. Around each wound the area was cleanly shaved. I looked at Clyde and said, "There were a lot more punctures than I saw."

"Yes, there was. We kept finding more. We counted over 30 punctures."

"Oh, no, that's awful. Poor Clyde," I said, stroking his head. He looked up at me with sad, brown eyes.

"Here's some medicine," he said, handing me a bottle. "Twice a day, two capsules."

"Okay, thanks."

"And keep him away from the other dog."

"I know, I know, we'll do our best." *One mistake with the door not closed completely, dogs outside and someone not knowing and letting the others out could mean disaster,* I thought to myself on the ride home. *How am I going to be 100% safe? Chrissy is a time bomb.* That's when the thought entered my mind briefly, *What if I have to put her down?*

The attack happened because Chrissy was surprised and surprising Chrissy was never a good thing. But it didn't explain the way in which she attacked instantly, no restraint, no warning. She didn't stop either, even when Clyde just tried to get away. Now I had a dog that was aggressive with bike riders, runners, dogs she didn't know, people in hats and hoods, and strangers. I had a very serious problem on my hands.

Chrissy seemed most aggressive when someone would come in when I was on the phone. Once, early on, Bryan had entered the office and barely got out without being bit. Another time a Pet Sitters client decided to come in the office without knocking and my office worker had to leap out of her chair and slam the door before Chrissy attacked. Yet another time she snapped at someone I was interviewing for a job. It was bad.

We continued to have some close calls. More than once one of us who was in the office would have to slam the door shut when someone tried to walk in. Even though there were signs all over saying "DO NOT COME IN! KNOCK!" people were used to an open door policy with us. We locked our office doors securely. We added a second safety lock on the outside of our kitchen door that we locked from the porch, ensuring when we let the foster dogs out that the porch door couldn't accidentally open. The glitch to that was that if we forgot to unlock it when the foster dogs were safely back in the offices anyone wanting to leave the house from the kitchen door couldn't. Our lifestyle had changed and our house would have to be a fortress.

But to people Chrissy knew she was 100% trustworthy. She was sweet, loyal and lovable. Many times she would put her front paws in my lap as I worked at my desk, her face soft and relaxed with her tongue lulling comfortably outside her mouth. I stroked her silky-soft head and massaged her muscular body. She closed her eyes, enjoying every minute of our exchange. I adored her and was deeply worried.

One morning I was talking to someone on the phone when I heard some commotion in the front office. I walked over to find Chrissy had cornered Connie, a volunteer. I grabbed Chrissy's collar and pulled her back, but not before she tried lunging one more time. "Did she bite you?" I asked.

"Yeah, she did."

"Oh, no!" I said, instantly beginning to shake. I pulled Chrissy to her crate and put her inside. I walked back to Connie. "Let me see."

Connie calmly pulled up her jeans to her shin and showed me a small bite, red and bruising already. "Oh, Connie! Do you need something for it? Do you want to clean it now?"

"It's fine," she said just a bit shook up. Connie was not a dramatic kind of person. "It's my fault. It was dark in the office and I peeked in through the window and didn't see anyone. I didn't even know you were here. I was just going to drop something off. I unlocked the door and came in. She came from the other room and just went at me. But I probably surprised her."

"I shouldn't have left the key in the lock. I didn't know anyone was coming over. And I was on the phone, which is when she's most aggressive." I was shaking badly now. I knew this was setting a ball in motion that would forever change my life.

"I feel terrible," Connie said.

"Me, too. But, Connie, don't blame yourself. She should never do that. Oh, I don't know how I am going to deal with this." I felt instantly spent, toasted and depleted. I worked very hard not to cry in front of Connie. She left a minute later.

After Connie left I went into full speed trying to think of whom I could call or e-mail to get help. Chrissy was looking at me lovingly through her cage as if nothing had happened. I e-mailed Joyce, my long-time volunteer that helped transport animals from shelters to safety.

Hi, Joyce:

Chrissy bit Connie today. I am beside myself. I don't know how I will ever find a home for this dog. She is dog aggressive, people aggressive and prey aggressive. If I have to put her to sleep I don't think I could keep doing this. I would melt into the ground, just want to disappear. My worst nightmare might be coming true. Do you know of a dog trainer who could help me?

Sandy

Logically I knew the likelihood of finding a trainer or behaviorist with more skills than me was probably not going to happen. Not that I was the best or the cure-all, but there are a limited number of trainers using the new style of training that uses behavior modification and praise, which was my style and the only type of training I believe is successful.

I used to be a trainer who used traditional methods, which included using choke collars, pinch collars and a heavy hand and voice. I knew that method would never work with Chrissy. Trying to suppress a dog's natural instincts through fear will only mask the problem and one day that dog will snap and there will be no warning. That would mean disaster. In addition, even if I did find a trainer, taking Chrissy somewhere wouldn't show the person her behavior in and around where she currently lived.

Even if I was able to manage where she was currently living, she was a foster dog and ultimately would have to live elsewhere. I couldn't possibly keep her. Introducing her to my personal dogs would surely be a blood bath. I knew my dogs, and Chrissy, a dominant, aggressive female dog, would never ever work in my home. Living long term like we were, always on guard and jumpy about locking doors, locking crates, who's where and when, would be a terrible way to live. Too many people came and went from my home to ever be 100% sure that Chrissy wouldn't bite again.

The trainers Joyce recommended used more aggressive training methods, such as jerking on the leash to "correct" the dog and hanging the dog (lifting the dog up off the ground by leash) when the dog was really bad. So I got online and began looking for a trainer or behaviorist that used my style of training and behavior modification. As my mind raced, trying to come up with a way to solve the problem, I decided what I needed was an evaluation and a second opinion. I knew in my head what the answer was, but my Animal Warrior's heart was not in sync with my head. I asked the universe for help, and taking a deep breath kept navigating the Internet.

Somehow I was guided to the web site of an animal behaviorist with 20 years of experience, plus many degrees in animal behavior. She lived outside the area but I thought maybe, just maybe she could help in some way. I called and left a message on her voice mail. Within an hour I received a call back.

"Hello, is Sandy there?" asked a friendly, warm voice.

"This is."

"Hi, Sandy, I am Helen Davis. You called about Chrissy, the dog you are fostering."

"Thanks so much for calling me." I was thrilled she called back. I wasn't even sure if she was going to. "Um, well, I am looking for a second opinion about Chrissy. I am a dog trainer but am at my wits end. I don't know what else to do to help her." I went on to explain all of Chrissy's behavioral issues. Then I said, "I am afraid she may, we may," I cleared my throat, "be at the end."

"Sometimes you do all you can and you can't do any more," she said softly.

"I just can't handle this," I said bursting into tears. "How could I put her to sleep? How could I end her life? I am supposed to SAVE lives," I sobbed.

"It sounds like you really love her. But some dogs are just wired wrong and it doesn't matter what you do."

"I know, I know. But this is my worst fear. When I started this whole crazy business I always had in the back of my mind that I might not be able to save all of them, but she loves me and I love her. How can

I look into her eyes and say 'I'm going to kill you.'"

"You have saved a lot of lives."

"But I want to save all the lives." I knew that sounded ridiculous. "I know that's not possible, but I don't think I'm strong enough for this."

"Let's take one step at a time," this stranger sent from heaven said.

"Yeah, I know." I forced myself to calm down. "I would like a second opinion. I'm willing to pay what I have to. Do you know anyone?"

"Yes, I work with a woman in your area. And I'll see if she will donate her time. If not then I'll pay for it." This woman was sent to me as a gift, I had no doubt.

"I am so grateful," I said sniffling.

"I'm grateful for what you do. Let me call Val and fill her in. She'll call you and set up a time to come out."

I looked over at Chrissy, relaxing quietly in her crate. "Okay, thank you so very much."

"Sandy, whatever the outcome you need to keep strong. Animals still need you out there."

"Yeah, I know." I wasn't convinced. All I could think of was my Chrissy and that her life was on the line.

The following afternoon I received a call from Val, a cheerful, upbeat woman, and we set up a time for her to come and do an evaluation. I contacted Lena, Bryan, Connie and Lena's mom, Lynn, and suggested that they join us for the evaluation. I didn't want to miss the opportunity to educate people.

Val came over on a dark, cool, late fall night. The rain was at bay and seemed an appropriate weather condition. Val spent a good hour teaching the volunteers about some training techniques, and she observed Chrissy first from her crate and then, after some time and many treats, outside. The volunteers left and Val and I continued our meeting for another half an hour. Many of the suggestions she had, as I anticipated, were management tools such as crating her when people came over and taking her for walks with a muzzle on.

We discussed medication to control her behavior. Val believed medication for her behavior would be very difficult to monitor and control since she had different aggression issues that included people, animals and objects. Each medication tended to work with one type of aggression, not all of them. While I could try it and observe her, the only way to see any change would be to slowly expose her to the stimuli that caused the aggressions. The time that would take and the delicacy of the process, not to mention the potential danger, made the idea of medication unrealistic to me.

After Val left I sat leaning over my desk, my hands cupping my forehead, completely depleted. I knew what I had to do but with Chrissy's eyes looking at me from behind, my neck burning with her stare, I decided to wait for Val's final written evaluation.

Meanwhile, Chuck suggested we do one more thing to try and save Chrissy. "Why don't you call the Rottweiler rescues and see if they'll take her?"

"Why would they want a dog that is such a huge liability? I would be embarrassed even to ask."

"It can't hurt."

"No way, they'll think I'm an idiot."

"Just ask. Who cares what they think? It's Chrissy's life."

Now that he said that I couldn't say no. "Okay, I will, but I already know the answer."

I wrote an e-mail to two local Rottweiler rescues and waited for replies. The first Rottweiler rescue wrote back a short time later. They sympathized with our situation and praised us for our hard work but they "could not possibly take a dog with such issues. We have our own problems." She went on, "Sometimes when you try everything you can, well, you can't save them all."

The second response was not so kind. They would not be able to help us and she added, "If you don't do the responsible thing by putting the dog to sleep, as hard as it might be, you are perpetuating the already negative attitude people have towards this breed. If that dog hurts someone it hurts a lot more than just the person the dog injured." As harsh as the letter read, she was right.

A long two days passed and I received the e-mail that contained Val's evaluation. It didn't tell me anything I didn't already know but validated what I had to do. I picked up the telephone, dialed the animal hospital and made one of the hardest calls I ever had to make. Chrissy's life would end the following day.

After I hung up with the animal hospital I sat at my desk and bawled and bawled. Words flashed in my mind: "You cannot give up." "Animals still need you." "It's for the best." "It's the responsible thing." So that day I tucked my heart away, went through the motions of life the next 24 hours like a robot and distanced myself emotionally from Chrissy. I knew in order to continue saving animals I could not be with Chrissy when they euthanized her. To do that I would walk away from it all and never look back. I knew my limitations. Chuck and Molly agreed to be with Chrissy when it was time.

David and Shari were aware of some of the issues with Chrissy, but they were not completely aware of all the issues Chrissy had. Shari was far less attached to Chrissy and she was older than David so after explaining to her the situation she understood. David, on the other hand, couldn't believe we were going to put her to sleep. He said, "Can't she just live in our offices?" I tried to explain to him the big picture but being 15 years old it was hard for him to understand. Ultimately, I think down deep he knew we wouldn't do something like that unless it was the absolute last resort.

The following day, at 4:00 p.m., I sat in my living room blankly staring at the TV screen. Meanwhile, Chuck and Molly took Chrissy to the animal hospital. While the vet stepped back, terrified of the lunging, snapping dog, Chuck placed the muzzle over Chrissy's face. Molly asked for a blanket, which she then laid on the floor. Lovingly they guided Chrissy to the blanket and gently but firmly forced her to lie down. Then the doctor injected the medicine that made her fall peacefully to sleep, and then he added the other medicine that stopped her heart.

As her spirit left her body my heart lay stomped flat on the living room floor. I looked up at the clock, its neon numbers clear. It was 5:15 p.m. and I knew my Chrissy was gone. For six months I had spent hours and hours determined to fix the unfixable. I sat there with thoughts running through my head. *There was no place in this world for Chrissy. She was a liability and a disaster waiting to happen. I did the right thing, making the decision to euthanize her.* "You can't save them all," played over and over in my head. But in all reality, as much as I tried to reassure myself, I felt broken, spent and used up.

So I spent the next week repairing myself. I visualized the next animal in need, the one locked in a dark basement or chained up outside. The animal that is cold, or so hot he can't breathe. The animal who is beaten and emotionally abused, as well as the one starved and ignored. I would find them and rip the chains free. I would then fix them and give them to people who would love them.

So I picked up my heart, slowly stood, dusting off the knees of my jeans, placed my heart in its proper place and took a deep breath. I blew a kiss into the air and told Chrissy maybe I would see her again someday and warned her that she is not to terrorize anyone in the next life. I did not win the battle, but I would continue to fight the war.

Not-So-Popular Michael Jordan

Michael Jordan, the former Chicago Bulls basketball player, is famous, wealthy and has people both near and far who look up to him and admire him. But I was soon to meet another Michael Jordan who, while named after the famous player, had a very different kind of life.

I received a call from a man who said that when he walked his dog past a certain house he always heard a dog barking in the garage. "Can people leave their dog in the garage?" he asked me.

"Unfortunately they can," I told him, "but the dog still has to have a safe and livable environment."

"I can't believe anyone would keep their dog in a garage. In our neighborhood. There are nice houses and nice people."

"I know, we'll check it out and make sure the dog's okay."

"Thanks, I appreciate it."

Dogs kept in garages are always a concern of ours. We live in the Midwest with harsh winters and hot summers. Most garages are not heated, nor do they have air conditioning, which could cause potential dangers for the dog. Also, there is always the concern there could be hazardous material around the dog that he could ingest or get on his skin—things such as oil, gas, cleaning fluids, paints and antifreeze, all items typically stored in garages.

On a chilly winter day I went with Cory, another humane investigator, to see what was going on.

The house was one of six styles of homes in a cookie cutter subdivision. It was a dark brown house that was nondescript, other than a hanging pot likely from the past summer that still hung next to the front door. I stood on the cement stoop and knocked. A minute later a middle-aged African American man answered the door.

"Hello, sir. My name is Sandy. This is Cory," I motioned to Cory behind me, "and we are humane investigators. We received a call about a dog in your garage."

A woman, presumably his wife, came up behind him. "So? What's the problem?"

"Well, it is not common for people to have their dogs in the garage. Does he live in there?"

"Yes. He's a German Shepherd."

"Okay, well, we just need to take a look at him, make sure everything is okay."

He looked over his shoulder at his wife. They both looked perturbed and then he said back to me, "Okay, hold on, I'll open the garage." With that he closed the door on us.

Cory and I walked over to the garage, the hum of the motor slowly lifting its door. The dark garage flooded with light as the door rose up. Standing inside, tethered to a rope, was a dog that looked like a Border Collie, with black and white markings, lanky legs and a long body like a Greyhound.

"This is MJ, short for Michael Jordan. My kid named him when he was a puppy."

"This is the German Shepherd?"

"That's what the farmer said he was when we got him."

"He's not a German Shepherd. He's more like a Border Collie mix," I stated.

The couple seemed genuinely surprised. *They don't even know what kind of dog they have.*

MJ lived in deplorable conditions. The garage floor had many urine stains and the odor in the air was foul. There were chemicals in containers on the floor as well as various sharp objects within his reach. A rusty pan with a copper-colored water stain in the bottom must have been his water bowl.

The man unsnapped the rope that tethered MJ. Freed, MJ happily headed to a bush in the front yard and promptly peed on it. He proceeded to trot around the front yard sniffing the grass while we talked to his owners.

"We need to see MJ's vaccination records," Cory said, "just to verify he's up to date."

"I don't know where they are," the man said flatly.

"I know where they are," the wife said and went inside.

Moments later she came back outside and handed me an ancient-looking rabies tag. It took a moment for me to make out the date. "This rabies tag is for 1997," I told them.

"Well, that's what we have."

"This dog hasn't been vaccinated since then?"

"I guess not," she stated defiantly.

"How old is MJ?" I asked.

"He's about 13."

"How long has he lived like this?" Cory asked.

"We moved here when the dog was one. He was very destructive. We couldn't have him in the house."

"So he's lived out here for 12 years?" I looked around the garage, noting the black sheets that covered the one window in the garage.

"Yes and he's fine. I let him out twice a day," the man stated. "Before work and when I get home."

"For an older dog that's not enough. He is peeing and pooing in here because he probably can't hold it that long."

The woman snapped, "We work. That's all we can do."

It was obvious they had no intention of changing MJ's living arrangements, so all we could do was issue them a notice of violation for the dog not having water and for picking up the dangerous items and moving them out of his reach. We suggested that if it became very cold on the cement floor that it was a good idea to provide MJ with a bed or blanket to lie on. As sad as it was I couldn't change the fact that he lived in a garage, on a cement floor, in the dark.

Three weeks later Cory and I returned to the home. Upon arrival we heard MJ barking in the garage. We knocked on the front door and heard the door from the garage into the house open and close. "Do you hear that? They're bringing him inside the house from the garage."

"Yeah, I hear it." We stood at the front door a few more minutes before deciding we were being avoided.

Undeterred by no one answering the door Cory said, "Let's go to the back door." We trudged through three-day-old sludgy muck–the remainder of a snowstorm the previous week–to the back door. Stepping onto a cracked patio we looked through the sliding glass doors. Standing beside the sink was the woman I recognized from our last visit there. I knocked on the glass. She walked towards us, a peeved look on her face, and slid open the door. "What do you want now?"

"We're back to see proof of a current rabies vaccine. And we need to see the garage," I explained in a formal tone.

She walked away from us and came back a minute later and handed me a piece of paper. "The dog lives in the house now." She thrust the paper at me.

Taking the paper I said, "I know you are lying. I heard you take MJ out of the garage and bring him into the house. I am not leaving without seeing the garage."

She rolled her eyes and sighed and told us to meet her at the front of the house. We walked back around to the front. The garage door came up and the owner stood by the door that led inside the house, her arms crossed over her chest and her lips pressed together thinly. MJ greeted us with enthusiasm, jumping up and down, wagging his big long tail. "Get down!" the woman yelled, annoyed. "The dog is always jumping up," she stated exasperated. "Get down!"

"It's okay," I told her. "He's just excited. I don't mind." I petted MJ's head. He looked up at me with loving brown eyes.

As I surveyed the garage I noted that it was in worse shape than before. Additional dangerous items and chemicals were littered around and numerous piles of feces were on the floor. Urine stains covered the area where MJ was tethered, the smell inside the stale room nearly unbearable. My eyes stunk from the ammonia smell that hung heavy in the air. Once again there wasn't any water for him to drink. This time the pan that had been there before was missing.

"The garage is worse this time," I told her.

"My husband's been out of town."

"We gave you three weeks to get the garage fixed up for him," I said.

"Look over there," Cory pointed at the antifreeze on the floor. "MJ could knock that over. The cap's not even on all the way. Antifreeze tastes sweet and a dog will drink it. It is poisonous and he would die."

"You have to move all these dangerous things," I said. "They have to be up high on shelves. Also, MJ is an old dog now. He really needs a blanket to lie on for his old bones. He likely has arthritis."

Trying to prove she was a good dog owner she blurted out, "He doesn't have heartworm. The doctor said so."

Not recalling seeing that on the medical records she showed me earlier, I asked her if I could see the paperwork again. She went inside and brought it back out to me. Reading over the paperwork, I said, "The only thing you did for MJ when you took him to the doctor was get his rabies shot, the bare minimum. This dog could have heartworm or anything else."

Standing in the garage I spotted something moving near the road and looked over. Walking up the sidewalk was a man with a Golden Retriever that looked like it had just been groomed. I was admiring the beautiful dog when the man made eye contact with me and mouthed, "Thank you." I smiled and he walked past.

I continued to pet MJ. "You know what," the woman said, "I don't have time for this dog anymore. My kids moved out. Just take him."

"Are you sure?" I asked, surprised that she blurted that out.

"Yeah, I'm sure. Just take him. What do I sign?"

I looked at MJ who was oblivious to the fact that his life, after 13 years, was going to change drastically. Cory said, "I'll go get it," and walked to the car.

She handed me the paper and wiped away a tear. *Why the tear?* I wondered. I went to my car and got a leash. While Cory finalized paperwork with the woman I led MJ to my car. Without looking back once at his owner, MJ hopped into my car. I closed him inside and walked over to Cory, who was walking away from the house. The woman had gone back inside.

"Everything okay?" I asked him.

"I have all the paperwork. What are you going to do with the dog?"

"I have no idea yet. And finding him a home at 13, I don't know…"

"Yeah, I know. If she would have just done better for him. It wouldn't have been hard."

"She didn't want him. She hadn't wanted him for a long time."

"Yeah."

"I'll take him to the vet first and get him checked out."

"Alright, well, good luck."

I walked back to my car and got inside. As I drove away MJ climbed onto my lap. He looked at me with loving eyes as if he was saying, "Thank you."

Stroking his cheek and muzzle I said, "I'm sorry it took us so long to help you. Your life from now on will be wonderful." But even as I said that I thought, *Who will adopt such an old dog?*

Arriving at the animal hospital MJ climbed out of the car and we headed for the door. Shortly thereafter he was examined and was tested for heartworm. While we waited in the waiting area for the results of the heartworm test I made some phone calls, looking for a foster home for MJ. Running out of options I called Merle, the owner of the doggy day care, and asked if she would keep MJ just until I could find a place for him to go. She said I could bring him over.

Hanging up I sighed with relief that I had somewhere for MJ to go for the night. Dr. Leonard came through the door from the back and walked over to us. "Well, I am sorry to say, but he is heartworm positive."

"Oh no, you're kidding." The treatment for heartworm is aggressive. "He's 13 years old. Could he survive the treatment?"

"I was thinking about it and I think the best course of action is to just give him his monthly heartworm medication, all year long. There is a theory that if you give them the heartworm medication the worms won't multiply. The adults currently in his heart have about a three-year lifespan and then in three years essentially they will die. And he's already 13…"

I nodded my head; I knew what he was implying.

"Right now he's not symptomatic, coughing or low energy, so I think that's the best way to go."

"Okay, that makes sense. I'd hate to put him at risk getting the treatment at his age."

Driving to the doggy day care I worried about MJ's future. Who would ever want to adopt a 13-year-old dog with heartworm? I stroked MJ's coat as we drove along, MJ looking up at me with appreciative eyes. He had an incredibly loving spirit.

After settling MJ into his temporary digs at the doggy day care I pondered where he would go next. He was an old man without a home and with a chronic medical condition. I was dreading the idea that I might be stuck with him at my house if I couldn't find somewhere for him to go. I was stuck with too many already. I was learning as time went on that running a rescue group meant that ultimately the person who called the shots either ended up stuck with animals that were nearly impossible to adopt out or they had to make a decision to euthanize some. For me, euthanizing animals that were not a danger to any person and were not suffering was not an option.

The next few days were busy as usual. I was finalizing all the details for our annual volunteer appreciation party the following week. Merle graciously agreed to let us have the party at her doggy day care. Volunteers and their families, as well as their dogs, were invited. I checked to be sure I had enough gifts for all the volunteers and decided on which volunteers would get which awards. I ordered the food and cake. It was going to be a nice afternoon.

The Sunday of the volunteer party I still hadn't found a place for MJ to go and Merle's almost daily updates said he was doing okay but "really needed to find somewhere else to go soon." I was looking forward to seeing MJ again and spending some time with him.

I arrived early for the party and busied myself setting up the tables and decorations. Displaying the silverware prettily I heard Merle's loud voice call the dogs out of their sleeping area. The herd of excited boarders barked and carried on, the stomping of their paws rhythmic on the mats as they raced towards the indoor dog arena. I looked up from the table and watched the dogs as they ran, bounded and leaped around.

Scanning the crew of ten or so dogs I spotted MJ. His mouth was open, his tongue hanging out, his ears back and his eyes just a little too big. *He looks stressed out.*

Watching him running around, clearly avoiding interacting or playing with the other dogs, I became concerned. Knowing his personality I surmised that he was trying to make the best out of a situation that he was not comfortable in. He was just that kind of dog. *MJ was isolated from everything his whole life and then I took him from that and threw him into what could be described as a huge dog party. Not good,* I thought to myself.

The festivities went underway and families and their dogs enjoyed an afternoon of food, fun and recognition. Near the end I noticed that MJ was still walking around everywhere and wouldn't settle down. *That dog needs to rest. This is not good for him.* I approached Merle. "MJ hasn't stopped moving. Is that how he's been the whole time?"

"Pretty much."

"That can't be good for him."

"No, it's not. I put him down for breaks sometimes but he's really restless."

"I have to get him somewhere else soon."

"The sooner the better," Merle said. "He's about at his limit."

By the end of the party I couldn't stand seeing MJ so stressed for one more day. I decided I couldn't wait anymore for someone willing to take him in, and as I loaded up the remainder of the party supplies I loaded MJ up into my car and brought him to stay at my offices.

On the porch I found some cushy blankets, folded them into a nice bed and laid them beside my desk. MJ promptly curled up into a ball on the fresh blankets and fell sound asleep. That likely could have been the first time in many years if ever that he had a soft place to sleep. That night when I went into the office to take him outside he had a hard time getting up. I kept encouraging him and because he wanted to please he gingerly got himself to his feet and walked stilt-legged outside.

The next morning I had to lift MJ into a standing position in order for him to walk outside, and he stumbled a few times along the way. He stood at the top of the deck stairs. He looked down the stairs and didn't move, as if he knew he couldn't make it down. So I scooped him up and hauled him down the stairs. Like the good boy he was he peed and then looked at me for approval. "Good boy, MJ," I told him. "You are my good boy." Helping him back inside he went right back to his blankets and plunked down.

By the afternoon he seemed to be getting worse. I had to pick him up to get him to stand and had to hover over him as he walked and catch him each time he started to fall. I called the vet and that afternoon went over there for the doctor to look at him.

"There isn't anything wrong that I can see," Dr. Leonard said after examining MJ. "His heart sounds fine. His limbs seem stiff, but he's an older guy so that's not a surprise."

"But he wasn't like this when I got him from his owner. I feel like he's giving up."

"Just keep an eye on him. Make sure he eats."

"He's eating some."

"Good."

"Okay, thanks."

So we headed home and I worried about my little pal. "It is not an option for the last years of his life to be like this," I told Chuck. "He's such a good boy. He deserves a good life for once."

I let MJ rest for the next few days and he continued to have a hard time getting up and walking. His eyes told me he was in pain. I worried nonstop about him. I sent out an e-mail asking for someone to donate a dog bed for him. By the end of the day a dog bed arrived at my door.

MJ loved his new bed. He spent the majority of his time lying on it. He had spent his whole life sleeping on dirty concrete; the feel of a comfortable bed must have been like heaven for him. But four days after bringing him to see the doctor I called and made another appointment for the doctor to take a look at him.

"He's dying. I know it," I announced to the doctor when he walked into the exam room.

"Why do you say that?"

"I can just feel it. He's giving up."

"Hum," he said, listening to his heart.

We were both silent for a minute pondering MJ's health.

"The only other thing I can think of," I said, "is that he was at the doggy day care for a week and a half before I took him and he was running around way too much. That's why I took him to my house and got him out of there."

"That could explain it then," Dr. L. said. "It's possible he's just incredibly sore. From what you told me about him he had very little or no exercise before."

"True. Gosh, why didn't I think of that? Poor baby," I said, stroking MJ. He looked up at me with loving eyes.

"If I had known that I would have told you not to have him on complete rest but to keep him moving a little. Now it's too late for that… I'll give you pain medicine and now just have him rest. We'll see if our theory is correct."

So for two weeks I coddled my sweet charge, massaging his lanky legs and slender body and taking him outside just for short potty breaks. On the 15th day when I came to get MJ for his morning potty break he sprung up from his bed on his own and walked with confidence outside. "Good boy!" I exclaimed. "You must be feeling better." He gave me one of his large-mouthed grins.

With the doctor's permission I began a slow but steady daily walk regimen with my boy. I made sure they were leisurely and short and gradually over time increased it. After a month MJ was mostly back to his old self. Now would be the difficult task of trying to find him a home. I contacted Claira, a pet photographer and volunteer and asked her if she would take a photo of MJ for our web site. She readily agreed.

After MJ's photo shoot I wrote a new bio for his web page and added the new picture. The picture was beautiful. It showed MJ's sweet and loving nature. His brown eyes looked wise and sparkled with light. The stark contrast of his black and white-colored coat made him look like a strikingly handsome guy. He had a blue handkerchief around his neck that read: Adopt Me. His bio said: MJ is a sweet, loyal and loving Border Collie mix. He lived his whole life in a garage until his owners decided they didn't want him anymore. He is 13 years old and has heartworm. But he deserves a chance for a new life. Won't you consider adopting this special boy?

It would take a miracle to find MJ a home.

Two days passed and I received a message on the office voice mail. "Hi, my name is Trudy. I saw MJ's photograph online and fell in love. My family and I would like to know what we have to do to adopt him." *Did they know he was 13 and had heartworm?* I thought.

I called the number Trudy left. A woman answered the phone. "Hi, is Trudy there?"

"This is Trudy."

"Hi, this is Sandy from Animal Education..."

"Oh! Is this about MJ?" she asked excitedly.

"Yes..."

"Oh, yes," she interrupted, "I was just browsing on the Internet and out of the blue this photo of this gorgeous dog came onto the screen. My heart just melted when I saw him. I wasn't even looking for a dog.

His photo, I swear, just came up and I don't know how it got there."

"You're kidding?" I said in awe.

"No, not at all. I already have two dogs. I don't need another, that's for sure. But I showed the photo to my kids and my husband and they fell in love, too."

"Did you read the description about him?" I asked, bracing myself to tell her his age and medical condition.

"Yeah, I did. I'm not afraid of his age or the heartworm. I am a hospice nurse and my husband is in a wheelchair. I don't get worked up about things easily."

"That's great." *Could this be a miracle?*

"What do I need to do to adopt him? I mean, I know we have to pass as a good family and all. I really do think MJ would be happy. We have one acre in a nice subdivision. We can have three dogs. I just want him to be happy."

"Okay." I smiled. "I understand. Well, there's an application online on our web site and then we would bring him to you to be sure the dogs get along. Would that work for you?"

"Yes! It would. I can't believe I am doing this. He just looks so sweet. I hope we pass."

I was touched almost beyond words. This woman saw MJ as a gem, an animal who was worthy, not a broken-down, old dog. "As soon as I get your application I'll go ahead and check your references and give you a call."

We hung up and I sat there, stunned. I didn't want to get my hopes up. But within 30 minutes I opened my e-mail and Trudy had already filled out the online application. I printed it off and began checking references. Each reference I called gave the family stellar recommendations. The next step was the home visit. Volunteer Becca and I drove the 30 minutes to Hawthorn Lakes, an upper-class suburban town. MJ sat on my lap the whole ride there, his body pressed against me, enjoying the continual stroking and sweet talk I showered on him. I was nervous and excited at the same time. I loved MJ so much and felt such a deep sense of commitment. I thought back to where he had lived in darkness and stench with barely any human contact, in a filthy garage, this sweet boy who only wants love. Then I remembered the terrible scare where I thought I would lose him.

We turned a corner and made a left onto a cul de sac with three houses on it, the green-grassed lawns expansive. It was a cool, early spring day and the dusk created long, dreamy shadows on everything outside. Standing at the end of a driveway was a tall, slender, woman. She was waving at us as we pulled in, a big smile on her face.

Becca parked the car and I opened the door and gently helped MJ off my lap and onto the ground. Trudy walked over to MJ and put her hand over her mouth. Removing her hand she said, "He's so, so handsome!"

I smiled. "Hi, Trudy, I'm Sandy. This is Becca."

"Hi," she said. She bent down to pet MJ. "Hi, sweetheart. It's nice to meet you." A lump grew in my throat. Then to us, "Come on in. My family's inside."

Trudy led us into her front door and into a huge living room covered with wall-to-wall carpeting. "Everyone, they're here!" Trudy called out.

Seconds later her two kids, a boy who looked to be around eight and a girl around ten, came into the room grinning and looking at MJ. "Go say hi to MJ," their mom coaxed.

The kids walked over to MJ and petted his head. MJ reacted with his open-mouthed grin, his eyes half closed in contentment. The kids' grins grew.

"What do you think of MJ?" I asked them.

They nodded their heads and the girl said, "Cute."

"How would you like the dogs to meet?" Trudy asked. "I have

them in my bedroom now."

"Let's have them meet in the yard."

"Okay, sounds good. My female can be kind of testy. That's my only worry, and the dogs have to get along. I don't know where my husband is." As if on cue her husband rolled himself into the room in an electric wheelchair. MJ wagged his tail. "There you are," she said to her husband. "Mike, this is Sandy and Becca, and this is MJ."

"Hi," Becca and I said in unison. MJ looked at Mike and wagged his tail.

"Hi," Mike said to us and wheeled over to MJ and petted his head. "Cute."

On the way with MJ to the backyard I noticed the many skylights and the big windows. We went out through sliding glass doors. *No more darkness for you, MJ,* I said to myself. The dogs met in the backyard without incident, and we all headed back inside. "Well, it sure looks like MJ fits in here," Trudy said. "We've been so excited."

I looked over at MJ, who was lying down on the carpeting, his body relaxed, and his mouth open in that silly grin. "He looks like he's always lived here," I commented, a lump heavy in my throat. *No crying,* I commanded myself.

After a little while longer I knew it was time to go. Becca and I stood and put on our coats. "Don't forget he needs the heartworm pills every month, year round," I said.

"I know, I won't," Trudy said.

I called MJ over to me and wrapped my arms around him. "MJ, I love you very much. Be a good boy and have a wonderful life." Then I kissed his muzzle loudly. Trudy walked MJ outside with us and back out to our car. MJ watched me get into the car. Unfazed by my departure, he turned around and headed for the front door. He knew he was home.

Two days later I received a short e-mail from Trudy: Just wanted you to know that MJ is doing great! I can't believe we've only had him two days! He follows me everywhere, including the bathroom. Luckily the bathroom is big enough for both of us. He sleeps on a dog bed beside my bed all night and never wakes me up once. He hasn't had any accidents in the house. He's the best dog ever. Just don't tell my other two I said that. Thanks for everything. We love him. Trudy

Miracles do happen.

I Am an Animal Warrior

A big part of my mission has always been to educate people about the welfare of animals. In particular I love to speak to kids about animals. Children are our future and can make all the difference in how animals are treated, long after my generation is gone. Most often when people neglect and abuse animals or don't spay and neuter, it's because they lack the education, often times many generations down the line. Education is the key to a better future for animals and to life in general.

In January of 2007 I was asked to be the speaker for a winter assembly for a school just 40 minutes north of my house. The school was in Oakworth, a depressed town far north of Chicago, near the Wisconsin border. I frequented Oakworth to conduct investigations because of the large number of abuse and neglect cases reported there. It was more common for people to have their dogs living in outdoor pens, living in a garage or tied to a doghouse, than it was for dogs to be warm and cozy living with their family inside the house. They also had a huge problem with pit bull fighting. Oakworth wasn't quite as crime-stricken as Robinson, but if things didn't change for the better within time it would be a close second.

Each time I drove through the town I saw where they were trying to better themselves–the occasional newly built home, the random houses that were well maintained and lovingly cared for. There were positive messages displayed on signs outside schools and churches. But by the large number of rundown houses, the struggle was apparent. I knew speaking to the children of Oakworth could make a difference.

Chuck, Connie and I caravanned there so Chuck could leave after he set up the sound and video equipment. It was an unseasonably warm day, the winter sun bright and cheerful. We had Peanut, Connie's mom's adopted Chihuahua mix, video equipment and miscellaneous literature with us, which we lugged inside the building. We were led to the gymnasium where we began setting up.

The school's students were from kindergarten through fifth grade, about 1,200 children total. As we were setting up more than one teacher came into the room, came up to me and discreetly warned me the "older kids might be challenging. They have a habit of not being respectful." After the third adult approached me I wondered what I was getting myself into. I slipped the chain holding my badge over my head and positioned it over my chest, hoping that it would help get me more respect. *I could play it tough if I had to,* I thought, *I am not intimidated. I like the challenge.* Chuck set up the equipment, showed Connie and me how to use it and left.

The first group of kids, kindergarten and first graders, filed into the room, their teachers directing them to sit in rows in front of us. I scanned the faces shaded in mostly colors of brown. There were girls wearing braids all over their heads, with colorful ribbons and barrettes, and the boys had closely shorn and shaved heads. After they were all seated the teachers gave the kids a three-finger sign, which meant to be quiet. After the chatter trickled to a stop, I began, "Hello, everyone!" I paused, waiting for a reply.

Finally, "Hello!" they shouted back.

I smiled. "Is everyone excited to be here today?"

"Yeah!!" they shouted back.

"Great!" I answered. Excitement made the noise level rise. The three-finger sign went up again to settle the kids down. "My name is Sandy Kamen Wisniewski. This is Connie," I motioned towards Connie, "and with Connie is Peanut."

"Peanut!" they all shouted. Hearing her name Peanut looked around at the crowd and wagged her stubby little tail. They giggled.

"Peanut had a very sad start at life."

I heard "oohhhs" and "ahhhs."

"She was found running loose in an area far, far from here and taken to a nearby animal shelter. Connie's son Bryan was working at the animal shelter with me and some other volunteers when he saw Peanut. And she was covered with over 75 ticks—little bugs that suck dog's blood."

"Ewwwww!!!!" they all cried.

"Yeah, it was really bad. But Bryan spent a very long time taking each tick out until they were all gone. Then he took Peanut home with him. Peanut went to the doctor, and because of the ticks she was very sick and it took a long time for her to get better. But it's a happy ending because Peanut got adopted by Bryan's grandma."

"Awww," the children sighed.

"I am going to show a video now, and then afterwards we are going to talk about how dogs and cats communicate with us and how to properly care for them. In the video I want you to look for Peanut, when she was at the shelter, and let me know when you see her."

The rest of the first program went smoothly and the kids were a joy, their innocent, enthusiastic energy contagious. The next group, second and third graders, came skipping and giggling into the room, excited to be there. I tailor made the program for their age group as well. I explained simply what the animal laws in Illinois were, why an animal should not live outside all the time and what spaying and neutering was and why it was important. I told them Peanut's story and sprinkled in stories of other animals we rescued.

The last group of kids, fourth and fifth graders, strutted, stumbled and shuffled into the gym, some laughing, some shoving others and some chatting with each other. The teachers of this group looked more tired and weary than the last two groups of teachers. The principal, her arms crossing her chest, a suspicious scowl on her face, looked more like a prison guard than a school principal. I took a deep breath.

The principal came over to me and whispered, "Did anyone tell you these kids can be more difficult?" She didn't wait for my answer. "But don't worry, we'll make sure they stay in line." I took another deep breath, determined to get to this tough crowd.

Once the students were sitting on the floor the teachers hissed, "Shhhh!" The students' noise in the room lessened and then rose back up like a wave.

"I need you kids to be respectful to these nice ladies," the principal shouted out. "Everyone quiet!" Another fall of voices, then a rise, the kids egging each other on, shoving, pushing. I stood there solemnly waiting.

"This is not respectful," the principal crossly hollered. "These ladies came out here to talk to you, on their time. Everyone needs to be quiet." The students began quieting down again. "One more time and we can all just go back to our classrooms." The noise trickled to a complete silence.

"Thank you, everyone," I said. "I expect that as I respect you, you will respect me. My name is Sandy Kamen Wisniewski. I am with Animal Education and Rescue." I paused, stood taller and pointed at the badge that hung from a chain around my neck. "You see this badge?" There was silence. I scanned the rows of young faces, eyes that told me they had already seen too much. Faces and bodies that looked slightly hardened, tired. "This says that I am a Humane Investigator. That means if anyone abuses or neglects an animal I will come to their home and do whatever I need to to help the animal.

"There are laws that protect animals. One," I said, "an owner of an animal must provide good, wholesome food. Two," I put up two fingers, "an owner must provide fresh water every day. Three," I held up three fingers, "an animal needs proper shelter from the elements. Four, an animal needs to be provided proper medical care as needed. That includes a yearly rabies shot."

I moved across the room, walked closer to the kids and said, "And people cannot hit or physically hurt their animal." The faces were watching me curiously. "If people don't obey the laws then they could receive fines, meaning have to pay money as punishment, have their animal taken away and possibly even go to jail, depending on the situation." I scanned the children's eyes. Some eyes were wide, others suspicious.

"This badge," I lifted the badge up for emphasis, "tells people I am there to protect animals and stop people from hurting them. Sadly, kids, your town has many people who don't take care of their animals. There is a pit bull I met yesterday, right here in your town, that was so skinny you could count all her ribs. Now, don't get me wrong, there are good animal owners in your town, but not enough.

"Last year there was a dog we rescued not six minutes from this building, Phoenix, a sweet, nine-year-old Border collie mix. That poor dog had such a bad skin infection he had lost most of his hair, and do you know six months later his skin's still not completely better? But lucky for both the dogs, I came along. Now they will get the care they need and deserve.

"Have you been lonely, hungry or scared?" I paused and looked around the room. A couple kids nodded. One boy looked down at his hands.

"Guess what? Animals can get lonely, hungry and scared. They can also be happy, like Peanut is today." I looked over at Peanut. "Well, I am here to protect them, make sure they're safe, make sure they don't suffer." I walked to the center of the room, scanned the faces again. I spoke louder, "You know what that makes me?"

"What?" a few kids called out, challenging me.

Even louder I said, "I am an Animal Warrior." I smiled widely. "But I am not the only Animal Warrior here." I raised my hand and then motioned to Connie. I asked her, "Connie, are you an Animal Warrior?" She nodded. "Connie here is an Animal Warrior.

"An Animal Warrior is a person who doesn't allow people to hit, hurt, abuse or starve an animal. They are people who shout out, I WILL NOT TOLERATE PEOPLE HURTING ANIMALS. Now," I paused again, walking closer to the group in front of me and looking the crowd up and down. Hands on my hips I said, "I want to make a change for the better for the animals in your community. Do you want to help me? I want to know right now–who here wants to be an Animal Warrior, a protector of animals?"

Some hands hesitantly raised, some voices said, "Yeah."

"If you want to be an Animal Warrior proclaim right now, in front of everyone that you are an Animal Warrior. Say it, I am an Animal Warrior!"

"I am an Animal Warrior," more children said.

"That's not loud enough. If you are going to be an Animal Warrior you have to be a Warrior. You are a protector of animals. Feel it in your gut. No more scared and lonely animals. Imagine not allowing animals to be neglected, hit, hurt, starved and think of saving them and shout, I am an Animal Warrior!"

"I AM AN ANIMAL WARRIOR!" they shouted.

"Again and louder." I cupped my hand to my ear.

The sound rose high, loud and powerful. "I AM AN ANIMAL WARRIOR!" I felt a surge of heat course through my heart, the same feeling I got when I was on my way to help an animal.

"One more time, my friends."

"I AM AN ANIMAL WARRIOR!"

"Now that's more like it." I smiled broadly. I took in a deep breath and let it out. "You are now all officially Animal Warriors."

My Favorite Animal-Related Websites

www.hsus.org
The Humane Society of the United States web site has tons of interesting information, resources and links.

www.aear.org
Animal Education and Rescue's web site shares stories and news about animals that are rescued along with dynamite video showing animals available for adoption as well as animals rescued from abuse and neglect.

www.DogWise.com
This site features books and videos for dog training and dog behavior. The site features books and videos using positive reinforcement training.

www.Petfinder.com
A web site that features animals all over the country that are available for adoption.

www.AdoptAPet.com
A web site that features animals all over the country that are available for adoption.

www.apdt.com
The web site for the Association of Pet Dog Trainers. The APDT promotes positive reinforcement training.

www.PetSit.com
The Pet Sitters International web site.

www.PetSitters.org
The National Association of Professional Pet Sitters.

www.PetSittersOfAmerica.com
My personal web site for my company, The Pet Sitters of America.

www.CompassionateDogTraining.com
My personal web site for dog training.